D0305713

MOSCOW 1941

A CITY AND ITS PEOPLE AT WAR

RODRIC BRAITHWAITE

PROFILE BOOKS

First published in Great Britain in 2006 by
Profile Books Ltd
3A Exmouth House
Pine Street
Exmouth Market
London EC1R 0JH
www.profilebooks.com

1 3 5 7 9 10 8 6 4 2

Typeset in Garamond 3 by MacGuru Ltd
info@macguru.org.uk

Printed and bound in Great Britain by
Clays, Bungay, Suffolk

A CIP catalogue record for this book is available from the British Library.

ISBN-10 1 86197 759 X
ISBN-13 978 1 86197 759 5

This book is about the men and women who lived and worked and stood their ground in Moscow in the autumn and winter of 1941. It is dedicated to the survivors who gave up so much of their time to tell me what it was like, and to their children, grandchildren, and great-grandchildren, who live in a very different city today.

And it is dedicated to Lev Parshin, who found so many of them for me. Without his tireless enthusiasm, energy, and ingenuity the book would have been a much poorer thing.

CONTENTS

Map 1: Central Moscow in 1941

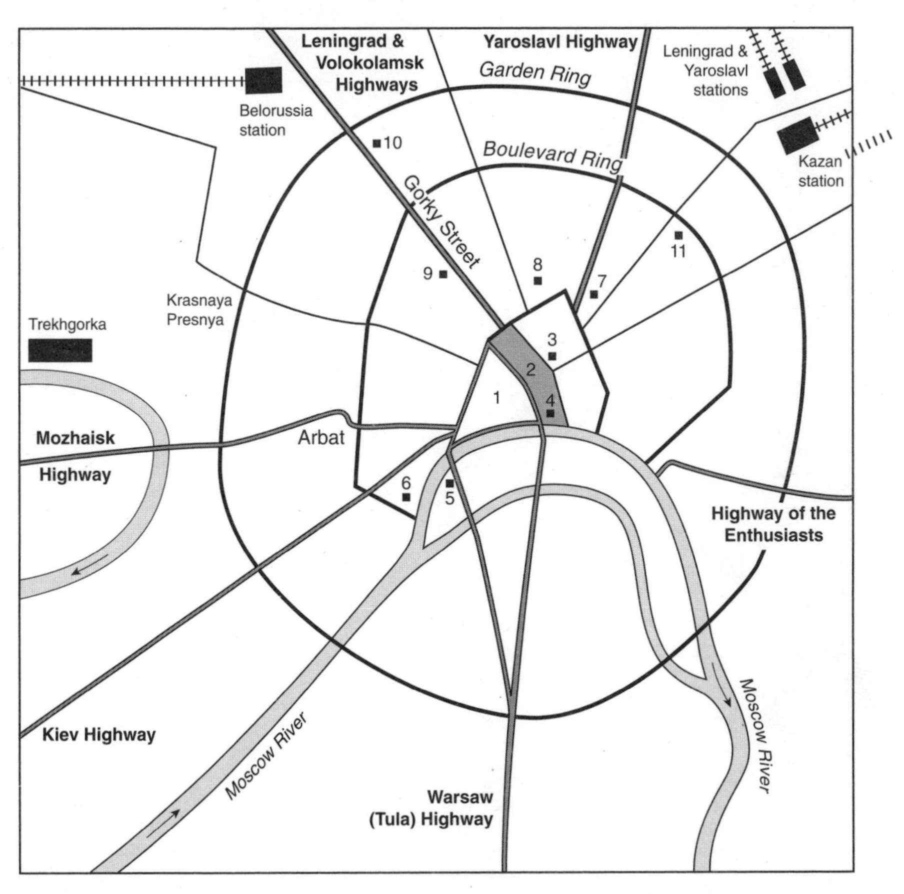

This map shows how the requirements of defence over the centuries imposed a concentric plan on the layout of Moscow, and how the main highways radiated outwards. The main German thrusts in 1941 were along the Mozhaisk, Leningrad and Volokolamsk Highways.

KEY:

1 The Kremlin
2 Red Square
3 GUM, the main universal store on Red Square
4 St Basil's cathedral
5 The House on the Embankment
6 The Palace of the Soviets, under construction on the site of the cathedral of Christ the Saviour
7 The Lubyanka, the headquarters of the NKVD
8 The Bolshoi Theatre (closed for repair on the eve of the war and damaged by a bomb)
9 The Moscow City Council (formerly residence of the governor of Moscow)
10 The Mayakovski metro station (where the anniversary of the Revolution was celebrated on 6 November 1941)
11 The Kirov metro station (the command post of the general staff during the war)

Map 2: The Invasion Route to Moscow

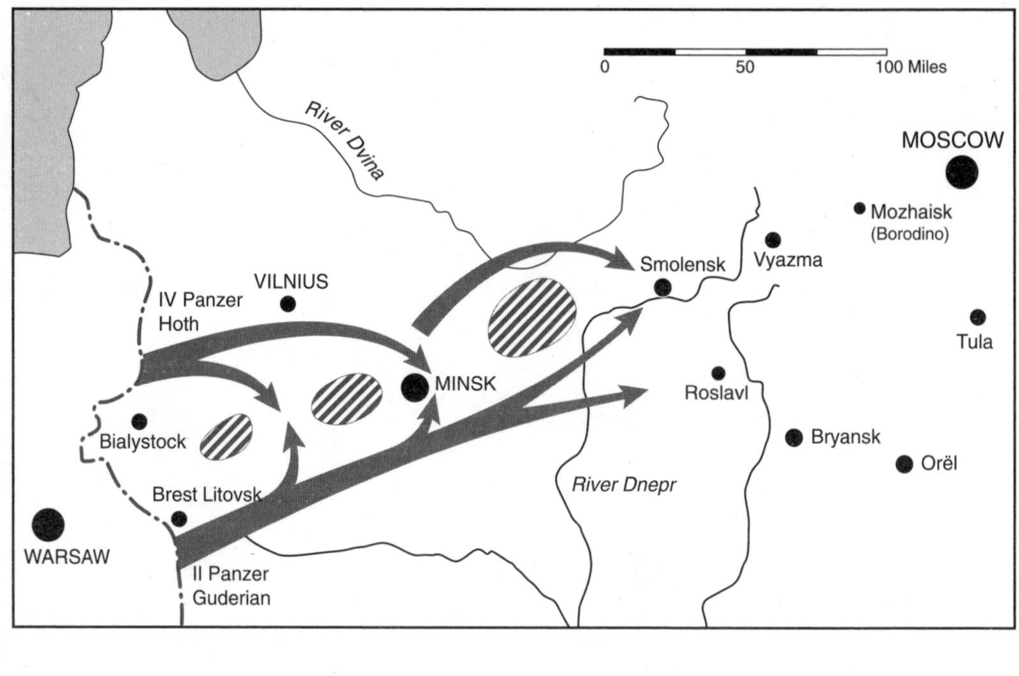

Distance from frontier *(miles)*		Napoleon 1812 *(days)*		Hitler 1941 *(days)*	
Crossing the frontier	0	Wed 24 June	0	Sun 22 June	0
Smolensk	412	16–17 August	54	18–27 July	35
Borodino	590	7 September	68	11–18 October	118
Moscow	670	14 September	129	5 December	166

The Poles in 1612, the French in 1812, and the Germans in 1941 all travelled along the same route to Moscow. On all three occasions the Russians stood and fought at Smolensk, and in 1812 and 1941 they stood at Borodino. The German army in 1941 was almost as dependent on horses as Napoleon's army, and took a lot longer to get to Moscow.

What distinguished the German invasion was the ability of the Wehrmacht to use fast moving armoured forces to surround and capture huge number of Russian soldiers. According to German figures, 324,000 men were taken at Bialystok and Minsk on 10 July, 310,000 at Smolensk on 6 August, 103,000 at Uman on 9 August, 84,000 at Gomel on 20 August, 665,000 at Kiev on 16 September, 107,000 at Azov on 11 October, 663,000 around Vyazma and Bryansk on 18 October.

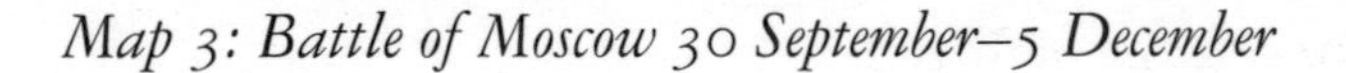

Map 3: Battle of Moscow 30 September–5 December

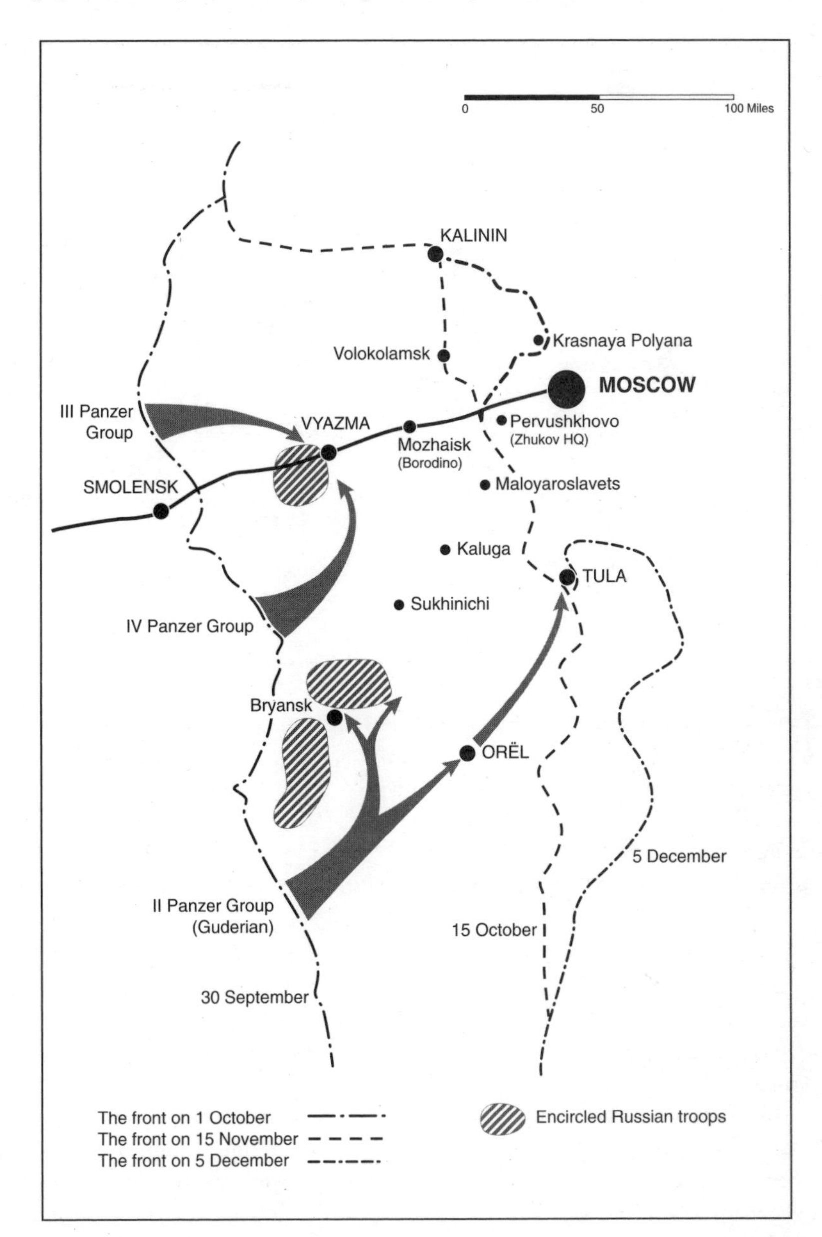

The Germans launched their assault on Moscow, Operation Typhoon, at the beginning of October. The Panzers of Army Group Centre outflanked the Russians from the North and the South, tore a hole three hundred miles wide in the Russian line, captured over 700,000 soldiers, and by the end of the month were only eighty miles from Moscow. After a pause, they resumed their advance on 15 November. But now the Russian resistance had stiffened. The final German thrust along the main Mozhaisk Highway petered out on 5 December, and the Germans were thrown back up to 150 miles by a Russian counteroffensive that their intelligence had entirely failed to predict.

NOTE ON TRANSLITERATION

I have not adopted any of the standard scholarly systems of transliteration, nor have I tried to be rigidly consistent. My system attempts to be simple, phonetic, and as easy as may be for the non-Russian speaker (Russian speakers will be able to work out the original spelling for themselves). The sounds should be spoken as written. Some sounds which do not exist in English are represented thus:

> 'kh', as in Khrushchëv, sounds like 'ch' in 'loch';
> 'zh', as in Zhukov, sounds like 'ge' in 'rouge'.

An 'e' at the beginning of a Russian word is usually pronounced 'ye'. Thus 'Yeltsin' not 'Eltsin'; but 'Mount Elbruz' not 'Mount Yelbruz' (because in Russian the 'E' in this case is a different letter).

I have used one special sign: 'ë'. The same letter is used in Russian; it is pronounced 'yaw'. It is usually stressed, as in KhrushCHËV, GorbaCHËV, YeRËMenko; but there are exceptions, as in TrëkhGORka.

I have used the English versions of names where these are more familiar: 'Moscow' not 'Moskva'; 'Gorky' for the writer (but 'Gorki' for the city); 'Peter' not 'Pëtr'; 'Alexander' not 'Aleksandr'; 'Tchaikovsky' not 'Chaikovski'; 'Mussorgsky' not 'Musorgski'. Except for such well-known Russian names, however, I have preferred to end Russian names in '-ski', which is more accurate. I prefer, inconsistently, 'Mikhail' to 'Michael'.

I have used the names of cities, streets, and other places as they were known at the time of the action. Where the place-names were changed by the Bolsheviks, I have put the original name in square brackets: for example, 'Kalinin [Tver]'.

NEW YEAR 1941

NEW YEAR 1941

Much of his life and the lives of those around him had been lives of privation, ordeal, and struggle. That was why, in the end, the terrible burden of the first days of the war was unable to break their spirit.

Konstantin Simonov, *The Living and the Dead*[1]

Most Muscovites were happy enough to celebrate New Year's Eve in the traditional fashion. They had saved up to buy their vodka and decorate their fir trees, and they now toasted the future and their families, sang songs to the guitar, and played silly games like 'What Have I Got in My Knickers?' Young girls looked into bowls of still water to catch a glimpse of their future husbands. People wrote their hopes and fears on bits of paper, and then set them on fire. And when the divination and the drinking were over, they went out into the town to go to the bars and restaurants or to walk in groups of friends to Red Square to hear the Kremlin chimes and see the changing of the guard outside Lenin's Mausoleum. The more prosperous – Party officials, soldiers, artists, writers, musicians – drank sweet champagne in their apartments or celebrated in their professional clubs and places of work. The Stalin Car Factory laid on a party for the military. Heroes of the Soviet Union, military commanders and ordinary soldiers (no doubt carefully selected) danced to the music of Johann Strauss and sang the Internationale. The Central House of the Merchant Marine entertained the sailors. The Komsomol, the Communist Youth League, put on a party for secondary school children in the Hall of Columns by Red Square (the same building which witnessed the show trials of 1937). The atheist regime did not of course recognise Santa Claus. But 'Grandfather Frost' wore his predecessor's long red robe and long white beard, and handed out his presents by a large fir tree decorated with candles and glass baubles in the old way.[2]

Once they had recovered from their hangovers, there was plenty for people to do on New Year's Day itself. The Bolshoi Theatre was putting on Rimsky-Korsakov's *Tsar Saltan* and Tchaikovsky's *Swan Lake*, as well as a couple of other operas. The Maly Theatre was performing Gogol's *The Government Inspector* and Ostrovski's *Crazy Money.* At the Moscow Art Theatre you could see Chekhov's *Three Sisters*, Dickens's *The Pickwick Club* and Mikhail Bulgakov's *The Day of the Turbins*, one of Stalin's favourite plays despite its sympathetic portrait of a White Guard family. Altogether there were forty different shows and concerts on in the city's theatres and concert halls that day. Among the twenty different films showing in the cinemas were *My Love* starring the popular actress Lidia Smirnova, and *A Girl of Character* with the equally popular Valentina Serova. For the more hardy there was fishing through the ice on the Moscow River, or skiing in the snowbound countryside outside the city.

The official newspapers that day (in the Soviet Union there were no others) assured their readers that all was well. The usual minor troubles apart – an underfulfilment of the plan castigated here, an incompetent official excoriated there – production and the arts were flourishing. Medals had been showered on the deserving – officials, artists, writers, workers from the factories and the new collective farms, those who had fought with distinction in the recent war against Finland, the airmen and aircraft designers who were Stalin's particular favourites. Millions of new citizens – so the papers claimed – had welcomed their incorporation into the Soviet Union following the annexations of the Baltic States, Eastern Poland, Bessarabia and part of Finland. The war now waging in the West was given wide coverage – evenly balanced between reports from the British and reports from the Germans. Every paper reproduced the good wishes (all couched in suspiciously similar language) which people from all over the country had sent to their great leader, Joseph Stalin, the 'Father, Teacher, Great Leader of the Soviet People, Heir to the Cause of Lenin, Creator of the Stalin Constitution, Transformer of Nature, Great Helmsman, Great Strategist of the Revolution, Genius of Mankind, the Greatest Genius of All Times and Peoples'.[3] All the papers – even the army paper *Krasnaya Zvezda* (*Red Star*) – contained long and sentimental poems and stories by well-known writers such as Konstantin Paustovski as well as by the regime's own hacks.

With a little bit of experience you could read behind the bland reports and the artificial enthusiasm of the leading articles to discover quite a bit about what was really going on in the world. Almost everyone in the artistic, political or military world had lost a relative or a friend during the recent purges. All but the most powerful lived in accommodation which was inadequate at best, squalid at worst. But ordinary people clutched at whatever grounds for hope they could perceive. Two years earlier Stalin had appointed Lavrenti Beria as Commissar for Internal Affairs to curb the excesses of the NKVD, the ubiquitous secret police. Arrests continued, of course, but – so far at least – things seemed better than they had been under his predecessor. There was now food in the shops again. Rationing had been abolished, and people were no longer hungry, as they had been only a few years earlier. And they were genuinely proud of what the regime had done for their city: the spectacular new Metro, the new schools, the new openings in higher education, the new jobs in the new factories, the official support for the performing arts, the glittering opportunities for writers and artists – at least for those who could adapt to the official line. Moscow was the city of opportunity in the First Country of Socialism.

Moscow was still a city of first and second generation peasants, people who had flooded into the capital in search of jobs and careers. They had not forgotten the horrors of collectivisation and famine. Some hoped that war would come and sweep away the hated collective farms which Stalin had imposed on the countryside. But the genuine enthusiasm which had fuelled the revolution twenty-four years earlier was still there despite the horrors which had succeeded it. Had not Stalin said that when you chop wood, the chips are bound to fly? After all, you could not make an omelette or forge Utopia without breaking eggs.

Most people in Moscow believed – or desperately wanted to believe – the official line that their country would keep out of the war which had engulfed the rest of Europe. If war came nevertheless, years of official propaganda had convinced them that the Red Army, with its huge air force and its fleets of tanks – more tanks than the whole of the rest of the world put together – would certainly repel the invader and carry the battle onto his territory in a matter of days.

Stalin and his generals were not as sanguine as they wanted the public to think. The Pact with Hitler in August 1939 had given the Soviet Union a new buffer zone to the West. It had been meant to secure a breathing space. But the overwhelming German victory in France had overthrown every calculation. For the last ten days in December 1940 the generals met in Moscow to draw the lessons. Most of them went home when the military conference ended on New Year's Eve. The most senior stayed behind to begin the business of putting the lessons into practice.

A white swan died late that night in the Moscow Zoo. It was the worst possible omen for the New Year to come.[4]

PART I

THE SLOW APPROACH OF THUNDER

- ONE -

THE SHAPING OF THE CITY

By one measure – the number of people involved – the Battle of Moscow was the greatest battle in the Second World War, and therefore the greatest battle in history. More than seven million officers and men from both sides took part, compared with the four million who fought at Stalingrad in 1942, the two at Kursk in 1943, the three and a half in the battle for Berlin in 1945. This was a scale never matched in the fighting in Western Europe and Africa. The Battle of Moscow swirled over a territory the size of France, and lasted for six months, from September 1941 to April 1942. The Soviet Union lost more people in this one battle – 926,000 soldiers killed, to say nothing of the wounded – than the British lost in the whole of the First World War. Their casualties in this one battle were greater than the combined casualties of the British and the Americans in the whole of the Second World War. This was the horrendous price they paid for inflicting on the Wehrmacht the first real defeat it had ever suffered. They fought the Germans to a standstill, bled them white, and hurled them back hundreds of miles from the very walls of their capital. The Wehrmacht went on to win more dazzling victories on the plains of Southern Russia in the summer of 1942. But in their hearts many Germans already knew that, if the Battle of Moscow was not the beginning of the end, it was most certainly the end of the beginning.[1]

Even today, Moscow – strangled by traffic, poisoned by the exhalations of decrepit factories, disfigured by the exuberant constructions of a vulgar and rampant capitalism – is a city which throbs with power. The focus and symbol of that power is still, as it always has been, the fortress of the Kremlin, the magnificent and awe-inspiring central point of an imperial city. Russia may now be bereft of empire, but the overwhelming aura of the Kremlin remains. The successors of the Tsars and the Bolsheviks still rule the country from behind the great walls of red brick that surround the offices, the grand palaces, and the glittering churches bearing the golden crosses of Russia's ancient Orthodox faith. Above the churches and the palaces, even today, the high towers of the fortress are crowned with the great red stars of illuminated glass, the symbols of a ruthless regime under whose banners the men and women of the Soviet Union held and then destroyed the German invader in the greatest war in history.

Beyond the Kremlin walls Moscow seems to be a rambling chaos of churches and monasteries, now once again crowned with golden cupolas which glow in the sunset, of great palaces and public buildings, of Stalinist fantasies, of drab offices and slums from the 1960s and 1970s, of exuberant post-Soviet kitsch. This is the city which has given Europe some of its greatest science, painting, music and literature. This is the city where Pushkin and Dostoevsky were born and where Tolstoy and Chekhov spent much of their working lives. Far more than the coldly formal city which Peter the Great built for himself amid the marshes of the Baltic Sea, Moscow is the core and the essence of Russia itself, sprawling, huge, unmanageable, a country both of Europe and apart from it. Moscow is a city which fascinates and obsesses the citizen and the stranger alike. Without Moscow European culture as we know it would look very different.

Beneath all its apparent chaos Moscow, like Vienna, is shaped by a simple logic, the logic of defence. Like Vienna, the core of Moscow is a defensive fortress on the bank of a river, protected by concentric lines of fortification, and joined to the outside world by great highways radiating to all the points of the compass. The course of the Battle of Moscow in 1941 was determined by the city's geographical position and climate, by the network of roads of which it was the centre, and by the shape of the city itself as it developed through the centuries in response to the actions of powerful men (see Map 1).

The countryside around Moscow – the Podmoskovie – undulates gently and undramatically across an endless sandy plain. The Moscow River and its tributaries wind across it, a place of fishermen and holiday-makers, of swimmers and sunbathers in times of peace, but an obstacle in time of war. The countryside has been partly cleared for agriculture. But even today, thick forests of silver birch and black pine still cover much of the land, dark and impenetrable except along the roads or paths that have been hacked through them. It is a landscape which does not impose itself on the observer. It has nothing of the wild grandeur of the Alps or the cultivated beauty of England or Italy. But it speaks to the deepest emotions of the Russian people: emotions which are captured, even for the foreigner, by Russia's landscape artists of the nineteenth century.[2]

Napoleon's veterans complained as they marched across these endless plains that the heat was as bad as it had been in Egypt. The dust cast up by the marching men and vehicles was so thick that the sun was sometimes reduced to a dim red disk and drums had to be sounded at the head of every battalion to prevent the rear from losing its way.[3] The dust killed Napoleon's horses and draft animals in their tens of thousands, and ground and clogged the engines of Hitler's tanks and lorries until they seized up.

The winters are as cold as the summers are hot. The snow starts in October or November and continues until April or May. The average temperature in December, January and February hovers around minus ten degrees centigrade. It can fall below minus forty degrees, but even that is manageable if your house is heated and you are properly dressed: for centuries people spent most of the winter indoors, asleep on their stoves. But the roads are hard once the frost takes hold, and if you have the right kind of transport you can move fairly freely.

The worst time of all is the moment when autumn gives way to winter and winter gives way to spring. This is the time that Russians call the *rasputitsa*, the 'time when roads dissolve', when the ground becomes waterlogged in the rain and the slush, and all but the most modern roads become a quagmire to any large number of men and vehicles. It was the mud, not the winter, which brought the armies of Napoleon and Hitler to a halt.

Small wooden villages and towns – Moscow and Tver (which the Communists renamed Kalinin), Tula and Zvenigorod, Mozhaisk and Volokolamsk, towns which were all to see bloody fighting in the autumn of 1941 – began to appear in these forests a thousand years ago. Almost every town had its own prince and, like Moscow, its own fortified kremlin. The princes were mostly related to one another, and to the ancient ruling family of Kiev – the reason, no doubt, why their tiny internecine wars were so vicious.

The men who founded Moscow in the twelfth century chose its position on a river ford because it was convenient both for trading and for defence against its princely neighbours, against outlaw rebels, against Tatars, Poles and Frenchmen. The fort which became the Kremlin originally consisted of no more than a dry moat and a palisade with wooden blockhouses, protected on the Southern side by the Moscow River itself. East of the fortress there grew up a settlement for traders and artisans. The open space between them became the Red (meaning 'beautiful' in old Russian) Square. The Southern bank of the river – the Zamoskvorechie, 'Beyond the Moscow River' – was flat, marshy, and unfortified. The Tatar horsemen who from time to time swept this far North to exact tribute and to carry off slaves would camp on this plain while they awaited payment. Sometimes they cut the process short by sacking the city and burning it to the ground.

The first ring of fortifications encompassed the market outside the Kremlin walls, the Kitaigorod. Later fortifications were razed as the need for them passed, and replaced by ring roads: the Boulevard Ring, the Garden Ring, the Earthen Wall. In 1900 an outer ring was constructed to carry the railway round the city; and in 1962 an orbital road – the Moscow Ring Motorway – was built to provide a similar facility for motor vehicles.

Apart from the cartwheel pattern imposed by the concentric system of defences, Moscow grew higgledy-piggledy. There were few planning rules beyond a requirement to leave occasional broad gaps as firebreaks between the houses. Even the great highways which led to the outside world degenerated into narrow and sometimes winding streets once they entered the city. The boulevards which are such a feature of Moscow today began to appear only at the end of the eighteenth century. The Boulevard Ring has retained much of its charm, but the Garden Ring is now a polluted and sclerotic battleground for modern foreign cars and ancient wheezing lorries.

It was along the great highways that Moscow's rulers set out to bring the neighbouring principalities under their sway, the first step by which Moscow was transformed from a minor settlement in a forest to the capital of an immense empire. The highways radiate outwards from the Kremlin, the spokes in the cartwheel. To the Northwest, one highway – now called the Leningrad Highway – led to Tver and on to the Free Republic of Novgorod, and in time as far as Peter the Great's new capital of St Petersburg. To the Northeast, a highway led to Yaroslavl and onwards to Russia's first maritime trading routes through Archangel to Western Europe. To the South lay the roads through Tula and Kashira, along which the Tatars came in their search for tribute. To the East the Vladimir Highway led towards the minerals and furs of Siberia and the Urals, a road known to the people as the 'Vladimirka', the 'Trakt'. Along it generations of criminals and political prisoners trudged painfully towards exile or worse in the Tsarist times. They were followed in the late autumn of 1941 by miserable conscripts on their way to their training camps, and refugees from a city apparently about to fall to the enemy.

But it was the roads to the West that had the greatest strategic significance in Russia's modern history: the Volokolamsk Highway, the Mozhaisk Highway, and the Minsk Highway which leads to the fortress city of Smolensk, to the Polish frontier and on to Warsaw. It was along the Mozhaisk Highway that the Poles and the French marched to capture Moscow in the seventeenth and nineteenth centuries, and it was along the last few miles of the Mozhaisk Highway that the Germans made their final desperate bid to break into the city in December 1941.

For centuries the Mozhaisk Highway entered Moscow through the Arbat, the name both of a street and of a quarter of the city, a place of craftsmen, artists and intellectuals until the middle of the twentieth century. The vanguard of Napoleon's army, a party of Württemberg Hussars under Marshal Murat, passed along the Arbat on their way to the Kremlin. It was here that Tolstoy's Pierre Bezukhov planned to assassinate Napoleon himself. Stalin used to drive along the Arbat on his way to the Kremlin from his dacha – the 'Nearby Dacha' – off the Mozhaisk Highway just outside the old city limits.

These ring roads within Moscow itself – the Boulevard Ring, the Garden Ring, the Earthen Wall, the Railway Ring; these great highways

– the Leningrad Highway, the Volokolamsk Highway, the Mozhaisk Highway; the rivers, the towns and the villages of the Podmoskovie; the Moscow River itself – all these shaped the Battle of Moscow in 1941, as they had shaped so much of Moscow's earlier history.

The face of this great city has been fashioned above all by the varying and often dubious taste of its rulers, from its founder Yuri Dolgoruki through a series of despots – Ivan the Terrible, Peter the Great, Catherine the Great and Stalin – to the sometimes bizarre caprices of Yuri Luzhkov, the mayor of post-Communist Moscow. Until well into the twentieth century, Moscow was a city built above all of wood. The grand buildings of the eighteenth and nineteenth centuries would have a facing of stucco. But the wooden framework was almost always there behind the façade; and this was the main reason why the domestic quarters of Moscow, and of most other Russian towns, burned down so regularly. When war came in 1941, the fear of a conflagration forced the authorities to mobilise much of the population of the city into a most effective, if brutally simple, system of fire-fighting.

Moscow's Kremlin and the churches and monasteries within its walls were rebuilt more durably of stone and brick in the fourteenth and fifteenth centuries. By the time Richard Chancellor visited it in 1553, Moscow was already twice the size of London. But, he thought, 'it is very rude, and standeth without all order. Their houses are all of timber very dangerous for fire. There is a faire Castle, the walles whereof are of bricke, and very high: they say they are eighteene foote thicke, but I do not believe it.'[4] Ivan the Terrible captured the Tatar capital of Kazan in 1552 and chose a singular, almost grotesque, new style for St Basil's, the cathedral he built on Red Square to commemorate the victory. At this time, too, six great walled monasteries were built in a ring around the city, defensive bastions to break up the assault of Moscow's enemies before they reached the walls of the Kremlin. Pre-revolutionary Moscow was dominated by its religious buildings: nine cathedrals, fifteen monasteries, ten convents, nearly three hundred Orthodox churches and another forty churches for the dissident Old Believers.

Moscow ceased to be the capital of Russia in 1712, when Peter the Great moved the government to his new city of St Petersburg on the Baltic. But as the decades passed, some of the richer citizens built themselves neo-classical town houses with something of a European elegance and the city began to acquire an overlay of Enlightenment taste. When the French entered Moscow on 14 September 1812, after the bloody Battle of Borodino on 7 September, which they still perversely regard as a victory, one of their number was 'seized with astonishment and delight. Although I had expected to see a wooden city, I found, on the contrary, almost all the houses to be of brick and in the most elegant and modern style. The homes of private persons are like palaces and everything was rich and wonderful.'[5]

By then the city was almost empty: the people of Moscow had fled along the Eastern and Northern highways. 'As far as the eye could see the entire Moscow road was covered with lines of carriages and people on foot fleeing from the unhappy capital. They jostled and overtook one another, and hurried, driven by fear, in carriages, cabriolets, droshkies, and carts. Everyone carried what he could. All faces were dusty and tearstained.'[6] The same scenes, on the same roads, at almost the same time of year, were to be repeated one hundred and twenty-nine years later as the Germans approached the Soviet capital.

And before the night was over Moscow was in flames, started spontaneously or on the orders of the Governor. The city burned for six days, and many of its grandest buildings were consumed. When the conflagration was over Napoleon announced, in horror or satisfaction, 'Moscow, one of the most beautiful and wealthy cities of the world, exists no more.'[7] It was an understandable, if not a pardonable, exaggeration. But it left the city uninhabitable for a large and increasingly undisciplined army. On Monday 19 October the French pulled out of the city and marched to catastrophe.[8]

Moscow was rapidly rebuilt, and by the end of the nineteenth century the centre of the city looked much as it does today. The huge Cathedral of Christ the Saviour, built to commemorate the victory over Napoleon, dominated the skyline of central Moscow. To make way for this overblown and debased pastiche of traditional Russian church styles an entire monastery was removed, on ground by the river to the West of the Kremlin. It was financed by money raised from the public. Much of the money disappeared into unknown pockets, and the Tsar had to make up the difference.

But even at this late stage, Moscow still resembled a great village in the most literal sense. People still kept their domestic animals in the courtyards surrounding their houses. There were still churches and monasteries everywhere. Most of the city was still built of wood. Cattle were still being driven through the streets, as they had been in London a century earlier. You could step through a gateway off almost any main street, and find yourself in a broad space like a farm courtyard, filled with trees, children, and animals.[9]

Unlike the medieval cities of Western Europe, Moscow never acquired an independent municipal culture with political institutions and influence of its own. Peter the Great set up its first municipal government, an inadequately financed and carefully packed body, closely monitored by a Governor General appointed by the Emperor. In the middle of the nineteenth century Alexander II introduced a small, fluctuating, but genuine element of representation. Moscow's new business class exploited these meagre opportunities to establish its political importance, a promise for the future which was cut short by revolution.

Russian education and culture in the Western sense developed late. When Peter the Great came to the throne in 1682, there was no provision for secular education, no provision for the printing of secular books, and no periodical literature in Russia at all.[10] Things changed with Peter and his successors. Moscow University – Russia's first – was founded in 1755. But it was with the rise of the new businessmen and industrialists that Moscow began to acquire something of the feeling of a modern European city. Once they had made their money and satisfied their taste for ostentation, they began to patronise architecture, painting, music, dance and literature with flair; they supported education, endowed scholarships, and set up specialised technical institutes; they contributed to charitable causes with great generosity, greater indeed than their contemporaries in Paris, Berlin, and Vienna.[11] Thanks to them, Moscow recovered much of the status as a cultural centre that it had lost when Peter transferred the capital.

In the nineteenth century, too, Moscow became a major industrial city. The Trëkhgornaya Manufaktura, the textile factory founded by the Prokhorov family in 1799, the year Pushkin was born, dominated the banks of the Moscow River in the Presnya district, where the Tsar and his boyars used to have their country estates.[12] Engineering and science-based enterprises proliferated. Professor Nikolai Zhukovski built one of the first wind tunnels in Europe there in 1902 and opened an aerodynamics laboratory at the Imperial Technical College in 1912. In 1909 the Duks Aviation Works, originally set up to make bicycles, built Russia's first aircraft, a Farman-4 biplane. In 1914 the Moscow Society of Aviators opened the Central Aerodrome beside the Tver [Leningrad] Highway: this became one of the bases for the fighter squadrons defending Moscow. The Russo-Baltic Wagon Factory – the builders of the *Ilya Muromets*, the first four-engined bomber in the world – was evacuated to Fili on the outskirts of Moscow in 1916 to escape the advancing Germans. By the eve of the 1917 revolution, much of Russian defence industry was located in Moscow.

In the Moscow of the first years of the twentieth century, the rich lived ostentatiously, the middle classes lived well, and the intelligentsia chattered, spinning revolutionary theories of the right and the left. But by far the largest proportion of the population consisted of workers and their families. Few of these were native to the city. By the time of the liberation of the serfs in 1861, half the people of Moscow were first generation peasants, and the proportion continued to rise. The men came first. But they kept their links with their villages and later on they brought their families to Moscow to live with them. Nine-tenths of Moscow's factory workers were former peasants.[13] Moscow before the revolution was a great village in its social make-up as well as in its appearance.

The worker-peasants who toiled in the new factories – dark, dirty, damp and dangerous – lived for the most part in Dickensian squalor. They worked seven days a week, and slept at night crammed promiscuously into wooden barracks erected by the factory owners, or on the factory floor by their machines. Later some moved to company housing, almost all of it in the newer suburbs outside the Garden Ring. The Trëkhgornaya Manufaktura, or Trëkhgorka as it was known, provided primitive communal housing and barracks for 3,900 of its 6,000 workers. Others crowded into tiny rented rooms in unsanitary apartment blocks. It is barely surprising that crime, disease and drunkenness all flourished.[14]

Health and safety remained at the abysmal level achieved by the early Victorians. Philanthropists and reformers – and there were many, even among the rich – could make little headway against the bone-headed conservatism of Tsar Nicholas II and the corruption and incompetence of his ministers. By the beginning of the twentieth century the workers were beginning to benefit from some primitive social legislation. But for the most part they were exploited by their employers and harassed and manipulated by the secret police. The situation in Moscow and Russia's other big cities was becoming explosive.

The peasants who flooded into the capital were neither as unthinking nor as ignorant, as 'dark', as their betters often assumed. They brought their passion for music and dancing and poetry with them. They were increasingly literate: by 1908 more than three-quarters of the men in Moscow and the surrounding province could read, and there were twice as many bookshops in Moscow as in the capital St Petersburg.[15] Village bards and musicians and storytellers improvised for hours to an enraptured audience. Maurice Baring, a member of the banking family and editor of the first *Oxford Book of Russian Verse*, got to know and respect the Russian peasant soldiers as a newspaper correspondent during the Russo-Japanese War. He was startled to discover that one of their favourite books was Milton's *Paradise Lost*.[16] He made enquiries and concluded that what attracted the soldiers was the sound of Milton's high-flown verse, the colourful story, and above all the Russian passion for seeing the world as a battleground between good and evil, between God and the Devil, between Christ and Antichrist.

These beliefs went back at least two hundred years, to the time when Peter the Great broke the power of the Church and finally nailed serfdom onto the backs of the peasantry. Many peasants concluded that Armageddon and the Last Judgement were at hand. The belief revived as Napoleon and his armies approached in 1812, amid rumours of Antichrist and the promise of freedom; and again when revolution loomed a century later.[17] The belief was not confined to the peasantry. The Russian literature of the last years of the old regime was shot through with images of Apocalypse.[18] They continued to transfix the emotions of peasants and intellectuals alike as the Four Horsemen – War, Famine, Pestilence and Death – stalked the Russian countryside for most of the first half of the twentieth century.

*

With time, perhaps, economic growth could have softened the lot even of the poorest. But defeat at the hands of the Japanese in 1904–5 proved to be the trigger for open revolt. In St Petersburg there was comparatively little bloodshed. A fleeting working compromise was established between liberals and the less extreme socialists, which successfully pushed Tsar Nicholas II to grant a measure of reform. On 17 October 1905 he approved the country's first – limited – constitution.

On the same day the Moscow printers went on strike. Others followed, and when the railway workers joined in, the city was isolated from the rest of the country. The socialist parties set up a Soviet or Council in November. At the beginning of December they voted for an armed uprising. The insurgents established their headquarters in the Trëkhgorka Textile Factory in Presnya. Four hundred workers from the factory took part in the fighting. The government brought troops and artillery against them. The factory was hit by several hundred shells, and when it finally fell to the government troops they shot fourteen people out of hand in the courtyard.[19] The fighting and destruction in Central Moscow were almost as bloody. The rising collapsed after ten days. Over one thousand people died.[20] One of the Bolsheviks' first acts on coming to power was to rename the district Krasnaya Presnya – Red Presnya – in honour of the revolutionaries of 1905.

The Bolsheviks in Moscow were slow to follow their comrades when Lenin and Trotsky seized power in the capital on 25 October 1917 (7 November according to the Western calendar). But they quickly rallied, invited the soldiers of the garrison to place themselves under their command, seized the Kremlin and other key points in the centre of the city, and began to put together an armed force from among the workers who lived in the industrial suburbs beyond the Garden Ring.

Moscow's City Council remained loyal to the Provisional Government in Petrograd. They had at their disposal about ten thousand students, army officers and cadets, well armed and trained, who rapidly recovered control of the city centre. The Bolsheviks remaining in the Kremlin were ordered to surrender. They obeyed, and many were immediately shot down.[21] But the Bolsheviks found rifles and artillery to arm their men, and began to press in along the radial roads. They brought their heavy guns into action, and the government troops threw in their hand.

When the fighting started, the writer Konstantin Paustovski was caught between two fires in his apartment at the Nikitski Gates, on the corner of Bolshaya Nikitskaya Street, another of the radial roads leading to the heart of the city, and not far from the Conservatoire.[22] The cadets had their headquarters in the Union Cinema, just down the road, and for six days Paustovski and his fellow lodgers sheltered in the little courtyard of their apartment, with cadets on one side of them and Red Guards on the other. When the shooting ended and he ventured outside he found blood frozen on the cobbled streets. A funereal blue flame still flickered from the shattered street lamps along the boulevard. Glass tinkled on the pavement as it fell from the smashed windows of bullet-riddled buildings. A fire was burning down by the Kiev Station.

The fighting in Moscow was over. The Bolsheviks admitted that more than two hundred Red Guards had died. As usual on these occasions, no one bothered to count the dead among the defeated or the civilian population.

On Sunday 10 March 1918, Lenin travelled with his wife and secretary from Petrograd – already threatened by the German advance – to Moscow in Special Train No. 4,001. The other members of the Bolshevik administration followed separately. The move was meant to be temporary. It became permanent, a symbol in the eyes of many that Russia had turned her back on Europe and become once again a barbarian Asiatic power.

Lenin and his wife moved into a government apartment in the Kremlin, where they had three large rooms, a servants' room and a kitchen on the third floor of the Senate building. The defence of the Kremlin complex was taken over by Lenin's personal bodyguard of Latvian riflemen. 'To appreciate the significance of these actions,' remarks Richard Pipes, 'one must imagine a British Prime Minister moving out of Downing Street and transferring his residence and office as well as those of his ministers to the Tower of London to govern there under the protection of Sikhs.'[23]

To make way for the other senior Bolsheviks, the Kremlin's existing inhabitants were expelled, including the monks and nuns from the Chudov and Voznesenski monasteries. But the Kremlin was not nearly large enough to take all the new arrivals. So they were accommodated in former official buildings, in hotels, in colleges, in the town houses of the bourgeoisie and in apartment buildings and schools. The secret police commandeered the large building of the Rossiya Insurance Company on Lubyanka Square, conveniently close to the Kremlin. Their headquarters have been known as the Lubyanka ever since.

It was the beginning of a new age. Paustovski christened it 'The Time of Great Expectations'.

- TWO -

FORGING UTOPIA

Now the Bolsheviks began to clamp their power upon the city. They cleansed it of the symbols of its Tsarist past and substituted symbols of their own. The Kremlin chimes were reprogrammed to play the Internationale. The imperial eagle was removed from the public buildings. Statues to the Tsars and to victorious Imperial generals were taken down in the public squares, and replaced by monuments to the new revolutionary heroes: Spartacus, Robespierre, Darwin, Herzen, Marx, Engels. A Special Commission was set up to rename the streets and highways. The Tver Highway was renamed the Leningrad Highway. The Vladimir Highway, the Trakt, along which so many had trudged to exile, was renamed, with no doubt unconscious irony, the 'Highway of the Enthusiasts'. The changes continued as new heroes emerged and old heroes were discovered to have been villains after all. The elderly were confused as the familiar names disappeared. Three generations later, after the Soviet regime had collapsed, most of the old names were restored. The elderly – and foreigners – were confused all over again.

Very few of the Bolsheviks had any practical experience of administration: they had spent their lives in political conspiracy and in intra-party intrigue. But the system of government which they now set up was remarkably effective. It reflected the duality of Party and State which was the peculiar mark of the Soviet regime. The Party called the tune, in Moscow as throughout the country; but under Stalin the secret police, the NKVD, played a powerful counterbass. Moscow was run by the Moscow Communist Party Committee and the Moscow City Council. The First Party Secretary of Moscow, the head of the Party Committee, was one of the most powerful politicians in the country. He was usually a member of the Politburo, the supreme body of the Party and the country's effective government: Molotov, Kaganovich and Khrushchëv each held the job at various times. The Chairman of the City Council was almost equally important. He too was usually a senior politician and sometimes a Politburo member.

The city was divided into Raions (districts). Each Raion had its own Party Committee, the RaiKom; its own Committee of the Young Communist League, the Komsomol; and its own Raion Council, the RaiSoviet. At first the Moscow Raions were based on the six political districts into which the Bolsheviks had divided the city during their years underground. The largest of the six was Krasnaya Presnya. It contained several major factories apart from the Trëkhgorka, the Conservatoire, the University, the Institute of Law, the Bolshoi Theatre, the Moscow Art Theatre, and the office of the Moscow Soviet. The Secretary of the Krasnaya Presnya Party Committee was often a rising politician of particular promise: the young Khrushchëv held the post briefly. When the number of Raions was increased to ten in 1930 and then to twenty-five in 1939 on the eve of the war, the size and political importance of Krasnaya Presnya were much diminished. But it retained a particular aura to the end of the Soviet period.

In addition to these Party and municipal bodies, in each Raion there was also an office representing the NKVD. Another, the VoenKomat (Military Commissariat), was responsible for recruitment, mobilisation, and local military training. These were the lowest formal bodies in the politico-administrative system. But below them was a network of Party Committees in people's places of work, and building administrators representing the Moscow City Council in their homes. Most of the building administrators doubled as informers for the NKVD.

This system, informed from top to bottom by the will of the Party and of its General Secretary, Joseph Stalin, was the carapace which kept Moscow together during the supreme crisis of 1941. At that time the men responsible for the city were two career Party officials: the First Secretary of the Moscow Party, Alexander Shcherbakov, and the Chairman of the Moscow City Council, Vasili Pronin. Shcherbakov became head of both the Moscow City and the Moscow Region Parties in 1938 and a Secretary of the Central Committee in 1941.[1] In 1942 he was further appointed to be Head of the Political Administration of the Red Army, Deputy Commissar for Defence and Chairman of the Council for Military-Political Propaganda. Pronin was a lesser figure. He is said to have helped purge the Moscow Party in 1938. After the war his career prospered for a while. But he faltered under Khrushchëv, who pensioned him off at the age of fifty-two. In the capable and energetic hands of these two men, Moscow's administrative arrangements proved remarkably effective at mobilising the people of the city for war.

The Bolsheviks moved rapidly to get their hands on the commanding heights of the economy and so consolidate their power. In Moscow the City Soviet seized the city's private banks, and combined them into one National Bank. Committees of workers had already taken over many of the bigger factories. The City Soviet took over the rest.[2] Factories, such as the Trëkhgorka, which had distinguished themselves in the revolutionary struggle, retained their old names. Others were drably redesignated: the Russo-Baltic Wagon Factory became Aircraft Factory No. 22; Yeliseev's famous grocery store on Tverskaya, the Moscow equivalent of Fortnum and Mason's, became Gastronom No. 1.

The proportion of Moscow's industry devoted to defence production continued to grow.[3] Old factories were reconstructed and new ones built. By 1940 Moscow was producing half of the country's automobiles, half of its machine tools and instruments, and more than 40 per cent of its electrical equipment.[4] All this would become a headache for the authorities as the Germans approached the city in the autumn of 1941.

The Bolsheviks were determined to bend not only the economy, but the very substance of the city to their own revolutionary image. The capital of the first Socialist state in history was to become a symbol of modern and rational living, a glorious demonstration of the power of the proletariat, the final proof that the revolution was here to stay. They launched into an orgy of destruction. Ancient churches and monasteries were torn down, even in the Kremlin itself. A proposal to destroy St Basil's Cathedral on Red Square was abandoned only at the last minute. In 1931 the Cathedral of Christ the Saviour was demolished in an act of destruction which reverberated down the years. The operation was filmed by Vladislav Mikosha, a very young man from Saratov on the Volga, who went on to become one of Russia's most distinguished cameramen. When he got home, his mother wept and said, 'Fate will not forgive what we have done – all of us. People should build – destruction is the work of Antichrist.'[5] Mikosha had a bad conscience ever after.

Brave men opposed the orgy of destruction. When even Khrushchëv protested that the wholesale destruction of ancient buildings was opposed by many people in the city, Stalin merely replied, 'Then you should blow them up at night.'[6] Many of the protesters were arrested, imprisoned, or shot. The destruction continued.

The most spectacular project in this new Socialist Moscow was to be a Palace of the Soviets: the tallest building in the world, to be erected on the site of the demolished Cathedral of Christ the Saviour. It was to seat twenty-one thousand people under a dome three hundred feet across, and be crowned by a massive statue of Lenin. The project was given to Stalin's favourite architect, Boris Iofan. Work began in 1935 and the foundation was completed three years later. But even by then the enterprise was already doomed. The site was wholly unsuitable for such a massive building. Water from the nearby river seeped into the foundations. Tombstones from the Moscow cemeteries were stuffed in to stabilise the ground. The steel framework had reached the eleventh storey by the time war began in June 1941. Stalin agreed that the building could be dismantled and its steel girders turned into tank traps. The work, he said, could be resumed when victory was won. It never happened. The site was turned into a vast open-air swimming pool, and the Palace of the Soviets now exists, an idealised wraith, only in the popular musical films produced in the last days of peace.

The most useful relic of Stalin's Moscow is the Metro. Khrushchëv was put in charge of its construction. A Figaro factotum to the whole city, he was already overwhelmed with work: supervising the construction of new factories, new bridges and new power plants, modernising sewage and water supplies. 'Comrade Khrushchëv,' Stalin rang to say on one occasion, 'rumours have reached me that you've let a very unfavourable situation develop in Moscow as regards public toilets [...] This won't do. It puts the citizens in an awkward position. Talk this matter over with Bulganin and do something about it.'[7]

Khrushchëv drove ahead with ruthless energy. By 1934 the Metro was the largest civilian construction project in the country. Nothing was spared: the stations were decorated with more than fifty types of marble, other rare stone, and white limestone stripped from the walls of the kremlin in the little town of Serpukhov, South of Moscow. Expensive English boring equipment was imported to drive deep tunnels which could serve as bomb shelters in time of war. Over seventy thousand workers were engaged on the project. Some were miners whom Khrushchëv brought in from the Donbass, where he himself had worked. But many were prisoners.

The first stretch of the Metro was opened by Stalin in 1935. Construction of new stations continued even during the war: three were opened in January 1943, and another four in January 1944. The maintenance workshops of the Metro produced ammunition, and built an armoured train which fought and was destroyed at the Battle of Kursk in 1943.[8]

The Bolsheviks inaugurated their new housing policy in Moscow with a declaration of class war. They moved thousands of workers and their families from their barracks in the industrial suburbs into better housing in the middle-class neighbourhoods in the centre. They forced the previous inhabitants – sometimes at gunpoint – either to move out, or to share their homes with strangers in the frictional discomfort of what came to be known as *kommunalkas*. Privilege remained. But Party loyalty, not money, now became the principle by which housing was distributed. If you fell out of favour, you lost your home – if you were lucky. If you were unlucky you lost your liberty or your life.

No one in Moscow now lived as well as the political, social, and commercial elite had lived before the revolution. But the top people did well enough, especially by comparison with those at the bottom of the pile. Most of the Politburo members stayed on in the Kremlin.

Anastas Mikoyan lived with his wife and their five sons in an eight-room apartment in the old Horse Guards building, surrounded by his colleagues, their wives, and their families. The Mikoyans and other Politburo members also had dachas outside Moscow. Stalin's own dacha was less than a mile away. But after his wife Nadezhda Allilueva shot herself in the Kremlin in 1932 Stalin built for himself a new dacha – the Nearby Dacha – at Kuntsevo just off the Mozhaisk Highway on the Western outskirts of Moscow. It was here that he lived during the war when he wanted to get away from his apartment in the Kremlin.

Senior officials for whom there was no room in the Kremlin took over large apartments in elite blocks of flats built before the revolution, such as the complex at 3 Granovski Street, where Molotov, Malenkov, Bulganin, Marshal Koniev and Marshal Rokossovski lived at one time or another. Shcherbakov lived there in an eight-room apartment together with his wife, father, mother, mother-in-law, and three boys. He and Pronin also had dachas in Ogarëvo about half an hour's drive from Moscow. Their staff lived in a sort of castle next door, which eventually became a country residence of President Putin.

Bolshevik housing policy also had an ideological motive: to transform the domestic manners of the Russian people, to condition them to communal, 'socialist' life, to liberate women from the 'obsolete domestic economy' of feudalism and capitalism by means of kindergartens, centralised laundries, and communal eating facilities.[9] The most prestigious symbol of these aspirations was Government House, designed by Boris Iofan, a huge constructivist building which still glowers darkly across the Moscow River. Its construction began in 1928 and it contained over five hundred apartments, each fitted out with telephone, constant hot water, and ponderous furniture marked with official inventory tags so that the inhabitants could not take it with them when they moved on. There was a universal store, a canteen, a sports hall, a library, a laundry, a post office and a savings bank. You could see the latest Soviet and foreign films in the Udarnik Cinema, watch vaudeville, or dance to a jazz band in the lobby.[10] Today the outside walls of Government House – the 'House on the Embankment', as it is now known after a very successful novella by the writer Yuri Trifonov – are lined with plaques in memory of those of its distinguished inhabitants who came to sticky ends during Stalin's purges.

*

Members of the former middle classes with no obvious claim on the new regime now lived in cramped circumstances, often in *kommunalkas*. In the early 1920s the Sakharov family, with their newborn son Andrei, the future physicist, moved into the house of Andrei's grandmother on Granatny Pereulok. The house was very old and the roof leaked. But it still had traces of its former grandeur: magnificent doors inlaid with Karelian birch, a broad staircase, and exquisite banisters. Here for the next nineteen years they lived with Andrei's grandmother, his Uncle Nikolai and his wife, Valya (whose second husband had been shot by the Bolsheviks), their daughter, Irena, Valya's mother, Sofia, and Uncle Ivan with his wife Zhenya and their daughter Katya, whose two brothers had died in the Civil War. Two other families shared the communal kitchen.[11]

Sara Litvin, a schoolmate of Anastas Mikoyan's son Stepan, also lived in a *kommunalka*. 'We and three other families lived in one apartment in a house with high ceilings and a marble staircase, which had been built before the revolution by a speculative landlord for rental. A single woman lived in a tiny room off the kitchen. We shared the kitchen and the bathroom, and there was a very strict timetable for using them stuck up on the wall. The water in the bathroom was heated by gas, and there was a meter in the kitchen. When somebody was using the bathroom, everyone else would check how much gas had been used, so that the person concerned could pay for it afterwards. Everyone had his own little electric light, which was separately metered. People had to dry their clothes in the kitchen. Families with babies had separate lines strung across the kitchen for the nappies. On one occasion the single woman lost her temper with this arrangement, and threatened to bash the baby's head against the wall. But on the whole people got on well enough, and helped one another out when necessary.'[12]

People could sometimes do better than that. Anatoli Chernyaev – Gorbachëv's future foreign policy adviser – lived with his father, a former officer now working as a minor official, his mother, an elder brother and a younger sister in Mariina Roshcha or 'Mary's Grove', a picnic spot in earlier times. They had three rooms, a kitchen of their own, and the luxury of a separate entrance in a new wooden house with two storeys, a grand entrance, elaborate wooden decoration around the windows, and a huge courtyard with lime trees, fruit bushes and a small orchard, a reminder of the days when this had been open country.[13]

But despite the Bolsheviks' grandiose slogans, the normal objective of municipal housing policy – to provide decent accommodation for ordinary people – was never high on their agenda.[14] The workers continued to live as badly as they had done before the revolution, in barracks or hostels provided by the factory, sometimes sharing a bed with the man on the next shift, sometimes even in a *zemlyanka*, an earthen dugout covered by a makeshift roof. More than a quarter of the accommodation in Moscow had no running water. In 1940 the living space each person was officially allowed to occupy was reduced to about forty square feet, less than two-thirds the living space people had had in 1912. These were the lucky ones. People lived in coal sheds, warehouses and cellars. One family of six lived under the stairs of their apartment block.[15] People entered into fake marriages in order to get a residence permit and a place to live. Divorced couples had to stay together because there was nowhere else for them to go. There was one ray of light: rents were fixed at very low levels. Sixty years later it was this that the elderly remembered above all, as they struggled to cope with the mysteries of the new market economy.

Food was chronically in short supply. In almost their first act, the Bolsheviks closed the markets down, the supply of food began to fail altogether and the workers prepared to strike. In 1921 Lenin bowed to reality and introduced a New Economic Policy (NEP), which allowed petty entrepreneurs (and crooks) to reopen small businesses and get rich. Moscow's economy began to perk up almost immediately.

For orthodox Bolsheviks this was an intolerable departure from the faith. Stalin abolished the NEP and put the so-called NEPmen in jail. The markets were once again closed down, this time for good. Once again food ran scarce, and the Moscow authorities had to ration first bread, then sugar, then potatoes, then meat and dairy products. In 1933 the average Moscow worker consumed less than half the bread, and no more than a fifth of the meat and fish, that he would have been eating at the beginning of the century.[16] His real wages had fallen by half in four years.[17] As always, things were better for those with money, who could shop in the high-priced 'commercial stores' or in special hard-currency shops. Those with official jobs or connections were awarded parcels of goodies at their places of work, the size of which depended on their seniority and the importance of their office.

In October 1928 Stalin launched his first Five Year Plan to industrialise the country and to create a defence industry which would soon give the Soviet Union more modern weapons than any other country in the world. The necessary capital and labour were squeezed from the peasants by driving them into collective farms. Moscow's RaiKoms sent armed squads into the countryside to enforce the Party's will. Those who resisted were arrested or exiled. The Secretary of the Moscow Party Committee, Karl Bauman, ordered that protestors were 'to be put down by all necessary means', including execution.[18] Millions of kulaks – the richer peasants who had a few cows and a decent house, and employed the odd labourer – were deported to the East. Many died on the way.

As this new serfdom was imposed and their way of life was destroyed about them, the peasants remembered their ancient beliefs. The Bolsheviks closed the village churches. But religious commitment increased: more than half the peasants took the risk of identifying themselves as believers in the 1937 census. Once again, tales of the forthcoming Apocalypse began to spread. The Reign of Antichrist was at hand, so the rumours said, and it would be followed by Armageddon and the Last Judgement. Soviet power would fall and the Communists would be massacred in another St Bartholomew's Night. The murder in 1934 of Kirov, Stalin's colleague in the Politburo, was a promising start.

The NKVD reported all this. And they reported talk even more worrying. Peasants were saying, 'Soon there will be war. The peasants do not want to fight, the Red Army men will refuse to go into the trenches.'[19] Perhaps, they hoped, rescue would come from outside: the sad belief that the Western Allies, if not the Germans, would abolish the collective farms persisted not only among the peasantry, but even among the Moscow intelligentsia, right until the end of the war. All this was disturbing news for a government that believed it was on the brink of war. After all, in 1812 peasants had not at first been hostile to the invading French, and peasant rebellion had run at twice the usual rate in that year.[20] How would the peasants react if it came to another great clash with an invader from the West?

*

Millions of the young, the intelligent, and the enterprising deserted the village for the town to find work in Stalin's new factories and better themselves through the new opportunities for education. The population of Moscow jumped from two million in 1927 to over three and a half million in 1934.[21]

'Life in the big cities,' Alexander Zinoviev remembered, 'offered irresistible temptations. Country life was primitive and boring. My family lived on the land. We had a large and comfortable house. In Moscow the ten of us had to make do with a single room of twelve square yards – just over one square yard per head. Can you imagine?! Yet, we preferred life in Moscow.'[22]

Zinoviev became a professor at Moscow University, a dissident and an exile, who spent much of his time justifying Stalin. His brothers made equally good careers. They were not exceptional. Vladimir Frolov and Yevgeni Anufriev also came from peasant families but ended their careers as professors at Moscow University. Frolov was born in the Tula province, South of Moscow, in a forgotten village far from the nearest main road. In September 1940 he won a place at Moscow University. Too poor to live in the student hostel, he stayed with an uncle who lived in one room with his wife and two younger sons. In the intervals of study he kept himself by working as a labourer.

Yevgeni Anufriev was born in 1923 near Rzhev in the Tver Region. From his grandfather, a former serf, Yevgeni's father Alexander inherited five cows, three horses, a timber business and a two-storey house. In 1928, as the collectivisation began, Alexander was sent as a kulak to the camps, and his house and property were confiscated. Yevgeni went to live with a sister in Moscow, in one room divided by curtains to accommodate four families. Despite their unpromising political background, Yevgeni and his siblings all made good careers. One brother became a deputy minister and worked on the first Soviet atom bomb. Another, a metallurgist, received the Lenin Prize. A third was a geologist in Siberia. Another was an architect who designed Khrushchëv's Congress Hall in the Kremlin.

Not all the immigrants rose to the top, or even wanted to. Antonina Savina, a lively and intelligent woman, never lost her class origins. She came from an earlier wave of peasant immigration. She was born in 1923 in a village in the Ryazan Province. Her father, a cobbler, moved to Moscow before the First World War, at first without his family. He worked as an orderly in a small hospital, the 'Misericordia', so called after a famous icon of the Virgin. His wife and children joined him in 1925. He died a year later, but his wife went on working in the hospital. The family lived in a cellar in the hospital grounds. They had no running water or electricity, the toilet was in the next building, the heating consisted of a stove in the party wall between their cellar and the one next door, and they cooked on a primus. They washed themselves in tubs in the room itself.

Before the war, Antonina remembered, it was still safe for girls to be out in the city at all hours of the day and night. She and her friends used to wander round Red Square or go to the open-air dance hall on an island on the lake in the nearby park. It cost five kopeks to get into the hall, but they never paid: they squeezed through a hole in the fence round the back. In the winter they went skating or to the cinema. Antonina and her mother and her sister spent the whole of their working lives in the hospital and living in the cellar. They did not get running water or gas until after the war.[23]

Stalin knew well enough that he could not preserve his power by terror alone, that he could achieve nothing with a people sunk in sullen apathy. He set out to inculcate a mood of popular optimism, patriotism, and support for the wider objectives of the regime. In December 1935 he proclaimed, 'Life has become better, Comrades, life has become more cheerful.'[24] These winged words were widely quoted throughout the country, sometimes ironically but often with blind faith.

To back Stalin's claim, the government ended rationing in 1935. They put money into the retail trading system, and new department stores began to appear. Prices went up to finance the scheme: for clothing they doubled. Once again it was the better off and the privileged who prospered.

But at least the Communists opened their new system to the talents, or at least to those who were willing to conform to their political and social demands. By 1939 they had practically eradicated illiteracy, and created a comprehensive system of universal education. At first they favoured working-class students: the proportion of working-class children in higher education rose rapidly. Workers' Faculties helped those with no secondary education to go straight to university: Khrushchëv was one of those who benefited. But the bias against middle-class students was relaxed in the 1930s when the government returned to the disciplines of the old Russian gymnasium system, which they thought would be better adapted to meet the needs of the Five Year Plans for a qualified 'technical intelligentsia' capable of building Socialism in one country.

The Bolsheviks had allowed much experiment in education in their early years, and it was often to schools where the ghost of an experimental tradition persisted that the new rulers sent their own children: the children of the generals Gamarnik and Uborevich and the politician Bukharin, all of whom fell victim to the purges; the children of Kaganovich, Khrushchëv, and Shcherbakov, who survived. School No. 110 was one of the most distinguished. It traces its origins back to a girls' boarding school founded by a French émigré at the end of the eighteenth century and a private boys' school set up in 1906.[25] The schools were amalgamated after the 1917 revolution and claim some remarkable alumni: Kavelin, who advised Tsar Alexander II on the liberation of the serfs; the poet Marina Tsvetaeva and her sister; the dissident writer Andrei Sinyavski; Andrei Sakharov, the physicist (very briefly); Yeltsin's foreign minister Andrei Kozyrev; Markus Wolf, the former head of the East German secret police; and Misha Sohlman, the Secretary of the Swedish Nobel Prize Committee.[26] It was another pupil of School No. 110, the sculptor Daniel Mitlyanski, who made Sakharov's death mask when he died in 1989. Daniel's classmate Irina Golyamina made it her life's work to preserve the memory of the boys who never returned from the war. Her best friend at school was Veta Gamarnik, who was sent into exile as a schoolgirl after her father committed suicide to avoid the purges.[27]

Although the supply of books and ideas was strictly controlled, in practice ordinary people could still get hold of Russian and Western classics if they really wanted to. The breadth of reading among Russian schoolchildren in the 1930s seems remarkable. By the end of his first year in college, Anatoli Chernyaev had read the Russian classics, and the major works of English, French, German, Polish and Ancient Greek literature. Vladimir Kantovski, whose father had worked in the embassy in Paris and been arrested in 1938, was one class behind Irina

Golyamina and Daniel Mitlyanski. By the time he reached the senior (tenth) class in 1940, he had read not only the Russian classics: he had also read Dante's *Divine Comedy* and – like Baring's peasant soldiers – the epic poems of Milton. He and his classmates discussed politics and literature with surprising freedom, and drew some risky conclusions. Stalin, they decided, had betrayed the ideals of Lenin. Collectivisation and the draconian new labour legislation added up to the reintroduction of serfdom. The Molotov–Ribbentrop Pact of 1939 was the 'Fourth Partition of Poland'.

Their history teacher was Pavel Dukovski. He was very strict and did not suffer fools gladly, but Kantovski and his friends adored him. He never departed from the official line. But he forced the pupils to think for themselves and to draw their own conclusions from what they were studying. He was arrested in March 1941, accused of anti-Soviet propaganda, of making threats against one of the Soviet leaders and – ironically, in view of the imminent German attack – of expressing doubts about the Molotov–Ribbentrop Pact. He died in a camp in April 1942.[28]

Kantovski and his friends Lena Sobol and Anya Bovshever decided something had to be done, and circulated a series of anonymous letters of protest. The language of the letters was fiery, emotional, full of references to the classics of Russian literature, the language of clever adolescents. They attacked the teachers who had taken over from Dukovski and mocked the NKVD and its agents in the school.[29] Four editions of the correspondence were circulated around School No. 110 between March and May 1941. There was no official reaction, at least for the time being.

The Bolsheviks shared the passionate belief of the Russian intelligentsia in the central importance of culture, but they were determined that culture should serve none but the cause of Communism. Writers, journalists, painters, composers, film-makers, actors, theatre producers, musicians were herded into professional organisations so that they could be controlled by a judicious mixture of sticks and carrots. For those prepared to conform, the practical rewards were immense. Favoured artists received the formal honours of the Soviet State: Orders of Lenin and a variety of lesser awards. They were given luxury accommodation in specially built apartment blocks and in dachas around Moscow. Some ran imported motor cars. They were allowed to travel on cultural delegations, even to the capitalist West.

These privileges had to be earned, not only by producing work according to officially approved patterns, but also by giving active public support to the regime. You had to serve on public bodies at the demand of the Party: among those elected to the Moscow City Council in December 1939 were the puppeteer Sergei Obraztsov and Alexander Goldenveizer, the Director of the Moscow Conservatoire.[30] You had to make public speeches praising the Party and its Great Leader, Joseph Stalin. And when one of your artistic or literary colleagues stepped out of line, you had to join the chorus of denunciation which was the prelude to his expulsion from public life or worse.

High office risked attracting the unfavourable attention of the authorities, and it was shunned by the prudent or the timid. When Goldenveizer was offered the directorship of the Conservatoire, he wrote in his diary, 'I feel that I shall be committing suicide, but it seems I cannot refuse.'[31] For some the strain was too much. Alexander Fadeev, a good writer and a notorious cultural bureaucrat, was made Secretary of the Union of Writers. Despite appearances, he was not tough enough for the job. He was forced by the censors to rewrite his wartime novel *The Young Guard*, took to drink, and committed suicide in 1956. In his suicide note he wrote, 'It is impossible for me to live any further, since the art to which I have given my life has been destroyed by the self-confident, ignorant leadership of the Party.'[32]

To survive you cultivated a necessary schizophrenia. Vasili Grossman, who was himself a member of the Union of Writers at that time, subjected the moral obliquities of life under Stalin to an unsparing and meticulous examination in his novel of Stalingrad, *Life and Fate* (*Zhizn i Sudba*). 'How many times,' one of his characters asks himself,

> had [he] said and written one thing, when in his heart there was something quite different? But while he was speaking and writing … he believed that he was saying what he thought. And sometimes he said to himself: 'In any case, that's what the revolution requires.' … To achieve its ends, the revolution had abolished morality in the name of morality, it had justified the Pharisees, the talebearers,

> the hypocrites in the name of the future, it had explained why the innocent had to be consigned to the pit in the name of the happiness of the people as a whole.[33]

Grossman, writing while the Soviet system still had more than three decades to run, compares Stalin's regime directly with Hitler's. With surprising naivety, he hoped his novel might be published in the more relaxed Soviet Union of the 1960s. It did not come out in Russia until the Gorbachëv years. But, unlike *The Young Guard*, it has become a classic of Russian twentieth-century literature.

Among those who profited from the new system was the young Kirill Simonov. His father, a Tsarist officer, disappeared without trace during the First World War. His mother was a Princess Obolenskaya. Her second husband was another former Tsarist officer, who was briefly arrested in 1931; Kirill and his mother were turned out of their official accommodation and sought refuge with a local peasant. Two of Kirill's well-born aunts were sent to Siberia. He changed his name from Kirill to Konstantin because he could pronounce 'r' only with an aristocratic lisp. By the mid-1930s he was a young poet on the threshold of a brilliant career, which was to rest on his talent as a poet, playwright and war correspondent, on his personal charm – as appealing to men as to women – and on his skill at manoeuvring in the slippery corridors of Soviet literary and political power. His affair with the popular film star Valentina Serova, the wildly popular wartime poem he dedicated to her, 'Wait for Me', his poem about the battles in July 1941, 'The Roads around Smolensk' – all these made him into a national figure.

Simonov rose to become editor of *Novy Mir*, the country's most prestigious literary journal, the Deputy Secretary of the Union of Writers and a multiple winner of the Stalin Prize. He travelled throughout the world praising the Soviet state and its treatment of the arts. He signed almost everything he was asked to sign and denounced almost everything and everybody he was asked to denounce. But it was a time of shaky moral compromises, and Simonov too was troubled in his conscience. He did his best – within the limits of prudence – to protect fellow writers who fell out of official favour. His novel *The Living and the Dead*, based on his wartime notes and published at the beginning of Khrushchëv's thaw in 1959, is still one of the best fictional accounts of the catastrophe of 1941 and was immediately made into a sobering film. In a later book, *One Hundred Days of War*, Simonov wrestled with the problem of historical truth as he tried to understand the fateful hold Stalin had exercised over him and his fellow countrymen. The book was too close to the bone to be published in the Soviet Union. It came out as he had planned it only in 1999, long after he was dead.[34] At the end of his life, Simonov was still working on a book, provisionally called *Chetyre Ya* (*Four Egos*), to describe the personalities warring within him. His career is an example and a warning of how talented, ambitious, and essentially decent people find themselves having to compromise their integrity in order to survive and make their way in a totalitarian regime. As his secretary remarked after his death, 'To understand Simonov is to understand our times.'[35]

Stalin, himself a voracious reader, took the closest interest in every detail of the country's cultural life, and occasionally overrode the censors and the policemen to order a work published or a writer saved. But on the whole he found the writers a troublesome lot. Where he thought it necessary his reaction was savage. The writers Boris Pilnyak and Isaak Babel were shot. The poet Osip Mandelshtam died in the camps. The avant-garde theatre producer Meyerhold was tortured and killed.

Stalin seems to have concluded that all this highbrow stuff was not what he needed to persuade ordinary people that life was indeed getting better, that it really was more fun. For this he turned, with considerable success, to popular music, popular song and the cinema.

Ballroom and Latin American dancing became all the rage. The new class of Communist bureaucrats and their wives, anxious to acquire the 'culture' for which their rank now fitted them, learned to do the foxtrot and the tango. Voroshilov, the People's Commissar for Defence, made dancing lessons mandatory for officers in the Red Army. Big-band jazz and mass-produced folk song spread like wildfire. The music of Alexander Tsfasman was a mixture of Glenn Miller and Latin American rhythm, and still sits easy on the Western ear. The music of Leonid Utësov was thinner and more sentimental, close to the nineteenth-century romances which still influence musical taste in Russia today. The speciality of Lidia Ruslanova, one of the most popular singers of the day, was the raucous village songs she had heard as a child. Chaliapin, who came from the same part of the world as she did, was reduced to tears when he heard her on the radio. Her song 'Katyusha' swept the Soviet Union, and during the war it swept the rest of the world as well.[36]

All these people became rich. Tsfasman was reputed to be one of the richest people in the Soviet Union. During the war Utësov personally donated two fighter aeroplanes to the 5th Guards Fighter Regiment.[37] When Ruslanova and her husband, one of Marshal Zhukov's generals, were prosecuted and imprisoned after the war for illegally acquiring valuable works of art, her defence was that she had paid for them out of her earnings.

The Bolsheviks believed that the cinema was their most powerful weapon of propaganda, and it was to the cinema that Stalin chiefly looked to help reconcile the masses to the Communist regime.[38] In the 1920s the films of Eisenstein, Pudovkin, and Kozintsev achieved and have retained the status of classics. Unfortunately, ordinary people preferred Douglas Fairbanks in *The Mark of Zorro* and *The Thief of Bagdad*. Under Stalin's eagle eye, a new kind of Soviet film began to emerge: uncomplicated, optimistic, sometimes heroic. The new films, such as *Chapaev* about a peasant hero of the Civil War, were often very good and remain genuinely popular even today. Aleksandrov's musical *Volga-Volga* (1938) was Stalin's favourite, and he spoke about the performance of its star, Liubov Orlova, on every appropriate and inappropriate occasion. Even the highbrow art directors gradually crept back into work. Eisenstein returned to favour in 1938 with his anti-Nazi film *Alexander Nevsky*, with music by Prokofiev.

Moscow in 1941 felt like a village not only because there were still courtyards and animals close to the city centre, but because it was also a place where everyone seemed to know everyone else, where people lived out their lives in tight communities, where they relied for mutual support on their family, their school, their colleagues at work and even on the professional organisations which Stalin created for their control.

This intimacy of everyday life existed at the apex of the pyramid as it did at the base. Stalin and his cronies, their wives and their children lived on top of one another in the Kremlin, in their elite apartment blocks, in their dachas, and on their holidays. This parody of Bloomsbury survived even the brutalities of the purges, when within Stalin's own circle parents were torn from children, wives from husbands, and slaughtered, while the survivors denounced their former friends and colleagues – sometimes even their spouses – as traitors to the great ideal of Communism.[39]

The pattern ran throughout society. The families of senior scientists lived together in specially built blocks of flats in Moscow, and spent their summers together in the same dacha settlements on the Moscow River. Officers in the armed forces joined together, trained together, were promoted together, and served together. Artists lived together in official studio-apartments in the courtyard of the Academy of the Fine Arts, opposite the old Post Office building. Actors, directors and scene-shifters spent their whole lives together in the same theatre company. Workers spent their childhood holidays at the factory's Pioneer camp, worked their whole lives where their parents had worked before them, and stayed on in retirement to run the factory's voluntary organisations. The professional criminals, the oddly named '*vory v zakone*' ('thieves at law'), banded together in solid and impenetrable groups to defy the state. Everyone knew everyone, everyone quarrelled with everyone, everyone slept with everyone, while their children played and grew up together. Nobody ever said, 'Mind your own business,' because the business of each was the business of all.

The Communist authorities regarded these group solidarities with mixed feelings. They were repelled by the idea that people might have loyalties to bodies other than the Party and the government. On the other hand, people were easier to manage if they were held together in a group. You could issue instructions to them through the Party organisations which each group contained. The control was never absolute. People continued to think for themselves – often the most subversive thoughts, as the NKVD regularly reported to their masters. But the ability to deal with people as groups and not as individuals – and the acceptance by ordinary people that this was natural and inevitable – was a considerable administrative convenience, and enabled the regime to mobilise the population of Moscow during the crisis of 1941 far more effectively than would have been possible under a more liberal system.

The first priority of ordinary people and of the ambitious alike – in peace as in war, even at the height of the Great Purge in 1937 and 1938 – was of course to survive, and to feed and clothe themselves and their families.

No one in Stalin's totalitarian society could entirely escape the evasions, the lies, the shabby compromises, the lesser and greater acts of cowardice and betrayal. But there was more to it than that. As she looked back on these times from the depths of old age, the distinguished critic Lidia Ginzburg wrote:

> People are wrong to imagine the calamitous epochs of the past as totally taken up by calamity. They also consist of a great deal else – the sort of things which life in general consists of, although against a particular background. The thirties is not just hard work and fear, it's also a mass of talented people with a will to carry things out.[40]

For decades after the revolution, a kind of revolutionary enthusiasm for the building of a new way of life remained, despite the privations, the Great Purge, the incessant demands which the Party placed on high and low alike. Intellectuals, scientists, industrial managers, generals, officials, convinced themselves that out of all the travail a new society would indeed be born. There was much to be proud of: the new factories, the spread of education, the social welfare system, the opportunities of advancement now open to people who would previously have remained at the bottom of the social pile. There were huge flaws, of course. But these were the inevitable flaws of a transitional society struggling to survive in a hostile world. Harsh measures and harsh discipline were unavoidable for the time being. The weaknesses, stupidities and even the crimes would surely pass, as Socialism was established at home and eventually abroad.

Russia's intellectuals, brought up on the ideas of Leo Tolstoy, believed that the ordinary peasant, the worker, the soldier, possessed a wisdom beyond that of their more educated 'betters', and this too undermined their capacity for critical and independent thought.[41] Even the sophisticated and much-travelled writer Ilya Ehrenburg half managed to convince himself that the doubts he felt about the way Stalin's regime was going were the doubts of an intellectual out of touch with the needs and psychology of the masses.[42] The 'dissident' Alexander Zinoviev, who fought in the war, was still convinced forty years later that 'Soviet life is imbued with a sense of common purpose, which imparts a firm orientation and a new and rich consciousness. It makes you feel that, despite all the failures, you are going somewhere.'[43]

The ordinary people themselves kept their counsel, except perhaps when they were drunk. Beneath the surface they were unpredictable and anarchic, as they had always been. A young woman called before the Komsomol committee at her factory to contribute to a 'voluntary' state loan simply turned her back, bent over, raised her skirt over her head, and walked off, saying, 'Comrade Stalin and the rest of you can kiss me just wherever you find it convenient.' In the embarrassed silence which followed, one member of the committee tittered nervously, 'Did you see she wasn't wearing any knickers?'[44]

– THREE –

WARS AND RUMOURS OF WARS

Marshal Rokossovski's wartime memoirs begin innocently enough, but with perhaps a touch of deliberately concealed irony: 'In the spring of 1940 I spent some time with my family in Sochi.'[1] How Konstantin Rokossovski, his wife Yulia and his daughter Ada happened to be at a holiday resort on the Black Sea at just that moment is a story in itself, which Rokossovski never told.

Rokossovski was one of the most successful of all Stalin's generals. His record of success as a Front commander from 1942 to 1945 was unbroken.[2] In 1999 an opinion poll in Russia rated him second only to Marshal Zhukov, the 'architect of victory' in the Second World War.[3] Molotov, Stalin's Prime Minister, thought Zhukov was the better man for a rough affair, but he put Rokossovski next. Marshal Golovanov, post-war commander of the Soviet long-range bomber force and a crony of Stalin's, rated Rokossovski above Zhukov, and put him in the same class as the great generals of the past, Suvorov and Kutuzov.[4] One of his long-time associates summed him up thus: 'He was likeable, elegant, generous, correct in his personal relationships, a highly knowledgeable soldier with a first class analytical mind.'[5]

Everyone remarked on his courtesy towards people of whatever rank, soldiers and civilians alike. The writer Ilya Ehrenburg thought him the most polite of all the generals he had met.[6] He never raised his voice in anger when dealing with his colleagues and subordinates at the front, and he never used physical violence against them, unlike many of his fellow officers. At the most his voice would take on a more steely note.[7] He was tall, erect, physically fit, a good dancer, especially of the polka. When he met the mother of his wartime chauffeur, he kissed her hand – a piece of gallantry which betrayed his Polish origins and which she never forgot. Not surprisingly, he liked women and they liked him. During the Battle of Moscow he was the favourite of the city's housewives: 'He'll show [the Germans] where the crayfish go in winter.'[8]

One of his more distant admirers was an Englishwoman called Mitzi Price, who lived in Ruislip outside London. She wrote to him in February 1945, to say that she had seen his picture in the British press. He looked just like a boyfriend that she had lost in the war. Thereafter she bombarded him with cards at Christmas and Easter and on Valentine's Day. She decorated a corner of her living room as a shrine in his honour. He kept her photographs. But he never replied to her letters, and she never met him.[9]

Konstanty Rokossowski was born in Warsaw on 21 December 1896, the son of a Polish father and a White Russian mother.[10] His father Ksawery Wojciech came from a family of minor Polish gentry going back to the fourteenth century which had fallen on hard times. His great-grandfather, Józef Rokossowski, rode with the Polish cavalry in the armies of Napoleon.[11] Rokossovski later spelled his surname the Russian way, and took the patronymic Konstantinovich because his father's name could not be bent to the Russian language.

Rokossovski's father died in an accident in 1902, and the boy spent his early childhood and youth in Warsaw – then under Russian occupation – living with his uncle Alexander Rokossovski and learning to ride in his uncle's stables outside Warsaw. He worked in a stocking factory in the Warsaw suburb of Praga, and later in a stonemason's business. He was already politically active, and for his participation in a May Day demonstration was briefly imprisoned by the Russian authorities in Warsaw's notorious Pawiak Prison, used by the Gestapo during the German occupation from 1939 to 1944.

Because of his skill on a horse, Rokossovski volunteered to join the Tsarist cavalry in 1914 and was rapidly promoted. He was twice wounded, and three times awarded the St George's Cross, one of Russia's highest awards for gallantry. As the tsarist army suffered one defeat after another during the second and third year of the war, Rokossovski retreated with it into Russia proper. After the revolution, he lost touch with his family, who were now living in the newly independent Poland.

Rokossovski fought with the Bolsheviks during the Civil War, and remained in the Red Army thereafter. He married Yulia Petrovna Barmina in 1923, and their daughter Ada was born shortly afterwards. Despite many later ups and downs, they remained together for the rest of their lives: a feat equalled by only one of Stalin's other Marshals.[12]

In 1936 he was sent to command the 5th Cavalry Corps in Pskov, in the Western Military District. In June 1937 a former colleague, a senior political commissar, recommended to Voroshilov, the Commissar for Defence, that he be investigated by the NKVD 'because of [his] suspected links with counter-revolutionary elements ... He is a Pole. His social background needs to be seriously examined. He has shown a desire to work abroad.'[13]

Rokossovski was put under house arrest, denounced by his brother officers, excluded from the Party, and imprisoned in the notorious Kresty Prison in Leningrad. Yulia was thrown out of her home, ostracised by her husband's former colleagues and their families, and forbidden to live in any of the country's main cities. When she came to rest in the small Southern town of Armavir, she was sacked from one job after another when her employers learned that she was the wife of an 'enemy of the people'. Ada was expelled from school for refusing to denounce her father in public.[14]

Rokossovski's interrogator confronted him with 'evidence' that he was recruited in 1916 for Polish intelligence by his friend and comrade Adolf Juszkiewicz, whom he had then helped to escape into Poland. Rokossovski pointed out that Juszkiewicz had been killed in 1920 fighting the White Army. The interrogator then accused him of spying for the Japanese during his service on the Manchurian frontier. He invited Rokossovski to sign the appropriate confession. Rokossovski refused to cooperate and was savagely beaten. He lost eight teeth, and they broke three of his ribs. In March 1939 he was put before the Collegium of the Supreme Military Court of the USSR. He again rejected the 'evidence' collected by the investigation, and demanded to be confronted with the witnesses. One had already been shot. Another was still alive, but he withdrew his evidence before the court, saying he had been tortured.

Rokossovski was not released: the case was simply postponed *sine die*. But by now the Red Army was getting desperately short of officers. Many had died during the Winter War against Finland. Many more were needed to staff the new formations created as the army quadrupled in size after 1939. Stalin ordered the release of officers against whom nothing had been found. Rokossovski was let out of prison in March 1940, reunited with his family, and sent down to Sochi to recuperate.

When he was fit enough, he was first sent back to his old command, the 5th Cavalry Corps in Pskov, and then to the 9th Mechanised Corps. When the ranks of General and Admiral were reintroduced in May 1940, Rokossovski was made a Major-General, along with ten other former prisoners.[15]

An oft-repeated story has it that Stalin called him in at about this time. 'Well, Rokossovski, I don't seem to have seen you around for some time. Where did you get to?'

'I was arrested, Comrade Stalin. I was sitting in prison.'

'A fine time you chose to go to prison!' Stalin laughed and got down to the business of the day.

The story may not be true, but it is certainly in character. Stalin was impressed by Rokossovski's independence of mind, the firm confidence with which he took decisions, and his ability to justify his decisions with sound arguments.[16] He addressed him by his first name and patronymic, Konstantin Konstantinovich – a Russian usage which manages to be both respectful and somewhat informal. Only Shaposhnikov, the ailing Chief of Staff, was similarly honoured. The rest of his generals Stalin called 'Comrade'.[17]

The Bolsheviks mounted their coup in October 1917 with no organised armed forces of their own. At first they had to rely on armed workers and military units who came over to their side. As White and foreign armies pressed in upon them, Trotsky, the Commissar for War, began to recruit professionals from the former Imperial Army. Among them were Georgi Zhukov, Semën Timoshenko, Semën Budënny, and Ivan Koniev. Many of those who had become Soviet Marshals by 1945 fought against the Germans in the First World War, against the Whites in the Civil War, against the Poles, the Spaniards, the Chinese, the Japanese and the Finns. They had thought hard about their experience and had done their best to draw the appropriate lessons. The Soviet high command in 1941 had far more recent experience in the conduct of actual operations than their French and British counterparts, who had been defeated by the Germans a year earlier. The disasters of the first year of the war sprang from different causes.

Georgi Zhukov was the most successful, and is now the most controversial, of all Stalin's Marshals. He came from a poor peasant family in the Kaluga Province, near Moscow. Like Rokossovski, he served in the cavalry during the First World War, was wounded and was twice decorated with the St George's Cross. He joined the Bolsheviks, and served under Timoshenko in the Civil War and under Rokossovski thereafter. He rose rapidly, successfully evading accusations of disloyalty at the time of the military purges in 1937. His reputation as the main architect of victory has been fostered by the Russian military, and is probably secure. But he is now much criticised for his excessive ambition, the poverty of his strategic thinking, his carelessness with the lives of his men, and his unwillingness to stand up to Stalin, especially on the eve of the German attack in June 1941.

Zhukov's reputation was made in 1939 in the course of a small war, forgotten by the outside world, which began when the Japanese invaded Russia's protégé Mongolia. The honours of battle in the first months were equal. Zhukov was sent to sort things out, and at the Battle of Khalkin Gol he combined his infantry, tanks and aircraft to inflict heavy losses on the Japanese, who were forced to sue for peace. Stalin was impressed. In January 1941 he made Zhukov Chief of the General Staff. It was a job for which Zhukov was not well suited: a German military appraisal described him as an 'outspoken man of action whose qualities are more those of the will than of the intellect'.[18] In August 1941 Stalin sent him back to the battlefield. After the war first Stalin and then Khrushchëv suspected him of excessive political ambition – the old Bolshevik fear of Bonapartism – and cut him down to size with great brutality.

Zhukov was married three times: he was rebuked by the Party for drunkenness and irregularities in his private life.[19] In his family circle he was charming, mild and warm.[20] But his style of command was ferocious, his language was abusive, he personally supervised the execution of officers for cowardice or desertion, and he was notorious for striking officers and men who displeased him (an old Tsarist military tradition followed by many of his fellows).[21] Rokossovski had once been his senior, but fell behind during his time in prison. He commented that Zhukov:

> had everything to excess – talent, energy, confidence in his own strengths ... We differed about the role of the commander, and the manner in which he should demonstrate the power of his will ... A demanding nature is a necessary, an essential characteristic of a commander. But an iron will should also always be combined with sensitivity towards subordinates, and ability to rely on their intelligence and initiative ... [Zhukov] did not always follow that principle. He was sometimes unjust in the heat of the moment.[22]

Three other future Marshals also played a major part in the battles before Moscow: Semën Timoshenko, Semën Budënny and Ivan Koniev. Like Zhukov, they came from simple families, served with distinction as NCOs in the First World War, and began to rise during the Civil War. Klimenti Voroshilov, who also became a Marshal, was not a professional soldier at all. But his close association with Stalin during the Civil War served him well until he was sacked for incompetence during the siege of Leningrad in 1941.

Two other men came from a different mould, and one of them met a very different fate. Boris Shaposhnikov's modest middle-class family was too poor to put him through university. So he got a scholarship as a cadet at a military college in Moscow, became an outstanding staff officer in the First World War and joined the Bolsheviks in 1917. He wrote a number of important works on military theory in the 1930s. He was Chief of Staff from 1937 to 1943, apart from a gap in 1941, when Zhukov took over. He became a Marshal in 1940.

Mikhail Tukhachevski came from a family with aristocratic and Polish connections. A linguist and a musician, he was a friend of the composer Shostakovich. He became an officer cadet in 1911, passed out top of his class in 1914, and entered the crack Semënovski Guards Regiment. In the First World War he was wounded and taken prisoner.

He too threw in his lot with the Bolsheviks. He drove the invading Poles from Ukraine in 1920, but was repelled in his turn on the outskirts of Warsaw. Like Shaposhnikov, he was a military intellectual, with advanced ideas about the use of armour in modern warfare. In 1935 he was one of the first to be made a Soviet Marshal.[23]

One group in the military were Stalin's particular favourites. The cult of the aviator was as strong in Russia in the 1930s as it was in America and Europe. Long-distance fliers, like the Russian Chkalov and the American Lindbergh, became national figures. So did the young airmen who made their names fighting as 'volunteers' in the Spanish Civil War. Many became Heroes of the Soviet Union for their exploits there. Press and propaganda called them 'Stalin's Falcons'. One, Serov, was the husband of the popular actress Valentina Serova: he was killed on a navigation exercise with the equally famous woman flier, Polina Osipenko. Two of them, Yakov Smushkevich and Pavel Rychagov, became commanders of the Red Air Force at the ages of thirty-seven and thirty respectively.

Smushkevich came from a small town in Latvia, one of seven children of an itinerant Jewish tailor. His studied for three years in an Orthodox Jewish elementary school, joined the Red Army in 1918, and switched to the air force in 1922. In Spain Ernest Hemingway knew him as 'General Douglas'. On his return to Moscow he became Deputy Commander of the Red Air Force. Stalin and Voroshilov insisted he adopt the patronymic Vladimirovich, since his correct patronymic, Vulfovich, betrayed his Jewish origin.[24] He and his family lived in the House on the Embankment, and were known for their cheerful parties, where the guests danced to fashionable Western music from a radiola which Smushkevich had brought back from Spain.

In 1938 Smushkevich was severely injured in a crash while practising for the May Day Parade. Both his legs were shattered, but he defied his doctors, learned to walk on crutches, and stayed in the air force. He managed the air campaign in Khalkin Gol for Zhukov and was made a Hero of the Soviet Union for the second time. Promoted to command the air force, he was responsible for the botched air campaign against Finland during the Winter War. But his career was apparently unaffected. He remained one of Stalin's favourites and in December 1940 he became Deputy Chief of the General Staff.

Pavel Rychagov was just twenty-five when he went to Spain. In 1938 he fought in China against the Japanese. In 1939 he was promoted Major-General, and fought against the Finns. In February 1941 he was appointed Deputy Minister of Defence and Commander of the Red Air Force. He was still only thirty. His wife Maria Nesterenko became deputy commander of a special services air regiment in 1940. The couple became popular public figures, always seen in the newspapers and in the Moscow theatres. They too lived in the House on the Embankment, that place of ill omen.

There was a remarkable group of women fliers as well. Marina Raskova was the first woman to qualify as an air force navigator. At the age of twenty-two she became the first woman instructor at the Zhukovski Air Academy. In 1938 she participated in an attempt to set a new long-distance record from Moscow to Komsomolsk in the Far East with two other women, Valentina Grizodubova and Polina Osipenko. Their plane, the *Rodina* (*Motherland*), a converted bomber, ran out of fuel shortly before reaching its destination. Marina Raskova, in the navigator's cockpit, baled out in accordance with the established emergency routine. The other two landed safely in a swamp. It was ten days before Raskova found her way to them through the forest. All three were rescued, and became instant heroines on their return to Moscow. They were met by Khrushchëv and Kaganovich, and paraded in triumph to the Kremlin, where they were greeted with kisses by Stalin. In his toast at the celebratory dinner he said, 'Today these women have avenged the heavy centuries of the oppression of women.' All three were made Heroes of the Soviet Union. Raskova was to turn her connection with Stalin to good use when the war broke out.[25]

In 1937 and 1938 Stalin's purges ripped through the military, as they did through all other parts of Soviet society, in an orgy of self-destruction. From the start the Bolsheviks had been convinced that the capitalist world would not rest until it had eliminated the first Socialist state in the world. The Soviet state was indeed surrounded by potential or actual enemies from the moment of its birth. Between 1918 and 1939 it was attacked by the Americans, the French, the British, the Poles, the Chinese and the Japanese. Émigré political groups continued to intrigue into the 1930s in the belief that Soviet power could not last.

The fears of the Bolshevik leadership were more than a mere obsessive fantasy. But there was paranoia as well. In Stalin it reached the proportions of a monomania.

To ensure his own supremacy and the loyalty of his people in the face of threats real or imagined, Stalin used terror without inhibition. In 1937 and 1938 about two and a half million people were arrested throughout the country. Stalin and his colleagues personally signed the documents which sent more than forty thousand people to their deaths or to the camps. Around eight hundred thousand people were executed for political offences in the country as a whole. Many more were killed without a hearing, or died under interrogation or in prison. Very much greater numbers died natural or unnatural deaths in the camps.[26]

In the four years before the war more than thirty-two thousand people died at the hands of the secret police in Moscow and the surrounding Region.[27] They included five previous heads of the Moscow City Party, two previous heads of Moscow City Council and thirty party secretaries of lower rank.[28] At first the corpses were disposed of inside Moscow. When the NKVD ran out of space, they set up two special burial 'zones' outside the city, disguised as army firing ranges for the benefit of inquisitive local inhabitants. One was in a stud farm in the village of Butovo. Nearly twenty-one thousand people were killed here in 1937 and 1938. They included priests, workers, peasants, Frenchmen, Americans, Italians, Chinese, Japanese, people from more than sixty different nationalities. Some were shot. Others were gassed in the specially converted lorries which brought them from the city. Butovo is now a burgeoning dormitory suburb of Moscow, and most of its inhabitants know and probably care little about what went on there seven decades ago.[29]

The other 'zone' was in the grounds of an NKVD dacha named after the Kommunarka State Farm next door. Most of the victims here came from the new elite: Lenin's colleagues, like Bukharin and Rykov; the wives of the murdered leaders of the Red Army; writers like Boris Pilynak; Sergei Efron, the husband of the poet Marina Tsvetaeva; and the leaders of the NKVD itself. Many of these executions were carried out by a squad under the command of Vasili Blokhin, a specialist in such matters. Blokhin is said to have personally killed the theatre director Meyerhold, the writer Isaak Babel and Mikhail Koltsov, the journalist and hero of the Spanish Civil War.[30] He took a major part in planning and implementing the notorious massacre of Polish officers in 1940, wearing a leather apron and cap and long leather gloves and using a German Walther pistol because, unlike the Soviet equivalent, it did not jam when it became hot with long use. He eventually became a Major-General: a photograph shows him in full uniform, handsome, dignified, and heavily bemedalled. But after Stalin's death he was disgraced by Khrushchëv, and stripped of his rank and uniform 'for discrediting himself during his work for the organs'. According to the account of one indignant patriot, he took himself home and hanged himself.[31]

Stalin's prime target among the military was Marshal Tukhachevski. His suspicions had already been aroused by earlier reports that a group of ex-tsarist army officers looked to Tukhachevski to lead a coup.[32] In June 1937 Tukhachevski was shot, together with three Army Commanders, Yakir, Uborevich and Kork, for conspiring with Nazi Germany against the Soviet Union.[33] Yan Gamarnik, head of the Political Directorate of the Red Army and editor of the army newspaper *Krasnaya Zvezda*, shot himself in his own apartment. Bliuma Gamarnik, Nina Uborevich, Yekaterina Kork, and Nina Tukhachevskaya were all arrested as wives of 'enemies of the people' and sent to the camps. Their daughters were sent to homes for the children of enemies of the people. When they turned eighteen, they too were arrested and sent to the camps.

Three of the Soviet Union's five marshals were executed during the purge. So were fifteen out of sixteen army commanders, sixty of the sixty-seven corps commanders, 70 per cent of the division commanders, and a large proportion of the senior political commissars. Many thousands of other officers were arrested. An unknown number died in prison or were shot. Thousands more were dismissed the service for non-political offences, though many were later reinstated.[34]

The figures are disputed, and the proportion of the total officer corps who were eliminated may have been comparatively small. But the willingness to take responsibility, to risk the unorthodox, if necessary to interpret or disobey orders in the light of changing circumstances – all this was knocked out of the survivors, in many cases literally, by the NKVD's interrogators. Every senior officer knew that the NKVD had files full of denunciations which could be used against him at the drop of a hat. All knew that if it came to war they could face summary execution on a whim. The wonder is not that they performed so badly when the crunch came, but that they performed so well.

In October 1938 the mood lightened. Stalin sacked Yezhov, the head of the NKVD, and replaced him with Lavrenti Beria. To make the point more clearly, he had Yezhov himself arrested and shot. He told a Party Congress in March 1939 that the domestic enemies of socialism had been crushed. The NKVD would in future direct its main efforts against spies, murderers, and saboteurs introduced into the country by its foreign enemies. For a while the number of arrests and executions declined. But this apparent relaxation, too, was a passing illusion: mass killing started again with the outbreak of war.

Stalin assumed that Hitler would sooner or later implement his much-publicised plan to expand Germany's living space by means of a crusade against Bolshevism. The failure of Britain and France in 1938 and 1939 to stand up to Hitler or to negotiate seriously with the Russians confirmed to him that they would not – probably could not – offer the Soviet Union effective military support against the Germans. He drew the reasonable conclusion that he should get what he could from Hitler. So in August 1939 he struck his deal: the Soviet-German Pact, under which he was assigned Eastern Poland and the Baltic States. From now on his was a policy of riding two horses: delaying the outbreak of war with Hitler by every possible measure of appeasement, and using the time to put the Red Army in shape to fight the Germans when the time came.

His calculations were entirely overthrown by the speed and completeness with which the Germans destroyed the French army and defeated the British in May and June 1940. It was the rudest possible shock. Hitler's generals had shown a mastery of armoured warfare which Stalin knew the Russians could hardly match. Now France was out of the war. The British were impotent and confined in their home island. It would not take Hitler long to finish them off. He would then be free to turn on the Soviet Union. The crisis was closing in on Stalin much more rapidly than he had bargained for. His appeasement of Hitler became increasingly desperate. What had originally been a sensible policy began to fall apart.

It was not that Stalin had neglected to prepare his country for war. It had been a constant theme of his speeches and he had given the Red Army huge numbers of modern guns and aircraft, and more tanks than the whole of the rest of the world put together. But the recent fighting in Spain, the Far East, Poland and Finland had shown up many weaknesses. The Soviet aircraft in Spain in 1937 were modern for their day, but the tubby little Il-15s and Il-16s were already trembling on the verge of obsolescence. The tanks were vulnerable to anti-tank guns, they could not be manoeuvred in the mass because they had no radios, and the arrangements for their support were inadequate. In the jackal's war of 1939 against a Poland already defeated by the Wehrmacht, the armoured columns ground to a halt for lack of fuel and maintenance.[35]

As for Finland, the Soviet leaders believed, according to Khrushchëv, that 'All we had to do was raise our voice a little bit, and the Finns would obey. If that didn't work, we could fire one shot and the Finns would put up their hands and surrender.'[36] The illusion was shattered when the Finns fought back with a skill the Russians could not match. They themselves were unprepared for winter warfare. They had no ski troops, they had no sub-machine guns for close-quarter fighting among trees, and their tanks rapidly bogged down in the snow. In one of a number of masterly operations, a small Finnish force closed through the forest on the Soviet 44th Motorised Division, trapped it on the highway, and cut it to pieces. The Soviet commander and his political commissar were among the few survivors to make it back to the Soviet lines, where they were court-martialled and shot.[37] In March 1940 Timoshenko eventually crushed the Finns with a costly offensive of overwhelming weight. Observing the shambles, Hitler concluded that the Soviet Union was indeed a paper tiger.

Stalin held a conference in April 1940 to draw the appropriate lessons. The army had been overconfident, he said. Its intelligence had been disgracefully poor, the artillery had lacked shells, the infantry had lacked mortars and automatic weapons, there were not enough tanks or aircraft. Too many officers believed that what had worked during the Civil War would be good enough for modern warfare. Thank God, he concluded, that the Red Army had got its baptism of fire from the Finns, not the Luftwaffe.[38]

Timoshenko now replaced the incompetent Voroshilov as Commissar for Defence and embarked on a far-reaching but inevitably rushed programme of reform. He immediately set up nine Mechanised Corps to match the German Panzers. Twenty more were planned in the early spring of 1941. The tank designers were already working on an innovative new vehicle which was to become the T-34. Artëm Mikoyan, the brother of Politburo member Anastas and co-designer of the MiG fighters, Alexander Yakovlev, Sergei Iliushin and other brilliant designers were developing new aircraft capable of matching their German equivalents and new factories were set up to build them.[39]

In the autumn of 1940 the General Staff began planning for a possible defensive war against Germany. The Western border of the Soviet Union was split in two by the Pripet Marshes, almost impassable to an invading force. Would the main German attack be to the North or the South of the marshes? Stalin believed that they were more likely to attack to the South, where Hitler would find the economic riches and the living space for the German people which he had so long demanded. It was here that the Soviet forces were eventually concentrated. Unfortunately, the assumption was flawed. In June 1941 the Germans attacked along three major axes, in the Centre and the North as well as the South.[40]

In January 1941 the Soviet High Command held two war games to test the ability of the Red Army to cope with a German attack. In the first, the Germans were assumed to have struck in the North and the Centre. In the second, they were assumed to have attacked in the South. Under both scenarios the outcome was a defeat for the defenders. Kirill Meretskov, the Chief of Staff, gave such a confusing account of the lessons to be drawn that Stalin sacked him on the spot in favour of Zhukov.[41] It was clearer than ever that war must be avoided at all costs until the Red Army was ready to fight.

That was all very well. But the practical problems were daunting. The Red Army had to be moved forward from its old defensive positions to cover the new territories that the Soviet Union had gained in Poland and the Baltic States. New military airfields had to be built from scratch, existing roads and railways extended, and supply depots constructed to accommodate the army's food, weapons, ammunition and fuel. Soviet troops were employed in building fortifications, stores, railways and roads, instead of training. This huge task was not completed by the time the Germans attacked: on 15 April 1941 the Staff reported to Stalin that many of the new fortified zones were unfit for war, unfinished and only partially manned by troops whose training was inadequate.[42] Nor was the Red Army able to fall back on its old defences as it retreated, for these had been abandoned and largely dismantled.

The Red Army needed time to master its new weapons. Commanders needed to learn how to organise and use the new armoured formations. The Russians had many more tanks than the Germans. But the older tanks were unreliable and many were worn out. The new KV-1s and T-34s were superior to the German machines. But they were only just coming into service. Most units still lacked wireless communications and had to rely on vulnerable field telephones. Where wireless was available, many officers did not know how to handle it. Many of their men were barely trained. Tank crews often had only a couple of hours' driving experience. Training accidents were destroying several aircraft each day. An analysis of the professional knowledge of commanding officers in the frontier military districts conducted in the winter of 1940–41 marked all as 'Poor', with the exception of the Odessa Military District, which was marked 'Average'.[43]

Officer training programmes were enormously accelerated as the Red Army expanded headlong between 1937 and 1941. But it was impossible to produce enough experienced commanders or men for the new formations. When the war began, three-quarters of the officers had been with their units for less than one year.[44] They had not had time to get to know their commands, and a surprising number were on summer leave.[45]

Stalin and his generals were well aware of what was in the wind. Intelligence of an impending German attack poured in relentlessly from the well-placed network of Soviet agents in Berlin, London, Tokyo, Washington and throughout Eastern Europe. The Russians had their people in the Luftwaffe headquarters and the economics ministry in Berlin. They had Anthony Blunt in London and Richard Sorge in Tokyo. Their embassies and military missions all over Eastern Europe counted the trainloads of heavy equipment moving eastwards. German reconnaissance aircraft began to appear over the Soviet frontier. Incautious

German officers boasted that the Red Army would collapse within days of attack: it would be a 'military stroll'.[46]

As the winter of 1941 turned into spring, the intelligence became increasingly detailed, accurate and timely. But even when the raw intelligence is good, all depends on the way in which it is interpreted and used.[47] The task of interpretation fell mostly to the Main Intelligence Directorate (GRU) of the Commissariat of Defence under General Filip Golikov. Golikov, 'extremely astute and well informed' in the eyes of British officers who met him, had to steer a careful path between assessing the intelligence objectively, and risking Stalin's displeasure if his interpretation failed to fit the dictator's preconceptions.[48] His predecessor, the airman Ivan Proskurov, had won his spurs in Spain and had stood up robustly to Stalin's criticism of the intelligence provided during the Finnish war. Golikov, more prudent or perhaps more servile, bent his judgements to serve his master. He has been much criticised. Other men in other countries have done the same, even though the penalties for independence of mind were usually less severe. Proskurov and two of Golikov's other predecessors were shot.

At first, the intelligence could reasonably be interpreted in two different ways. Either Hitler was intending to attack the Soviet Union in short order. Or he was intending to blackmail the Soviet Union into further economic and political concessions while he pursued his war against Britain to a conclusion, an interpretation assiduously promoted by the Germans to divert attention from their real objective. For Stalin, the second interpretation was by far the most attractive, since it could give him the time he needed to put the Red Army in shape to fight the Germans when the moment came. His optimism was bolstered by Beria, who had his own stream of reporting through the NKVD.

As the months went by, the evidence moved increasingly against Stalin's optimistic interpretation. In October 1940 the NKVD concluded that two-thirds of Germany's infantry and mechanised divisions were now deployed against the Soviet Union.[49] At the end of December 1940 General Tupikov, the Military Attaché in Berlin, forwarded a report by his agent 'Aryan' that the Germans were planning to attack in March.[50] Hitler had issued his Directive 21 for 'Operation Barbarossa', the codename for the German attack, ten days earlier. There was no attack in March, and Stalin's belief that Hitler was bluffing was reinforced as other deadlines came and went without a German move. But Soviet agents were now reporting that the Germans believed that Britain could be brought to its knees by submarine warfare alone. They could therefore move on Russia with no worries about their rear; and the Red Army would collapse within eight days. The British passed on an unilluminating piece of intelligence about German troop movements from their *Enigma* code-breaking operation, and a more substantial Swedish report which named 20 May as the day for the German attack.[51] The Russians suspected a plot: when Hitler's deputy, Rudolf Hess, flew to Britain, they immediately assumed that he had gone there for some nefarious and probably anti-Soviet purpose. 'The majority of the intelligence reports which indicate the likelihood of war with the Soviet Union in spring 1941,' Golikov emphasised in a report at the end of March, 'emerge from Anglo-American sources, the immediate purpose of which is undoubtedly to seek the worsening of relations between the USSR and Germany.' He concluded that 'the most likely timing for the beginning of military operations against the USSR will be after a victory over Britain or after the conclusion with her of an advantageous peace.'[52]

It was entirely in the British interest that hostilities should break out between Germany and the Soviet Union, and Stalin had no intention of falling for that trick. He concluded that the Germans' threatening posture was at least in part a bluff, that any attack would be preceded by an ultimatum, and that they would strike only if he refused to meet their demands.

This was of course what he wanted to believe. It was neither a stupid nor an irrational conclusion. The conclusions of the intelligence analysts in London were very similar. Both thought a war between Germany and Russia was likely in the longer run. Both thought Hitler wanted to finish off the British before he turned on Russia. In April 1941 a War Office official concluded, 'There seems to be no reason whatever why Germany should attack the U.S.S.R.'[53] A month later the Joint Intelligence Committee issued a key judgement: 'Whereas a few weeks ago rumours were current throughout Europe of an impending German attack on the U.S.S.R., the contrary is now the case. There are some indications which suggest that a new agreement between the two countries may be nearly complete.' The JIC supported their judgement with sophisticated argument. The Germans, they believed, needed more economic help from Russia. They could get it either by agreement or by the uncertain instrument of war. 'The advantages [...] to Germany of concluding an agreement with the U.S.S.R. are overwhelming.' The movement of German troops to the Soviet border was an instrument of blackmail. The British analysts sympathised with Russian policy: 'The natural course of the Soviet Government is to endeavour by every means in her power to avoid a clash by yielding to German demands.'[54] They repeated and refined their arguments at the end of May, three weeks before the German attack. Thus the wishful thinking in Moscow was a mirror image of the worst-case analysis in London: Stalin's hope was Churchill's nightmare. Neither took sufficient account of the vagaries of Hitler's mind. But for the British this had no short-term consequences. It led Stalin very close to catastrophe.

Timoshenko and Zhukov, by that time Commissar for Defence and Chief of Staff respectively, could not afford to be complacent. As the evidence of an imminent German attack multiplied they became increasingly desperate. As cautious professionals, they were bound to look at the worst case, and to take a bleaker view of the available intelligence than the political leadership. Despite Stalin's determination to do nothing that Hitler could see as a provocation, they got him to take some discreet measures of preparation. At the end of April he agreed to call up eight hundred thousand reservists, and to move substantial forces from the Urals, Siberia and the Far East to the Western border. The deployment was to be completed by 10 July. Many of the troops were still on the move when the Germans attacked. At the last minute, on 14 June, Timoshenko sent a desperate message to the commanders of the forces on the Western frontier. Recent inspections had shown, he said, that their troops and especially their radio operators were poorly trained. Their new Mechanised Corps were disorganised, their tanks, guns and infantry incapable of operating together, and they lacked the tractors they needed to move their heavy weapons. All these defects were to be eliminated by the end of the month.[55] This wholly unrealistic and indeed absurd order was a measure of the extent to which the military as well as the political leadership had failed in their duty to prepare the country's armed forces for war.

On 4 May 1941 Stalin took over Molotov's job as Prime Minister. He thus combined in his own hands both the highest Party and the highest governmental position, a greater concentration of formal power than Lenin had ever aspired to. It was a measure of the seriousness of the international crisis which he knew he faced.

The following day he delivered a major speech on the international situation at the annual reception in the Kremlin for military cadets. He claimed that the right lessons had been drawn from the recent campaigns of the Red Army. The process of re-equipping it was now complete. One-third of the army's divisions were now mechanised, and of these one-third were armoured. Soviet industry was now producing the most modern aircraft in vast numbers. To exploit this new equipment, commanders needed to master the very latest in military art. They had not yet done so, and it was up to the military schools to pull themselves together.

The Germans had learned from their defeat in 1918. They had developed a modern doctrine and modern weapons. They now had the best-organised and equipped army in the world. They had concluded that it was fatal for Germany to fight on two fronts. This time they had not gone to war before ensuring that Italy was on their side and that the Soviet Union was a benevolent neutral.

Hitler's determination to overthrow the unjust provisions of Versailles, said Stalin, had won him support at home and some sympathy abroad. That sympathy had evaporated when the Germans had overwhelmed Yugoslavia and Greece a few months earlier. They were now showing the dangerous arrogance which comes with victory. They had come to believe that they were invincible. But there was no such thing as an invincible army. The Germans' technical advantage was fading. But with the decline of Britain and France, 'only the USSR and the USA have the necessary resources. These world powers will determine the outcome of the struggle.' Stalin concluded that the Soviet policy of peace and security was at the same time a policy of preparation for war. 'There is no defence without attack. We must educate the army in the spirit of the offensive. We must prepare for war.'[56]

It was a skilful speech, expressed with all Stalin's habitual force and logic. He knew very well that the Germans were gathering for attack and that the Red Army was by no means as well prepared as he claimed. His soldiers had warned him earlier in the year that all the talk of peace was lulling the nation into complacency.[57] He had to strike a difficult balance between caution, the overriding need not to provoke the Germans, and the upbeat language that his predominantly military audience would naturally expect. As so often, Stalin's purposes were veiled. Neither those who heard him, nor subsequent historians, have been able to agree what exactly he meant.

On 15 May Zhukov and Timoshenko devised a radical way out: an immediate offensive to seize the initiative from the Germans while they were still deploying. The idea does not seem to have been proposed officially. If Stalin saw it, he did not endorse it, perhaps because he rightly believed that the Red Army was hardly in a shape to prepare and execute a successful preventive attack even with the advantage of surprise. In his cheerfully provocative *Icebreaker*, the émigré Russian historian Viktor Suvorov put the opposite argument with a wealth of circumstantial detail. Stalin, he claimed, was intending to attack Hitler when Hitler got his blow in first. To the fury of more orthodox historians, Suvorov sold millions of copies of his books in his former homeland. The argument will run until somebody produces a clinching document.[58]

In the last weeks and days Stalin's mind was increasingly closed to reason as the rationale for his policy ebbed away. When Timoshenko and Zhukov presented their evidence of German plans, Stalin threw it back in their faces. Sorge, the Soviet spy in Tokyo, had 'deigned to report the date of the German attack as 22 June. Are you suggesting,' Stalin asked indignantly, 'I should believe him, too?' When 'Starshina', the Soviet spy in the Luftwaffe headquarters, reported that the final measures for the attack had been taken, he scribbled furiously, 'Starshina should be sent to his fucking mother. This is no source but a disinformer.'[59] On 15 June Timoshenko and Zhukov asked him for permission to move the covering forces on the frontier to more favourable defensive positions. Stalin rejected their request outright: 'We have a non-aggression pact with Germany. Germany is up to her ears with the war in the West and I am certain that Hitler will not risk creating a second front by attacking the Soviet Union. Hitler is not such an idiot and understands that the Soviet Union is not Poland, not France, and not even England.'[60]

Stalin told his generals to take their line from the communiqué which TASS put out on 14 June. The rumours of an 'early war' between the Soviet Union and Germany, said TASS, like the rumours that Germany had presented both territorial and economic claims to the Soviet Union, were 'nothing but clumsy propaganda put out by forces hostile to the USSR and Germany and interested in the extension of the war'. TASS strongly implied that the 'hostile forces' were the British government and their ambassador in Moscow, Stafford Cripps.[61] The readers did not know what to make of it. Some were lulled into inactivity. Those who believed that official communiqués usually meant the opposite of what they said saw it as a sign that war was indeed on the way. Many in the army took it as one more indication that they would be punished if they took any defensive initiative.

In the very last days of peace Stalin's dogged confidence began to crack. On 17 June he ordered his advisers to summarise their intelligence. They produced a list of forty-one reports received from Berlin over the previous nine months. Some were the usual gossip that agents are prone to pass on. Some were red herrings. Some were contradictory. But taken as a whole the weight of the intelligence was clear. Alas, by the time it was ready, the document was already only of historical interest.[62] It reached its readers after the Germans had already attacked.

On 18 June Timoshenko and Zhukov tried once again to persuade Stalin and the Politburo to put the army on full alert. The meeting lasted for three hours. The more Zhukov spoke, the more irritable Stalin became. He accused Zhukov of warmongering and became so abusive that Zhukov fell silent. But Timoshenko persisted. There would be havoc, he said, if the Wehrmacht struck the troops in their present positions. Stalin was furious. 'It's all Timoshenko's work,' he told the others. 'He's preparing everyone for war. He ought to have been shot, but I've known him as a good soldier since the Civil War.' Timoshenko reminded Stalin that he had told the cadets on 5 May that war was inevitable. Stalin replied furiously, 'I said that so that people would raise their alertness. But you have to understand that Germany on her own will never fight Russia. You must understand this.' He stormed out, then suddenly put his head round the door and shouted, 'If you're going to provoke the Germans on the frontier by moving troops there without our permission, then heads will roll, mark my words.' In Stalin's mouth that was not a figure of speech.[63]

Stalin's wishful thinking had become a catastrophic obsession. As Churchill was acidly to remark, 'Nothing ... pierced the purblind prejudice and fixed ideas which [he] had raised between himself and the terrible truth ... The wicked are not always clever, nor are dictators always right'.[64] But even in the last minute before the storm, Stalin was not alone in thinking that it could be averted. On 21 June 1941, the very last day of peace, the Swedish ambassador in Moscow wrote:

> No one either knows or is prepared to say a thing about what is happening, if anything is indeed happening on the diplomatic front. One suggests that negotiations are under way, a second that there won't be any negotiations but an ultimatum. Some say that the demands, whether they have been made or not, concern the Ukraine and the Baku oil wells, while others suggest they are concerned with different issues. Some suggest that the demobilization and disarming of the Ukraine are part of the demands. Most believe that war is inevitable and imminent; some believe that a war is intended and desired by the German side. A few think that there won't be a war, at least not presently, and that Stalin will make extensive concessions in order to avoid the war. The only certain thing is that we face either a battle of global significance between the Third Reich and the Soviet Empire or the most gigantic piece of blackmail in world history.[65]

Ordinary people had been told often enough by their leaders that war would come eventually. People gossiped about the lengthening queues for salt, matches, thread, sugar, and tinned food: always a sign of impending trouble. Raisa Labas, who had once been married to the well-known painter Robert Falk, lived in one of the studio apartments in the Academy of Fine Arts opposite the old Post Office with her small son Yuli and her sister, the one-legged actress Aleksandra Granovskaya. She had been thinking of spending the weekend in her dacha. But when a military friend told her that he was being sent urgently to the Far East, which could mean that the Japanese as well as the Germans were planning an attack, she wondered whether it made sense to go away after all.[66] Others drew their own conclusions from the shambles in Finland and the obvious unreadiness of so many Red Army units. The year before, Anatoli Chernyaev had visited his father, who was serving with his reserve division right on the new frontier with the Germans. The division's equipment came from all over the place – some from the Tsarist army, some from the French, some captured from the enemy in the First World War and the Civil War. The men were as old as the equipment, men like his father, who had been mobilised in a hurry. Their discipline, tactical skills and general bearing were far below those which prevailed in Chernyaev's own university cadet corps. It did not bode well for the war which was bound to come.[67]

But most people believed the message hammered home by years of propaganda. The popular film *If War Should Come Tomorrow* had shown them that if the Germans attacked (no one doubted it would be the Germans), the Red Army would carry the fighting into the aggressor's homeland within days, the German workers would rise to greet them, and victory would come with a minimal expenditure of blood.[68] What else could they believe, after all the sacrifices that they had made to give the Red Army more tanks and as many planes as the whole of the rest of the world put together? They felt that lightening of the spirit that always accompanies spring after a long Russian winter. They got on with their lives, went to the cinema, planned for their summer holidays, thought about what they would do when they started their new jobs or their new university terms in the autumn. The young women went with their friends to the theatres and to the cafés to eat ice cream: they could not afford to go to restaurants, even if it had been proper for them to go to such places by themselves. It had been raining heavily for days. But that Saturday was 21 June, Midsummer's Day, and that weekend the summer began in earnest. Those who could, left to relax in their dachas, to cultivate their vegetable gardens, to picnic and to fish in the Moscow River. Those who could not afford such luxuries, who were pinned down by their work, or who still had their exams to take, stayed behind in the city. In the memories of survivors, that last day of peace has the golden quality of an idyll.

But on that last Saturday night of peace the generals at Headquarters in Moscow knew that the storm was about to break. They knew of the mood in the ruined villages. And they wondered. When the time came, would the peasant soldiers fight?

PART II

THE STORM BREAKS

- FOUR -

22 JUNE 1941

When the storm broke, people turned to Tolstoy. 'During the war,' wrote the critic Lidia Ginzburg, 'people devoured *War and Peace* as a way of measuring their own behaviour (about Tolstoy they had no doubt: his response to life was wholly adequate). The reader would say to himself: Well then, so what I am feeling is right: that's just how it should be.'[1] *War and Peace* was the only book the writer Vasili Grossman had time to read while he was a frontline correspondent, and he read it twice. It was broadcast on Moscow Radio, complete, over thirty episodes.[2]

For Russians the war of 1812 was always 'The Patriotic War'. The newspapers immediately adapted the old name to the new conflict and called it 'The Great Patriotic War'. Parallels multiplied as summer turned into winter. Paradoxically it took the Germans nearly three months longer to get to Moscow than it had taken Napoleon. For despite their deserved reputation for lightning armoured warfare, the Germans were almost as dependent as Napoleon on horses and on the stamina of their men on the march.[3] It turned out to be their greatest weakness, for neither the men nor the machines which had performed so well in the confines of Northern France were able, in the end, to cope with the vast expanse of Russia.

The force that was poised on the Soviet frontier at midnight on 21

June was six times as large as Napoleon's Grande Armée. Over three million men, nearly two thousand aircraft, more than three thousand tanks, and three-quarters of a million horses were organised into three Army Groups. Field Marshal von Leeb was to take Army Group North through the Baltic States, and then to capture Leningrad in cooperation with an army of vengeful Finns. Army Group South under Field Marshal von Rundstedt was to capture Ukraine, its rich agricultural and industrial resources, and its capital Kiev.[4]

The main task was reserved for Army Group Centre, the most powerful of the three. Field Marshal von Bock and his men were to thrust along Napoleon's own invasion route, through Minsk, the capital of Belorussia; through the fortress city of Smolensk, which had held out for two bloody days against the Grande Armée in August 1812; across the battlefield of Borodino where Kutuzov's army had fought Napoleon to a standstill in September; and then on towards Moscow itself.

Huge though it was, the invading force was not overwhelming. Overall the opposing forces were almost equal in numbers of men and equipment. The Russians had 170 divisions and four million men – many still on the march from the East. They had more guns and mortars. They had more than twice as many tanks, including a number of modern KV-1s and T-34s, better than anything the Germans could put against them. They had three and a half times as many serviceable aircraft, though few were of the latest model.[5] These forces were arranged in five Fronts. These were roughly the equivalent of the German Army Groups, though they were substantially smaller. The Northern Front under General Popov and the Northwestern Front under General Kuznetsov faced von Leeb; the Western Front under General Pavlov faced von Bock; the Southwestern Front under General Kirponos and the Southern Front under General Tulenev both faced von Rundstedt.[6]

The Germans were well enough aware of the line-up in front of them. They knew much less about the Russians' immense reserves of men and industry in the Urals and Siberia, far beyond the range of German reconnaissance. But they relied in Russia, as they had done in France, on the shock of surprise, manoeuvrability, and superior skill to destroy the Russian will to fight, topple the Soviet regime, and impose a Carthaginian peace long before the Russians could bring their resources to bear. It was a fatal miscalculation.

In the Kremlin the last illusions were finally being stripped away. Throughout Saturday, the pace of activity in the highest echelons of the government and the military had accelerated to fever pitch. Towards the evening, Zhukov received an urgent call from the headquarters of the Kiev Special Military District. A German sergeant-major had just crossed the border: the Germans would attack the next morning. Stalin summoned Zhukov and Timoshenko to the Kremlin. His first thought was that the Germans had sent the defector across in a deliberate move to provoke a conflict. A desperate Molotov summoned the German ambassador, von Schulenburg. Why, Molotov asked, had the staff of the German embassy suddenly left Moscow? Why had the German government not responded to the olive branch offered by the TASS announcement of 14 June? Was Germany dissatisfied with the way the Soviet Union had been behaving, and if so why? These questions were by now irrelevant. Von Schulenburg could give no sensible answer.

The Politburo began to assemble. Stalin asked Timoshenko what should be done. Timoshenko suggested that the forces on the frontier should take up their battle positions. Stalin still resisted: 'It's too soon ... Perhaps we can still solve the problem by peaceful means.' He ordered Zhukov to draft a short general warning to the frontier armies. The result, Directive No. 1, was a deeply confusing document. The troops were warned that a German attack was possible at any moment. They were to occupy their firing positions in secret. They were to disperse and camouflage their aircraft. But they were 'to avoid provocative action of any kind which might result in serious complications'. They were to do nothing more without specific instructions.[7]

It did not matter. The message was far too late. It did not reach Pavlov's headquarters at the Western Military District until just before 1 a.m. on 22 June. It was passed on to subordinate units only at 2.30 a.m. Some commanders had already risked Stalin's fury by taking their own precautions, but such initiative was the exception rather than the rule. An earlier attempt by General Kirponos of the Southwestern Front to move his troops into their battle positions was specifically overridden by Zhukov on 11 June. On the very eve of the war Admiral Kuznetsov told the navy to fire if they were attacked. But for the most part the soldiers were wholly unprepared.[8] Most of the frontline troops did not get Directive No. 1 until after the Germans had already attacked.

Shcherbakov and Pronin, the two most senior officials responsible for Moscow itself, were warned that a German attack was possible, and were told to make sure their senior officials stayed in town. Stalin himself left for the Nearby Dacha at 11 p.m. Molotov and other members of the Politburo are said to have joined him there to watch a film. They left at midnight.[9] At about that time General Kirponos telephoned Zhukov and Timoshenko at the ministry to say that a deserter had told the border police that the attack would start at 4 a.m. Stalin was informed immediately. He was little moved and went to bed.[10]

At 3.15 a.m. on Sunday 22 June 1941 German bombers attacked Soviet air bases on the Western frontier. The Red Air Force lost over twelve hundred aircraft in the first morning of the war, most of them on the ground.[11] German special forces – many wearing Soviet uniforms – had already infiltrated into the Soviet rear and were cutting telephone lines, attacking headquarters, and seizing key bridges. As the sun rose, chaos had already taken a grip of the defenders. One forlorn group of men radioed a desperate plea for instructions: 'We are being fired on. What shall we do?' The reply was rapid and decisive: 'You must be insane. And why isn't your signal in code?'[12] The bewildered frontier guards stood fast and died – many with their wives and children – as the Germans swept over them.

The Panzer divisions now moved forward. Army Group North rapidly sliced through to capture the bridges over the Western Dvina. Army Group South stumbled over difficult terrain and ran into the substantial force that Stalin had placed there in the belief that this was where the Germans would make their main thrust.

The threat to Moscow came from Army Group Centre. Von Bock had fifty divisions, including nine Panzer divisions and six motorised divisions. He was supported by the 2nd Air Fleet of Field Marshal Kesselring with fifteen hundred aircraft, many of which had flown under the same commander in the Battle of Britain and the London Blitz. The tanks went first. The Second Panzer Group was commanded by Heinz Guderian, the distinguished military thinker whose theoretical insights had been outshone by his brilliant practical performance in the field at the head of a Panzer Corps in France the year before. Now Guderian raced ahead on the Southern wing of the advance, while General Hoth's

Third Panzer Group matched him to the North, closing in behind the defenders, blocking off their line of retreat, and leaving them to be cut to pieces by the advancing infantry. The Germans planned to repeat this manoeuvre again and again along the six hundred miles which lay between the frontier and Moscow, until at the last the Soviet capital lay open before them (see Map 2).

General Dmitri Pavlov, the commander of the Western Front facing von Bock, was on his way back from a concert party when the Germans attacked. There was no one responsible on duty at his command headquarters. He himself did not get there until 4 o'clock in the morning. It was only then that he saw Directive No. 1, authorising him to put his forces on alert. But by that time communications between Front headquarters and its subordinate armies were being disrupted by the German raiding parties. Orders to units could not be sent or received, still less implemented. Pavlov could form no coherent idea of what was going on. He soon lost any real control of his troops.

For the first four hours the generals at Headquarters in Moscow had no idea how, if at all, the soldiers at the frontier were performing. General Voronov, the chief artillery commander, admitted years later that he had heaved a huge sigh of relief when the news finally filtered through that the peasant army was fighting after all, despite the overwhelming odds. The British historian John Erickson wrote, 'On that simple, but by no means inevitable, fact rested the possibility of victory, however far into the future'.[13]

The first reports of the German attack started to come into the Commissariat for Defence at 3.30 a.m. Zhukov rang Stalin right away. The duty officer asked sleepily, 'Who's calling?' 'Zhukov. Please connect me with Comrade Stalin. It's urgent.' 'What, right now? Comrade Stalin is sleeping.' 'Wake him up immediately. The Germans are bombing our cities.' Three minutes later Stalin was on the telephone. Zhukov reported the situation, and was answered by silence. 'Did you understand what I said?' Zhukov asked. Again there was silence. Then, finally, 'Tell Poskrëbyshev to summon the whole Politburo.'

Poskrëbyshev, Stalin's executive assistant, sent out the messages. Stalin was the first to reach the Kremlin, his pockmarked face drawn and haggard. The others arrived soon after.[14]

Timoshenko reported bleakly, 'The German attack must be considered an accomplished fact. The enemy has bombed the main airfields, ports, and major arterial junctions.'

Then Stalin began to speak slowly, choosing his words with care. Occasionally his voice broke down. Even now he tried to argue that the German attack was a provocation by the German military. 'If it were necessary to organize a provocation, then the German generals would bomb their own cities,' he muttered. 'Hitler surely does not know about it.' When he finished everybody was silent for some time, and so was he. Then he said, 'We must get in touch with Berlin again and ring the embassy.'

The German ambassador came to the Foreign Ministry, barely able to conceal his own distress, to tell Molotov that the German government had declared war: there was no scope for further negotiation.[15] Molotov returned to Stalin's office and gave him the news. Stalin said calmly, 'The enemy will be beaten all along the line.' Then, turning to his generals, he asked, 'What do you recommend?' Zhukov replied, 'Order the troops on the frontier to attack along the whole front and halt the enemy – he's gone too far too fast.' Timoshenko said aggressively, 'Not halt – destroy.'[16]

So the meeting ordered the frontier armies to attack the enemy and destroy him wherever he had violated the Soviet frontier. They themselves were not to cross that frontier unless specially authorised. The Red Air Force was given more forceful instructions: to destroy German aircraft on the ground and to bomb German cities, including Koenigsberg, up to ninety miles behind the line. This was Cloud Cuckoo Land. By the time the order was issued, the Soviet air forces at the frontier had largely ceased to exist. Pacing up and down the office, Stalin asked in furious disbelief, 'Surely the German air force didn't manage to reach every single airfield?' 'Unfortunately,' said Timoshenko, 'it did.' 'How many planes were destroyed?' 'Around seven hundred at a first estimate,' replied Timoshenko. 'That's a monstrous crime,' said Stalin. 'Those guilty of it should pay with their heads.' And he immediately ordered Beria to investigate.[17] He was even more furious when he heard that all contact had been lost with Pavlov, the commander of the Western Front, and that the Germans were already threatening Minsk, the capital of Belorussia. 'Your Pavlov needs to be asked some difficult questions!' he snapped. He ordered Shaposhnikov to fly immediately to Pavlov's headquarters to find out what was going on, and sent Zhukov to Kirponos' headquarters at the Southwestern Front for the same purpose.

Orders were issued for the mobilisation of all men born between 1905 and 1918. The children of the leaders were among the first to respond to the call of duty. Stalin's son Yakov was captured in the first days of the war and died in a German camp. Timur Frunze, one of Stepan Mikoyan's best friends and the son of the man who helped Trotsky create the Red Army, Leonid Khrushchëv, and Volodya Mikoyan were all killed fighting in the air. Those who survived included Stalin's second son, Vasili, who flew when he was not incapacitated by drink, Stepan and Aleksei Mikoyan, and Shcherbakov's eldest son, Alexander. They too were all airmen.

That evening Stalin held another meeting. Timoshenko had still not been able to make contact with Pavlov. 'Some of these generals have been getting fat. But they've learned nothing,' said Stalin. He gave the unfortunate Timoshenko twenty-four hours to get matters under control.[18] Yet another directive – Directive No. 3 – was sent to the desperate commanders at the front. It admitted that the Germans had 'achieved considerable success, while suffering heavy losses'. It ordered the Northern and Western Fronts to encircle and destroy two German groups which had broken through the Russian defences. It told the Southwestern Front to hold the Germans on the frontier.[19] These instructions bore no more relation to the state of affairs on the ground than their predecessors. The generals and their political masters still had only the sketchiest idea of what was happening at the front, and little conception of the extent of the catastrophe. They did not know where the Germans were, where their own troops were, or how to communicate with most of their commanders. They were battling with shadows, simulating decisive action lest they gave way to panic, still believing – or forcing themselves to believe – that the Germans would be defeated within a matter of days.[20]

Just before 5 o'clock that afternoon Beria, the last of Stalin's official visitors, left him and he went home to the Nearby Dacha.

The first care of the Soviet leaders was to secure the capital. The Dzerzhinski Division was ordered to move to Moscow as soon as the news of the attack came through. The 'F.E. Dzerzhinski – Order of Lenin Motor Rifle Division for Special Tasks' originated in the mobile detachment set up to guard the Soviet government in 1918. It fought in the Civil War, helped to put down the peasant rising in Tambov in 1919–21, and protected Lenin as he lay dying in a grand country house in the Moscow countryside in 1924. By the 1930s it had become a formidable military force, with three motor rifle regiments, a cavalry regiment, an independent artillery regiment, a tank battalion, and its own communications, engineering, chemical and other companies. The Division's normal peacetime role was to preserve law and order in the capital and protect the leadership. But it was also available as an instrument of force inside the city or beyond. It participated in the deportation of the Chechens in 1944 and in the siege of the Russian parliament in 1993. The role of the Division remains unchanged. But it is now much reduced, and its name has been changed to the 'Independent Division for Special Tasks of the Ministry of the Interior of Russia'.[21] It is, as it always has been, stationed at Reutovo just to the East of the capital.

Sergei Markov, who later became the head of Zhukov's bodyguard, had only been in the Division for eight months when the war began. He came from a village in the Novgorod Region halfway between Moscow and Leningrad. He and his twin sister were the youngest of seven children. One of his brothers was killed in the Finnish war, and another in the battles around Staraya Russa in 1942. He himself joined the NKVD forces in October 1940: his mother and sister were in tears when they saw him off at the station. He and his fellow recruits took two days to travel by cattle truck to Reutovo. He was given two months' basic training, was posted briefly to serve in Moscow's Lefortovo Prison, and was sent to camp for summer training in May 1941.

The Division's seventeenth anniversary fell on 22 June itself, and the men of the Division had spent the last few weeks preparing to celebrate it. Sergei Markov was on sentry duty on the night of 21–22 June when an officer appeared at the crack of the summer dawn and told him to report with his kit and weapons to the transport park. His comrades were hauled from their beds, kitted out, armed, and sent in short order into Moscow. No one told them that war had begun: that they learned only when Molotov spoke. They started to patrol the streets right away, with instructions to guard important buildings, enforce public order, and mop up enemy parachutists, saboteurs, people signalling to the enemy, spreaders of panic and rumours, and those breaking the blackout discipline. They were supported by Destroyer Battalions (Istrebitelnye Bataliony) set up by the NKVD offices in each Raion. These, despite their menacing name, were auxiliary policemen inadequately armed and with a modicum of hasty military training, whose task was to catch parachutists, saboteurs, and spies, tackle fires, help the militia maintain order and guard buildings, and at a pinch to throw grenades and destroy tanks.[22] Sergei Markov and some of his fellows briefly returned to Lefortovo for training as NCOs, and were then sent to join the Division's 2nd Rifle Regiment, quartered in Moscow's Petrovski Barracks. Thereafter they spent the first weeks of the war patrolling the streets of the capital, except for five days in July and August when they were sent off to build defences on the Western and Southwestern approaches to Moscow at Naro-Fominsk, Mozhaisk, and Volokolamsk.[23]

The news that war had come reached the ordinary people of Moscow in several ways. Vladislav Mikosha, the cameraman who had filmed the destruction of the Cathedral of Christ the Saviour, was one of the few to have a short-wave radio. He was at home and suffering from insomnia when he turned it on at about 5 a.m. that morning. There was nothing on the Soviet wavelengths, but fiddling around he heard news in German, French and Polish listing a number of cities near the frontier – Minsk, Odessa, Kiev. He could not understand the languages, but he deduced that they had been bombed by the Germans. He woke his mother, but she told him not to talk nonsense and they went back to sleep.[24]

Ilya Zbarski was the son of the man who had developed the process for keeping Lenin's corpse in decent order, and worked with him in the Mausoleum laboratory. He too had a short-wave radio. He was woken up in the small hours of the morning by Sergei Mardashëv, a colleague at the laboratory, who asked him if he had heard the news. He rushed to his set: it was only the usual rigmarole about the successes of the socialist economy. Back he hurried to the telephone. 'I can't hear anything special,' he said. 'You must be on the wrong wavelength,' replied Mardashëv. Zbarski caught a news bulletin on a German station.

A voice – it seemed to be Hitler's – was proclaiming that the USSR was just 'a conglomeration of ill-assorted races and nations threatening European civilisation'. He scanned the airwaves and managed to pick up another voice in English giving details of the German concentration on the frontier. Later he heard Churchill broadcast his support for the Soviet Union.

Before the war all radio receivers had been registered with the authorities. Now the authorities ordered them to be handed in. Zbarski was given a receipt. But of course he never got his radio back.[25] One radio ham handed in his receiver together with his home-made transmitter. But he had kept a whole pile of valves and radio parts. They were discovered by a local NKVD informer. The police arrived just as he was leaving for the front. They let him go.[26]

Apart from the leadership, the men already fighting at the front, and those who were suffering from insomnia and had their own radios, most Soviet people still had no idea that they were at war. The Politburo turned its attention to drafting an announcement. The final text bears the marks of Stalin's brutally direct style, and he was the natural person to read it. Instead he told Molotov to read it over the radio at noon. It may have been a failure of nerve. But it was also a neat tactic. There was some difficult explaining to do. The Germans had attacked despite the Pact. Molotov had signed the Pact. Let him carry the can.

Yuri Levitan, the country's most distinguished and best-known radio announcer, had first made his name by reading Stalin's speech – all five hours of it – to the XVIIth Party Congress in 1934.[27] Now, in the middle of the morning on that first day of the war, he warned the people of the Soviet Union to listen to a special announcement at midday. All over Moscow people stopped what they were doing to hear Molotov's words over the round black loudspeakers – half a million of them – which were strung out on the streets, in public places, and in factories throughout the city.

'Citizens and Citizenesses of the Soviet Union!' said Molotov in an uncertain voice. 'Today, at 4 o'clock in the morning, without addressing any grievances to the Soviet Union, without a declaration of war, German forces fell on our country, attacked our frontiers in many places, and bombed our cities – Zhitomir, Kiev, Sevastopol, Kaunas and others

... an act of treachery unprecedented in the history of civilised nations.' The Germans – not the German people but their bloodthirsty leaders – had broken their faith with the Russians, who had fulfilled all their obligations under the Pact of Friendship. The Red Army and Fleet, and the valiant falcons of the Red Air Force would drive back the aggressor. 'Our people's answer to Napoleon's invasion was a Patriotic War ... The Red Army and the whole nation will wage a victorious Patriotic War for our beloved country, for honour, for liberty ... Our cause is just. The enemy will be beaten. Victory will be ours.' [28]

The final phrases were Stalin's own. They immediately entered the vocabulary of Soviet wartime propaganda and remained there until the end. But Molotov was not the man to inspire the people. Stalin looked in on him afterwards. 'Well,' he said, 'you sounded a bit flustered, but the speech went well.'[29]

People listened with patriotic emotion, tears and shock. A photographer captured the scene on Gorky Street: it is one of the most poignant images of the Russian war. One old woman in the crowd picked on Molotov's claim that the Germans had broken faith. 'It was the Communists who broke the faith, so God has punished them.' A man with a sack told her, 'Not that faith, grandmother, not faith in God but faith in the treaty with the Germans. That's the faith we are talking about!' 'But who ever had faith in Hitler, that Herod?' asked the old woman.[30]

People could not believe what was happening. Krylov, an official from the Commissariat of Finance, was travelling home by tram when an elderly woman told the passengers that war had begun. A well-dressed man sitting beside him accused her of provocation, and said she should be taken off to the police station. He shut up when a policeman got on at the next stop and said he had just heard Molotov's broadcast. When the news sank in, there was a wave of anger at German treachery, of passionate patriotism, and of confidence that the Red Army – with its glorious traditions and its modern equipment – would quickly see the Germans off the field. The war would be over in a month, or at the most by the end of the year. Krylov overheard one young man explaining to his girlfriend that modern technology meant that nowadays long wars were technically impossible.[31] One factory director went too far: he announced to his workers that the Red Army had already captured

Warsaw. He was arrested, but the rumour swept Moscow.[32] It was left to those who remembered the First World War to warn that beating the Germans might not be so simple. Most people set aside their reservations about the regime: it was their country which now had to be defended from the German assault. They flocked in their tens of thousands to volunteer their services. Pictures of universal patriotic enthusiasm flooded the press.

The enthusiasm was not very evident to foreigners living in Moscow. They were struck by the apparent absence of patriotic demonstrations, whether organised or otherwise. They dismissed the patriotic resolutions passed by workers in their factories. They too wondered why Stalin had not spoken. The British embassy believed that Stalin had preferred not to speak on such a grave national occasion because he knew that ordinary Russians found his thick Georgian accent somewhat comic. But why then, the embassy wondered, had Stalin not issued a personal call to the people through the press?[33]

Some people – like the bewildered villagers in Vladimir Voinovich's satire *The Adventures of Private Ivan Chonkin* – simply waited for the government to tell them what to do. Others were angry that the government had given them no inkling of what was likely to happen. Some, especially among the dispossessed peasantry, secretly hoped that the German attack heralded the destruction of a hated regime. Everyone asked one question above all: How could the government have allowed itself to be caught by surprise? Why were they not warned by the Soviet intelligence agencies? Even today the question refuses to go away. But in the 1990s most of the documents were published and people could begin to make up their minds for themselves on the basis of solid evidence.

The authorities needed not only the picture that was presented to them by their own propaganda, but also some way of gauging what people were really thinking. It was the job of the NKVD to provide the answer. They put together reports based on tapped telephones, censored letters, and gossip and rumour collected by agents. Such piecemeal and clandestine methods inevitably produced uncertain results. The British Government was making the same attempt, and finding it just as difficult to quantify attitudes: there were no opinion polls or focus groups at that time. But what the NKVD reports make clear is that there was considerable criticism of the Soviet Government, its policies, and its prospects, from the very first day of the war; and that the criticism was often expressed with surprising – and surprisingly incautious – freedom, force, and perspicacity.

Despite the general optimism, based on years of propaganda, that the Germans would quickly be beaten, many people did not believe the war would be a walkover. Workers in one factory commented sourly that it was the fault of the Pact: the government had fed the German hand that had now bitten it.[34] A doctor called Grebeshnikov remarked that the prisons were full, the peasants were ill-disposed and half the population was opposed to the government. It would be hard to get them to fight. A woman worker, Makarova, said that it was just as well the war had begun as life in the USSR had become unbearable. Everyone was sick of famine and forced labour; the sooner it was over the better. Kurbanov, who worked in the tourist agency Intourist, argued that during the Civil War people had fought for freedom and for their rights. But now there was nothing for them to die for. The Soviet regime had brought people to a pitch of anger.

A former Social Revolutionary called Spund said that it was the Soviet Union that had started the war, to distract attention from popular discontent with the Soviet dictatorship. A woman factory worker, Lokshina, said that the country was badly organised; domestic confrontations would complicate the conduct of what was bound to be a bloody war. An official called Loginov remarked that Litvinov, the pre-war Commissar for Foreign Affairs, had been right to try to reach an accommodation with England and France. Now the country was unprepared for war, and people were panicking. Another official called Danilov believed that the Germans had already captured five cities and that they had reduced Kiev and Odessa to ruins: 'Now at last we can breathe freely. Hitler will be in Moscow in three days and the intelligentsia will be able to live properly.' Tobias, a military doctor, thought that after a good deal of suffering the war would certainly be lost. The military technology was available, but the country as a whole was badly prepared. That was what Hitler was counting on.

As news of the débâcle on the frontier seeped through, the questions became more insistent: Why was the Red Army, the finest and largest army in the world, the army that was intended to carry the war onto the enemy's territory as soon as the shooting started – why was this army surrendering one Russian city after another to the German invaders? Was it that the peasant soldiers were unwilling to fight for the regime that had destroyed their way of life? A Polish visitor thought that the war was a consequence of Hitler's demands that the Soviet Union hand over its heavy industry, its oil fields, and the ports in the Black and Caspian Seas. Epifanov, an electro-mechanic on the Moscow–Donbass railway, got quite close to the truth when he remarked that the government had been split between those, like Timoshenko, who considered that the Soviet Union should have launched a pre-emptive strike at the Germans while they were tied up in Greece, and those who thought that the confrontation should have been postponed because the country was insufficiently prepared.

Kiun, a former factory owner, thought that the full responsibility for the war lay with the Soviet Union, which had mustered 160 armoured divisions on the frontier with Germany. Disagreement between the two countries had blown up even before Molotov had gone to Berlin to demand the cession of the whole of Finland, a demand which Hitler had categorically rejected. The Soviet Union had then broken its agreement with the Germans not to sovietise the Baltic states. Now the main thrust of the German attack would be towards Kiev and Leningrad, where 30 per cent of the country's military industry was concentrated. The Soviet government had never been elected by the people, and the people would pass their own verdict upon it. Kiun was arrested. So was Mauritz, a woman of German origin, who said that the peasants would be happy at the news of the war, because it would free them from the hated Bolsheviks and the collective farms. Although Russia was strong, she said, it was not strong enough to stand up to the Germans, who would bomb it to pieces in a trice.

Information was not readily available to ordinary people, and they were sometimes muddled as to the facts. But they expressed themselves intelligently and their analyses were often remarkably sophisticated. Their controversial ideas about the cause of the war still echo among historians today.

These disquieting views were immediately reported to his superiors by Major Zhuravlëv, the head of the Moscow NKVD.[35] His men had prepared lists well in advance, and were already rounding up those of dubious political, social, or national antecedents: over a thousand individuals listed under the categories of 'terrorism, sabotage [diversion], wrecking, German, Italian and Japanese espionage, other forms of espionage, bacteriological sabotage, Trotskyism, former members of anti-Soviet political parties, sectarians and conscientious objectors, various anti-Soviet elements'. Confirmed criminals were also rounded up: a thousand inhabitants of Moscow's prisons were sent off to camps to make way for them. A special camp was set up to house three hundred foreign internees.[36] Pogonin, an eighteen-year-old railway-car attendant, was arrested for handing out leaflets on the train calling on people to struggle against the Soviet regime and its leaders. A band of seventy 'criminal bandits and counter-revolutionaries' was arrested the following day.

Major Zhuravlëv also reported that there were hiccups in the arrangements for mobilisation. Each Raion had its own recruiting station. Some of them were badly organised. The Shchelkovo Station, for example, had failed to arrange the vehicles needed to take conscripts to their units. A senior engineer from the Hammer and Sickle factory had been arrested for trying to persuade other recruits to refuse to serve. Similar incidents had happened in the Novosëlov and Kirov stations. In the Kuibyshev centre a recruit had committed suicide rather than join up.

A run on the shops had already begun. Queues of up to three hundred people had formed. In some shops there was no sugar, salt, or grain products. Others were sold out by midday. The manager of the grocery store in the House on the Embankment – Gastronom No. 21 – complained that its privileged inhabitants were spending their savings on buying up the stocks. Others followed suit, and the savings banks began to run out of cash. Savings accounts had to be frozen for a while, and thereafter people were allowed to take out 200–300 roubles a month.[37] The savings banks were given twenty-six million roubles by the State Bank to keep them liquid.

The queues outside the food shops began to diminish after the first couple of days. But the shortages of salt, sugar, grain products, matches and kerosene continued. Bread began to run short because the bakers had been conscripted and there was not enough flour: one bakery produced only a third of its normal output of bread on 23 June. People had started to hoard: one shop sold fifteen tons of salt on 23 June, compared with four and a half tons on 21 June. The NKVD began to arrest people for hoarding and black-marketeering. Forty speculators had been arrested by the end of the second day of the war.[38]

Attitudes to the Germans were complex. Pre-war propaganda had succeeded in convincing many Soviet citizens that ordinary Germans, unlike their leaders, were friendly to the workers' state. Even when these ordinary Germans appeared in uniform as aggressors on Soviet soil, many people could not get used to the idea that they were now the enemy. One artillery officer later told Ilya Ehrenburg that when he ordered his men to fire on the Germans, they replied, 'We should let the Germans get close, and then try to explain to them that they should come to their senses and let us help them rise up against Hitler.'[39] A few days after Molotov's speech the *dvornik* (odd-job man) in Raisa Labas's apartment building asked her, 'What have we got to be afraid of? The Germans are civilised people.'[40] These were not at all the emotions of patriotic hatred which the authorities expected and needed. Stalin himself spoke on May Day 1942 of the 'placidity and indifference' towards the enemy which had existed among the troops in the first months of the war. These feelings, he claimed, had now been replaced by hatred as the enemy had revealed the depths of his barbarism.[41]

The day before the war began Yevgeni Anufriev, the aspiring young peasant from Rzhev, sat his last exam, got his school-leaving certificate and went off to celebrate with his friends. 'I didn't wake up until midday on the following day. That was when I learned that the war had begun. My friends and I discussed what to do next. I went to volunteer, but the recruiting officer rejected me because I had lost the tip of my trigger finger in an accident. This probably saved my life, since I would otherwise have served in one of the volunteer divisions which were wiped out in the opening stages of the battle for Moscow. Instead the recruiting office used me and my friends to deliver call-up papers. We were surprised how many of the recipients tried to hide so that they wouldn't have to accept the papers. There was no enthusiasm for the war at that stage.'[42]

Anatoli Chernyaev, Gorbachëv's future foreign policy adviser, heard Molotov's speech as he was walking home from a brief look into the university. Military convoys were already driving along the Garden Ring, lorries were towing anti-aircraft guns, both were being overtaken by cavalry. There were patrols on the street corners: unimpressive groups of three men in strange uniforms with unfamiliar weapons. In the evening he went to a meeting at the university. The auditorium was full to overflowing. People were making patriotic speeches one after another. One of the most fiery orators was Chernyaev's fellow student Misha Gefter, in those days an enthusiastic Communist and a leading figure in the Komsomol, though he later became a dissident. The meeting went on until well after midnight. It was still hard to grasp the extent of what had happened. Surely it was a misunderstanding, something that would soon be cleared up? But when Chernyaev went to take his exams the next day, his professor, Valentina Dynnik, was in tears and awarded all the boys top marks. For some reason it was this that first gave him a glimmering of what was at stake; this and the way that, in the next few days, the wooden gates and fences of Mariina Roshcha were dismantled, and the look of the place spoiled for ever.[43]

Because of Stalin's belief that the main German thrust would be into the Ukraine, most of the new Mechanised Corps were deployed with General Kirponos' Southwestern Front. These newfangled armoured formations were supposed to rectify some of the failings identified after the Finnish war. The idea behind them looked back (without attribution of course) to the theories of Tukhachevski and the brilliant practice of the Panzer divisions. But as so often in Soviet practice, Stalin and his generals had gone for speed and quantity rather than quality. The new formations were spatchcocked together far too quickly. They were ill-equipped, ill-trained, and ill-manned. Even those that were well led were no match for the German Panzers.

General Andrei Vlasov was in command of the 4th Mechanised Corps, based in Lvov, in what had recently been Poland. A bespectacled bear with the air of an intellectual, Vlasov was a regular soldier with a high reputation. He was one of the youngest Major-Generals in the army, he had been awarded the Order of Lenin on Army Day in June 1941, and the training and discipline of his division were singled out for praise by the military authorities and in *Pravda*.[44] He was to distinguish himself in the battles on the frontier, the forlorn defence of Kiev, and the counterattack before Moscow in December and January.

One of the most junior officers in the divisions under Vlasov's command was Lieutenant Pavel Gudz. Twenty-one years old and newly commissioned, with the face of a girl and a gentle voice, he came from the Western Ukraine, a part of the world where people spoke only Ukrainian. His father went off to work in the port at Vladivostok at the other end of the country, where the money was better, and Pavel was brought up by his mother, Stepanida. Life in the village was still run by the village elders in the old patriarchal manner. Young men who behaved badly were given two warnings. On the third misdemeanour the offender would be given a piece of bread, a chunk of bacon fat, and some onions – one for each year that he was to stay away from the village and make his own way in the world.

In 1934 – the same year that his father was killed in an accident – Pavel left the village school, and went to study literature in secondary school. After two years he was sent to work in the local House of Culture, and was then appointed as a school inspector. To enable him to get around, he was given a horse and a pony and trap – the equivalent, he used to say in later years, of a Mercedes today. In August 1939 – not yet twenty – he was called in by the local Party secretary and asked if he would like to go for training in the Second Heavy Tank Academy in Saratov on the Volga.

Gudz still barely knew the Russian language and until he travelled to Saratov he had never even seen a train. His first test at the Academy was to take dictation. It was an excerpt from a speech by Stalin, of whose existence he was barely aware. He made forty mistakes, and was called before the Academy's political commissar, who asked him sarcastically whether with a bit of effort he couldn't have made even more mistakes. 'Probably,' he answered. But the school had evidently already marked him down as outstanding material, and the commissar took him at his word when he swore that he would bring himself up to scratch very soon.

On 1 September 1939 the training began with a briefing about the German attack on Poland. The cadets trained at first on the T-28 tank, a good machine with a substantial cannon and three machine guns, but mechanically weak. Later they went on the KV-1, a heavy tank named after Klim Voroshilov, which was superior to anything the Germans then had available.

Gudz finished his course with distinction. He was commissioned as a lieutenant on 10 June 1941 and given a splendid uniform. Two days later he and twenty other young officers were sent to the Kiev military district. He was assigned to the 32nd Tank Division in Lvov. The division had three hundred KV-1 tanks and was commanded by Colonel Pushkin. He and the NCOs were all long-term professionals. Stalin had said that war was impossible, so no one in Saratov had been allowed to talk about it. But on their arrival at Lvov, the young officers were greeted by the divisional chief of staff, Captain Yegorov, who told them laconically, 'Things will start happening very soon. So there's no point in you finding accommodation in the town. Set yourselves up in the barracks.'

The 32nd Division had been ordered by the Southwestern Front to check the state of the roads between Lvov and the frontier, on the grounds that they had been damaged by heavy rain. There was no trace of rain: it was a cover story to allow the officers of the Division to patrol up to the frontier along the likely German line of attack. This was another of Kirponos' discreet measures to ensure that the Southwestern Front was not entirely unprepared when war came.

Gudz was given command of the regimental headquarters platoon, which consisted of five KV tanks, two T-34s, two armoured cars, and four motorbikes. He was fortunate enough to have as his driver Galkin, an experienced man who until recently had been testing the new tanks at the Kirov factory in Leningrad. On Saturday 21 June 1941, he was regimental duty officer. That evening, as the sun was setting, a German aircraft flew over the town and left without being fired on. As dawn broke the following morning, German planes appeared overhead and attacked the Lvov airport. The Soviet aircraft were lined up wing-tip to wing-tip, and Gudz could see them burning. Some of the German aircraft peeled off to bomb the barracks of the 32nd Tank Division, and a couple of bombs hit the maintenance shops.

On his own initiative, Gudz called out the troops, even though one of the senior sergeants warned him not to: 'Stalin says there will be no war.' Gudz replied, 'Let's go and fight.' Captain Yegorov and the battalion commander, Captain Khorin, supported him. The Division set out for the frontier with Gudz and his headquarters platoon at their head.

The Germans started bombing the column. German troops deployed ahead of them. Khorin ordered Gudz to attack. Gudz was still, alas, wearing his best uniform. A shell from a German anti-tank gun bounced off the tank's heavy armour. The damage was negligible, but Gudz smelled the peculiar smell of scorched armour for the first time. Gudz, who was the tank's gunner as well as its commander, fired a single shot in return and the gun was destroyed. He and his platoon went on to knock out five German tanks, three armoured personnel carriers and several cars. The Germans retreated, but Gudz was told not to pursue them across the frontier.

The platoon then set out to rescue some Soviet infantry that had been surrounded. They were too late – all were dead, including a nurse who had evidently been shot in cold blood as she was bandaging a wounded soldier.

After lunch the Germans attacked again. Gudz knocked out three more tanks. His driver Galkin rammed another German tank, dislodging its caterpillar track and forcing it into the ditch. The fields were covered with burned-out tanks and dead Germans. The weather was so hot that the fields of corn caught fire under the shelling, and the corpses swelled up almost immediately.

But the Germans continued to push ahead. Within days the Division was forced to retreat – first to Lvov, and then to Kiev. The Germans were systematically destroying the Russians' supply lines from the air, and the Division soon started to run out of fuel and ammunition. Outside Kiev Gudz and his comrades had to burn their tanks: the tracks were worn out and they had no more fuel. The surviving men of the Division were put on trains and sent to Moscow.

Rokossovski's new command, the 9th Mechanised Corps in the Kiev Military District, was fully up to strength in men. But it had less than a third of its tanks and motor transport. The officers were raw and over-promoted, and many of the drivers had had only a few hours' experience with their vehicles. As a mechanised formation the 9th Mechanised Corps was, Rokossovski had to conclude, unfit for military operations. He nevertheless began to prepare for the coming war. He reconnoitred possible German lines of advance. He accelerated work on the half-finished defensive works. He refused to allow his artillery to be sent away for summer training. He husbanded his tanks, worn out in earlier training exercises. He forged close links with the civilian organisations which were meant to supply extra transport on mobilisation.

These measures were by no means complete when, after finishing his work on 21 June, Rokossovski invited his divisional commanders to go fishing the following morning. But that evening his staff were told that a corporal in the German army, by nationality a Pole from Poznan, had deserted to the frontier forces and told them that the Germans would attack on 22 June. Rokossovski put his commanders on the alert. The duty officer rang him at about 4 o'clock the following morning with the order to open his secret emergency instructions. They told him to deploy his men for war. He said a quick goodbye to his wife and daughter and left for the front.

Rokossovski and his corps immediately started to move towards the battle positions that he had already identified. The promised civilian transport did not arrive, and on the very first day the Infantry marched thirty miles, carrying all their own weapons and ammunition. By evening they were so worn out that they lost all capacity to fight. Thereafter they were asked to march only twenty miles a day. As they travelled, strange groups of people stumbled towards them, trying to make themselves scarce when they saw the officers. Some wore only their underwear, others wore shirts and trousers of military cut, or worn-out peasant clothing and torn straw hats. They were men who had escaped from encirclement or who had cut and run in the shock of battle. They came from many different military units. Two men turned out to be from the engineering platoon which had been sent ahead to set up Rokossovski's new headquarters.

A tattered general was brought to Rokossovski, worn out, his uniform torn, without his personal weapon. He had gone to find out what was happening at the front. Lorryloads of troops had passed him in the opposite direction. He had stopped one lorry to ask the men where they were going and what unit were they from. Instead of answering, they dragged him into the lorry, declared that he was a German agent in disguise, took away his documents and his weapon, and sentenced him to death. He managed to jump out of the lorry as it was moving and hide in the thick corn by the roadside. Other officers who tried to stem the panic were less lucky, and were shot out of hand.

The fugitives produced a variety of excuses: their units had been wiped out and they were the only survivors; they had been attacked from the rear by parachutists; they had been harassed by enemy soldiers dressed in the uniform of Soviet militiamen, frontier guards, the NKVD, even of senior officers. Some had lost all faith in the possibility of resisting the enemy. Some mutilated themselves to escape battle. Some committed suicide. One officer in Rokossovski's own corps left a note saying: 'I am haunted by a feeling of fear that I will not be able to cope with battle, and that has forced me to kill myself.' Whole units panicked when they were attacked from the flank by a small group of enemy tanks and aircraft. But Rokossovski saw that those who had good leaders were willing to fight.[45]

General Kirponos' other Mechanised Corps were equally hampered by shortages of equipment and inadequate training. But here and there they had their successes. Rokossovski himself ambushed a German Panzer division and inflicted heavy losses. The Panzers were not invincible after all.[46] A veteran of Khalkin Gol remarked to him, 'We can beat the Germans, just like we beat the Japanese.'[47] But two whole years and many defeats passed until this sentiment became an uncontested reality at the battle of Kursk in the summer of 1943. Like Lieutenant Gudz and the 32nd Tank Division, Rokossovski was soon forced to fall back.[48] By the end of the first week of the war, most of the Red Army's brand-new Mechanised Corps had lost nine-tenths of their strength.[49]

A week passed before Rokossovski heard that his wife and daughter were safe. It had taken them seven days to get by train from Kiev to Moscow, a journey which usually lasted about fourteen hours. In Moscow they had not even had time to tell their relatives what was going on before they were put onto another train and sent off to Kazakhstan. He wrote a quick note in blue pencil: 'Dear Lulu! I hear you've left. I'm glad you won't be in danger. But I'm worried where you will live and in what conditions. I am well and cheerful. Don't worry about me. I kiss you hard and Adulya too. I love you, Kostya.'[50] He did not make contact with his family again for nearly a year.

By the end of that first day of the war, the Germans had already forced the Nieman – the river whose crossing had marked the beginning of Napoleon's invasion on Wednesday 24 June 1812, just 129 years earlier.[51]

Despite the doubts which some expressed in private, the public mood was still sanguine. Professors of history published articles pointing out that foreign invaders – Frenchmen, Swedes, Poles, Tatars, and indeed Germans – had always been driven from Russia in defeat. Surely, people thought, that was bound to happen again once the mighty Red Army summoned up its strength. Few expected that Hitler's armies too would reach the gates of Moscow.

Foreign observers were not so sure. Within twenty-four hours the War Office in London had concluded, with a wealth of technical argument, that 'German armoured divisions might reach the line ROSTOV–MOSCOW in three weeks or less, though allowing for a reasonable resistance by the Russians they would probably take as much as five weeks.'[52]

One Moscow schoolboy was particularly resentful at the way things had turned out. For him the outbreak of war could not have been worse timed. He had only got two out of five for his end-of-term examination. 'If Hitler had started the war a bit earlier,' he complained, 'perhaps the exams would have been cancelled.'[53]

– FIVE –

THE RUSSIANS FIGHT BACK

Stalin was already back at work in the Kremlin by 3.30 a.m. on the second morning of the war. A major item of the day's business was the creation of a Stavka ('General Headquarters') of the Supreme Command, consisting of Molotov and Voroshilov; Timoshenko, Zhukov and Budënny for the army; and Admiral Kuznetsov for the navy. Timoshenko was its first chairman, an anomaly rectified on 10 July when Stalin was 'persuaded' to take over.[1]

Timoshenko reported that the Soviet forces were regrouping to check the enemy's advance. Stalin: 'You mean you are no longer getting ready, as you were previously, to smash the enemy quickly?' Timoshenko: 'No, but after we've concentrated our forces we shall undoubtedly smash him.'

Stalin's particular fury was directed against Pavlov, the commander of the Western Front, which stood in the direct way of von Bock's relentless thrust towards Moscow. 'He says the order reached him late. Shouldn't an army be ready to fight even if it hasn't been ordered to?'[2] Though Pavlov had lost his head, and was to pay for it, this was wholly unfair. Stalin had made it clear beyond any doubt in the run-up to the war that any exercise of initiative by his commanders would be severely punished. Pavlov had done what he could to prepare for the war. He was hampered at every turn by Moscow. In February he pleaded to Stalin for the wherewithal to construct proper defences. He suggested that school leavers and students should be mobilised to build fortifications during their holidays, so that his soldiers could do their training instead of working as labourers. His pleas were not answered. By the beginning of the war less than a fifth of the planned defensive works had been completed.[3] His own intelligence officers gave him an accurate picture of the build up of German forces opposite his front. He had been afraid to tell Moscow that war was imminent. But on 21 June he had asked for permission to move his troops to their fortified field positions. Timoshenko had refused.

On 26 June Pavlov withdrew his headquarters to Bobruisk and then to Mogilëv, in the mistaken belief that German tanks had broken through. Still lacking telephone or radio communications, he sent liaison officers to the units at the front with orders to withdraw. His alternative mode of communication was the U-2, a small and elderly biplane capable of flying just over eighty miles an hour at a height of no more than 5,000 feet.[4] Despite these unmilitary characteristics, the U-2 could fly at treetop level and land on a halfpenny, carry a gun and a load of bombs, and was used throughout the war for liaison, the evacuation of the wounded and night bombing.[5] Pavlov sent one U-2 to carry his orders to each army. He sent armoured cars and dropped liaison officers by parachute for the same purpose. All the U-2s were shot down and all the armoured cars were knocked out by the Germans. Two of the parachuted officers got through to the 10th Army. They were arrested as spies. The 10th Army cipher clerks were unable to decipher the coded orders, because the codes had been changed the previous day. The two officers were handed over to the NKVD Special Section and shot on the spot.[6] Pavlov plunged back into the line to save something from the wreckage. Stalin and Zhukov lost track of him for six whole days. Stalin sent Shaposhnikov and Kulik to see what was going on. They too were unable to take control. Kulik went off to the 3rd Army and disappeared from view. Aircraft and armoured vehicles were sent to track him down.[7] Pavlov's Chief of Staff, Major-General Klimovskikh, responded to all questions with the despairing reply, 'The commander is at the front.' What that meant, Klimovskikh had no idea. As soon as Pavlov reappeared he was summoned to Moscow and Timoshenko was appointed in his place.[8]

On 29 June 1941, as Minsk was about to fall to the Germans, Stalin took Molotov, Malenkov, Beria and Mikoyan with him to the Commissariat for Defence. Zhukov was already in Timoshenko's office. The generals were quite unable to say what was going on at the front. Stalin flared up into a rage and took it out on Zhukov. 'What kind of Chief of Staff panics as soon as the fighting starts, loses contact with his forces, represents nothing and commands nobody?'

Zhukov left the room in tears. He was brought back by Molotov after a few minutes. Things calmed down, and the meeting ground to a subdued conclusion. As Stalin left the building, he said to Mikoyan and the others, 'Lenin founded our state, and we've fucked it up!'

It was at this point that Stalin succumbed to the nervous strain of the past week. His authority had been catastrophically undermined by his shattering misjudgement of German intentions and his refusal to accept advice that did not square with his obsession. He must have feared that his close colleagues would take the opportunity to get their revenge for years of terror and humiliation. At first he had continued to spend twelve to fourteen hours a day in his office, apparently calm, certainly in unchallenged control, and receiving a constant stream of ministers, party officials, military men, foreign diplomats, industrialists, designers and testers of tanks and aircraft.[9]

Now he took himself off to the Nearby Dacha in what Molotov later told Mikoyan was a state of prostration. The telephones in his office fell silent. He summoned no one. His staff were increasingly alarmed. Lev Mekhlis, a Deputy Prime Minister and Stalin's unpopular and sinister troubleshooter for the military, tried to ring the Nearby Dacha but got no answer. The work piled up. Stalin's office manager took urgent papers to Voznesenski and Molotov for signature. Both refused to take any decisions on Stalin's behalf: after all, nearly four centuries earlier Ivan the Terrible had also withdrawn from the Kremlin into seclusion, and had turned horribly against those who had been incautious enough to think they could grab for power in his absence. Stalin's absence too, might be a device to test his colleagues' loyalty.

But the business of the war could not be delayed. On 30 June the members of the Politburo decided unanimously to visit Stalin in the Nearby Dacha. He seemed to crumple in his chair as they came in, and asked in a strange and anxious voice, 'Why have you come?', evidently fearing they were there to arrest him. Molotov said that a new mechanism was needed to concentrate power and prosecute the war. 'Who should head it?' asked Stalin, and seemed surprised when Molotov told him that he should of course head the new body himself.[10]

Unless some intimate account by Stalin himself emerges – a diary perhaps, or a personal note – we cannot know whether he had really been shaken to the core, as any other man would have been, or whether he was indeed subjecting his colleagues to a loyalty test. His remarks four years later to his victorious generals give a clue. 'Any other nation,' he then said, 'might have said to its government: you have not justified our expectations, you should now depart so that we can install another government, which will conclude a peace with Germany and assure our well-being.'[11] Given the evidence of public unease which the NKVD put to him from the first day of the war, his apprehensions were understandable. The decision of the Politburo to stick with him may not have been mere pusillanimity: the overwhelming need to organise against the Germans would have been severely and perhaps fatally disrupted by a crisis over the succession. But Stalin doubtless concluded that his colleagues lacked the courage to operate without him and the *cojones* to strike down the man who had exploited and terrorised them for years, as he would have done if the positions had been reversed. His confidence in himself and his contempt for his entourage must have been greatly boosted.

He never seriously wavered again. He immediately resumed his duties with all his old energy and determination. His first act was to implement Molotov's suggestion of a supreme body to manage the conduct of the war. The State Committee for Defence, the Gosudarstvenny Komitet Oborony or GKO, was set up to 'concentrate the full range of state power in [its] hands ... All citizens and all Party, Soviet, Komsomol and military bodies [are to] carry out the decisions and provisions of the State Committee for Defence without question.'[12] These decisions thus had the force of law. Infractions were punished immediately and ruthlessly.

The Committee consisted of Stalin as Chairman and Molotov as Vice-Chairman. The other members were Voroshilov, Malenkov and Beria. Voznesenski, Kaganovich and Anastas Mikoyan joined the

Committee in February 1942. The responsibilities of each member of the Committee were carefully defined. Molotov was in charge of tank production, and was a success despite his weakness for holding interminable bureaucratic meetings.[13] Kaganovich was responsible for transport, Malenkov for aircraft production, Mikoyan for supply (including, at a later date, Lend-Lease supplies from the Western Allies). All the other branches of the economy were in the capable hands of Voznesenski. The Committee played a crucial role in subordinating the whole life of the country to the single goal of achieving victory. It took strategic responsibility for the supply and armament of the Red Army. It gave broad direction to the conduct of military operations, paid close attention to all military appointments of any significance, and managed the partisan war behind the German lines. It took many economic decisions as well, including instructions about the production of sledges and horseshoes.[14] The Committee met informally in Stalin's office in the Kremlin. It kept no minutes: its proceedings were recorded in the ten thousand-odd decisions it issued in the course of the war. Stalin himself signed most of the military decisions. Many of these he wrote out himself, others he dictated, others were submitted to him in draft and substantially rewritten.[15]

On 10 July Stalin became Commander in Chief. In addition to chairing the GKO, he was by now also Secretary General of the Party, Chairman of the Council of People's Commissars (the Government) and People's Commissar for Defence. Even Stalin, with all his stamina, energy, intelligence, and willpower, could not master all these bodies. Some lost significance: the Politburo met irregularly, and the only plenary meeting of the Central Committee of the Party during the war took place in October 1941, and Stalin himself did not attend.[16]

Bad news continued to pour in. By 10 July the Western Front had lost 4,799 tanks, 9,477 guns, 1,777 combat aircraft and 341,000 soldiers.[17] In less than three weeks von Bock's Army Group Centre had captured the whole of Belorussia and had advanced nearly four hundred miles along the road to Moscow.

Russian soldiers surrendered, in huge numbers, in formed units, without firing a shot. By 28 June the Germans had encircled two Soviet armies and elements of two others around the Belorussian capital of

Minsk, rounding up a force roughly comparable in size to the British Expeditionary Force which escaped at Dunkirk.[18] Nearly half a million more men were captured in August in Smolensk, Uman in Ukraine, and Gomel in Belorussia; 665,000 were taken around Kiev in September; in October 107,000 fell into German hands in the South and 663,000 on the approaches to Moscow in October: more than two million in all.[19]

The German High Command had expected to take millions of prisoners. But it had made no plans to feed them. In May 1941 Hitler's economic experts had reported that the war could only be sustained beyond the end of 1941 if the German soldiers were fed from Russian supplies. 'Doubtless tens of millions of people,' the study concluded, 'will starve to death.'[20] Even an army which adhered scrupulously to the provisions of the Geneva Convention would have found it hard to feed, house, care for and guard such vast numbers of bewildered and defenceless men. The Germans were not prepared to divert the necessary resources, and very soon the prisoners began to die like flies.

And yet within days of beginning their triumphant advance the Germans noticed something which ran entirely counter to their expectations. In 1940 the French and the British fought for as long as they thought prudence and honour required. They then retreated to fight another day, or surrendered: by the end of the campaign in France the Germans had taken 1,900,000 prisoners.[21] The Germans had assumed that things would be even easier in the East. The Russians would not fight for their hated regime. A demoralised Red Army would crumble before them. It would be a walkover.

But even on the first day of the war the Germans saw with surprise what General Voronov had heard with huge relief: the Russians were fighting back. They stood their ground, or advanced into futile counter-attacks launched by officers who were inexperienced, incompetent, terrified of their own superiors, or all three. They threw themselves in suicidal waves on the German lines, and were mown down in their thousands. It was a frightening experience even for soldiers who had already fought in France and Poland.

The Russians went on fighting not only when fighting had become pointless, but even when it had become physically impossible. Encircled, outnumbered, disorganised, often without their commanders, without ammunition, fuel, medical supplies or food, they were cut down or surrendered only when they had nothing left to fight with. Even then, substantial numbers melted into the forests to make their way back to their lines or to join the partisan bands that were already beginning to form.

The Germans had misjudged their opportunity and missed their chance. An elderly Tsarist general told Guderian in Orël just after the city had fallen to the Panzers at the beginning of October:

> If only you had come twenty years ago we should have welcomed you with open arms. But now it's too late. We were just beginning to get on our feet and now you arrive and throw us back twenty years so that we will have to start from the beginning all over again. Now we are fighting for Russia and in that cause we are all united.[22]

At the end of July, the Politburo took a decision of great symbolic and political importance: to move Lenin's body from the Mausoleum on Red Square to a place of safety in Tyumen, deep in Siberia and well away from big industrial centres that were likely to be bombed. Poskrëbyshev informed Kuptsov, the Regional Party Secretary in Tyumen, that an 'object' of exceptional importance would soon be arriving in his town. But the only person among the senior staff in the Mausoleum itself who was told of the decision was Ilya Zbarski's father, Boris.

Ilya Zbarski and his colleague Mardashëv knew nothing until 3 July. They were then ordered to go that very evening to the Yaroslavl Station to care for Lenin on his way to safety. Lenin had been placed in a wooden coffin covered with paraffin, its lid moving on grooves greased with Vaseline. The coffin was in a large wooden crate, and a consignment of accompanying equipment was assembled, including two large glass baths and the necessary chemicals and equipment. The windows of the special train were curtained off, and the body was guarded night and day by Kiryushin, the officer responsible for guarding the Mausoleum, and a detachment of officers and men from the Kremlin guard. It was a hot July evening when the train finally pulled out of the station. All along its route to Tyumen there were soldiers stationed by the tracks, and at the stations through which it passed more soldiers were posted to keep back the desperate crowds of refugees trying to travel to the East.

The train reached Tyumen on 7 July, a quick journey even in

peacetime, and quite remarkable in the tremendous dislocation which had already gripped the overstretched railway system. The train was greeted by local dignitaries, who by now had learned that the 'special object' was none other than Lenin himself. The next day the coffin was moved to a two-storey building belonging to the local agricultural college. It was by no means ideal: it was in a filthy state, the plumbing had to be restored, and distilled water and other essential supplies had to be brought from Omsk, several hundred miles away. But Lenin was safe.

Back in Moscow the Mausoleum was surrounded in metal scaffolding and covered with black tarpaulin as a form of camouflage.[23] Ordinary Russians assumed that Lenin was still there, a symbol of resistance and eventual victory.

Stalin finally spoke to the nation on 3 July, eleven days after the war had begun. Over the loudspeakers which hung in streets, in factories, in buildings throughout the country, his listeners heard Stalin walk with heavy steps towards the microphone, fill his glass with water and begin.[24]

'Comrades!' he said, speaking slowly, calmly, tonelessly, didactic as always, without rhetorical flourishes, and with a strong Georgian accent. 'Citizens! Brothers and Sisters! Warriors of our Army and Fleet! I turn to you, my friends!'

The treacherous Germans were continuing their attack, he went on, even though some of their best divisions and some of their finest squadrons had already shattered themselves against the heroic resistance of the Red Army and found a grave on the battlefield. They had already captured Lithuania, part of Latvia, parts of Western Belorussia and Ukraine. They had bombed the country's main cities in the West.

Did this mean that the Germans were invincible? No, it did not. History showed that there was no such thing as an invincible army. Napoleon's 'invincible' armies had been defeated by the Russians, the British, and (an odd reference in the context) the Germans. The armies of Wilhelm II had been eventually defeated by the Russians, the French and the British. So it would be with Hitler, whose armies had never until now met serious resistance on the continent of Europe. The Germans' initial success in Russia was explicable. They were at the height of their readiness, while the Soviet forces were still redeploying towards the new frontiers. And they had gained surprise by treacherously breaking their Pact with the Soviet Union.

The Soviet people must understand the full extent of the danger which threatened their country. A ruthless enemy was bent on enslaving them. They must abandon the soft ways of peace, arm themselves for a battle to the death, and show no mercy to the foe. The Army, the Fleet, every citizen must defend each inch of Soviet territory, and be ready to offer up the last drop of their blood. The whole country must be mobilised to produce the weapons and munitions they needed. Everything must be subordinated to the demands of the front.

Nothing should be left behind for the enemy where the Red Army was forced to retreat: not a single vehicle nor a single animal, not a kilogram of bread nor a litre of fuel. Anything that could not be removed should be destroyed. Partisan detachments should stay behind to make life unbearable for the enemy.

But this war was not a war in defence of the Soviet Union alone. It was also a war to liberate the peoples of Europe – including the enslaved people of Germany itself. It was a war in which the Soviet Union would stand shoulder to shoulder with the peoples of Europe and America to fight for independence and democratic freedoms. 'Comrades!' Stalin concluded. 'Our arrogant foe will soon discover that our forces are beyond number ... Forward – to Victory!'[25]

This telling speech set the themes which were to dominate political discourse and propaganda in the Soviet Union for the rest of the war: the overriding aim was victory in a war of liberation, everything was to be ruthlessly sacrificed to this end, the Soviet Union had powerful allies in the struggle. People were deeply stirred by their sense of Stalin's strength, his willpower and his inflexible courage. They were moved above all, many to tears, by his warm reference to his friends, to his brothers and sisters. He had never used such language to them before. But many reacted, above all, with a sense of relief. Now at last there was an open admission of what everyone on the ground knew to be true. The fantasy of rapid and inevitable victory had been blown away. This new understanding was bitter enough. But it was better than the uncertainty that had preceded it. Stalin's willingness to tell the truth was a sign of strength. The more reflective, such as the writer Konstantin Simonov, wondered of course why Stalin had not spoken earlier. Had he decided to remain silent until he had a clearer view of what was happening? After all, he could not risk getting things wrong and having to eat his words. Or had he needed time to identify the scapegoats against whom to divert criticism? But for almost everyone, the speech was a masterstroke. It ended all the speculation about Stalin's apparent absence from public life. It rallied morale and strengthened the popular determination to resist. It was, in its way, one of the turning points of the war.[26]

The speech was immediately read out at meetings in factories, offices, and other institutions throughout Moscow, and the reaction was fed back to the Party through its own channels and through the NKVD. The Lenin Raion Party Committee hurried to report that listeners had dutifully expressed 'their love, their devotion to our great and beloved Socialist Motherland, to our best friend, father and teacher, Comrade Stalin'. One worker after another – men and women – had risen to express their hatred of the German invader, and their determination to exceed themselves in producing weapons for the army. Several had volunteered on the spot for the people's militia.[27]

There were of course the usual sceptics, as the Moscow NKVD reported, those who felt that the situation was even worse than Stalin had admitted. One man thought that the Soviet government had been taken entirely by surprise: it was this that had led to the string of defeats and to the colossal losses of men and aircraft. Stalin's call for a partisan war – an extremely unreliable form of warfare – was a sign of desperation. It was foolish to hope for help from Britain and America. The USSR now found itself in a hole from which there was no visible way out. Several people thought that Moscow would be abandoned and that the Soviet regime would then collapse. Everything that had been constructed in the last quarter of a century, they said, had turned out to be a myth.[28]

Writers and journalists were mobilised to sustain the public mood. They got off to a slow start. On 22 June itself the papers carried no news at all about the catastrophe that had befallen the Soviet Union early that morning: the Soviet press did not work to that kind of deadline. There were technical pieces about military affairs in *Krasnaya Zvezda*, an article on lessons to be drawn from the British and Italian use of armour and aircraft in the Libyan desert, and an account on the sports page of the first round of the USSR football championship: Dinamo had lost its game the previous day in Moscow. *Pravda* reprinted Lermontov's famous poem about the Battle of Borodino in 1812 – not because there was now a new war, but because it was the centenary of the poet's death in a duel. Tucked away on the back page was a report that physicists in Leningrad were trying to split the atom.[29] Moscow's own evening paper, *Vechernyaya Moskva*, did not come out at all. The next day the press was no more informative: like the government and the High Command, they had no idea what was going on. They printed large pictures of Stalin, Molotov's speech, some official decrees, and accounts of patriotic meetings in fighting units and in factories, where soldiers, airmen and workers swore to defend their country to the death.

In later years David Ortenberg – at that time still deputy editor of *Krasnaya Zvezda*, the army newspaper – used to say that for him the war began a day early, when he was summoned on Saturday 21 June by Mekhlis, the Deputy Prime Minister and former editor of *Pravda*, his journalistic mentor and political patron. Mekhlis was in the full uniform of a general. 'What's going on?' asked Ortenberg. 'The war is just about to begin,' Mekhlis answered. 'The Germans are going to attack us. I have been reassigned to head the Main Political Administration of the Armed Forces.' He told Ortenberg to go home, put on his own uniform and come straight back to accompany him and Timoshenko to visit the Headquarters of the Western Front at Minsk. By the time Ortenberg returned Timoshenko and Mekhlis had gone to see Stalin in the Kremlin. At 5 o'clock in the morning of 22 June Mekhlis rang Ortenberg: 'The war's already begun. Our trip to Minsk is cancelled. Go to your office and put out the paper.'

Ortenberg promptly commissioned a patriotic poem from Vasili Lebedev-Kumach, who wrote many of the songs for the film comedies of the 1930s. It was called 'Arise, O Mighty Country'. Within three days, the words had been set to music by Alexander Aleksandrov, whose Red Army Chorus immediately performed it to soldiers setting off for the front from Moscow's Belorussia Station. Thereafter it was played every morning on the radio to start the day and became one of the defining theme songs of the war. It can still raise a lump in the throat even of those too young to remember. In those first days, more than a hundred new patriotic songs were composed in Moscow alone.[30]

Ortenberg, like Mekhlis, was Jewish. When Mekhlis told him at the end of June that he was being promoted chief editor of his paper, he tried to wriggle out of the job. Editing a national newspaper in the Soviet Union was a risky business: three chief editors of *Krasnaya Zvezda* had disappeared in rapid succession during the purges. But Mekhlis said the appointment had been approved by Stalin. He added that Ortenberg was to use the byline 'Vadimov', concocted from the name of his son Vadim, and suitably un-Semitic. Ortenberg was convinced that even now, a week after the German attack, Stalin still wanted the names of Jewish journalists to be disguised, lest Hitler be offended.[31]

Though the government already exercised close control over the press, something more was needed. On 24 June they set up the SovInformBuro, the Soviet Information Bureau. The ubiquitous Shcherbakov was put in charge and given undisputed authority. He made it an absolute rule that no news should be printed in any newspaper until it had appeared in a SovInformBuro bulletin. But the SovInformBuro's own correspondents rarely strayed beyond the Front headquarters, and their reports often simply regurgitated what they were told there. Ortenberg, who wanted to report the news directly from the front in an interesting and timely fashion, was often at daggers drawn with Shcherbakov in consequence.[32]

By now Konstantin Simonov was up at the front. He had covered the campaign in Mongolia as a young war correspondent. But that campaign had been victorious. Now he found himself observing something very like defeat. One incident among many struck him so forcefully that it appeared in many of his subsequent writings. A week after the war began he was travelling from Mogilëv along the forest road to Bobruisk, in the line of the German advance, when fifteen TB-3s flew slowly and peacefully overhead. These were the four-engined bombers built at Aircraft Factory No. 22 in the Moscow suburbs – the old Russo-Baltic Wagon Factory which had produced the revolutionary *Ilya Muromets*. The TB-3s, too, had been revolutionary in their day, but by now they were practically obsolete. The fifteen bombers had no fighter escort. German fighters shot down six in a matter of ten minutes: they would fasten on the tail of one aircraft, there would be a rattle of machine-gun fire, the bomber would catch fire and fly on before it crashed into the forest, and the Messerschmitts would then latch onto the next victim.

Simonov picked up two of the survivors in his truck. One was a captain, wearing a medal of the Winter War. The other was a lieutenant with a broken leg. Shortly afterwards yet another TB-3 flew overhead and shared the fate of its predecessors. The scene repeated itself a few miles further on. This time, as the bomber was beginning to fall on fire, one of the two attacking Messerschmitts reared up and began to fall in its turn: it had been hit by fire from the bomber's rear gunner, still serving his weapon even though his plane was burning. The German pilot bailed out. So did five of the crew of the bomber: but not the rear gunner. The strong wind carried the parachutes far off. The TB-3 blew up as it hit the ground with three heavy explosions. The incident became one of the most dramatic scenes in Simonov's novel about the first six months of the war, *The Living and the Dead*.

Years later Simonov went to the archives to establish what had happened. General Pavlov had ordered every available plane into the air to try to hold the German tanks. So the TB-3s were sent on a daylight tactical mission for which they were entirely unsuited. Ground observers confirmed the claims of the survivors that they had achieved a substantial success. The next day the bombers were ordered up again. Their commander asked for fighter cover, and dive bombers to suppress the German anti-aircraft guns. But too many fighters had been destroyed on the first day of the war. Once again the low-flying bombers, with their vast bulk and modest speed, went to their targets without cover, a splendid target for the Germans. They had no choice but to struggle and die. Twenty-one TB-3s were lost that day.

The Soviet bombers did not only have to contend with the enemy. The war had barely begun before Timoshenko had to deal with several gross cases of friendly fire. One group of TB-3s returning from a mission, which had successfully beaten off the German fighters, was then shelled by Soviet anti-aircraft guns and attacked by Soviet fighters. One aircraft was forced down and crashed on landing. Two TB-3s were shot down by their own side near Minsk. These mistakes – Timoshenko's people called them 'shameful' – were all the more indefensible since no German bomber had more than two engines, and none remotely resembled the lumbering TB-3s.[33]

These disasters were not, of course, reported in the press. Simonov looked at the old files for one summer's day in 1941: 19 July, the day he returned briefly from the front to Moscow to file his stories. The papers on that day carried no place-names, no names of units, no news of German successes nor of the loss of key cities. They described successful individual actions between Soviet partisans, aircraft, tanks, artillery, and their German opponents, and gave the deliberate, though false, impression that the Soviet forces were inflicting heavy casualties on the Germans, while suffering few of their own. Most unreliable of all was the reporting on the Red Air Force. Its huge losses and its lack of modern aircraft were ignored. The SovInformBuro entirely suppressed the bitter truth that in the summer of 1941 the Germans had enjoyed almost continuous air superiority.

Simonov could never finally decide where the boundary lay between necessary and unnecessary secrecy. He felt some sympathy for the authorities, who had to manage the news as the Red Army suffered one disaster after another. He himself felt unable to tell even his closest friends in Moscow what he had seen at the front. His mother had believed the pre-war stories about the superiority of 'Stalin's Falcons' and their aircraft, and she believed what the newspapers now told her about the successes of the Red Air Force at the front. She would have found the truth an unbearable shock.[34] Simonov came to an ambiguous conclusion. 'Even though the phraseology of those years is shot through with elements that to us today are unacceptable ... the pages of those newspapers reflect the grandeur of those days, a grandeur which one can only fully appreciate today, quarter of a century later.'[35] He would perhaps have sympathised with the Home Office official in wartime London who wrote:

> The people must feel that they are being told the truth. Distrust breeds fear much more than knowledge of reverses. The all-important thing for publicity to achieve is the conviction that the worst is known. [...] The people should be told that this is a civilian's war, a People's War, and therefore they are to be taken into the Government's confidence as never before.

But he would probably also have shared that official's conclusion: 'It is simpler to tell the truth and if a sufficient emergency arises, to tell one big, thumping lie that will then be believed'.[36]

*

In that summer of 1941, surrounded by the evidence of panic, defeat, incompetence, cowardice, and dogged courage, Simonov – the atheist and the Communist – began to look at the Russian countryside around him with new eyes:

> The villages were small, and next to them, usually on a small rise alongside a dilapidated little church but sometimes, even where there was no church, you would see large graveyards, with the old wooden crosses each looking like the next. The disproportion between the number of houses in the village and the number of those crosses shook me at the time, and that feeling has remained with me to this day. It was then that I understood how strong within me was the feeling for my Motherland, how much I felt that the land itself was my own, how deeply rooted within that land were all those people who lived there. The bitterness of the first two weeks of the war convinced me that even though the Germans might get as far as this, it was impossible to imagine that the land itself could become German. Whatever happened it was and would remain Russian. In these graveyards lay so many unknown ancestors, grandfathers, great-grandfathers, old men whom we had never seen, that this land seemed Russian not only on the surface but downwards for yard after yard into the depths.[37]

His emotions crystallised into one of the most popular poems of the war, 'The Roads around Smolensk', a poem drenched in passion for the ancient Russian land, the land of Christian Orthodoxy, the land for which Russians had fought since the days of the Tatars:

> *By the graves on the edge of every small village,*
> *Guarding the living with the sign of the cross,*
> *Our forefathers gather together to pray,*
> *For their grandsons who no longer believe in a God.*

Simonov had understood a simple truth. The soldiers would fight not for Stalin and his regime, but for the Russian land and the Russian people, for the living and for the ever-present spirits of the dead.[38]

– SIX –

THE VOLUNTEERS

'*Narodnoe opolchenie*' is a phrase which resonates through Russian history. It means 'popular levy', the raising of military units from among ordinary people to support the regular army in times of national trouble. The *opolchenie* helped to expel the Poles from Moscow in 1612, and to fight Napoleon to a standstill in 1812. The *opolchenie* raised in the summer of 1941 from Moscow and the surrounding countryside played a desperate part in halting Hitler's armies on the very outskirts of the capital. Ill-armed and hastily trained, they died in their tens of thousands. Their fate is still a matter of furious controversy between those who believe they were uselessly sacrificed by a ruthless Party and incompetent generals, and those who see their self-sacrifice as a tragic but inescapable part of the defence of the city, and a symbol of the courage of its people.

As soon as the news of the German attack came through people flocked to volunteer at their places of work and their colleges, at the army's recruiting stations and at their local Party and Komsomol offices. They came from many backgrounds: from the old intelligentsia, from the 'new class' of government and Party officials and 'technical intelligentsia', from among the peasants who had poured into the capital after their old way of life was destroyed by collectivisation. Students, workers, dancers, actors and musicians volunteered in groups, together with their teachers and bosses. It was like Britain in 1914, and as in Britain those who volunteered together too often died together.

Although there was a good deal of moral pressure to volunteer, not everybody felt bound to conform. Yuri Averbakh, who in the fullness of time became one of the Soviet Union's most distinguished grandmasters of chess, missed volunteering by a series of fortunate accidents which probably saved his life. A precocious child, he entered the Bauman Higher Technical Institute in 1939 at the young age of seventeen. He was therefore in the midst of his studies and exempt from immediate call-up when the war began. Instead of joining a volunteer division, he was sent to work at a tank repair base outside Moscow. When the Germans broke the Russian front outside Moscow in mid-October, Shcherbakov issued a panic call for volunteers for a new wave of militia units. There was no avoiding the call this time. Averbakh turned up in the most suitable civilian clothes he had. The recruiting sergeant took one look at his light summer boots and told him to buy something more suitable. He went round all the shops, but no one had anything to fit his unusually large feet. So once again he missed the war.[1]

Viktor Merzhanov was finishing his studies at the Conservatoire when the war began. At first he was lukewarm about it, but his mood changed when he heard Stalin's speech of 3 July. He attended the meeting in the Conservatoire at which his fellow students and teachers volunteered. But before going to the war, he wanted to say goodbye to his parents in the provincial city of Tambov. He and three others refused to volunteer, and got away with it. He never did see action. He was sent first to the aviation academy in Tambov as a percussionist in the military band and later as a horn player in a military band in Central Asia, where he stayed until the end of the war. He was demobilised in time to prepare for the Conservatoire's piano competition at the end of 1945, when he tied for first place with Sviatoslav Richter. He was still pursuing an active career as a concert pianist as the twenty-first century began.[2]

The authorities were already overwhelmed with the task of organising the mobilisation of reservists and conscripts. They were not at first sure what to do with this huge influx of volunteers. For the most part they simply took their names, and told them to go home to await instructions.

They did mobilise two special categories from the start. Nine hundred Moscow Party officials were sent to the army at the front as political instructors and even as ordinary soldiers, in the belief that this would raise morale. Many were killed in the first weeks of the war. Zhilenkov, the secretary of the Rostokino Raion Party Committee, was made a member of the Military Council of the 32nd Army. When the 32nd Army was surrounded at the beginning of October, he went over to the Germans. He eventually became the chief ideologue in General Vlasov's 'Russian Liberation Army' under German command.[3]

Volunteers who already had military qualifications were inducted straight into the army. The senior class at Vladimir Gurkin's school did regular military training, and their names were kept on a list at the VoenKomat, the recruiting office. The patriotic propaganda, the physical training, the highly developed competition between schools, all helped to prepare the boys for war. Even before leaving school, Gurkin had been offered a place in the Krasin Artillery School. This was one of the five Military Schools in the Moscow area: the others were the Podolsk School, the School of the Supreme Soviet, the School of Engineering, and the Military-Political School. Cadets from all of these took part in the Moscow battle.

On the evening of 21 June Gurkin and his class celebrated the end of school exams by going to Red Square. When he eventually woke up the next morning, he went straight to the Artillery School, which was having an open day. On the tram people looked tense, and they weren't talking to one another, but it was not until he got to the School that he discovered that the war had started. He and the other boys spent the whole day being tested on their knowledge of maths and other subjects relevant to the artillery. They all passed and were sent straight off to start their military training as cadets. For Gurkin it was the beginning of a lifelong career with the military, which he ended as a general in the Historical Section of the General Staff.

When peace came, Gurkin and his classmates had a reunion with their teachers. Most of the girls turned up. But only five boys had survived out of twenty-two.

The authorities were also picking out men for special forces units. One which became famous was the OMSBON – the Otdelnaya Motostrelkovaya Brigada Osobogo Naznachenia or Independent Motor-rifle

Brigade for Special Tasks. This brigade came under the NKVD, and was composed of a mixture of volunteers and regular troops. The volunteers were selected by the Komsomol, who looked in particular for athletes because of the physical demands that long-distance special operations would make. The new unit was made up of four battalions.[4] The first consisted of regular NKVD troops and militiamen, the second of men who had fought in Spain, including some Spanish Republicans exiled after the victory of Franco. The third and fourth contained students and teachers from the Central Institute of Physical Culture, more than eight hundred athletes altogether.[5] At first the recruits were not told what kind of unit they would be joining. They were sent for a medical examination to the Dinamo Stadium on the Leningrad Highway. Then they were sent to an NKVD training camp at Mytishchi, just North of Moscow, and began to learn map-reading, parachuting, sniping, and the use of explosives.

One of the early volunteers for OMSBON was Yevgeni Teleguev, a man with a highly intelligent face and a twinkling eye, who ended his career as a general in the KGB. His father and mother had been reasonably prosperous peasants in Siberia, but his father had later joined the army and worked in a construction regiment. There were no proper schools in the obscure places where his father was serving, so Yevgeni spent two years in a boarding school in Chita, beyond Lake Baikal. His father had wanted him to go back to the land as an agronomist when he grew up: he would live in the open air and be able to go hunting. But except for singing, he had always got top marks in all his school subjects and was particularly good at mathematics and physics. So he had thought it worth trying to get into an institute of higher learning in Moscow. On 20 June 1941 he left Irkutsk with his mother for Moscow to study at the Institute of Power. He was still on the train when he heard the announcement that war had begun. He went straight to the recruiting office when he got to Moscow, but was told he was too young. He therefore went to the Komsomol, who were more interested. After ten days he was invited to the Komsomol Central Committee in the main Party building on Old Square. There they asked him what use he thought he would be. He told them that he had been good at sport at school, and that he had done a lot of duck shooting. So they took him.

Teleguev was familiar with the military because of his father, and at the Dinamo Stadium he quickly realised that he was not joining a normal army unit. He was assigned not to a section in a platoon, but to a 'link' (*zveno*) in a 'detachment' (*otryad*) – terms not used in the regular army. The specialised instruction he received at Mytishchi was very methodical, and by the end of September he and his fellows were thoroughly well trained. He later realised how lucky he had been not to end up in a volunteer division, where the heavy casualties were exacerbated by the soldiers' lack of proper training.[6]

On 22 June Vladimir Frolov, the former peasant from Tula, was preparing to go off to Siberia on a geological expedition. When he heard Molotov's speech he was shocked but excited: he looked forward to fighting and winning a war that would be over by the end of the year. The only pessimist among his friends was Ivan Novikov, a sailor from Odessa, who had fought in the Spanish Civil War, and did not believe that the war would be over that quickly. Novikov later joined the 8th (Krasnaya Presnya) Volunteer Division, where he was made a junior commander because of his previous experience, and was killed in the fighting around Vyazma. The other students in the Faculty of Technology and Mathematics all agreed to volunteer. Even those whose attitude to the regime had been unenthusiastic and ironic were carried away by the surge of patriotism. Frolov volunteered for the OMSBON. He was called to the Dinamo Stadium a few weeks later, given his uniform, and sent off for training.

Yevgeni Anufriev, who had initially been rejected because of the accident to his trigger finger, now volunteered again. Like Frolov, he was sent to the Dinamo Stadium, kept his finger hidden, and passed. Next day he reported for duty, was given his uniform, and sent home to say goodbye. During his training at Mytishchi he was decently paid, learned to fire his weapon with his third finger, and was surrounded by interesting people. The Spanish Republicans taught him how to cook frogs, there was a company of Finns, some Georgian girls whom the soldiers called 'Beria's eyes' in honour of their fellow countryman, and even some Germans who had been working for the NKVD.

As the enemy approached Moscow in October, training ceased, and the OMSBON was moved into the city, billeted in schools, and set to helping the Dzerzhinski Division and the militia retain control as the capital hovered on the brink of panic and collapse. When the Soviet counteroffensive began in December, they were sent through the lines to harass the retreating Germans.

Moscow's young women volunteered as enthusiastically as the men. They served in the front line as telephonists and signallers, or as nurses and doctors. Forty per cent of the Red Army's frontline doctors and all of its frontline nurses were women: seventeen became Heroes of the Soviet Union, ten of them posthumously.[7]

Tatiana Milkova was studying chemistry at the Timiryazev Academy. She was also taking extra courses in nursing at the Botkin Hospital: since the Finnish fiasco she had been sure that war would come. On Sunday 22 June, like so many others, she was finishing her examinations. Suddenly the examiner was called from the room. He came back to say that Molotov had spoken, and that the war had begun. Everyone immediately volunteered to give blood. She finished her medical examinations on 12 July, and with some of her fellow students was then sent straight to Army Hospital No. 10/74 at Khimki, on the Leningrad Highway just outside Moscow.

This hospital received seriously wounded cases from the field hospitals at the front, operated on them if urgently necessary, and otherwise sent them to the rear. At first the situation was chaotic. The wounded often arrived without any documents, and the first thing the nurses had to do was to establish their identity. Milkova quickly apologised to one soldier whose inability to answer her questions had made her angry. She always remembered the names and faces of soldiers from those days. The first time she saw a soldier die after an operation she was deeply upset: the chief surgeon Alla Dementieva took her into another room to comfort and embrace her. Afterwards she got used to terrible sights: soldiers arriving with frostbitten limbs black from gangrene, the bloody operations, and the great boxes filled with amputated limbs.[8]

Liubov Vostrosablina came from the Arbat in the very heart of Moscow. Her father was a lawyer who used to work in the Moscow court, but when the revolution came he lost his job, and played the fiddle in a theatre orchestra. She had two sisters, and when her father left her mother in 1936 they had to go to live in a *kommunalka* in Malaya Bronnaya. She started work as a draftsman at 300 roubles a month. But in May 1940 her mother got her a job in the Lenin Library.

She took a cut in pay, but remained there for the next fifty years. Like Milkova, Vostrosablina thought that in the aftermath of the Finnish war, and despite the pact with Germany, war was inevitable sooner or later. Throughout 1940 she trained as a nurse.

But although Vostrosablina had been expecting a war, her hands shook when she heard Molotov speak on 22 June 1941: the only other time her hands shook so badly was when she took her exams. She went straight to the Library. At that time, the new building of the Lenin Library was not yet finished, though it had been under construction since the early 1930s. The staff were immediately put onto a 'barracks regime', which meant that they had to sleep at their place of work. The regime was strictly applied. Her boss refused to allow her to attend her father's funeral when he died in October 1941. He told her brutally that she wouldn't have been able to get back to the funeral if she had been at the front; there was no call to make an exception for her just because she was living in Moscow.

Everyone in the Library wanted to go straight to the front. One of the most beautiful of her colleagues, a young woman called Valya Serafimova, was killed almost as soon as she got there. Vostrosablina herself was sent for a while to a military hospital. Some people helped with the wounded by reading to them or writing their letters, but she was put to cleaning the toilets.

The library remained open throughout the war. Soldiers came in to read there and the older librarians did little bits of research. But the most valuable books were evacuated by train to Perm. All the books except one were returned to the library after the war. Many of the staff accompanied the books to Perm, but Vostrosablina refused to go. She was on air-raid duty from the beginning. On one occasion she was at home when the air-raid warning went. She ran all the way from the Malaya Bronnaya to the library because she was terrified of being punished for being absent from her air defence team. She had to work during the day, and in September she and about a hundred people from the Library were sent to dig anti-tank ditches on the Western outskirts of Moscow, on the Poklonnaya Gora, where Napoleon waited for the surrender of the city in 1812. The trolleybuses were still running, and she caught the No. 2 from the Arbat, then walked the rest of the way. When she and the others were attacked by German aircraft, they threw themselves into the ditch they were digging and covered their heads with their spades.[9]

Praskovia Sergeeva was at the other end of the social scale. She came from a village in the Kalinin [Tver] Region North of Moscow, studied in a local medical technical school in 1937, and then started to work in a village hospital. She volunteered as soon as the war started, despite her mother's tears. Seventeen other nurses also volunteered. They all went to Moscow, to Red Square, in order to bid it farewell. Then she returned to Kalinin where a volunteer division – the 242nd – was being formed, and joined its medical battalion. She saw action almost immediately. On 14 July the division was sent to the Western Front near Smolensk. It was involved in heavy fighting, and Praskovia had her first experience of coping with large numbers of wounded. Her subsequent military career took her through the Battle of Moscow and on to the storming of Koenigsberg and the meeting with the Americans on the Elbe.[10]

Yelena Volkova also served as a nurse. She was born in Moscow but the family later moved to Mogilëv, where her father was the administrator of the main theatre. 'I came back to Moscow to live with my grandmother in a *kommunalka*. I was keen on all kinds of sport and spent the winter playing ice hockey, and the summer rowing on the river and learning to fly a glider. I was fourteen when I started my training at the Aeroclub in Taininka aerodrome outside Moscow. At school I was already learning elementary nursing, fieldcraft and the use of the rifle and the machine gun.

'I was out at the airport on the morning of 22 June. We had no radio and did not hear the news that war had begun until it was brought out to us by a man on a motorbike. I went back into Moscow and with a couple of girl friends went straight to the VoenKomat. I lied about my age: I was only seventeen, one year below the call-up age. All the instructors and students from the Aeroclub had already been called up, and they wanted me to go back there as an instructor. But I was called up on 26 June, and assigned to Hospital Train No. 95. We evacuated wounded from the front to Moscow. We gave them first aid on the train, and sorted them into categories for further treatment.

'At the beginning of October I was wounded during an air attack on the train, and sent first to a hospital in a former school in Mariina Roshcha in Moscow and then to a hospital in Siberia near Kemerovo. It was at about this time I heard that my father had been hanged by the Germans in Mogilëv. My mother had escaped and been evacuated to Alma Ata, where before long she died of grief.

'After I got out of hospital I served as a nurse with the 71st Marine Infantry Brigade, which later became part of the 25th Guards Division. During my time at the front I was twice decorated for recovering wounded men under fire. I was also decorated for helping to capture a German prisoner for interrogation, although it was forbidden for nurses to take part in active military operations. At one point the food supply at the front got so bad that we had to eat seeds that we found in a storeroom in a village.'[11]

Many other women served not as nurses, but as combatants in fighting units. Graduates of the Central Women's School for Snipers are said to have killed twelve thousand Germans in the course of the war. Ludmila Pavlichenko, whose personal claim was 309 Germans, made a triumphant wartime tour of North America. Women contributed their savings with their friends to buy the tank they later fought in. Irina Levchenko, another former inhabitant of the House on the Embankment, served first as a frontline nurse, and later became a distinguished tank commander and a Hero of the Soviet Union. Altogether 800,000 women served with the Red Army during the war.

Women had a particularly distinguished combat record in the air force, flying combat missions on a wide variety of fighters, bombers, and ground-attack planes (the lethal Stormoviks). On 8 September 1941 Marina Raskova, the heroine of the *Rodina* flight, publicly called for women 'pilots who are ready at any moment to sit down on a combat machine and plunge into battle ... [to] stand in the ranks of the warriors for freedom'. A woman of great personal charisma, she used her influence with Stalin to turn this stirring call into reality. On 8 October, Stalin ordered the creation of the 221st Aviation Corps, to be commanded by Raskova and manned by women. The three regiments in the Corps were the 586th Fighter Regiment, flying Yak-1 fighters; the 587th Bomber Regiment, flying the latest Pe-2 dive bombers; and the 588th Night Bomber Regiment, flying the ancient U-2 biplane. Volunteers were recruited through the Komsomol and by word of mouth.

Polina Gelman, who later became a navigator in a U-2, heard the call while she was building defences to halt the German breakthrough.

'All the [university] students were digging antitank ditches along the Belorussian road near Moscow. Among the students the rumour was going around that girls were being taken into aviation. My girlfriend was studying at the Moscow Aviation Institute. She said that she had already received orders. The next morning, I submitted all the paperwork to the Komsomol Central Committee.'[12]

Marina Raskova set up her headquarters at the Komsomol building, and interviewed all the volunteers personally. Galina Dokutovich, who served as a navigator in the 588th Night Bomber Regiment, wrote in her journal on the first anniversary of her regiment's frontline service: 'They came from all over the capital – from colleges, from offices, from factories. They were of all kinds, lightheaded, noisy, calm, reserved; some with close cropped hair, some with long thick pigtails; mechanics, parachutists, pilots and ordinary members of the Komsomol who knew nothing about flying.'[13] Those who had already learned to fly at the flying clubs around the city were assigned as pilots. Women students were assigned as navigators. The mechanics and the armourers were recruited from women with practical experience in factories. There were no men. The women were issued with men's uniforms which were too large for most of them. On 17 October, the day after the great Moscow panic, Raskova and her people were evacuated to Engels on the Volga to complete their training. The journey took them nine days. In May 1942 they were assigned to their squadrons, and saw action until the end of the war.

The twenty-year-old Lidia Litviak was a highly skilled pilot even before she joined the 221st Aviation Corps. Even though, at five feet, she was almost too small to fly a modern fighter, she later became the highest-scoring woman ace with twelve kills. She disappeared without trace during a battle in August 1943. Her body was not found for more than forty years. She was posthumously made a Hero of the Soviet Union by Gorbachëv.

Another volunteer was Rufina Gasheva, the granddaughter of a provincial priest, who opposed the destruction of his church, died in exile, and was sanctified by the Orthodox Church in August 2000. Rufina's family moved to Moscow in 1930, and she was in her third year at the Mathematical-Mechanical Faculty of Moscow University when the war began. She became a navigator in the 588th Night Bomber

Regiment, flew 848 combat missions and was twice shot down. On the first occasion she and her pilot made their way back to the Russian lines. On the second they bailed out and landed in a minefield. Rufina survived, but her pilot, Olga Sanfirova, stepped on a mine and was killed. Rufina was made a Hero of the Soviet Union in February 1945 in a ceremony presided over by Rokossovski. She ended the war as a major.[14]

Nadezhda Popova was nineteen years old when she joined Raskova's unit. By then she had already qualified as a flying instructor and an air force navigator. She too was assigned to the 588th Night Bomber Regiment, of which she eventually became the deputy commander. In August 1942 she was shot down, and made her way back to her unit with the crowds of soldiers and civilians who were retreating from Rostov-on-Don as the Germans swept towards Stalingrad. Among the crowd was a wounded fighter pilot, Semën Kharlamov, who was sitting on a tree stump reading Sholokhov's novel *Quiet Flows the Don*. Popova flew 852 combat missions and she too was given her medal as a Hero of the Soviet Union by Rokossovski. In one of a mounting series of coincidences, Kharlamov became a Hero of the Soviet Union on the same day.[15]

Raskova herself was killed in a flying accident in January 1943. She was buried in the Kremlin wall. But her three regiments distinguished themselves throughout the war. They were employed on exactly the same missions as men. Two of the three became Guards regiments. At least thirty-three women pilots and navigators became Heroes of the Soviet Union.[16] The 588th Night Bomber Regiment entered into legend: the gallantry of the pilots and navigators flying their fragile aircraft over the German lines, sometimes making eight or nine sorties in a single night, caught the public imagination. The Germans called them the 'Night Witches', a name which stuck and became a term of affection. At least two feature films touched on their exploits.[17] In 1943 the regiment was renamed the 46th Taman Guards Division. It lost thirty-one people – 27 per cent of its aircrew – in the course of the war.[18] It finished the war in Berlin, where its members added their message to the graffiti scratched on the walls of the Reichstag: 'Hurrah! The 46th Women's Guards Regiment flew as far as Berlin. Long live Victory!'[19] Popova and Kharlamov, who had met up again in Berlin on the day after the victory, added their own contribution: 'Nadia Popova from Donbass. S. Kharlamov. Saratov'. They were married soon after.

Women in the fighting forces were grudgingly received by commanding officers, at least until they had proved themselves in action. The army was unprepared, and often unwilling, to provide for the accommodation, sanitary arrangements, or medical care of its women soldiers. The Moscow air defence organisation was one of the honourable exceptions: it provided medical advice, 'hygiene rooms' run by women medical orderlies, and extra supplies of soap and cotton wool.[20]

There were other obvious hazards. One commander said: 'You have chosen to fight, girls. Very well, but don't do anything else. Don't lower yourselves.' Some viewed pregnancy as a breach of military discipline. Much of this was simple hypocrisy. Sex in the Soviet Union was surrounded with prudish official silence, which led incautious foreign observers to believe that Russians were somehow more puritanical in their behaviour than people in the decadent West. This was of course not so. As in all the combatant countries, the disruption of war led to the break-up of many established relationships and the formation of many new and often transient ones. Because so many women served in the Soviet armed forces as doctors, nurses, radio operators and clerks, and as combatants in fighting units, liaisons were often formed between them and their superior officers, sometimes voluntarily, sometimes less so. Galina Dokutovich, the navigator from the 588th Night Bomber Regiment, commented in bitter despair: 'Everything around me is so disgusting. Even the best senior commanders are debauched scoundrels! The way that the best and worst characteristics can be combined in the same person is really terrible and absurd.'[21]

In the autumn of 1941, at the height of the Battle of Moscow, Zhukov was assigned a personal doctor, Lt Lidia Zakharova. She became his mistress and remained with him until well after the war. She finally left him when he was posted to Sverdlovsk in the early 1950s and took up with Galina Semënova, who eventually became his third wife.[22] This did not prevent Zhukov from sending a furious note in February 1945 to his subordinate, the distinguished tank commander General Katukov:

> I have reports ... that Comrade Katukov is completely idle, that he

> is not directing the army, that he is sitting around at home with some woman, and that the female he is living with is impeding his work. Katyukov ... apparently never visits his units. He does not organise the operations of the corps and army, which is why the army had been unsuccessful recently. I demand ... that the woman immediately be sent away from Katukov. If that is not done, I shall order her to be removed by the organs of Smersh [NKVD counterintelligence]. Katukov is to get on with his work. If [he] does not draw the necessary conclusions, he will be replaced by another commander.[23]

The unsympathetic called these women 'Field Service Wives' (Pokhodno-Polevye Zhëny or PPZh). Konstantin Simonov wrote a compassionate poem about them in which he contrasted the fate of the legal wife of an officer killed at the front, basking in his glory and enjoying a pension to bring up his children, with that of his former campaign mistress, struggling to bring up her son in obscure poverty. The poem is sentimental and by modern standards politically somewhat incorrect. But it still captures the imagination of Russian women.[24]

Life was not so conveniently organised for the ordinary soldiers, so they took their opportunities where they could. On one occasion Anatoli Chernyaev's platoon was in reserve about six miles behind the front. There was a row of huts in the next field, inhabited by village girls picking up the gleanings from the previous year's harvest. The soldiers would pounce on them in broad daylight and either take them there and then or, if they were more bashful, drag them off into the neighbouring bushes.

One junior lieutenant dragged a girl from a hut, and immediately began to assault her. She proved unwilling and started to shout. Another girl jumped on the officer's back and started to beat him over the head, crying out the while, 'Bastard. Get off her! What are you doing! Stop!', all the time crossing herself and asking God to forgive her sinful soul. The lieutenant took no notice. A third girl, shouting and swearing, tried to drag him off by the feet. In the end he was rescued by some passing soldiers, and ran off holding up his trousers.[25]

But the main problem in those first days of the war was to deal with the many thousands of Muscovites who simply wanted to get to the front as quickly as they could. The GKO decided on 4 July 1941 to raise twenty-five volunteer divisions, one for each of Moscow's Raions. Two hundred thousand volunteers aged between seventeen and fifty-five were to be mobilised in Moscow itself, and another seventy thousand in the Moscow Region. Each Raion was also to set up a reserve regiment, to provide replacements for casualties. A troika consisting of the Raion party secretary and representatives of the local NKVD and VoenKomat (recruiting office) would handle the practical details. Divisional and regimental commanders and their chiefs of staff would be regular soldiers. Some regulars were also put in charge of regiments and battalions. Company commanders were mostly officer cadets. Platoon commanders were elected by the volunteers themselves, and often had no military experience at all. The political commissars were supplied by the Raion Party Committees.[26]

The plan was to accommodate the volunteers initially in local schools, clubs and other buildings. The municipal authorities were responsible for equipping them with vehicles, motorcycles, bicycles, entrenching tools, knapsacks, cooking cauldrons and mess tins.[27] The Moscow Military District was responsible for supplying their weapons and ammunition. Their pay would reflect their peacetime earnings. Their eventual widows would get pensions at the standard rate.[28] For some, these financial advantages, and the prospect of being kept by the government, were sufficient reason to volunteer. Some of the volunteers from Pavlovski Posad outside Moscow believed that the Raion authorities had promised that they would not actually serve at the front: they would be used for support tasks not far from home, building defensive works, guarding military sites, hunting down saboteurs. When she heard that the volunteers were being loaded onto wagons at the station, Klavdia Markina, a teacher, went to see off her husband, Vasili. He was walking up and down nervously. 'We've been deceived,' he said. 'We're being sent to the front.' Viktor Laskin, a worker at the Kolomenskoe Locomotive Factory, who also told his wife that he had been deceived, served with many of his fellow workers in the doomed 8th (Krasnaya Presnya) Volunteer Division.[29]

Although they may not all have realised quite what they were letting themselves in for, most of the new recruits were genuine volunteers. But some joined under intense pressure from over-zealous Party officials anxious to make up the numbers. Specialists were taken who would have been more use continuing in their civilian jobs. Medical students were signed up as ordinary soldiers, though they at least were mostly released again in July, finished their studies, and became military doctors. Without consulting the military authorities, the Komsomol enlisted men who were subject to the draft, so that those already serving in one of the volunteer divisions – or already dead in battle – were later called to the regular army and posted as deserters when they did not appear. Some were recruited even though they had medical exemptions. There were rumours that some were simply taken off the streets.[30]

Given the speed with which it was done, it is not surprising that the enlistment process was a shambles. The headquarters of the 18th (Leningrad) Division were in the Sovietskaya Hotel on the Leningrad Highway, an overblown neo-classical building of red sandstone, where visiting grandees stayed in more normal times. The volunteers came from the Second Watch Factory and the Zhukovski Aviation Academy in the Petrovski Palace. There were teachers from the local institutes of higher education and children from the upper forms of the local schools. One teacher from the Academy of Art volunteered with his whole class: at the end of the war one of the pupils, Mikhail Volodin, was given the task of saving the pictures in the Dresden Gallery.[31] The senior officers in the new division were for the most part regulars and teachers from the military academies with some experience in battle, some under Zhukov against the Japanese in 1939. The junior officers had just emerged from their training schools. The young lieutenant in charge of one anti-tank platoon was given two captured guns, each with two shells. It was the first time he or his soldiers had seen such things. But by 8 July the division could muster nearly seven thousand men. They were quartered for the time being in the school and clubs of Leningrad Raion.

The staff of the 8th (Krasnaya Presnya) Division, under its commander Brigadier Skripnikov, assembled in a building on Herzen [Bolshaya Nikitskaya] Street, next to the Conservatoire. The volunteers signed on in three of the Raion schools. They came from all over the Raion. They came from the Institute of Law and from the Theatre of the Revolution. Over a thousand came from Moscow University.[32]

Four hundred workers volunteered from the Trëkhgorka.[33] Two of the teachers from School No. 110, Ivan Kuzmin and the chemistry master Vainstain, volunteered along with several of their pupils. Kuzmin was killed.[34]

In the Kiev Raion, where the 21st Division was being formed, three hundred volunteers came from the studios at MosFilm. Many brought cameras with them, and ran a trench journal throughout the war. Vasili Ponomarëv, who had just finished his 9th grade at School No. 56, volunteered for the division with twenty-nine of his classmates and his headmaster. His future platoon commander, Zastrovski, brought a number of his colleagues in from the Vakhtangov Theatre.[35]

By 5 July twelve divisions had been formed. Each was given a number and the name of the Raion where it had been raised. Altogether the twelve divisions contained more than 68,000 soldiers and nearly 10,500 officers and NCOs. This was a remarkable achievement, though it was well short of the target of two hundred thousand which had been set by the GKO.

For the first few days, the men were trained in their recruiting centres, the schools and institutes of their native Raions. But they were soon marched out into the countryside to learn elementary tactics. Their wives and mothers saw them off as they left to the sound of military music. They were dressed in whatever came to hand, with rucksacks and suitcases, sacks and briefcases, in boots and shoes, some even in sandals. When they reached their training camps many of them simply collapsed where they stood from exhaustion. Seven hundred men from the 18th (Leningrad) Division had to be sent home for medical reasons; three thousand five hundred were weeded out of the 2nd (Stalin) Division.[36] In these early days the volunteer divisions had no proper weapons or even uniforms. Four divisions were armed with Polish rifles, for which there was no ammunition. Some were given elderly French rifles. Two divisions had French machine guns, artillery pieces and mortars. All were short of rifles, ammunition, overcoats and vehicles. Fidelman of the 9th (Kirov) Division complained: 'We were given ancient foreign rifles of various types, and captured ammunition which occasionally did not fit. The commissars and commanders were given Colt revolvers from the time of the Civil War. There were shells for the guns, but the guns themselves were promised for later.' Between them, the seven thousand men of the 18th (Leningrad) Volunteer Division had twenty-one machine guns, not quite three hundred rifles, a hundred or so pistols and revolvers, and a few thousand grenades and Molotov cocktails.

A large part of the volunteers' exhausting working day was taken up not with military training, but with the digging of trenches and anti-tank ditches. Mitrofan Merkulov of the 2nd (Stalin) Division wrote to his mother on 19 July: 'Mama, I don't have any time at all. We're training the whole time. We get up at 4 o'clock in the morning and go to bed at 11 o'clock at night. I am writing this letter on a box full of rifles. They have now given us our rifles and everything else. We all have uniforms.'[37]

The 8th (Krasnaya Presnya) Volunteer Division contained an unusually large number of writers, musicians, and historians. The writers were put together in the 3rd Company of the 1st Battalion of the Division's 24th Regiment. Many were already men with established reputations, members of the Writers' Union. Others were still making their careers. Some were in their mid-twenties. Pavel Balkin had been a member of the Bolshevik Party since 1903, and had taken part in the revolution of 1905.[38] Viktor Rozov was an actor in the Theatre of the Revolution who after the war wrote the screenplay for the internationally successful film *The Cranes are Flying*. Alexander Bek, whose ancestor had been brought by Peter the Great from Denmark to set up Russia's first postal service, had fought in the Civil War, and carried a copy of Clausewitz's *On War* wherever he went.[39] He had made his reputation as a writer of documentary reportage based on extensive interviews, which served him in good stead when he came to write his masterpiece *The Volokolamskoe Highway* about the fighting before Moscow in the last months of 1941. In those early days, however, he rapidly acquired a reputation as the Good Soldier Schweik of the 3rd Company, a notorious joker and spectacularly scruffy: 'He wore great big boots, puttees which kept on unwinding and trailing on the ground, a grey-coloured uniform, and most absurd of all, a forage cap which sat on top of his head like a bonnet – not to speak of his spectacles.'[40] Like some of the other more experienced writers, Bek was withdrawn from the Division before the fighting started to serve as a war correspondent.[41] Perhaps the youngest member of the 3rd Company, which inevitably became known to history as 'The Writers' Company', was Vera Dëmina, who was accepted into the Division even though she was under age, and in due course became the Chairman of the Veterans' Association of the Division's few survivors.[42]

Two hundred and fifty musicians from among the staff and pupils of the Conservatoire joined the Division, urged to volunteer by the Pro-Rector, Abram Diakov. They were put into the 1st Battalion's 2nd and 3rd Companies.[43] They included the violinist David Oistrakh and the pianist Emil Gilels. The Division's recruiting officer, Captain Saraev, a biologist with previous military experience, took it on himself to send thirty of the musicians back to finish their studies and they survived the war.[44] But Diakov was still with the seven and a half thousand men of the Division when it was encircled and annihilated outside Vyazma in October. One of the finest pianists of his generation – some of his recordings are still available – he never returned and died either with the partisans or in a German prisoner of war camp.

Lev Mishchenko was studying physics when the war began. His background was unpromising: his Ukrainian grandfather had opposed the Tsarist regime and his parents were shot by the Reds during the Civil War. But he managed to get into Moscow University in 1935, where he studied physics, met his future wife Svetlana, and became an orthodox member of the Komsomol. He volunteered in the first days of the war. 'Altogether fifty students from the Physics Faculty of the university joined the Krasnaya Presnya Division,' he remembered. 'Many of the other volunteers in the division were professors and teachers, scientists from the Krasnaya Presnya observatory and from the local factories. Many had no military experience at all. I and some of my fellows had qualified as platoon commanders through the university's part-time military training scheme, and we were assigned to positions of junior command in the new Division. But few of us were given jobs which matched our specialities. I was put in charge of supplies. Two of my colleagues from the Physics Faculty, who had been trained as aerial observers, were sent off as private soldiers to a communications platoon. No one took any notice of our protests.'

Many of the youngest members of the Krasnaya Presnya Division had just graduated from the History Faculty of Moscow University. Moisei Ginzburg, Alexander Ospovat, Yakov Pinus and Igor Savkov were assigned to the Division's artillery regiment, and Ginzburg and

Pinus were each given the command of a gun. They began their training outside Moscow, and lived in huts which they built for themselves. Towards the end of July they were marched thirty miles to another camp, staggering under their rifles and their heavy rucksacks, their feet blistered from the unaccustomed exercise. In their new location they were comfortably accommodated in a large peasant house, and given their uniforms, riding breeches and tunic, which at first they wore with awkward embarrassment. They got used to firing their guns, and the crews of Ginzburg and Pinus were both commended for their performance. In mid-August they suffered their first casualty: one of the battery commanders was killed by a stray bullet from some infantry exercising nearby. Once the rains started in September they were given horses to pull their guns through the gathering mud. Wholly unaccustomed to animals, they had to learn how to look after them from scratch. Moisei Ginzburg wrote to his girlfriend Galina Rashkovskaya that, as commander of a gun, he was to be given a horse of his own. He looked forward to wearing a sabre and spurs, but within days he had already fallen off his new mount twice. Once they had learned how to manage the horses, he told Galina, they would be moved to the front. It would be one of the quietest parts of the line.[45]

The 5th (Frunze) Division contained even more intellectuals than the 8th Division. Abram Gordon was finishing his studies at the State Pedagogical Institute when the war began. He and his classmates were hurriedly furnished with diplomas to show that they had finished the course. On 4 July they were summoned to a meeting by the Komsomol Committee of the Frunze Raion and invited to join the new Division. They volunteered with enthusiasm, in the firm belief that the Germans would soon be defeated.

On 9 July the 5th Division moved out with its horse-drawn artillery to its training ground twenty-five miles from Moscow. Gordon had never walked more than five or six miles in his life. He barely made it to the new camp, and when he got there his feet were covered with blisters. The volunteers were then given Polish rifles without ammunition and dressed in black shirts which made them look like Italian fascists. They were such a comic sight that one of them was taken for a German spy by a crowd of elderly women outside a bread shop, and was rescued with difficulty by his comrades.

Gordon had been assigned to the Division's reconnaissance company. He and his fellows were given horses. Like Moisei Ginzburg, he too had never ridden before. But he and his fellows were ruthlessly schooled by a reserve officer, Lieutenant Kovalenko, who made them ride bareback until they were bloody. They quickly learned to ride properly, and once they went into action Gordon was grateful that he had been so well taught.

Whatever plans the leadership may have had to give the volunteer divisions time to train properly were soon overwhelmed by events as the Germans continued to advance. On 16 July the GKO ordered the construction of a defence line at Mozhaisk, to be manned by a new Reserve Front consisting of five NKVD divisions, and ten volunteer divisions formed into two armies of five divisions each, the 32nd and 33rd.[46]

It was about this time, in the middle of July, that Konstantin Simonov stumbled across some of them, still barely armed and still in civilian clothing.

> In the next village we met units from one of the Moscow volunteer divisions, apparently the 6th [the Dzerzhinski Division]. I remember that they produced a gloomy impression on me at the time. I later realised that this was the moment when those hastily recruited July divisions were thrown in to plug the gap, because something – anything – had to be thrown in, at whatever price, to preserve the front which the reserve armies were preparing further to the East, nearer to Moscow, from being shattered to pieces. There were good reasons for that, but at the time I found it hard to bear. I thought: do we really have no other reserves besides these volunteers, dressed anyhow and barely armed? One rifle for two men, and one machine gun.
>
> For the most part they were not young: forty or fifty years old. They marched without supply wagons, without the normal regimental and divisional support – naked men, to all intents and purposes, on naked ground. Their uniforms were second- or third-hand tunics: some had once been dyed blue. Their commanders were not young either, reservists who had not served for many years. They all still needed to be trained, formed, made to look like soldiers.'[47]

The volunteer divisions were now to be reorganised as regular rifle divisions with the full complement of artillery, anti-aircraft guns, engineers, signallers and medical support.[48] At the end of August the volunteers were given proper uniforms and took the military oath, and each division was given its battle flag in a ceremony of great solemnity. By now the 18th (Leningrad) Division could muster nearly eleven thousand men, the normal size for a Soviet division. And by now, at least, three-quarters of them had rifles. They had well over a hundred heavy machine guns – the Russian version of the Maxim gun mounted on two little wheels, with a metal shield to protect the gunner. They even had a fair number of anti-aircraft guns, field guns and mortars, fourteen radios and a motley collection of cars, lorries, tractors and other vehicles.[49]

But as they moved up to their new positions during August, many of the divisions were still undermanned and underequipped. The lucky ones went by train. The rest marched twenty-five miles a day until they got to their destinations. Much of the time they were under attack by German bombers. They marched through the heat of the day and cool of the night, thirsty because the wells in the villages through which they passed had run dry. They took up defensive positions near Vyazma, and busied themselves once again with training and with the digging of trenches and dugouts.

Lev Mishchenko described how the 8th (Krasnaya Presnya) Division went to war. 'We were given no proper uniforms before we were sent off to the front. We were armed at first with rifles captured after the campaigns in Poland and the Baltic States. There were only two worn-out trucks in my battalion, and they kept on breaking down. We marched at night, and after a brief sleep were drilled and given political instruction during the day. At first I was sent back to Moscow to pick up supplies for the Division. As we got closer to the front, I was told that the local collective farms had been ordered to supply us. I went round a couple of dozen farms, but none of them had anything to spare. Not only did the farmers have no meat: they even had to bake their bread from potatoes. Even their children saw no milk. Everything had been delivered to the state. It was a stark contrast to all the propaganda we had been fed about happy peasants on flourishing collective farms. My underfed soldiers simply requisitioned supplies from the farms that lay on their line of march. At first I was troubled in my conscience. But in practice there was no other choice, and I reconciled myself to what was little more than looting.

'I had believed what I had been told about the fighting ability of the Red Army, and was confident that the war would soon be over. But as we marched we could see the state of the countryside for ourselves, and we had already worked out what was happening in the frontier battles. Our political commissars continued all the old claptrap about the superiority of the Soviet system and the invincible Red Army. They claimed that the German tanks were running out of fuel, and that their soldiers were so badly equipped that they were taking rifles on the battlefield from the Russian dead. It was pointless lying.'[50]

As they stumbled forward into their final positions, along routes that had not been properly reconnoitred towards an enemy whose strength and position were unknown, the men of the 8th (Krasnaya Presnya) Division found the roads hopelessly blocked by refugees: people, cows, carts, an impenetrable mass of people fleeing from the Germans. Their commanders had almost as little idea of what was going on as they did. One of them asked a four-star general where he could find his Division. 'Young man,' the general replied, 'we don't even know where our armies are, let alone our divisions.'[51]

By the end of September the volunteer divisions were no longer the ragged and motley crew of subsequent legend, untrained and barely armed civilians, thrown without compunction into the meat-grinder, able to die courageously but not to fight. Five of the divisions that survived the murderous round of fighting in October went on to become Guards Divisions, among the elite of the Red Army.[52] They had received a good deal of the equipment they needed, and were beginning to look like a real fighting force: in many ways they were not all that worse off than some of the ill-equipped and ill-trained formations that were being scraped together for the regular army. But a great deal remained to be done. General Vashkevich, the commander of the 2nd (Stalin) Division, later wrote that his division's performance when they finally went into battle was significantly undermined by the lack of anti-aircraft weapons, radio sets, tractors and even horses to pull the guns.[53] The commissar of the 9th (Kirov) Division, a regular officer, thought that his men needed another three months' training before they could be considered proper soldiers.[54]

In 1940 the British scraped together a motley collection of enthusiastic Local Defence Volunteers to oppose a German invasion. They have gone down in legend as 'Dad's Army'. It is hard to see what account they could have given of themselves if they had been put to the test. The Moscow volunteer divisions were a good deal better than that. But unlike Dad's Army, they were about to face the Germans in battle.

– SEVEN –

MOBILISING THE MASSES

The Soviet government had had a good deal of practice in moving large masses of people all over the country. They deported many thousands of class enemies from Moscow and Leningrad in the 1920s. They deported millions of kulaks to Siberia and Central Asia in the 1930s. They knew how to manage the railway schedules and muster the rolling stock for the trains. They were less concerned about how their involuntary passengers should be fed on the way or accommodated at their destinations, and many died as a result from disease, malnutrition, exhaustion or the casual brutality of their guards.

Mobilising large numbers of ordinary people for comparatively benign official purposes was, moreover, a normal feature of everyday Soviet life. People were mobilised for a day at the weekend to clear up the city, or for a week in the autumn to help out with the harvest. They were mobilised with a fanfare of rhetoric from Government and City authorities, from the RaiKoms and the Komsomol, by Party Committees in the factories, in the offices and in the colleges, from the building administrators in their homes – fine words about the voluntary devotion of the people to building Socialism. So the Moscow authorities already had plenty of relevant experience when the war made it necessary to move people in large numbers for many pressing reasons. They moved students and women to build defensive works. They evacuated key workers, officials, artists, women and children into the interior. They helped the army muster its recruits and sent them off to training camps far to the East of the city.

Within weeks – days even – of the German attack, the authorities realised that the inconceivable could become reality, that Moscow itself might be at risk. So they ordered the construction of a series of grandiose works to defend the capital in depth. These works – anti-tank ditches, trenches and foxholes, concrete pillboxes and machine-gun posts – were built in the greatest haste, often by untrained civilians and often by women, mobilised en masse and working twelve hours a day and more, living in the most primitive conditions, and often subjected to bombing and machine-gunning by the Germans.

In June and July some fifty thousand Moscow students, many of them girls, were sent off to build defences on the distant approaches to Moscow – around Roslavl, Smolensk, Vyazma, Bryansk and elsewhere. Some came from the University, the Moscow Pedagogical Institute and the Energy Institute. Young women from the Medical Institute dug trenches and helped look after children being evacuated. The Bauman Higher Technical Institute sent three hundred students to help construct the Vyazma defence line. They left as a formed battalion and had their first brush with the reality of war as they passed through the little town of Sukhinichi, to the Southwest of the city, which had just been bombed. Students from the Construction Engineering Institute supervised the work of the less skilled.[1]

Anatoli Chernyaev was at home on 27 June when Kolya Gauzner, a fellow student and a Komsomol activist, called in to say that there would be a meeting at 5 o'clock in the Historical Faculty: everyone was going to dig anti-tank ditches. Chernyaev thought that this would be a lark. But his grandmother, the only other person in the house, burst into tears. The faculty was in turmoil. Chernyaev and his colleagues, about two hundred of them led by Misha Gefter by virtue of his position in the Faculty Komsomol, were loaded onto tramcars and taken to the Kiev Station, where the girl students saw them off.

The train travelled only at night and they were still on their way when they heard a rumour that Stalin had spoken on the radio. That night – 3 July 1941 – they were unloaded into a field. They shuffled into some kind of order and marched in fits and starts until they came to a large village on the banks of the River Snopot, a tributary of the Desna, about twenty-five miles from Roslavl.

Here they hung around for several days, doing nothing. At last they were set to digging an anti-tank ditch three yards deep along the bank of the river. It was hard work, but they were well fed: the constant streams of refugees, driving their flocks of sheep, cows, and pigs, gave them milk and meat. It was at this point that Chernyaev noticed that, apart from Gefter, there was no one from the Komsomol there: the Young Communists had all found themselves more interesting things to do. The day after their arrival a small boy from the nearby village drowned in the river. It seemed a tragedy at the time, but that was before life became cheap.

After a couple of weeks a military unit took up position behind their ditch, and began to erect barbed-wire entanglements. German reconnaissance aircraft flew overhead. The students were not bombed, though there was a heavy raid little more than a mile away from them.

The atmosphere grew more oppressive. The students saw the village boys gathered by the church, loading up carts, collecting provisions, wooden boxes, horses – preparing to go into the forests as partisans. To the North and West they could already hear the sound of guns. Chernyaev and some of the others asked Gefter for rifles to defend themselves with. He wrung his hands: it wasn't permitted, and anyhow there were no rifles to spare.

When they had finished the trench they were taken by lorry some ten miles to the rear. The guns were getting nearer and every night fleets of bombers flew overhead towards Moscow. The students were withdrawn again, and then again, each time leaving their trenches unfinished. Increasingly they heard the guns to the side of them and even, it seemed, to the rear.

And so they retreated steadily until the beginning of September. Then one day they were bundled into a train and rushed back to the Kiev Station, from where they had started more than two months earlier. Chernyaev was furious. The efforts of tens of thousands of Moscow students had been wasted. They were young, enthusiastic, already bound by ties of comradeship. Most of them had done some military training in college. Instead of constructing useless defensive works which the Germans simply outflanked, they should have been formed into mobile shock detachments. It would have been dangerous work. But most of the students were killed anyway, fighting in second-rate units among poorly trained soldiers, where their military capacity never had a proper chance to show itself.

Moreover it was only the second, third, and fourth year students who were brought back to Moscow. The first year and fifth year students – including Gefter – were left behind to dig ditches. Most were surrounded by the Germans, and were captured or died. Gefter fought in the battles around Rzhev, escaped encirclement, and managed to make his way through to Moscow. The Germans were shooting any Communists they captured, and Gefter sensibly destroyed his Party card. But for that crime against Party discipline – amounting almost to blasphemy – he was inevitably punished. He was forced to serve throughout the war as a private soldier and then as a sergeant. His Bolshevik enthusiasm was extinguished once and for all.[2] He became a professional historian, but found the Party line increasingly unacceptable. He was officially reprimanded, narrowly escaped expulsion from the Party, and was no longer published. He continued to write as a dissident, without hope of publication, until Gorbachëv's perestroika allowed him to see the light once again. He died in 1995.[3]

After the Germans reached Smolensk in July, the construction project gathered much greater speed. In July and August nearly two hundred thousand people were mobilised to construct a further line of defences, the Mozhaisk Defence Line, about sixty miles from the capital. The supply of spades ran out: the Moscow administration allocated a thousand tons of sheet steel to produce another half million.[4] The Mozhaisk Defence Line was still not complete when the Germans came up against it at the beginning of October. Its four fortified defensive zones contained less than half of the planned gun emplacements and only half the planned anti-tank ditches, and the planned escarpments and barbed-wire entanglements had not been built.

At the last minute work began to fortify the approaches to Moscow itself. Nearly three-quarters of those who built Moscow's inner defences were women. Antonina Savina was working, not in her mother's hospital, but as an apprentice seamstress to an atelier attached to the Moscow

Military District. Here she sewed dresses for the wives of officers and then, when the war started, equipment for the military. She continued to live with her mother in the Misericordia hospital. Because they got full rations as workers, they were fairly well fed. But they often had to spend all night in the bread queue to be sure of getting anything.

Antonina was sent off several times to what everybody called the Labour Front. She had to dig deep anti-tank trenches while living on one sausage and a small roll of bread a day. At Serpukhov, little more than a mile behind the front line to the south of Moscow, she was lodged in the local club with seven other girls and two boys. They slept on the floor on the blankets and cushions they had brought with them. The woman in charge refused to supply them with heating, and there was no electricity or water for washing. Then they discovered that they had got lice: Antonina picked them out from her hair and under her bra, and burned them in the candles. Eventually, after they complained to their squad leader, water was laid on. The boys and girls all stripped off together and scrubbed one another down. It was not enough. When she got back home, her elder sister shaved off all her hair and burned all her underwear before she would let her back into the house. The labour obligation continued even after the Germans had been thrown back. The following spring Antonina was sent off with a party of girls to produce firewood in the forests round Moscow. This was unsuitably heavy work for girls: you had to load the logs as well as cut them. You had to produce ninety cubic feet of wood a day and your ration of 600 grams of bread was reduced to 500 if you failed to meet the target. It was very hot, and all they had for drinking and washing was a barrel of water a day for the whole team. But they managed.[5]

Although so many people were being moved out of the city for military, industrial or other reasons, many factories remained and the workers there continued their pre-war occupations. At the beginning of the war some six thousand people were working at the Trëkhgorka. Many of their parents and grandparents had worked there too: there were whole dynasties of Trëkhgorka workers whose forebears had worked in the factory when it still belonged to the Prokhorovs. Most of them were women, who worked at the spinning and weaving machines. Maintenance, transport, technical and supervisory jobs were traditionally reserved for the men. But when the men went off to join the Krasnaya Presnya Division and the regular army – thirteen hundred men in all – the women took their places.

Klavdia Leonova was one of a family of seven children from Krasnaya Presnya. After leaving school she wanted to become a teacher, and studied for a while in a technical training college (*tekhnikum*), where she also received a thoroughly enjoyable training in first aid and air defence.

'One of my brothers was captured at the frontier on the outbreak of war, my sister went off to be an army driver, and my mother – by now a widow – was evacuated. I stayed behind in Moscow and succeeded in getting into the Trëkhgorka, where I was trained to operate a textile machine.

'During the war the factory worked two shifts of twelve hours each. I made army tunics, parachute material, camouflage netting, bandages, and foot wraps [*portyanki*]. The workers were fed by the factory: we were given badly baked bread, and a kind of porridge [*kasha*] of burned wheat which was brought to us as we worked, so we did not have to waste time standing in queues. We did not starve, but we were always very hungry and often ate potato peelings to supplement our diet.

'We slept at home, not in the factory as workers elsewhere often did. But we had no life of our own outside the factory. Sunday was in theory a day off, but the factory Party Committee often called on us for outside work, such as digging trenches or bringing in timber from the forests around Moscow. The women were organised in brigades of four, our food was brought from the factory, and each brigade ate a bucket of potatoes a day. We had to load lorries with pitprops which were so heavy they would have been a burden even for a professional weight-lifter. There were German prisoners there as well. We got on with them well enough. They stood around showing photos of their families and flirting, but they did not work nearly as hard as we did. We lived with the peasants and discovered to our surprise that the peasant cottages didn't have proper chimneys – just holes in the roof to let the smoke out. The peasant women regularly abused the regime. They abused us too, because we collected berries and mushrooms in the woods, which they had hoped to sell to us.'

Lidia Robel also worked at the Trëkhgorka throughout the war, but had a somewhat easier time of it than Klavdia Leonova. Lidia was born in the Arbat, but soon moved with her family to Krasnaya Presnya. 'I had three sisters, and lived with my parents and my grandmother in a house which had formerly belonged to a prosperous man with a German wife. Maria Karlovna continued to live in the house: she taught us German and was very strict about our behaviour.

'I worked in the technical maintenance department of the Trëkhgorka as an electrician. This meant that I worked an eight-hour day, doing work that had previously been done by men. Sunday was the busy day for my team, since that was when they could maintain the machinery – much of it dating from the Prokhorov days before the revolution – so that it would be in good order for the Monday shift. Saturday was my day off, and unlike the production workers in the factory, I was often free to go out in the evening to the theatre or elsewhere. Later in the war I was taught to use a sub-machine gun, and learned to operate a radio. But I was not trained in the use of ciphers, because I was thought to be too young to be reliable. When the men returned from the front, they were much more uninhibited in their ways. They used to give me the eye when I was up a ladder. They would not have done that before.' Klavdia Leonova broke in to scold Lidia Robel for saying that: the heroes who returned from the war would never have behaved with so little respect towards their women fellow workers.[6]

The regime conscripted the country's artists and writers as ruthlessly as they did the rest of the population. Many were simply called up into the armed forces, and many of them lost their lives. No one of either sex had exemption from digging defence works around Moscow or doing fire duty on the roofs during air raids. The male dancers at the Bolshoi Theatre immediately began to do military training on the stage of the theatre itself. Two of the stars of the ballet, Mikhail Gabovich and the Georgian Mikhail Sulkhanishvili, joined volunteer units. Gabovich survived to partner Ulanova, and to create the roles of the Prince in Prokofiev's *Cinderella* and Romeo in his *Romeo and Juliet*. Sulkhanishvili started his career in the Opera House in Tbilisi, and was highly acclaimed for his elegant, colourful and individual style. In the early 1930s he moved to the Bolshoi, where he danced the lead role in *Demon* and became Secretary of the Theatre's Komsomol. He was killed near Vyazma in the autumn of 1941.[7]

That autumn, Pronin drove with Shcherbakov to see the work on the outskirts of the city.

> We went up to an anti-tank ditch. At the bottom of the trench, in glutinous mud, we saw about fifty wet figures. We slid down, and asked what organisation they were from. They answered: artists and workers from the Bolshoi and other Moscow theatres. Their faces were tired and wet. And all of them asked one thing only: What's happening at the front? They asked us to help them get better spades and firewood to dry their clothes. We suggested sending workers from other organisations, instead of theatre people. They were insulted. 'What, do you take us for deserters? It's worse at the front. We'll survive, we'll put up with everything, so long as our people can hold Moscow.'[8]

The more sensible officials realised that digging ditches was not the best way of using the artists' skills: they were better employed supporting the war effort by bolstering morale. Moscow's theatres were kept open, and some continued to operate despite the evacuation of the main companies during the October panic.[9]

Tens of thousands of musicians, actors, singers, and dancers were deployed in nearly four thousand travelling 'brigades' to entertain the troops. The repertoire ranged from classical music, ballet, and Shakespeare to folk dancing and popular song. The brigades often performed right in the front line, sometimes under fire, to audiences ranging from three to three thousand people.[10] The artists included Liubov Orlova, Stalin's favourite film star, and Lidia Ruslanova, the popular folk singer.[11] Leonid Utësov gave more than two hundred concerts at the front with his band and his daughter Edit as vocalist.[12] The film star Valentina Serova performed in the Moscow hospitals. The NKVD had its own jazz band. Obraztsov, the puppet master, put on special anti-fascist shows at the VoenKomats, hospitals, and even on a barge full of children being evacuated.[13]

The bandmaster Alexander Aleksandrov put together a concert brigade consisting of stand-up comics, singers and dancers from the Bolshoi and the Operetta, and set off along the Mozhaisk Highway to perform to the troops. Lidia Ruslanova was among them. A difficult woman, unused to having to work in a team, she began by exchanging barbed comments with the other stars, but calmed down once she got to the front. Later she led her own concert brigade. In May 1942 she performed before the Second Guards Cavalry Corps, and within two weeks had married its commander, Lieutenant-General Vladimir Kriukov, a long-time colleague of Zhukov. She was the star in the legendary concert which took place on the steps of the Reichstag in Berlin in May, the background to Stalin's idealised appearance at the end of the film *The Fall of Berlin*. It served her little: within a few years of that concert she and Kriukov were arrested for corruption, and she spent five years in prison until she was released by Khrushchëv.[14]

The ballerina Susanna Zvyagina, who came from Smolensk, joined the Bolshoi ballet company in 1937, and lived in the hostel next to the theatre in the building where the scenery was built and stored. In April 1941 she danced in the last performance of *Swan Lake* before the theatre was closed for repair. The next day she was sent with a concert brigade to perform to the soldiers still stationed in the Mongolian desert after the battles with the Japanese two years earlier. The artists lived in tents and performed on the back of a lorry. They returned to Moscow as the war began. Zvyagina performed in the front line during the Battle of Moscow, and later on all the major battlefronts of the war. At Stalingrad, she crossed the Volga under fire to perform to the soldiers in the trenches. On one occasion she came under German mortar fire. She fell flat in the mud, and was stuck there for six hours. She gave the first concert in liberated Rostov-on-Don. Everywhere there were German bodies, barefoot because their boots had been taken by the Russian soldiers. The corpses of Soviet prisoners of war who had tried to escape were still hanging on the wire in a nearby concentration camp. They had burned to death when the Germans set the camp on fire. She too performed in Berlin after it was captured.[15]

Ivan Petrov had just begun his career as a soloist at the Bolshoi when war broke out; he went on to sing all the bass roles in Russian opera. In the first days he did his share of air-raid duty, and performed in the VoenKomats and at the railway stations as the soldiers left for the front. As the Germans got nearer to Moscow, he sang in innumerable concerts at the front itself. The dugouts where he performed were very low for a man of his height. On one occasion he had to sing sitting on an ammunition box with his arm wrapped round the wooden central support of the dugout. On another, the concert was so close to the front line that the Germans could hear it too. When it was over, they mortared the Soviet positions by way of applause. On a third occasion, a sergeant left the bunker halfway through the concert with a few soldiers, and returned almost immediately with a German prisoner. The sergeant offered the prisoner to Petrov as a present, saying that they had no other way of expressing their appreciation for his singing.[16]

In the eyes of Stalin and his colleagues the giants of Soviet literature in 1941 were Aleksei Tolstoy and Ilya Ehrenburg. Stalin was determined that these two at least should be preserved and they were not permitted to go too near the fighting. Neither was a typical product of the Bolshevik revolution. Aleksei Tolstoy, a distant relation of Leo, emigrated to Paris in 1918 but returned to the Soviet Union in 1923. He was known as the Red Count, and as the man with a bottomless bank account. His novel *Peter the First* was particularly pleasing to Stalin, who saw the Tsar as his predecessor. His first wartime article appeared in *Pravda* on 27 June. But the closest he got to the real thing was in August 1941, when he was permitted to visit a fighter regiment to meet Victor Kiselëv, who had just downed a German aeroplane by ramming it.[17] Like others, Tolstoy was concerned by the naïve friendliness which even some Soviet soldiers appeared to feel towards the Germans. This had to change if the war was to be won. He wrote a piece for *Pravda* entitled 'I Call for Hatred' and another entitled 'The Face of the Hitlerite Army', with eyewitness accounts of German atrocities.[18] For *Krasnaya Zvezda* he wrote uplifting articles with titles like 'An Army of Heroes', 'Russian Warriors' and 'Why Hitler Will Be Beaten'.[19] As the Germans approached Moscow in the autumn, Stalin peremptorily ordered him to take himself off to safety in Gorki [Nizhni Novgorod] on the Volga.

Ilya Ehrenburg lived in France in the 1920s, and several of his major works were written there. He was in Spain during the Civil War and in Paris when the Germans entered in 1940. He was as liberal as it was safe for a prominent man to be in Stalin's Russia. The wartime pieces he wrote for *Krasnaya Zvezda* were often inflated in their language, though they were popular enough with the soldiers. Like Vasili Grossman, he became increasingly conscious of his Jewishness during the war: the two men collaborated on a minutely detailed book about German war crimes which fell foul of the authorities. He was rebuked at the end of the war for being excessively anti-German at a time when Stalin was already planning to incorporate Eastern Germany into his empire. His short novel *The Thaw* played an important, though cautious, part in the process of mild liberalisation which followed Stalin's death in 1953. His memoirs *Years, People, Life* were one of the sensations of the Soviet publishing scene in the early 1960s, and remain an essential witness to Russian literary and political life in the first half of the twentieth century. He died as Khrushchëv's thaw was being brought to an end by Brezhnev.

Ehrenburg and Aleksei Tolstoy were only two among the brilliant team of writers David Ortenberg, the new editor of *Krasnaya Zvezda*, assembled when the war began, all of them talented and some of them major figures in the history of Russian literature: Vasili Grossman, Andrei Platonov, Alexander Avdeenko, Konstantin Simonov, and a host of others. Under Ortenberg's leadership, *Krasnaya Zvezda* became the most popular wartime paper in the Soviet Union, delivered to the front in the most difficult circumstances, and greedily devoured by the soldiers. Eighteen correspondents from *Krasnaya Zvezda* were killed in the course of the war. Ortenberg was a cautious man, always careful to remain in good odour with the authorities: he would not otherwise have long remained in his job. But he would occasionally wangle onto his staff even a writer who had got into a political scrape, if he was good enough.[20]

Vasili Grossman was originally one of the more orthodox of Ortenberg's writers. He was born in Berdichev in Ukraine, went to school in Kiev, and to Moscow University to study chemistry in 1923. His first novel, written in 1932, received a mixed reception. In 1933 he was called into the Lubyanka for interrogation when a cousin was arrested and exiled to Astrakhan. In 1937 he became a full member of the Writers' Union. His mother was trapped in Berdichev when the Germans captured it. Overwhelmed with guilt at having failed to get her out, he volunteered for the army. Instead, Ortenberg took him on as a war correspondent. He was made a 'Quartermaster of the Second Rank' (the bizarre rank given to war correspondents who were not Party members), taught to fire a pistol, and sent off to observe the fighting.[21]

In some of the most distinguished reporting of the war, he covered the German breakthrough before Moscow, the Battle of Stalingrad, the discovery of the German extermination camp at Treblinka in Poland, and the fall of Berlin. His novel of Stalingrad, *Life and Fate* (*Zhizn i Sudba*) and his passionate denunciation of the whole Bolshevik experiment in *Forever Flowing* (*Vse Techet*) were not published in Russia until the late 1980s.

In 1942 Grossman asked Ortenberg to take Andrei Platonov under his protection. Platonov started life as a convinced Communist. His budding literary career ground to a halt when Stalin attacked him in 1931 for a story about village life. He then lived in poverty until, on Grossman's recommendation, Ortenberg called him in, appointed him as a special correspondent, and put him in uniform, the first decent clothing he had had for a long time. Platonov went straight off to the front, and proved a brilliant and courageous correspondent. Ortenberg expected a thunderbolt from Stalin at any minute. It did not come. But after the war Simonov, by then editor of the prestigious literary journal *Novy Mir*, published one of Platonov's masterpieces, the short story *The Return* about a man who comes back from the war to discover his wife has had an affair with a local official. The 'slanderous story by Platonov' was attacked viciously and at length by *Literaturnaya Gazeta*. Platonov was not published again in his lifetime.[22] But his reputation continued to grow, at first underground, and then openly, until he too was eventually recognised as one of the most important Russian writers of the twentieth century.

Not nearly as significant a writer as Platonov, but with an even more complicated history, was Alexander Avdeenko. Avdeenko was a miner who became a successful novelist in the 1930s. He did everything to keep on the right side of authority. He was elected a member of the Supreme Soviet. In his maiden speech he said, 'If I ever have a son, the first word I will teach him to say will be: Stalin.' And then his film about the 'liberation' of Bessarabia from the Romanians in 1940 fell foul of the authorities. Avdeenko, said Stalin, was 'a man in a mask, an enemy, a racketeer'. He was expelled from the Writers' Union and from the Party. He, his wife, his sick son and his elderly mother were thrown out of their apartment and had to live in a corner of a factory storehouse. He went back to working in the mines.

In 1943 articles signed 'A. Avdeenko' started arriving in the *Krasnaya Zvezda* editorial office. Ortenberg did not print them. But he made enquiries. Avdeenko was serving as a second lieutenant on the Leningrad Front and had fought with distinction. Ortenberg asked him to write a piece on an officer who had been sent to a punishment battalion, where he had redeemed himself in action. Shcherbakov grumbled, but Ortenberg wangled permission direct from Stalin for the piece to be published. From then on Avdeenko became one of Ortenberg's most useful correspondents.[23]

The inflated wartime writing of Ehrenburg and Aleksei Tolstoy was not always popular with the fighting men. One of them later wrote, 'Tolstoy may have written well about the fate of the Russian emigration, because he had lived through all that. But when he started to write fairy tales about the heroes at the front without leaving his comfortable dacha, the result was laughable and shameful.'[24]

The ordinary Russian soldier preferred Alexander Tvardovski's *Vasili Tërkin*. Tvardovski, like his hero, the soldier Vasili Tërkin, was born a peasant in the countryside around Smolensk. He wrote about his hero in a simple and attractive verse which owes much to the rhyming couplets of the *chastushki*, the raucous and often improvised rural verse which was and is used to comment, often disrespectfully, on people and events in the village and even – Moscow itself being still partly a village – in the capital. Occasionally – as in the dialogue between Death and the wounded soldier on the battlefield – *Vasili Tërkin* rises to the height of real poetry. Unlike much Soviet wartime writing, the tone is never pretentious, the word 'Soviet' appears only once in the whole poem and the word 'Stalin' not at all. Tvardovski writes as much about Tërkin at rest, in hospital, playing the accordion, as he does about the nature of courage, the meaning of patriotism, the experience of battle itself. His attitude is half affectionate, half ironic. Sometimes he writes about Tërkin as if he were a real person. Sometimes he lets other characters in the poem treat Tërkin as a literary figment.

Tërkin and his comrades could be of any age – the soldiers in the First World War, the soldiers that Maurice Baring met in the Far East during the Russo-Japanese war, the soldiers who repelled Napoleon. Vasili Tërkin is lightly idealised, like Baring's soldiers, like Alyosha Skvortsov, the young hero of Grigori Chukhrai's moving film *Ballad of a Soldier* (1959).[25] But like them he also has a convincing reality about him: Tvardovski was bombarded throughout the war with letters from the front asking whether Tërkin actually existed or not. Tërkin was, above all, the image that the soldiers wanted to have of themselves: cheerful, stoical, comradely, sensibly brave where necessary, but sensibly convinced that (as the NCOs in the British Army used to say) it is not your duty to die for your country, but to make the enemy die for his. From 1942, when the poem first started to come out as a serial in the Soviet press, it was a huge success. Tërkin became, and has remained, the archetype of the ordinary Russian soldier, on a par with Leo Tolstoy's modest heroes, the men who fought at the siege of Sevastopol and Captain Tushin in *War and Peace*.

The stars of MosFilm dug trenches and watched for incendiary bombs just like everyone else. When the war began, Liubov Orlova and Grigori Aleksandrov were in Riga. They struggled to get first to Minsk, already under bombardment from the air, and then to Moscow. Orlova was immediately set to digging slit trenches outside the MosFilm studio. Aleksandrov was knocked unconscious by the blast of an exploding bomb while he was on fire duty. But the glittering couple still had time to receive the American photographer Margaret Bourke-White and other foreign journalists in their luxurious dacha in Vnukovo.

Lidia Smirnova was in the middle of filming Simonov's *A Boy from Our Town*. She was terrified of fire-watching, but no one asked her what she felt, so she too picked up the incendiary bombs with her asbestos gloves. When she was off duty, Smirnova and the other actresses collected woollen gloves and socks for the soldiers. When the men from MosFilm went to join the 21st (Kiev) Volunteer Division, the actresses organised concerts at the VoenKomats to see them off.

Smirnova's husband Sergei Dobrushin did not volunteer immediately. But one day – a couple of weeks after the war began – he came home from the paper where he worked, very upset. The female Party Secretary had asked him sarcastically, 'What's a fine young fellow like you doing sitting around at home, instead of going to the front to defend the Motherland?' He went straight off to put his name down at the recruiting station, and was called up a couple of weeks later. Smirnova packed his things – woolly socks and some stamped addressed postcards for him to send off wherever he was, to let her know how he was getting on. They set off for the recruiting office at 5 o'clock the next morning. When they got to the Garden Ring, Sergei told her to leave him and go home without looking back. She ran home weeping.

The next day she was back filming, digging trenches during the day, and going to the shelter during the night. For a whole month she heard nothing from Sergei. Then she had three days off and decided to look for him. The Tatar watchman at the recruiting station recognised her from her films and said, 'I can't promise you anything. But tomorrow morning some lorries will be going out along the Mozhaisk road. If you want to risk it, the last lorry will stop to pick you up.'

So the next morning she sat waiting on the Mozhaisk Highway, just where Kutuzov decided to abandon Moscow to the French in 1812. Sure enough, a small column of lorries drove up, carrying mattresses roped on the back. The driver of the last lorry told her to hop on. She lay on the mattresses, clinging to the ropes, and getting steadily whiter from the dust until she looked like a photographic negative.

She was eventually dropped off at a village where the middle-aged commander of her husband's unit had set up his headquarters in the local school. The colonel said sarcastically as she appeared, 'Oho, the first swallow has arrived. Now all the wives and mothers will be coming to look for their men.' But he allowed her and Sergei to spend the night together under a lorry, and the next morning he sent Sergei back to Moscow to pick up a consignment of motorcycles for the regiment. Smirnova and Sergei spent their last night together in their own home, ignoring the raids.

Marina Ladynina, another rising star, had had to learn how to cope with dozens of live piglets on the set of *The Swinemaiden and the Shepherd*, a light-hearted musical directed by her husband, Ivan Pyriev, about the star-crossed romance of a champion pig farmer from the Russian North and a shepherd from the mountains of Dagestan, who meet in the fairyland surroundings of Stalin's permanent *Exhibition of the Achievements of the National Economy* in Moscow. In May 1941 the team went to film on location in the Caucasus, dragging their equipment up to the high pastures on the backs of donkeys and oxen, and gasping in the thin air. They were on their way back to Moscow by train when the conductor came in to tell them that war had broken out. Was it right, they wondered, to go on making a comedy when people were already fighting and dying? They decided to end the project, and several of them volunteered for the front. But they were overruled by higher authority. Filming continued for the next four months. It was an emotional time. Ladynina's parents were caught in Vyazma when the Germans arrived. The actresses were often red-eyed and tearful as the bad news flooded in. Pyriev swore at them: 'Stop crying, God damn it!' – because you couldn't make a comedy if you were weeping. For 26-year-old Vladimir Zeldin, playing the shepherd, the decision to continue filming was a godsend: it was his first major breakthrough as an actor. He was given exemption from military service so he could finish the film. Thereafter he too gave performances to the troops at the front. In 1942 he rejoined MosFilm in evacuation. He continued his acting career in one of Moscow's main theatres until well into the new millennium.[26] *The Swinemaiden and the Shepherd* was first shown on 7 November 1941, on the day of Stalin's Red Square parade. It became an instant hit with the soldiers at the front, and has remained a hit ever since.

In 1944 Pyriev and Ladynina made another musical comedy, *Six o'Clock after the War*. This time it was about a gallant young lieutenant and a teacher-turned-anti-aircraft gunner, who get engaged, lose one another at the front, return separately to their rendezvous on the bridge over the Moscow River from Red Square on Victory Day, and are happily reunited. The songs are by the musical bureaucrat Tikhon Khrennikov and the text – this being Russia – is in rhymed couplets throughout. For years after the war the film was regularly shown on television on the anniversary of the Victory.

On 22 June the government mobilised all men born between 1905 and 1918 to replace the divisions and armies that were already being consumed at such a frightening rate in the West.[27] By the end of June over five million reservists had been called up. Thirteen new armies were created in July, fourteen in August, one in September and four in October. Eight more armies were provided for the defence of Moscow in November and December, and another ten new armies were created the following spring. By 1 December nearly two hundred new divisions had been created, including the volunteer divisions raised in Moscow, Leningrad and elsewhere.[28]

The Moscow Military District commanded by General Artemiev had overall responsibility for calling men to the colours in the capital. The VoenKomats in each Raion sent out the call-up papers. It was to the VoenKomats that conscripts reported for duty and it was there that they were given their preliminary medical examination before being assigned to their training units. The call-up papers were served either by post or by messenger. One teenager delivering call-up papers was surprised to discover that by no means everyone was pleased to see him.[29]

Reservists were sent straight off to the new divisions being formed, or to the front to replace losses in existing units. Except for those who joined elite units such as the OMSBON, the youngsters who were joining the army for the first time were sent off to training camps well to the East of the city. The journey was not pleasant. The training camps around Gorki [Nizhni Novgorod] lay some two hundred and fifty miles from Moscow. There was no transport, so the recruits had to walk – driven, one of them remarked, like cattle to the slaughterhouse. The provisioning often broke down, and they would have to march for a day or more at a time, existing on what the army could give them – sometimes no more than a handful of crusts a day, some dried soup and some porridge, on what they could buy at greatly inflated prices in the markets they passed through, or on what they had brought with them from home. The peasants in the villages through which they passed were as hungry as they were, unwelcoming and unwilling to provide them with billets for the night: in one village the militia had to be called in to make the villagers provide shelter for the exhausted men. To make matters worse, rumours spread along one column marching in late autumn to their camp outside Gorki that typhus had broken out there.

The more sophisticated recruits drew their own conclusions. One wrote home that, for the third time in the twentieth century, the Russian nation was being destroyed in the name of a doubtful idea, in defence of interests which were certainly not those of the people themselves. Another drew a resonant historical parallel with those who for generations had trudged to Siberia along the Vladimir Trakt:

> I am marching along the same road along which so many different

> people have passed before me: idealists of all kinds, the Decembrists [who rose against the Tsar in 1825], revolutionaries of every stripe, political charlatans, criminals and convicts, passing from West to East, into the unbounded expanse of Siberia, distant and mute like the Russian soul. I don't remember from the official biographies whether S[talin] and M[olotov] travelled along the same road, and what conditions they met, but I suspect that their exile was much less arduous than our heroic journey in the battle to defend their glory. S[talin] recently said that the home front is now stronger than it was before. Good luck to him! If he had gone through the kind of places I am going through, he would have spoken differently.[30]

Soon after his return from digging trenches, Anatoli Chernyaev decided to join the regular army rather than one of the volunteer divisions. At the VoenKomat he asked to be sent to flying school. He did not tell the recruiting sergeant that he was already suffering from severe bronchial asthma: it was in remission and the medical examination did not pick it up. He was nevertheless rejected for flying training, so he asked to be sent to a ski battalion because he had won a number of prizes for cross-country skiing at the university. He then suffered his first humiliation: they shaved his head bald. They did allow him to keep his moustache, but a sergeant later made him shave that off as well.

Next he was sent with fifteen other recruits including Gaft, a fellow history student, to a training camp at Grokhovetsk on the Volga. Here all his romantic enthusiasm for the military was wholly overthrown. The camp consisted of a very large area covered with huts dug into the ground. Each hut was sixty yards long. Inside thousands of recruits from all over the country lounged listlessly on bunks carved out of the earth. Even in bright sunshine the tiny windows gave almost no light. The food in the canteen was foul. Chernyaev was not yet so hungry that he was prepared to eat whatever came his way, so he lived on the supplies he had brought with him from home. The so-called 'latrine' was a nightmare: a clearing in the nearby wood about thirty yards wide, with no facilities at all, the whole area one mass of excrement. He and Gaft agreed that this was not what they had joined the army for. Unlike the other recruits, they were volunteers. It was from this point that

Chernyaev dated his contempt for the officers under whom he would have to fight. Neither then nor later did he understand what military or educational purpose was served by treating like cattle those who were in any case about to risk their lives at the front.

After a week the new recruits were roused in the middle of the night and marched to another camp on the outskirts of Gorki. Many of them fell out from exhaustion on the way. Most had bloody feet by the time they arrived. The new camp – ironically it was called Mariina Roshcha, the same as the district of Moscow in which Chernyaev had grown up – had been built only recently. There had not yet been time to reduce it to the state of the camp they had just left.

The humiliation and terror began immediately. Open courts martial were held in public, at which 'deserters' were sentenced to death. The victims were not men who had deserted on the battlefield, but recruits who had broken away to see their families as they were being marched to the training camp.

Their training as ski troops began. The other recruits came from small towns of European Russia. Only one, Chugunov, was a peasant and he was the only one with whom Chernyaev became friends. Chernyaev was put in the mortar platoon of a ski battalion, and was soon promoted sergeant. He already knew the drill at least as well as his instructors as a result of his three years of military training at the university. And again he asked himself: what did the military think they were doing, putting trained students among a mass of half-educated recruits from the provinces?

The recruits had no idea what was happening in Moscow or at the front. But after six weeks their platoon commander began to treat them much better. Chernyaev concluded that they were soon bound for the war: everyone had heard from wounded soldiers in the nearby hospitals what happened to unpopular officers in battle. Soon they were kitted out with their skis, and with distinctive new uniforms which gave rise to adverse comments from other soldiers when they finally arrived at the front. Then they marched to the station, applauded by the people.

For the first time Chernyaev felt himself to be a worthy defender of the Motherland.[31]

1. Gorky Street – The Beginning

22 June 1941. Listening to Molotov announcing the outbreak of war.

2. Moscow before the revolution – the Cathedral of Christ the Saviour

The Cathedral of Christ the Saviour was built to celebrate the victory over Napoleo in the Patriotic War of 1812. It was intended to be financed by public subscriptior but the money vanished into unknown pockets and the project was in the end pai for by the state. Construction lasted from 1839 until 1883. In 1931 the Cathedra and the older churches around it were demolished on Stalin's orders. A replica wa erected in remarkably short order by Mayor Luzhkov in a mere four years, an consecrated in 2000.

. Moscow between the wars

'op: The House in the Embankment seen from across the river. It was built for the :ommunist elite, many of whom suffered in the purges. The Church of the Adoration f the Mother of God in the foreground was destroyed together with the Cathedral of :hrist the Saviour in 1931.

3ottom: The Kazan Station was completed in 1926. The station and Komsomol Square n front of it were packed with people fleeing Moscow on 16 October 1941.

4. Film Stars

Clockwise from top left: **Marina Ladynina**, the star of *The Swinemaiden and the Shepher* and *Six O' Clock after the War*; **Valentina Serova**, Konstantin Simonov's partner, and th object of his popular wartime poem *Wait for Me*; **Lidia Smirnova**, the star of *A Boy fror our Town*, and many other films and plays, who was still working in her eighties and wa awarded a high decoration by President Putin on her ninetieth birthday; and **Liubo Orlova**, seen in her role as the heroine of *Volga-Volga*, Stalin's favourite film.

5. The Dukovski Affair

Pavel Dukovski was the history teacher at School No 110. Adored by his pupils, he was arrested in March 1941 and died in a camp. His pupils Vladimir Kantovski and Anya Bovshever organised an anonymous campaign of protest. The authorities did not stir until the outbreak of war when the children were arrested. Below are the NKVD mug-shots of Vladimir and Anya, both were sentenced to ten years forced labour.

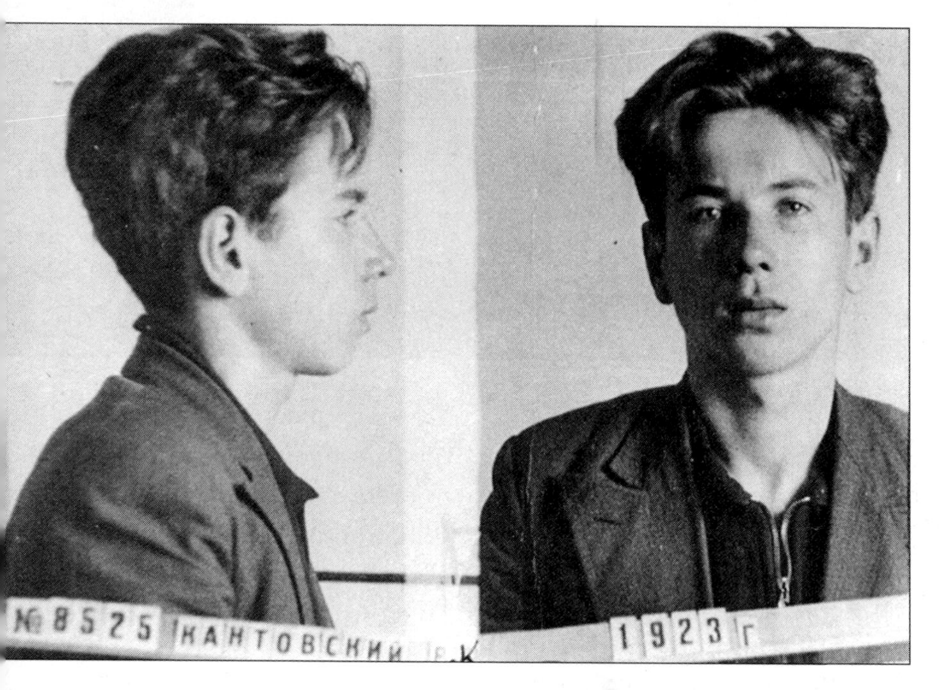

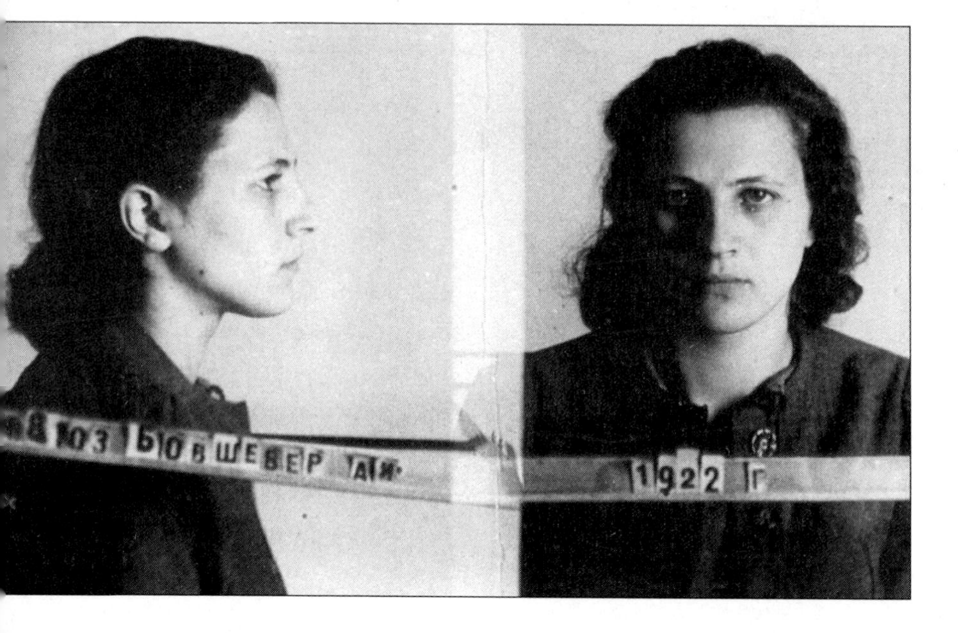

6. Governing Moscow

Top: Alexander Scherbakov was th quintessential Party functionary, a ma of energy and ruthless administrativ skill. In 1941 he was the First Secretar of the Moscow Party, a member of th Politburo, Head of the Main Politica Administration of the Armed Forces and Head of the SovInformburo, th official agency for war news. He wa thus by far the most powerful man i the Moscow administration at the time He died on 9 May 1945, the day of th Victory itself. With such a work loa that was perhaps hardly surprising.

Left: Mikhail Nemirovski was chairma of the Raion Council for Krasnay Presnya, one of the twenty five district into which Moscow was divided. H was responsible for the detailed runnin of his district, and was one of the ke members of the municipal apparatu headed by Vasili Pronin, the Chairma of the Moscow Executive Council.

. Going to the Front

8. The People Join the War

Top: Signing on for the 18th (Leningrad Raion) Volunteer division. This division survived the early fighting, and served successfully throughout the war.

Bottom: The inhabitants of No 31 Suvorov Street learn how to fight fires.

. The Trëkhgornaya Textile Factory

The Trëkhgornaya Manufaktura, the 'Trëkhgorka', was founded by the Prokhorov family n 1799 on the banks of the river in the district which is now called Krasnaya Presnya, and t is still going strong. Its workers played an important part in the 1905 revolution. The *top* photograph shows the factory as it looked in the 1890s. The *bottom* photograph shows some of the four hundred workers who joined the ill-fated 8th (Krasnaya Presnya) Volunteer Division, which was wiped out in the fighting around Vyazma in October 1941.

10. Defending the Kremlin

Top: MiG-3 fighters flying over the Kremlin. Red Square, the department store GUM and St Basil's Church can all be seen in the top photo. The Bolshoi Theatre is in the middle distance. There are few multi-storey buildings: in 1941 Moscow was still a village of largely wooden buildings.

Bottom: The Kremlin is silhouetted against the massive volume of fire put up by the defences to deter the German bombers. The white line on the right marks the path of a descending German flare.

1. Sheltering in the Metro

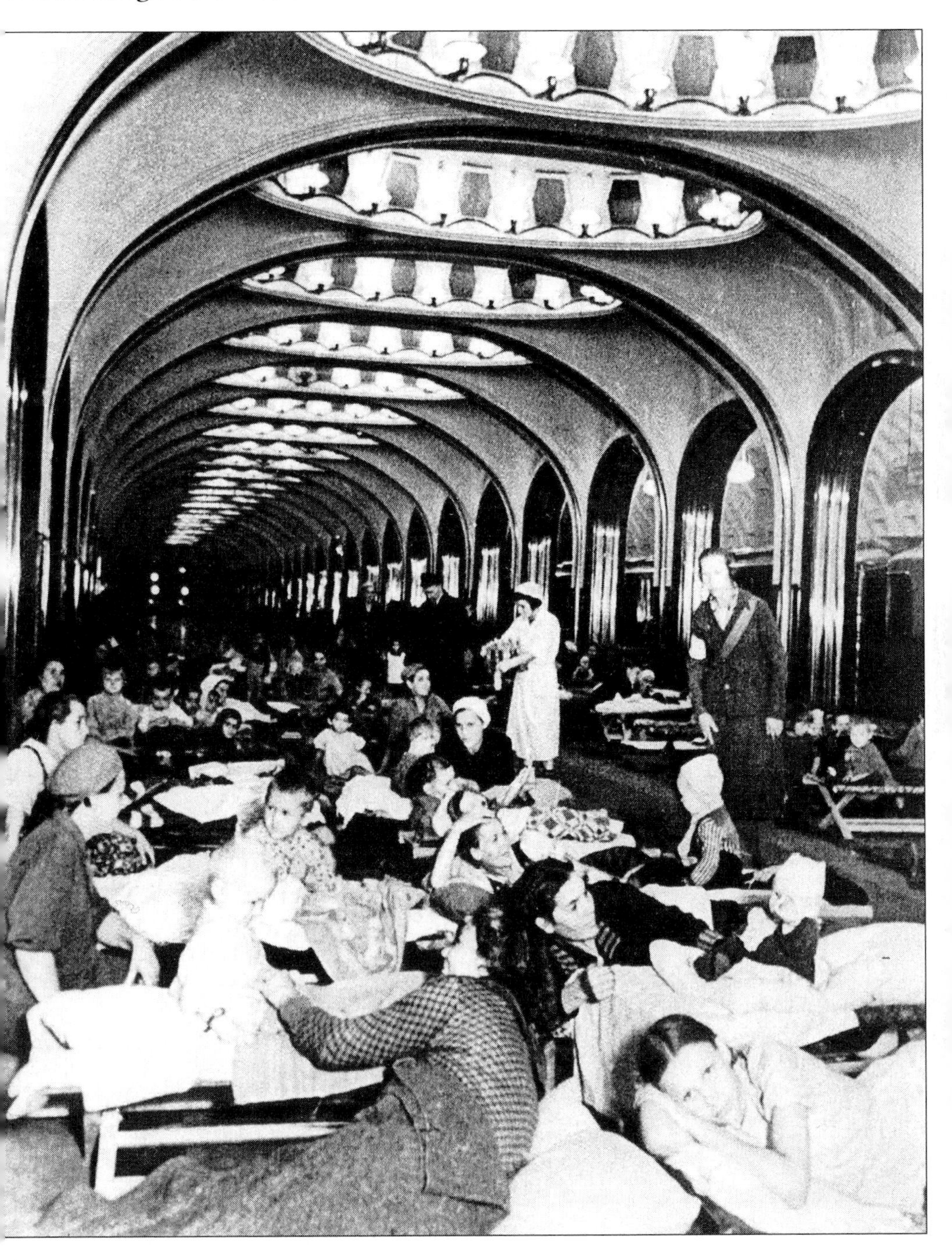

The Moscow underground system was opened by Stalin in 1935. Construction of new stations continued even during the war. They were intended from the start to serve as shelters in the event of war. The British authorities, on the contrary, tried to prevent the London Underground from being used to shelter from the Blitz, but they were unable to resist public pressure.

12. Balloons

As in London, the barrage balloons were intended to force the German bombers to fl
high, and to spoil their aim. When not in the air, they lurked on almost every ope
space in the city.

3. Rationing

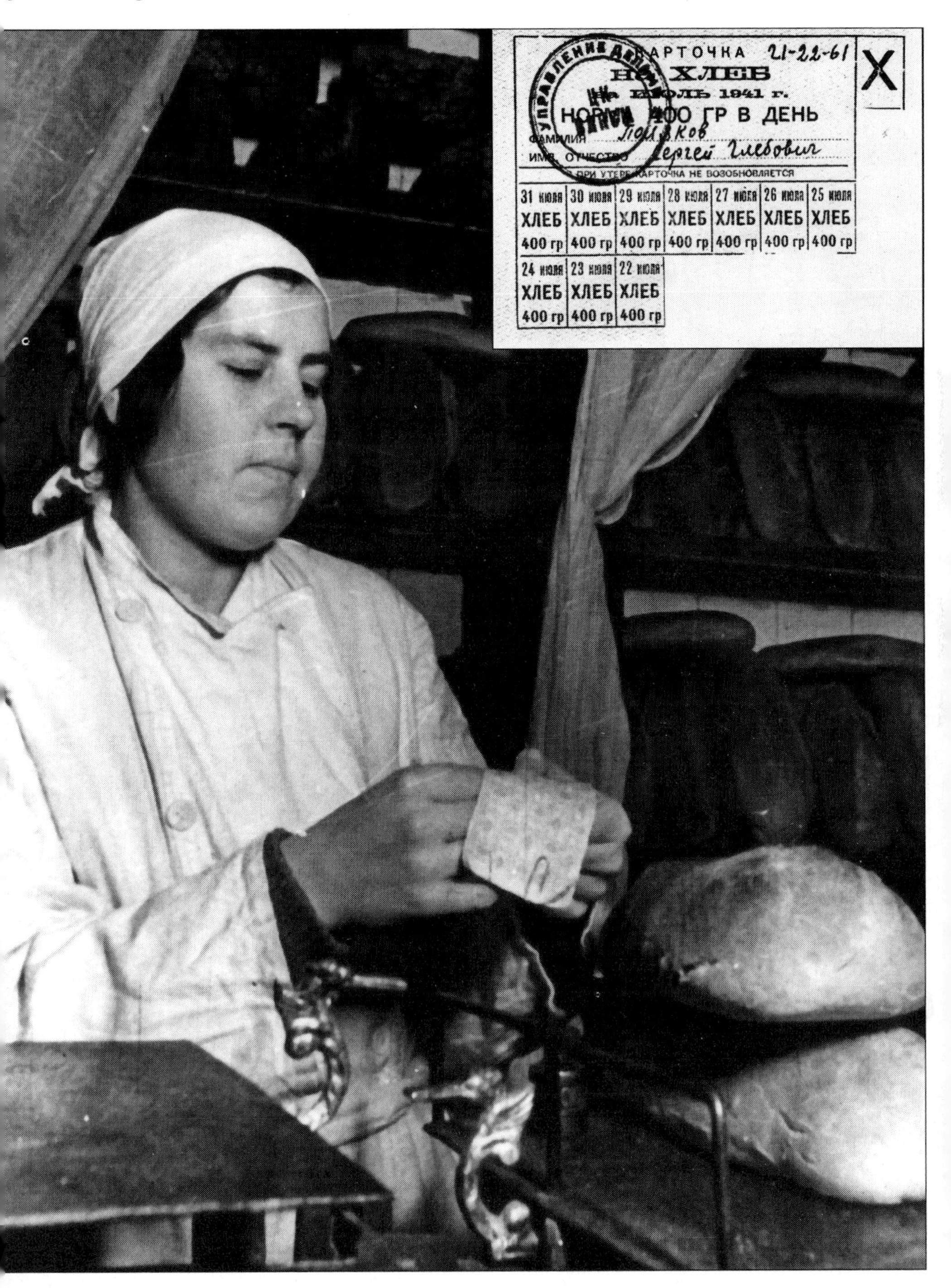

Bread was the most important part of the wartime ration. The size of your ration depended on the work you were doing. Heavy workers got 600 grammes a day – in theory, and provided it was available. Children and dependents got 400 grammes a day. The card on the right belonged to Sergei Polyakov, who only got 400 grammes a day.

14. General Rokossovski

Konstantin Rokossovski was born in Warsaw in 1896 of a Polish father and a Whit
Russian mother. He was decorated for gallantry several times while serving in th
Tsarist cavalry during the First World War. He then joined the Red Army, where h
spent the rest of his career except for three years after his arrest during the 1937 purge
He was reinstated in 1940, became one of the most successful of all Soviet generals, an
ended his career as a Marshal. He played a key role as commander of the 16th Arm
in the Battle of Moscow: this picture is a still from the documentary film *The Defea
of the German Forces before Moscow*. Rokossovski had the reputation of being particularl
courteous to his subordinates. A recent poll in Russia rated him second only to Marsha
Zhukov.

5. Generals

Clockwise from top left: **Lev Dovator**, the Jewish cavalry commander who was killed during the Russian counteroffensive in December 1941; **Ivan Panfilov**, the commander of the 316th Division which distinguished itself on the Volokolamsk Highway: he was killed in November 1941. **Andrei Vlasov**, who won a high reputation in the fighting on the frontier and outside Moscow, but was later captured and went over to the Germans in July 1942; and **Georgi Zhukov** at his headquarters in Pervushkhovo outside Moscow during the battle.

16. Soldiers

Clockwise from top left: **Anatoli Chernyaev** was graduating from the Historica Faculty of Moscow University when the war began. After a couple of unsatisfactor months digging trenches, he volunteered for the army and finished the war as a lieuten ant outside Riga: this uncharacteristically glum picture comes from his army identit card. In 1985 he became Gorbachev's foreign policy adviser. **Yevgeni Teleguev** wa travelling from Siberia to study in Moscow when the war began. He volunteere for the OMSBON, the special forces unit of the NKVD, and operated for two year behind German lines. He ended his career as a general in the KGB. As a regular office **Alexander Pyltsyn** commanded a platoon of disgraced officers in the 8th Punishmen Battalion of Rokossovski's 1st Belorussian Front. He remained in the army and retire as a Major-General. **Lev Mischenko** joined the 8th (Krasnaya Presnya) Voluntee Division from the Physical Faculty of Moscow University. He was taken prisoner an sent to the camps for ten years on returning to Russia.

– EIGHT –

STALIN TAKES A GRIP

The patriotic emotion which overwhelmed most Russians on the first day of the war, and which drove so many of them to volunteer on the spot, was intense and genuine enough. But the mutterings of the people and the chaos in the army must have convinced Stalin that the fate of the country, and the fate of his own authority, were hanging by a thread. He reacted with his usual ferocity.

But first of all, even before the war began, he turned on his old favourites, the falcons of the Red Air Force.

The airmen were not of course immune from the purges of 1937 and 1938. The commander of the Red Air Force, Yakov Alksnis, was arrested in 1937 on his way to a diplomatic reception in Moscow and executed.[1] By 1946 four of his five successors had been arrested and beaten, and three had been shot. But the fury with which Stalin turned on the airmen in the summer of 1941 seems to have been triggered by a number of particular events.

Stalin took a particular interest in the development of the new aircraft designed to replace the obsolete fighters and bombers that had fought in Spain. He had strong and often misguided views on technical details, which he did not hesitate to impose on his subordinates. Because of his determination that the new aircraft should be produced in massive quantities and very soon, he was also prepared to cut corners, and to blame others when the results did not come up to expectation. One absurdly counterproductive consequence was that hundreds of aircraft designers, engineers and specialists were interned between 1934 and 1941. They included Andrei Tupolev, one of the most distinguished of all Soviet aircraft designers. Three hundred of these men worked in *sharashkas* – prison laboratories and research units. One hundred died in the Gulag, and fifty were executed.[2]

Stalin was interested above all in the speed and range of the fighters. A requirement was issued that fighter aircraft were to have a range of six hundred miles. To convince Stalin that this range was attainable, the MiG factory used a special fuel mixture for a demonstration flight at high altitude by their test MiG-3. This achieved the range but ruined the engine. Stalin was tipped off to the deceit.[3] He then fell foul of General Filin, the head of the Scientific Test Institute for the air force, in a separate dispute about aircraft radios. In 1941 Soviet bombers were fully equipped with wireless. But not all of the fighters had receivers, only a few had transmitters, and there was no adequate system of control from the ground. Filin rightly insisted that all aircraft needed proper radios, but Stalin objected because the extra weight would lead to a loss of performance.

The forced development of the new aircraft also led to an increase in the number of flying accidents. In April 1941, Timoshenko and Zhukov complained to Stalin and demanded the removal of several senior air force officers.[4] The problem was discussed at a meeting on the eve of the war. As usual, Stalin was walking up and down, smoking his pipe, as the discussion proceeded. Rychagov, the young commander of the Red Air Force, went red in the face and burst out, 'The accident rate will go on being high as long as you make us fly in coffins.'[5] There was a moment of absolute silence. Stalin stopped walking up and down, took his pipe out of his mouth, went up to Rychagov, and said slowly and quietly, 'You shouldn't have said that.' Rychagov was relieved of his duties, and sent to the General Staff Academy to cool off.[6]

The war in Finland had shown up the inadequacies of the Soviet air defence system, and the military leadership had given repeated orders for improvement. They were equally dissatisfied with the results of the air force training programme for the winter of 1940–41.[7] But little was done, and things seem to have come to a head when General Pumpur, the commander of the Moscow air defence system and a hero of the Spanish war, sent his deputy, Colonel Sbytov, on a tour of inspection of the airfields in the region in March 1941. In one after another Sbytov found that there was no fuel and no munitions. The obsolete fighters were lined up wing-tip to wing-tip on the ground, and they were not camouflaged. The station commanders argued that everything could be sorted out if a war began. Sbytov reported back to Pumpur, but Pumpur brushed him aside: it could all be dealt with after the May Day parade. Sbytov took it to the politicians, and went to see Shcherbakov, the Secretary of the Moscow Party. Shcherbakov immediately called a meeting of the senior air force commanders on 3 May. The officers explained that the pilots were retraining on new types of aircraft. The politicians thought this an inadequate excuse for neglecting Moscow's defences. Stalin noted on Malenkov's report of the meeting: 'The guilty parties should be court-martialled.'[8] Sbytov's career prospered, and he eventually became a general. Many of his fellow officers never forgave him for his role in this affair.

An incident on 15 May 1941 may have been the last straw. On that day a German Junkers 52 flew without permission from German-occupied Poland to Moscow. The air defences failed to react. Timoshenko and Zhukov investigated, and on 10 June they issued a furious Order. Ground observers, they said, had mistaken the (three-engined) Ju 52 for a scheduled (two-engined) Soviet DC3. The Bialystok airfield had failed to inform the local air defence units of the intrusion because their communications had broken down. The people in Moscow had not only failed to stop the aircraft; they had given it permission to land there. Timoshenko and Zhukov called for remedial measures, reprimanded those responsible, and – surprisingly belatedly – ordered that silhouettes of German aircraft should be distributed to all ground observers.[9]

The arrests and the beatings started almost immediately. Pumpur was arrested on 31 May. Rychagov was arrested on 24 June. His wife, the airwoman Maria Nesterenko, was arrested the next day, for 'failing to denounce a state criminal [...] Being his beloved wife she could not but have known of the treacherous activities of her husband.'[10] General Shtern, another hero of the Spanish war, commander of the air defences for the country as a whole; General Loktionov, a former commander of the air force now in charge of the Baltic Special Military District; General Arzhenukhin, the commandant of the Air Force Academy; General Gusev, the commander of the air force in the Far East; the air force commander of the Southwest Front; the air force commander of the 7th Army; and for good measure the Chief of Communications of the Red Army, General Trubetskoi – all were arrested on the eve of the war, or in the days immediately thereafter. So was General Proskurov, the distinguished airman who had served in Spain and was Golikov's predecessor as head of Military Intelligence.[11]

Yakov Smushkevich, the former air force commander who was now Deputy Commissar for Defence, was back in hospital for further operations on his shattered legs. On 7 June Yelena Burmenko, a surgeon at the hospital, came home very upset and told her husband, David Ortenberg, 'This morning, when I was in Smushkevich's ward, three NKVD officials came in, and took him away, though he was barely able to walk.'[12] That night Smushkevich's fifteen-year-old daughter Rosa was asleep in the family apartment in the House on the Embankment, when she and her mother were awakened by an electric torch flashing in their faces. The bedroom was full of men under the personal direction of Beria's deputy Bogdan Kobulov, who had helped to organise the murder of the Polish officers at Katyn. The Smushkeviches' extensive library was torn apart: each book was inspected individually and then thrown on the floor. All the mattresses and cushions were removed, so that Rosa and her mother had to sleep on the floor. All the money in the place was taken away. The search continued for thirty-six hours.[13]

A number of devoted friends rallied to support the two women. Admiral Kuznetsov, the Commander of the Navy, who had been close to Smushkevich in Spain, contacted Poskrëbyshev, Stalin's Executive Assistant, who suggested that Rosa should write to Stalin. She did so, but got no immediate answer. She telephoned Poskrëbyshev, who said, 'Rosa, Comrade Stalin is taken up with very important government business and can't meet you. But somebody will certainly see you.'

A few days later an unknown colonel turned up at the House on the Embankment and told Rosa's mother, 'I need to take your daughter away for a while. There's nothing to worry about.' Rosa was driven to the Lubyanka to see Beria himself. He was sitting in a huge room at a desk under a table lamp with a green shade.

'Was it you who wrote to Comrade Stalin?' asked Beria.

'Yes, it was me.'

'Well, Comrade Stalin has asked me to have a word with you ...'

Rosa interrupted him to ask, 'Tell me, please, has papa been arrested for political reasons or not?'

'I don't know. I can't tell you. But do you believe that your papa is a good, honest man?'

'Yes, I do believe that.'

'Well, so you should. Everything will be investigated and everything will be all right. But don't ask me any more questions.'

Then Beria pressed a bell, and Kobulov appeared. Beria gave him a severe dressing-down for leaving Rosa and her mother with no money and nothing to sleep on. By the time Rosa got home, the mattresses had already been returned, and the money came back soon afterwards.[14] The women settled down to wait. So did Stalin: for the time being he left the fate of the prisoners on one side, while he concentrated on more urgent matters.

Once the war had actually begun, repressions in the military started up again in earnest. Commanders, junior officers, and simple soldiers were executed for incompetence, panicking, cowardice, or simple bad luck. Commanding officers shot their men to get them to fight, to gain a reputation for ruthlessness, or to divert attention from their own failings. Brutal measures were taken from the first days of the war to keep men in the line and control the rear areas. On 17 July 1941 military security units were redesignated 'Special Sections' and transferred from the army to the NKVD.[15] A platoon-sized Special Section of NKVD troops (about forty men) was to be assigned to each division, a company-sized Section to each army, and a battalion-sized Section to each Front.[16] Their tasks were to prevent soldiers leaving their battle positions; to check and if necessary arrest officers and men suspected of abandoning their posts; to execute deserters on the spot; to carry out the sentences of courts martial, if necessary by executing those found guilty in front of their comrades.[17] These instructions were soon expanded to include the arrest and interrogation of soldiers who had been taken prisoner by the Germans and to keep under constant observation those deemed fit to return to fighting units.[18]

In early September a counterattack Southwest of Moscow by General Yerëmenko, then commanding the Bryansk Front, failed with heavy losses at least in part – so he claimed – because of panic among the soldiers and their officers. On 12 September the Stavka issued a Directive, signed by Stalin, authorising all commanders to set up blocking detachments.[19] Under pressure from the Germans, the Directive said, whole divisions panicked, cried 'We are surrounded', went into headlong retreat, and abandoned their equipment. This would not happen if commanding officers and political commissars were sufficiently strong and reliable. But too many of them were not. Blocking detachments should therefore be organised in each division within five days. They should be up to a battalion in size, fully armed, and equipped with transport and tanks. They should not hesitate to use their weapons against those responsible for inciting panic, though they should spare decent soldiers who had simply been swept away.

Some veterans, and some historians, claim that blocking detachments never fired indiscriminately on retreating men. Even at their height, the size of the blocking detachments was small in relation to the size of the army as a whole, and it is not surprising that many veterans say they never saw them in action. But Alexander Yakovlev, Gorbachëv's reforming partner in the last days of the Soviet Union, took part in one incident as a young marine on the Volkhov Front North of Moscow in May 1942. 'We marines had a fearsome reputation as fighters. People called us the Black Devils. One night our two battalions of marines were ordered out of the line. Luckily the Germans never found out, because we left the whole sector undefended. We were taken at the double through the darkness to a nearby village. We dug trenches and set up machine guns to cover a neighbouring wood. A division of NKVD troops – mostly conscripted policemen – had broken at the front, and they shortly emerged from the wood in disorder. Our Commissar, a man called Ksendz, told us to fire over their heads. He took a loudhailer and shouted at the fugitives to lie down. They did, and that of course stopped the panic. Ksendz was then able to sort them out into their platoons and companies, rally their officers, and send them back into the line. There were no casualties, but he told them that next time they panicked, the machine-gunners would shoot to kill.'[20]

According to the NKVD's own figures, NKVD blocking detachments detained nearly seven hundred thousand officers and men between the beginning of the war and 10 October 1941. They returned most to active duty. But they arrested nearly twenty-six thousand, and shot more than ten thousand, over three thousand in front of their comrades.[21] While in Leningrad in September 1941, Zhukov personally ordered machine guns to be turned on retreating battalions. A few days later – egged on perhaps by Stalin, who had ordered him not to spare Russian civilians who were being used by the Germans as human shields – he went even further and ordered that the families of those who surrendered to the enemy were to be shot.[22]

Stalin was as ruthless with the army's senior commanders as the NKVD were with the rank and file. He moved quickly to deal with those who had presided over the catastrophe on the frontier. On 16 July 1941, the GKO announced the arrest of the commanders of the Western, Northwestern, and Southern Fronts. 'It is ... our holy duty,' said the Order, 'to punish panicmongers, cowards and deserters, and restore military discipline, if we wish to preserve unsullied the high name of warrior of the Red Army.' Nine generals had been arrested and were to be court-martialled. The nine were Dmitri Pavlov, the former commander of the Western Front; his Chief of Staff, Major-General Klimovskikh; his Chief of Communications, Major-General Grigoriev; and six lesser generals.[23]

Pavlov and his associates were tried on 22 July 1941, in the middle of the first German air attack on Moscow. It is said that they asked to be sent to the front as ordinary soldiers, to atone with their blood for the defeat of their armies.[24] If so, their plea was rejected. On 28 July Stalin announced that the Supreme Court had found Pavlov and Klimovskikh guilty of cowardice, passivity and incompetence, allowing their forces to disintegrate, abandoning their weapons and supplies to the enemy, permitting units of the Western Front to abandon their defensive positions without authority, and thus enabling the enemy to break through the front. Grigoriev was convicted of panic and criminal negligence, failing to establish reliable communications between the staff of the Western Army Group and its constituent formations, and thus contributing to the loss of control over their actions. The four senior generals, said Stalin, had been stripped of their rank and sentenced to be shot. The sentence had already been carried out.[25]

Major-General Kopets, the air commander of the Western Front, a hero of the war in Spain who had been promoted in three years from the rank of captain, had already taken another way out. He shot himself on the evening of the first day of the war, overwhelmed by the catastrophe that had overtaken his command. The *Journal of the Military Operations of the Western Army Group* contains a sneering reference to his fate: 'The commander of the Air Force of the Western Front, Major-General Kopets, who was mainly to blame for the loss of the aircraft, obviously in a desire to avoid punishment, shot himself on the evening of 22 June without waiting to learn the full extent of the losses. The other culprits received their just rewards later.'[26] Simonov later wrote his epitaph: 'Kopets was one of our finest fighter pilots. ... [He] may well have shot himself not so much because he feared punishment, but because he was oppressed by the terrible responsibility which lay upon his shoulders. From the psychological point of view that is entirely understandable.'[27]

To get a more comprehensive grip Stalin issued Order No. 270 on 16 August 1941. It was couched in his own distinctive style: grinding, rhetorical, repetitive, brutally logical, almost an incantation. The Order began by describing the gallant actions of those who fought to the last. 'But,' it went on, 'we cannot hide the fact that in the recent past there have been a number of shameful examples of surrender to the enemy.' Generals were as guilty as ordinary soldiers of unsteady, mean-spirited and cowardly behaviour. Commanding officers hid in their slit trenches or their headquarters, instead of directing the battle. At the first sign of difficulty they tore off their badges of rank and deserted. Could such people be tolerated in the ranks of the Red Army? No, they could not. Those who surrendered should be destroyed by all means available, from the air or from the ground, and their families deprived of all benefits.[28] Those who deserted should be shot on the spot, and their families arrested. Commanders who failed to direct their soldiers effectively in battle should be demoted or reduced to the ranks, and replaced by NCOs or soldiers who had distinguished themselves in action. The Order was not published either then, or for many years afterwards. But it was read to all units, and to senior Party and Government officials throughout the country.[29]

Even those who had suffered found themselves applying Order No. 270 in all its rigour. Meretskov, who made way for Zhukov as Chief of Staff after his poor performance at the war games in January, was arrested at almost the same time as Pavlov. He was accused of conspiring with his fellow generals and beaten very severely because, one of his interrogators said even after he had been restored to favour, 'he was a dangerous and obstinate conspirator. We did not spare him.' He confessed to all the charges against him, and went on to denounce Pavlov, whom he accused of having attempted to stand up for some of the officers who had been purged in 1937. Pavlov admitted that he and other officers had written to Voroshilov and Stalin to say that the arrests were unjustified, and were undermining the confidence of the soldiers in their own officers. He was forced in his turn to denounce Meretskov and his links with the 'traitor' Uborevich. Later Meretskov was confronted with Loktionov, the former air force commander who was his alleged co-conspirator. Loktionov was covered with blood, and he was beaten again in front of Meretskov. At first he too admitted that he had been linked with Uborevich, but he refused to sign a confession, despite Meretskov's urgings. Unlike most of his colleagues, Loktionov wavered but never finally broke.[30]

Later Stalin, remembering Meretskov's existence, said, 'He's been cooling off long enough,' and had him released. In his memoirs, Meretskov describes how he was called in by Stalin a few weeks later.

Stalin: 'Hello, Comrade Meretskov! How are you feeling?'

Meretskov: 'Hello, Comrade Stalin! I feel fine. Please give me my orders.'[31]

Two days later, Meretskov was on his way to join Bulganin and Mekhlis on the Military Committee of the Northwest Front. Soon he too was judging his fellow officers. On 11 September 1941 he and Mekhlis sentenced General Goncharov, the Artillery Commander of the 34th Army, to death for cowardice. Goncharov was shot in the late afternoon in the village of Zaborie, in the presence of twenty-three members of his staff. Colonel Saveliev witnessed the scene:

> By order of Mekhlis the members of the staff of the 34th Army were lined up. [Mekhlis] strode rapidly along the line, until he came to the artillery commander. Stopping in front of him, he shouted:

> 'Where are your guns?' Goncharov gestured vaguely in the direction where our units were surrounded. 'I'm asking you, where are they?' shouted Mekhlis and then, after a brief pause, began the standard phrase: 'In accordance with Order No. 270 of the People's Commissar for Defence ...' He ordered an elderly major on the right of the line to carry out the sentence. Unable to overcome his emotion, and greatly daring, the major refused. A firing squad had to be summoned instead.[32]

Meretskov ended the war as a Marshal, a Hero of the Soviet Union and one of the commanders of the Soviet campaign against Japan in 1945. Like Rokossovski, he never spoke of his time in prison.

Several generals listed in the preamble to Order No. 270 were beyond Stalin's reach. Generals Ponedelin and Kirillov had been taken prisoner, and were sentenced to death in their absence. They appear to have behaved well in captivity. The two men were liberated by the Americans at the end of the war, and handed over to the Soviets for repatriation. At first they were allowed to resume their former ranks. But in October 1945 they were arrested, held in prison for nearly five years, and then tried and executed in 1950. They were rehabilitated – posthumously – in 1954.

General Ponedelin's father and his second wife were arrested and exiled.[33] His daughter Alla, a classmate of Stepan Mikoyan, recalled: 'My father met my mother in the civil war, when he was billeted on her upper-middle-class family. He came from a peasant background, but rose to command a brigade during the First World War. In 1923 he was sent to study at the Frunze Academy in Moscow. We lived in the Academy's hall of residence. My father's pay was so poor that my mother had to sell her jewellery to keep the family going. In 1927 my father was posted for two years to Stalingrad to command a regiment. He then returned to the Frunze Academy, this time as a lecturer. We lived for four years in a *kommunalka*, where each family had three rooms but shared a common kitchen. One of our close family friends was General Timashkov, who was also on the teaching staff. My father then commanded a corps during the Finnish war, and in the spring of 1941 he was posted to command the 12th Army in Ivano-Frankovsk in Western Ukraine.

'My mother and I remained in Moscow, and the family split up when my father took up with another woman. But we were on good terms, and he invited me to visit him in Ivano-Frankovsk in the middle of June. Just a week before I was due to travel I got a telegram from him telling me not to come.

'As I had received top marks in my school leaving exam, I was able to go straight to the Mechanical Mathematics department of Moscow University in 1940. But at the end of my first year at university I only got a 3 for physics. That was serious because it meant I wouldn't get a scholarship for my second year. But the war started the next day, and that no longer seemed very important. I spent a few weeks helping to bring in the harvest at a state farm outside Moscow and took some courses in nursing. I did fire duty on the top of the cupola of the old university building: I was lucky enough not to be there the day the building was hit by a bomb and a number of the firewatchers were killed.

'In August I got a phone call from General Timashkov. He said, "Your father has been captured, and has been condemned as a traitor, along with Generals Kirillov and Kachalov. I've heard that the NKVD are going to arrest you as a member of his family, but I've managed to put them off. Don't tell anyone who your father is, and when you have to fill in any forms, say that your father is in the military, not that he is a general."

'This seemed to work. I continued to study at the university. When it was evacuated I stayed on in Moscow and joined a construction team building air-raid shelters. I'd only been there a week when the foreman tried to assault me, and warned me, "Don't make a fuss: I know who your father is." I got myself transferred to another job in the personnel department of a trading company. Then a friend who was working as a typist in the staff of the 214th Ground Attack Division of the air force told me that they were recruiting radio operators for the meteorological section. I applied for the job, but was assigned instead to the personnel section of the division as a casual employee [*volnonaemnaya*], which meant among other things that I never formally wore uniform. In November 1942 the Division was assigned to the Stalingrad front. I was moved to the operational section of the staff, and put in charge of handling all the division's operational documents. One day General Rybanov, the divisional commander, called me in and asked, "Do you know General Naidënov? He's asked me why I am employing the daughter of a traitor in such a sensitive post." Rybanov gave me three months' paid leave to make myself scarce, and suggested I go back to Moscow to resume my studies. He offered to take me back again when things had blown over, but I decided it was safer to stay on in the capital.

'During this whole time I never changed my name, even though it is very rare – there is still only one Ponedelin in the Moscow phone book.

'My father was in a German camp until the end of the war. They tried to recruit him to the Russian forces under German command, but he refused. At the end of the war he and other generals were taken to Paris, and there handed back to the Soviets. He was held for five years in Lefortovo Prison. The interrogators were never able to prove that he had acted treacherously. There is a story that after some years in prison he wrote to Stalin to protest his innocence. Stalin had forgotten about him, and when he got the letter said, "Is that man still alive?" Whatever the truth of the matter, my father was shot in 1950.

'General Timashkov was arrested as a friend of a "traitor", and his family had to live in a cell in the Donskoi Monastery when they were thrown out of their apartment.'[34]

Stalin continued to refine his brutal system as the war went on. Order No. 270 was followed a year later by Order No. 227, issued on 26 July as the Germans lunged towards Stalingrad and the Caucasus and the Red Army was once again in headlong retreat. Order No. 227 became more notorious, but was no more savage, than its predecessor. Once again it bore the unmistakable mark of Stalin's personal style. The Soviet people, he said, had always admired and loved the Red Army. Now they were losing faith in it and cursing it for abandoning ordinary people to the German yoke, while saving itself by retreating ever further to the East. Those who argued that the Red Army could not be beaten because it could retreat indefinitely into the vast spaces to the East were talking rubbish. The country had already been forced to give up to the enemy seventy million people and much of its production of grain and metal. It could not afford to lose any more. From now on, the army must retreat not one step more. Panicmongers and cowards should be shot on the spot, and commanders who abandoned their positions without authority should be treated as traitors.

Individual commanders had set up punishment units in the first months of the war.[35] Stalin now ordered them to be systematised. Each Army Group should establish up to three punishment battalions for officers and senior NCOs convicted of cowardice and similar crimes. Each Army should establish up to ten punishment companies for convicted soldiers and junior NCOs. These units of *shtrafniki* should be sent to fight on the most difficult sectors of the front, so that they would have the opportunity to 'wipe out their crimes before the Motherland with their blood'.

The details were fixed by Zhukov a few weeks later. Service in punishment units varied from one to three months. Before being posted to a punishment unit, the soldier or officer would surrender all his medals, which would be kept until his return to normal duty. Regardless of previous rank, he would serve in the punishment unit as a 'private-*shtrafnik*', but could if necessary be promoted as far as sergeant. The families of *shtrafniki* continued to receive the financial support to which they had been entitled. The officers commanding these units were regulars. They received no special training for the task, but their service was counted extra for pensions purposes. Over four hundred thousand men served in these punishment units.[36]

Order No. 227 further reinforced the system of blocking detachments, which were to be stationed immediately behind 'unreliable divisions', with the power to shoot panicmongers and cowards on the spot 'and thus assist the honest soldiers in the division to fulfil their duty to the Motherland'. In March 1943 Rokossovski complained that nineteen men from one of the punishment units under his command had deserted to the Germans, and ordered his commanders 'to employ penal subunits only in situations that permit detachments to be deployed immediately following them'.[37]

By the summer of 1944 the men of the blocking detachments were performing a random variety of tasks. They were being used to defend headquarters; as telephone linesmen; even as cooks, cobblers, tailors, storemen and clerks.[38] Blocking detachments were formally abolished on 29 October 1944. But both blocking detachments and punishment units continued to exist in practice until the end of the war, long after the tide had turned against the Germans.[39]

Order No. 227 was read to Chernyaev and his comrades when they were resting in reserve. It cut very little ice with them. They already knew perfectly well that the situation was desperate, and the threats of dire punishment no longer frightened them. They trusted one another, no one had ever panicked, and no one ever thought of abandoning the battlefield. If the order had any meaning, they concluded, it must relate to someone else.[40]

There are plenty of eyewitnesses to the way the punishment units functioned. In the summer of 1942 Lieutenant Zia Bunyatov was arrested by a Special Detachment of the NKVD as his unit retreated towards Rostov-on-Don. He and a number of other officers were driven to a large farm in the village of Vesely. They were taken one at a time into a house where three men were sitting at a table. Each prisoner gave his rank, and was then asked what had happened to his unit. Most replied that the whole line had crumbled, and that as junior commanders they were in no position to stop the rot. Half were sentenced, led behind a pigsty, and shot. The rest, including Bunyatov, were assigned to punishment units. Bunyatov's unit at times numbered as many as seven hundred men. But after each major engagement it was usually reduced to a few dozen.[41]

Semën Aria was sentenced to serve in a punishment unit as a result of a bizarre misfortune. He was called up in 1940, and had just completed his first year's training when the war began. 'I was immediately sent to join a motor rifle unit on the Western Front outside Moscow. I had only spent three days at the front when I was blown up and severely concussed. I was in a military hospital until August 1942. After three months' training as a T-34 tank driver I was posted in December 1942 to a tank brigade on the North Caucasus Front. There my unit saw heavy fighting as the Germans retreated. At one point we were redeployed to another sector – a forced march of twenty miles. My tank fell off a wooden bridge and turned upside down. We managed to extricate it, but after another twenty miles the engine began to leak oil and then seized up. We were exhausted and spent the night in a barn, leaving one member of the crew as a sentry. He fell asleep too. When we woke up, our tank had disappeared. We later learned it had been salvaged by a passing repair team.'

The commander of the tank, Lieutenant Kutz, and Aria were both arrested and put in a freezing cellar. Another of the cellar's inhabitants was a major from the staff of the 44th Army who had been a gangster in Leningrad before the war. He had been arrested for machine-gunning five hundred German prisoners, on the grounds that he had no one to spare to guard them. He rather expected to be shot, but hoped that he might get off if he could persuade the court that he was only following Stalin's order 'to liquidate the German invaders to the last man'.

Kutz and Aria were sentenced to seven years' hard labour for losing a major piece of military equipment. The sentence was suspended and, together with another soldier they did not know, they were posted to the 683rd Punishment Company. This was now at the front 150 miles away, near Taganrog.

'We were given our documents, no supplies and no transport, and were told to make our own way as best we could. Quite soon I was separated from my companions. I never saw them again. I was starving and freezing. I had to beg my way from farm to farm. The peasants had already been overrun twice, first by the Germans and then by the Russians, and they were not at all keen to see another soldier. I was terrified the whole time that I would be picked up by the NKVD, who would think I was a deserter.

'When I finally arrived at my destination, I was attached to a platoon under Lieutenant Leonov. Our doctor, Major Artashev, had previously commanded a medical battalion but had been relegated to lesser duties when the nurses, who had joined his personal harem, fell out with one another and the whole arrangement was denounced to the authorities. We froze in broken-down trenches, and we were literally starving because the supply system had broken down. We were in no condition to fight. Luckily the sector was quiet, although one night we were roused out to be told that a sentry had been found asleep on duty. He was led straight off to be shot.

'Then things began to change. Officers with periscopes began to study the German positions, well dug in several hundred yards away up a frozen hill. We were given vodka and meat for the first time. That night we were told to attack the German line, break through, and capture the village beyond. Leonov led us at a crawl towards the German positions. We were almost there before the Germans discovered us. Between bursts of machine-gun fire we rushed forward. Then we ran into a minefield. Leonov gave the order to retire. Our platoon lost a third of its strength.

'It was obvious that the attack had been a feint. Our commanders had known of the minefield. They never expected us to break through it: they were simply trying to get the Germans to reveal their positions. A couple of days later I was called to the company commander, Captain Vasenin. He told me that my sentence had been annulled: Leonov had reported that I had shown exceptional courage in the battle, though I couldn't remember any such thing. I asked if I could say goodbye to Leonov before I left. No, said Vasenin: Leonov had already been shot on the orders of the divisional commander for withdrawing from the battle without orders. I was only in the punishment company for three weeks.

'I was then sent to the rear for further training. I was posted to a Katyusha rocket unit in the 51st Guard Regiment and fought my way through Ukraine, Romania, Bulgaria, Yugoslavia, Hungary, and Austria. I was wounded twice. My final military action in the war was to bombard the big wheel in the Prater in Vienna. I returned there many years later and was amused to see that the wheel has a plaque saying that it was shelled by Soviet artillery. I was demobilised a year after the end of the war, went to live with my mother in Moscow, and took an external law degree.'[42]

Like Semën Aria, Vladimir Kantovski reached his punishment unit by a route both circuitous and bizarre. After their anonymous protest against the arrest of their favourite history teacher, he and his classmates were left to finish their exams in peace. But as soon as the war broke out, he was arrested. So were his two girl accomplices, Lena Sobol and Anya Bovshever.

One of the first people he met in the Lubyanka as they both underwent the routine humiliating body search was Sergei Shcheglov. Shcheglov was two years older than Kantovski. He came from a poor family in the provincial town of Murom. His mother was very religious, and his schoolmates teased him because he sang in the local church.[43]

In 1937 his father was arrested and shot and his mother was sent to a camp. He went to live with an aunt. He and his school friends set up a 'Political Economy Discussion Group' to study Marx's *Capital* and discuss the Soviet economy. Shcheglov was called in by the NKVD and asked to spy on the group. He refused as tactfully as he knew how.

In autumn 1940 Shcheglov got a scholarship to study at the Moscow Region Pedagogical Institute. He passed his first-year exams on the morning of 22 June 1941, and started planning for his summer holiday.[44] Still ignorant that the war had started, he went off to have his hair cut. The loudspeaker in the corner of the barber's shop was playing soft music when it was suddenly interrupted, and Molotov spoke. A girl hairdresser burst into tears: her boyfriend was in a military unit on the Western frontier. Shcheglov's spirits rose: from now on every hour would be significant, every day a milestone of history.[45]

The next morning he went to the Komsomol to volunteer. He was told to return to his institute and wait to be called. He got back to find everything in chaos. Books, rolls of maps, diagrams, posters were piled up on the floor. Students were removing tables, benches, stands, lecterns, lamps from the teaching rooms and the lecture halls. The institute was being turned into a military hospital.

The secret policemen had not forgotten Shcheglov's earlier refusal to cooperate. Amid all the confusion, he was called to the Rector's office. A man in the uniform of the secret police was sitting on the sofa. Two civilians were by the window, one in a grey suit, one in a brown. He was asked for his identity card and his Komsomol card, told that he had been arrested, and shown the warrant. The two civilians searched him efficiently, and laid his possessions out on the Rector's table: a penknife, a notebook, a pencil, a union card, a couple of dozen roubles, a savings book, a cigarette case which the policeman returned. He was driven off in a van to his hostel, his possessions there were searched, and he was told to take them all with him. He was then delivered to the Lubyanka.[46]

Shcheglov and Kantovski soon struck up a close friendship, which lasted into old age. They struggled to make sense of their arrest. Kantovski believed there was a fascist plot to undermine the Soviet state by persuading its leaders that they were surrounded by traitors. Shcheglov thought the regime was bound to assume that they had become enemies after the arrest of their parents. Kantovski criticised Stalin, his destruction of the old Bolsheviks, the mass arrests, the accusations of treachery. He was so vehement that Shcheglov began to suspect that he might be a provocateur. He told Kantovski he was too young to judge such matters. Kantovski retorted that he was the same age as many of the Bolsheviks were when they began their political careers.

The two were moved to the prison in Omsk in Siberia, where Dostoevsky had been incarcerated a century earlier. Eighty inmates were now housed in cells that had been constructed in Tsarist times for six. Shcheglov's interrogators tried to get him to admit that his discussion group at school was a cover for the meetings of an anti-Soviet conspiracy. He doggedly denied the charge, and the interrogators were unable to make it stick. They sent him off to a labour camp in Norilsk in the Far North, where he remained for the next five years.

Kantovski was interrogated once only. 'My interrogator had all the letters that we had circulated, and it was an open and shut case of counter-revolutionary conspiracy. In December 1941 Anya Bovshever and I were sentenced to ten years' forced labour; Lena Sobol was given a five-year suspended sentence. I was transferred to a labour camp near Omsk where we were set to build an aircraft factory. The conditions were freezing, the food was barely enough to survive, scurvy and pneumonia were rife. Prisoners died like flies.

'I bombarded the authorities with letters, asking to be sent to the front. Eventually I was posted to a punishment company. At that point in the war the Red Army was forming units from national groups – Czechs, Poles, Lithuanians, Latvians, and so on. The people at the Omsk VoenKomat were delighted to discover that I was technically a Latvian. I was given a travel pass and rations, and sent off on my own by ordinary passenger train to one of the military camps near Gorki, where reinforcements were being trained for the 43rd Latvian Guards Division.

'But the authorities in Gorki could not decide whether to treat me as a Latvian guardsman or as a criminal with my sentence still to run. For safety's sake, they posted me to a punishment company on the Northwest Front.' Once again Kantovski was sent off on his own, by ordinary passenger train, without an escort, a journey across Russia at war worthy of the Good Soldier Schweik which lasted for a whole month.

'After some hanging about, our unit was sent into an attack ahead of the main force, presumably to draw the Germans' fire and get them to reveal their positions. The tanks we were given in support only got fifty yards before they were pinned down or destroyed. I was badly wounded in the arm, and crawled back to the Soviet lines with difficulty. Out of my company of 250 men, I was later told, only seven survived unwounded: they were all given medals. I was discharged from the army because of my wound, and resumed my studies.'[47]

Alexander Pyltsyn did not serve in a punishment unit as a prisoner: he was assigned as a lieutenant in 1943 to command a platoon in the 8th Punishment Battalion of Rokossovski's 1st Belorussian Front. Men under his command were former officers, more experienced and older than he was. He worried about his ability to exercise authority over them. But they were a disciplined lot on the whole, though they did have a distressing tendency to laugh at military policemen who incautiously threatened them with time in a punishment unit if they misbehaved.

Punishment units, said Pyltsyn, were formed on a simple basis: you could always find enough 'guilty' people if you looked. Many of the soldiers serving in punishment companies had been released from the camps and prisons. Although some officers were sent to punishment battalions on the arbitrary decision of a superior, most had been sentenced for military offences by court martial. One man in Pyltsyn's own unit was captured by the Germans at the beginning of the war. He escaped, got back to his own people, and went on fighting. When Order No. 227 came out, he was sent straight off to a punishment battalion. Another had been involved in a battle for a village in which he had lost half his men. Once the fighting was over, he had sent his sergeant back to collect the rations, but omitted to point out that his ration strength was sadly diminished. He handed out the extra food and vodka to the survivors; they toasted the memory of the dead – and someone denounced him for stealing government property. Another had been in charge of a workshop for repairing ships' radios. He had picked up a broadcast in German. It was Goebbels. His colleagues asked him to translate. He was sent to a punishment battalion for spreading enemy propaganda. Another officer had called home after lying in hospital wounded, to find his wife with another man. He had killed them both. He too was sent to Pyltsyn's unit.

Casualties in punishment units were very high. But at no point in the war was a blocking detachment ever posted behind Pyltsyn's unit. As with ordinary units, the level of casualties depended on the situation on the ground and the competence of the commanding officers. At the beginning of 1944 Pyltsyn's battalion was attached to the 3rd Army under General Alexander Gorbatov, who had himself been in a camp and released, like Rokossovski, on the eve of the war. The battalion was ordered to break through the German line so that the rest of the army could move forward. The operation was successful. Out of eight hundred and fifty men in the battalion, only forty were killed. Gorbatov arranged for all to receive medals, and many were restored to their former ranks. But in October 1944 Pyltsyn's battalion was transferred to the 65th Army under General Batov. To recover a position which the Army had recently had to abandon, they were sent across what the staff knew was an uncleared German minefield. They achieved their objective, but only one man in five survived.[48]

In the initial weeks of the war, when everyone from Stalin downwards was in a state of shock, anything seemed justified if it would help to stem the onrush of the Germans. Harsh though these measures were, they were not in principle either unprecedented or unnecessary. Some process of filtration was unavoidable as men streamed back from encirclement: it was not a myth that the Germans were trying to persuade their prisoners to go back through the lines as agents. And the killing of panicky men by their officers to get the rest to return to the battle has been practised by all countries in all wars. The provisions of Order No. 270 have their equivalent in the military codes of other nations. Communicating with the enemy, failing to engage the enemy, failing to give chase to an enemy, attempting to surrender, refusing to obey an order, desertion, mutiny, failure to denounce a conspiracy to mutiny, striking a superior office, wrecking one's ship, sleeping on duty, robbery, sodomy and buggery – all these were crimes for which, until well into the nineteenth century, officers and men of the Royal Navy 'being convicted thereof by the sentence of a court martial, shall suffer death'.[49] Nor were these matters by any means always settled by due process. One British officer, who ordered the machine guns to be turned on his fleeing Portuguese allies, became a pacifist and wrote a book to ease a conscience troubled by the number of his own men he had shot out of hand on the battlefields of the First World War. Even so, he never wavered from his belief that

> Men will hold out, and do hold out, in isolated posts, to the bitter end – till all are dead or wounded. But when once put on the run – by surprise or weight of metal or numbers – panic will at times overtake the very best, particularly when isolated and only partly trained and raw. It is then that the situation can only be saved by a well-aimed shot. You see, *the line must be held at all costs*.[50]

But the executions in the Red Army were on such a massive scale that they were counterproductive. One of the perverse consequences was that ordinary soldiers began to wonder whether the army was indeed riddled with treachery, and whether it made sense to trust their own officers. By the autumn of 1941, the situation had reached such a pitch that Stalin himself felt moved to intervene. In his Order No. 391 of 4 October 1941, he criticised commanders for resorting to abuse, physical assault, and 'repression' (a euphemism in this case for shooting), often to cover their own panic and confusion on the battlefield.[51] 'Repression,' he said, 'is an extreme measure, allowable only in circumstances of direct disobedience and open resistance in conditions of battle, or in cases of malicious violation of discipline and order by people who are consciously attempting to undermine the orders of their commanders.' Discipline and morale could only be maintained by a proper combination of persuasion and compulsion. Unjustified repression, illegal shootings, arbitrary behaviour and the use of personal physical violence by commanders and political commissars were evidence of lack of will and lack of ability, and often produced the opposite of the results intended. They contributed to a decline in military discipline and in the morale of the troops, and could push wavering soldiers into running away to the side of the enemy. Stalin could not resist concluding these sensible remarks on a characteristically severe note. Those who disobeyed the principles he had laid down would be court-martialled. His order was to be brought to the attention of commanders from the rank of colonel upwards.

These admirable sentiments by no means brought the exercise of harsh and arbitrary discipline to an end. Only nine days after Stalin had called for a more measured approach Zhukov said, in his first Order to his soldiers on taking over the Western Front, that 'cowards and panic-mongers, who abandon the field of battle, who retreat without permission from their positions, abandon their weapons and vehicles' were to be shot on the spot.[52]

Figures for those who were sent to punishment units and for those who were executed on the battlefield or following sentence by court martial are unclear. A conservative study concluded in 2001 that nearly a million members of the armed forces were sentenced by the courts during the war, more than a third for desertion. More than four hundred thousand of these men had their sentences suspended, and were sent to punishment units. The study confirms that casualty rates in punishment units were particularly high: in 1944 three to six times higher than those in normal units. Of the remainder of those sentenced, 135,000 were shot, the equivalent of thirteen divisions of infantry.[53] These figures take no account of those who were executed on the battlefield or behind the lines without any formal proceedings at all.

Stalin claimed in Order No. 227 that the idea of punishment battalions was taken from German practice. In the last months of the war, at least, the Germans' repressive measures against their own soldiers were indeed as savage as those of the Russians. Tens of thousands of German soldiers were sent to penal battalions, nearly 45,000 were sent for court martial in October 1944 alone, and there were 15,000 recorded executions – to say nothing of those that were not recorded.[54]

– NINE –

THE EYE OF THE STORM

As soon as he heard that the war in Russia had begun, the British journalist Alexander Werth was determined to get to it. He had covered the fall of France, the Battle of Britain and the London Blitz. Born in St Petersburg, with Russian as his first language, he was not a Communist. But he was prepared to recognise the regime's achievements and was occasionally too ready to apologise for its failings. Sentimental and sometimes gullible, he had a strong sense of the Russian people, of their literature, and of the cities and the countryside in which they lived. He understood what the war meant to ordinary Russians, and it was this which enabled him later to write *Russia at War*, still one of the most vivid accounts in the English language.

Moscow at the beginning of July 1941 was still in its summer dress, still surprisingly untouched by the war, almost in a holiday mood. In the rosy sunsets and the clear blue skies the Moscow River had an almost Mediterranean colour. Because it was hard to evade the official barriers and get at the real news, Werth spent his time wandering around the streets, admiring the girls in their white blouses, going in and out of the second-hand bookshops. He visited the Hermitage Garden with its well-kept flower beds, with its three separate theatres and its concert hall, its buffets still selling cheese and ham and sausage and sandwiches and sweets and chocolates and plates of tomato and cucumber and sugar buns. He found his way down nondescript streets with buildings from the 1860s, past wooden cottages looking like something out of a seventeenth-century print, and out along the Highway of the Enthusiasts ('They do give absurd names to streets'), the highway to the East along which panic-stricken crowds would try to escape from the city four months later.[1]

Though he knew the language, Werth imagined, like so many travellers, that he could judge the politics of the country from the expressions on people's faces. It was all much better than he had expected. Moscow looked surprisingly prosperous, food seemed plentiful, the people were well dressed:

> These people do not look unhappy; and since ordinary living conditions have improved so much in the last two or three years, they felt that they were owing a great deal to the regime ... The shoe shine girl rubbing the white shoes of a citizen was joking and laughing. There were crowds around the lemonade stall and queues for newspapers, but none for cigarettes, which are plentiful.

Dr S. G. Dreitser, who worked in the capital's first aid service, was noting sourly at about the same time: 'It's getting harder to buy food. Ice cream is still being sold everywhere. The elegant Moscow cafés have become common eating houses: the tablecloths have disappeared, the spoons are now made of tin, and the waitresses have become ruder.'[2]

From time to time the journalists were taken by their minders in the Foreign Ministry on carefully managed forays into the countryside. Werth and his colleagues were driven out along the Leningrad Highway to the monastery town of Istra, where Chekhov had practised medicine and some of the fiercest fighting of the Battle of Moscow was later to take place. All the signposts had been removed.

> There were many small rivers and ponds along the roadside, where naked little boys were bathing and waving at us. ... Along the road, lorries, camouflaged with foliage and crowded with smiling, fairly cheerful soldiers, were moving towards the front. There were also many soldiers in the main square of Istra. It was a rather nondescript town, with a fruit shop, where they sold some tins; two or three

> lemonade carts, and an ice-cream stall, for which there were queues of soldiers and boys. We drove out of Istra along the same road. We passed through villages, where the hens were scuttling and the geese ambulating along the road … And everywhere there was the same contrast between old and new. Striking was the enormous number of children, all healthy and cheerful-looking; the smaller ones waved as we drove past. Women were going about carrying large rye loaves, and cows sometimes got in our way and there were many goats and kids grazing by the roadside.[3]

The theatres and the cinemas were still operating at full flood: on Sundays there were fourteen different theatrical shows. Not everyone was happy with the wide range of work on offer. Gridaspov, the Deputy Director of the Department for Artistic Affairs in the Moscow City Council, was appalled by the way the theatre repertoire had been polluted by plays openly hostile to the Soviet ideology. In the course of 1941 he succeeded, despite the opposition of some quite senior officials, in banning fourteen plays. They included *The Motherland*, a play which (claimed Gridaspov) preached Zionism; Aristophanes' pacifist *Lysistrata*, which incited women to oppose war; *Trilby*, based on George du Maurier's novel, a clear example of 'mystical deviation'; J. B. Priestley's *Time and the Conways*, which masqueraded as an attack on the decadence of the bourgeoisie, but was actually intended to give the spectator a taste for the most perverted eroticism. Gridaspov disapproved even of Konstantin Simonov's inoffensive *Story of a Love*. As a result of his energetic purge, Gridaspov reported proudly, by 1942 one-third of the works performed in the Moscow theatres dealt with patriotic themes. Sadly, there had been much backsliding on the part of managements and performers alike. He had been compelled to intervene forcefully when the management of one theatre attempted to replace Simonov's patriotic play *Russian People* with a romantic comedy, on the excuse that the lead actress, Valentina Serova (Simonov's partner), had left for Sverdlovsk. Things were pretty bad at the opera too. It was difficult, admitted Gridaspov, to object to such established classics as *The Queen of Spades*, *Tosca*, and *La Traviata*, although these pessimistic works aroused the audience to quite inappropriate emotions. But why did no one perform a patriotic piece such as Rossini's *William Tell*; or for that matter Shakespeare's *Henry IV*, or the unjustly forgotten plays of Corneille, with their theme of the citizen's duty towards the state?[4]

Alexander Werth went to see everything he could, as fascinated by the audience as by what he saw on the stage. The evergreen *Chapaev* was still on at cinemas throughout the town, six years after its première. The young people watching *Volga, Volga* screamed with laughter throughout. The film was 'very good fresh fun, with a nice touch of craziness'. Werth thought it would make excellent Russian propaganda if it could be shown in England, though he personally did not much care for Orlova. When the audience cheered Stalin during the newsreel he concluded, 'He must enjoy general popularity among the ordinary people here; for people don't cheer in the dark unless they really feel like it.'[5]

At a performance of *Anna Karenina* at the Moscow Art Theatre on 16 August,

> The theatre was sobbing; I looked back – two young girls behind me were weeping buckets, really *enjoying themselves.* How much sentimental *tendresse*, natural human expression, there is in these ordinary Soviet girls; their souls haven't been toughened by the hard fire of Stalinist propaganda; they haven't been made impervious to ordinary human emotion ... When the curtain dropped, after Anna had been duly run over by the railway train ... hundreds of young girls swarmed to the front of the stalls, shouting frantically for Anna. How much youthful spontaneity, what a fund of generous instincts there is among these young people of Russia![6]

The Bolshoi Theatre was still closed for repair. But the performance of Tchaikovsky's *Eugene Onegin* in the theatre's Annexe in Pushkin Street was the highlight of Werth's summer. As the lights went out he was keyed up for the opening melody on the woodwind, but instead

> there was a blare of brass, and the curtain went up on a patriotic chorus of women dressed up in sarafans, and bearded warriors in glittering helmets and mailed armour, and resting with both hands on enormous swords. It was the patriotic prologue to Glinka's *A Life for the Tsar*, now called *Ivan Susanin* ... Kozlovski, the sweet tenor [who

> sang Lenski in *Eugene Onegin*], is the idol of the youth of Moscow, or rather one of the two idols, the other being the tenor Lemeshev; and Moscow is really divided into two camps, the Kozlovski fans and the Lemeshev fans. There is a parallel feud among the ballet-goers, between the worshippers of Ulanova and those of Lepeshinskaya, the two rival *prima ballerinas*. Only in a country where the theatre is really part of life, and not one of the frills of life, can people feel so strongly about such matters.

Werth's romantic belief in the universal devotion of the Russian people to their national culture was dented by his neighbour, 'a lanky, rather stupid-looking lad of twenty-five or so, in an embroidered shirt. ... He said he was a house-painter, and was working on the present repairs at the Bolshoi Theatre. After the first act he suddenly asked me what was "going to happen now and what this play was all about?"' Werth was shocked to discover that the house-painter had never seen the opera nor read the Pushkin poem on which it is based.[7]

It was the calm at the eye of the storm, an illusion. Despite the outward appearance of normality, Moscow was, of course, already a city at war. When Werth tried to buy a map of Moscow, he was surprised to be told by the startled shop assistants that there was none available. A Western colleague told him he was lucky not to have been taken for a spy.[8]

There had already been one false air-raid alarm by the time Werth arrived, and the Muscovites were preparing for the real thing. Trucks were delivering sand all over the city for people to put into sandbags. One of them dumped a large pile of sand outside Werth's apartment. A young couple started to fill bags. A pompous elderly man with an official badge shouted at them that they had no right to take the sand, which belonged to the state. A crowd gathered to support the two young people, who took no notice of the official, whoever he was. Similar tussles over firewood, sandbags, rubbish bins, building material for shelters, took place throughout the city.

New censorship regulations had already been introduced. It was forbidden to communicate any military, economic or political information, to send postcards with views or photographs, to correspond in

Braille, to transmit crosswords or chess problems. The military censorship read all correspondence and either inked over or cut out any passage it disliked. Letters to and from the front were sent without envelopes or stamps: they were simply folded into a triangle. This made life simpler for the censors.[9] By November 1941 the NKVD censors in Moscow alone were reading nearly three million incoming letters a fortnight, at a time when the British censors were only managing to get through two hundred thousand letters a week. Both the NKVD and the British used their reading of people's correspondence to form an estimate of the state of their morale.[10]

People were already hoarding salt, matches, buckwheat, sugar, canned food, flour, stuffing them into their cupboards, their bathtubs, and every spare space they could find. Elderly women laid in stocks of vodka, not to drink themselves, but to serve as currency when things got scarce. On 17 July the Moscow City Council formally introduced rationing of bread, flour, cereals, macaroni, butter, margarine, vegetable oil, meat, fish, sugar, confectionery, and consumer goods. The cards were issued at one's place of work. Dependants and children received them at home from the building administrator. The daily ration of bread for all manual workers was 800 grams, for office workers 600 grams, for children and dependants 400 grams. The monthly ration of buckwheat and macaroni was two kilograms for a worker and 1.5 kilograms for the rest. The monthly ration of meat was 2.2 kilograms, 1.2 kilograms and 600 grams respectively. Blood donors were given a worker's ration card in addition to their own, as well as various supplementary coupons. Food cards were given out once a month, cards for consumer goods once every half-year. You had to register as a customer in a particular shop, and could not use your cards elsewhere. The cards could not be renewed if they were lost. If you lost your card, or if it was stolen, you risked starvation. [11]

Most people's rations fell well short of minimum nutritional levels. The shortfall fell especially hard on white-collar workers and on dependants, particularly children over twelve years old. Rationing was almost as strict in Britain. But in wartime Britain you could be reasonably sure of getting what you were entitled to. In wartime Russia this was not so.

> The rationing system in the USSR during World War II was thus not simply a matter, as elsewhere, of distributing the available food in such a way as to achieve a balance of economic efficiency and social fairness. It also meant the authorities being forced to take decisions about whom to preserve and whom to abandon of a kind comparable only with those familiar to food relief workers in the midst of major famines today.[12]

But the ice-cream woman still came every morning to sell her wares to the small boys waiting for her on the corner of Gorky Street.

Privilege continued. Party officials, scientists, creative and performing artists, and sportsmen, together with their close relatives, could do their shopping in special closed stores and canteens. Academicians and People's Artists got a monthly parcel of food from their place of work worth 500 roubles: meat, fish, macaroni, fat, sugar, potatoes, vegetables, soap, tea, tobacco, vodka or wine. The next category down, Corresponding Members of the Academy of Sciences and the like, got parcels worth 300 roubles.[13] It was of course the same system that had operated before the war.

As in Britain, the introduction of rationing generated a whole range of new crimes and spawned a whole class of new criminals. For one thing, the system was not easy to administer. The authorities were slow to issue the cards. People leaving Moscow legally or illegally gave or sold their cards to those who stayed behind. For a suitable bribe, officials could get extra cards by simply failing to report that people they were responsible for had already been evacuated. The shop assistants took an age to count up the coupons, weigh out the goods, and sell them, and they were not above cheating their often semi-literate customers.[14] Building administrators exploited their position by swapping spare ration cards for gold, fur coats, carpets and rare porcelain. They were regularly arrested by the militia. But their successors were equally tempted and soon succumbed.[15] One building administrator, Maria Glinkina, specialised in robbing the apartments of those who had been evacuated. When her own apartment was searched, the police found among other things ten gramophones – worth some 300 roubles on the market. She was sentenced to be shot, but the sentence was commuted to eight years in prison.[16] The more ambitious moved from fraud to forgery. Kolya Leonov, a sixty-year-old artist from the Stalin Car Factory, photographed and printed ration cards for bread, which he sold on the black market. Others forged Moscow residence passes for those who had no permission to live in the city. One man who was caught was sent to a punishment battalion and died in battle.[17]

By the beginning of August the government was pulling out all the emotional stops to touch chords in the Soviet people which went beyond the clichés of Communism. In a passionate and deeply un-Marxist address to his congregation at the Bogoyavlenski Cathedral in Moscow on 10 August, the Metropolitan of Leningrad, Aleksi, drew the inextricable and intimate connection between Russian patriotism and Russian religion. Had not Alexander Nevsky proclaimed that 'God is not Power but Truth' when he smote the Teutonic Knights at the Battle on the Ice? Had not Dmitri Donskoi sought the blessing of St Sergei of Radonezh before going to defeat the Tatars at the Battle of Kulikovo Field? Had not two of Russia's most revered saints died in that battle? God had led Napoleon to the walls of Moscow as if to give the Russian people the chance to show what they could do when their Motherland – the land of Mary the Mother of God – was in danger. Now once again the Russian people were called upon to save themselves and the whole civilised world from the madness of a tyrant. Now once again it was their noble mission to rid the world of the evil of fascism, to liberate the nations which it had enslaved, and to restore to the world the peace which fascism had so crudely violated.[18]

On 24 August the Soviet Union's most distinguished Jews met to issue a similar appeal to 'Brother Jews of the Whole World!' Among the participants were the film director Sergei Eisenstein, the physicist Peter Kapitsa, and the architect Boris Iofan. The theatre producer Solomon Mikhoels was there too, and others who were to die in Stalin's anti-Semitic campaigns after the war. Ilya Ehrenburg delivered a key speech, which touched on themes felt increasingly strongly by Russian Jews:

> I grew up in a Russian city. My mother tongue is Russian. I am a Russian writer. Like all Russians, I am now defending my homeland. But the Nazis have reminded me of something else: my mother's name was Hanna. I am a Jew. I say this with pride. Hitler hates us

> above all. And that is our distinction [...] I appeal now to the Jews of America – as a Russian writer and as a Jew. There is no ocean behind which to take cover. ... Do not shut your ears, do not close your eyes! [...] We Jews are the main target of the beast! Our place is in the first ranks. We will not forgive those who are indifferent. We will curse those who wash their hands [...] Let each do all he is capable of. Soon he will be asked: what did you do? He will answer to the living. He will answer to the dead. He will answer to himself![19]

Aleksei Tolstoy addressed himself at another meeting to fellow Slavs: Ukrainians, Belorussians, Poles, Czechs, Slovaks, Serbs, Croats, Bosnians, Bulgars, Slovenians, and Ruthenians. The Slav unity he invoked was not, he hastened to reassure them, the same as the Pan-Slavism of the Tsars, that instrument of Russian nationalism. But the moment had now come for all Slavs, bound by their common origins and their common struggle, to unite as equals to throw off the fascist yoke. Hitler had said in *Mein Kampf*, 'Who can deny my right to destroy millions of Slavs, who multiply like insects?' The Germans had given the world wonderful music, poetry, philosophy. They now needed to cleanse themselves of the filth of Hitler's fascism. One hundred and sixty million Eastern Slavs – the peoples of Russia, Ukraine, Belorussia – were fighting alongside the powerful and freedom-loving people of Britain. The Slavs must now go united into battle, under the cry: Victory or Death! Death to fascism![20] The final document of the conference repeated the now universal slogan: Blood for Blood! Death for Death![21]

The newspapers, too, set out to build morale. *Krasnaya Zvezda*, the army newspaper, published lists of soldiers who had been awarded medals, articles from a partisan unit behind the German lines, and a 'Song of the Commissars' complete with score.[22] The Moscow evening newspaper *Vechernyaya Moskva* carried a peaceful picture – it could have appeared in any summer before the war – of a pretty girl sitting on the embankment watching skiffs compete on the Moscow River.[23] But editors had to watch their step. Even the most positive material could attract critical attention from those above them. At the end of August Stalin rang Ortenberg, the editor of *Krasnaya Zvezda*, out of the blue.

The message was crisp: 'Stop printing so much about Koniev.' Koniev's 19th Army had been operating successfully in the Yelnia counterattack. Ortenberg had run a series of reports with headings such as 'Successful Operations by the Units of Commander Koniev' and 'Koniev's Glorious Troops Have Destroyed an Enemy Division'. Who Koniev was, or whether he commanded a battalion, a brigade, or an army, was kept deliberately obscure so as to give nothing away to the enemy. Ortenberg was baffled: what had he done wrong? Later that night Mekhlis rang with an explanation. Stalin thought that foreign correspondents had been blowing Koniev's operations out of proportion, at a time when things were going badly for the Red Army elsewhere. That did not seem to Ortenberg a sufficient reason to pass over the Red Army's few successes. But he did not print Koniev's name again.[24]

On 22 August the GKO took the formal decision to allow each soldier on active duty a ration of one hundred grams of vodka a day.[25] It was doubtless a welcome decision, though it is hard to believe that the soldiers had not already found their own ways of laying hands on the stuff.

Apprehension began to grow as July turned into August. Despite the absence of reliable official information, Werth noted in his diary on 11 July that the big offensive against Moscow was expected at any minute. Fighting flared around Smolensk, on the direct route to the capital. People began to say that Moscow itself might have to be abandoned. An officer in the British Military Mission told Werth that the Russians would have difficulty saving their troops: he was no longer sure that 'we' would stay in Moscow. Vera Maximovna, Werth's neighbour, thought that the Russians, who had gone through the Great War, the Civil War, and years of famine, would not be able to stand this war for very long: 'They can't stand as much as the British.' Such defeatist remarks were hotly resented by many Russians. But morale was beginning to wobble: 'If a girl said no nowadays, the lad replied: "Saving it up for the Germans, eh?"'[26]

But the moment of maximum danger for Moscow had not yet struck. In the middle of July Hitler and his generals took a crucial, perhaps an inevitable, decision which postponed the crisis for more than two months.

Smolensk is two hundred and fifty miles from Moscow, on the banks of the Dnieper River. It is one of Russia's oldest cities, a key barrier to any army invading Russia from the West. Appropriately its coat of arms is a black cannon on a golden carriage, with a bird of paradise perched on top of it. The city was massively fortified at the end of the sixteenth century, with walls thirty-six feet high, fifteen feet thick, and four miles long. It held out against the Poles from 1609 to 1611. It was at Smolensk that Napoleon met the first serious resistance on his road to Moscow, and the city was burned to the ground after an overwhelming artillery bombardment. In July 1941 the Russians prepared to make a stand there once again.

Timoshenko was now in command of the Western Front in place of the disgraced Pavlov. The forces at his disposal were a motley lot. The bedraggled remnants of the Western Front were still falling back. They were being joined by two new armies: Koniev's 19th Army from the Southwest and Lukin's 16th Army from beyond the Urals. Timoshenko had barely two hundred tanks and less than four hundred battered aircraft at his disposal. But inadequate though these forces were, German intelligence had not identified them all, and the Germans had a harder fight of it than they expected.

The Germans followed their well-tried plan. Hoth's Third Panzer Group enveloped Smolensk from the North. Guderian's Second Panzer Group crossed the river to outflank it from the South. The Russians launched a series of desperate counterattacks. The legendary General Dovator – Jewish, a dashing commander, a hero to his Cossack (and traditionally anti-Semitic) troopers and to the Soviet public at large – led a cavalry raid deep into the German lines. It was in vain. Smolensk itself was captured on 16 July. Lukin, Koniev, and Remizov's 20th Army were trapped in a rapidly diminishing pocket to the North and West of the city. The Germans closed in for the kill.

Timoshenko was ordered to hold open an escape route for the encircled armies. Rokossovski was brought up from the South to Yartsevo, Northeast of Smolensk, to take over one of four 'Operational Groups' cobbled together for the purpose. He brought with him his staff from the 9th Mechanised Corps: Malinin, his Chief of Staff; his artillery commander, Kazakov; his communications officer, Maksimenko; and his tank commander Orël. Some of the divisions he took over were very run down: one consisted of no more than 260 men, another even fewer. He supplemented them by collecting together whatever disorganised bits and pieces of units he could find. Many of the soldiers who reached him from encirclement had no weapons. He organised raiding parties to go behind the lines to pick up weapons abandoned by the retreating soldiers. In this way he was able to rearm most of his men. He also had some multiple rocket launchers, nicknamed 'Katyusha' after the song which Lidia Ruslanova had made so popular before the war. These formidable new weapons had just seen action for the first time, but they were still so secret that there were crippling restrictions on their use, less they fall into German hands. Rokossovski set the restrictions aside so that he could use them effectively.[27]

On 31 July Guderian struck at the Operational Group commanded by General Kachalov and all but destroyed it. On 4 August, as his people got bogged down, Kachalov commandeered a tank, took himself right up to the front line to get a better grip, and failed to return. One of his staff, Captain Pogrebinski, reported that Kachalov had been joking about German leaflets calling on Soviet soldiers to surrender. Stalin concluded that Kachalov had gone over to the Germans.[28] He was pilloried in Order No. 270, stripped of his rank and honours and condemned to death *in absentia*. His wife and mother-in-law were arrested and sentenced to eight years in prison, and his son was sent to an orphanage. Much later, rumours began to emerge that Kachalov had been killed in his tank and buried in a common grave by the inhabitants of a village called Starinka. A commission went to the village after the liberation, and exhumed the remains. Kachalov had been a big man, and his body was easily identified.[29]

Despite the best attempts of the Germans to close the gap, Rokossovski was able to hold a corridor open for the vestiges of the three armies trapped at Smolensk to escape. Lukin was wounded in the breakout. Rokossovski therefore combined the poor remains of Lukin's 16th Army with those of his own Operational Group to re-form the 16th Army. This Army too was consumed in the fighting over the next few weeks. Rokossovski put together yet another 16th Army in the second week of October, which performed with particular distinction under his command in the autumn and winter fighting before Moscow.

In the middle of August the new Bryansk Front under Yerëmenko and the Reserve Front now commanded by Zhukov attacked the salient which the Germans had carved out for themselves at Yelnia, Southeast of Smolensk. After much bloody fighting, the Russians expelled the Germans from the salient. But they had too few tanks and aircraft to hold it, and the Germans took it back when the front rolled towards Moscow in the autumn. The Yelnia operation thus had no strategic significance. But it was one of the first Russian successes since the catastrophe on the frontier, and Stalin hailed it as a significant victory. Four of the divisions involved were renamed 'Guards Divisions', the first use of a title which became widespread as formations and units distinguished themselves in the fighting to come. For the first time Alexander Werth and his fellow correspondents were taken to the front to see a battlefield for themselves.[30]

The Yelnia operation reinforced Zhukov's reputation with Stalin as a ruthless commander, the right man for a rough affair, in Molotov's phrase. He was the obvious man to go to Leningrad, where the local political and military leaders seemed unable to prevent the Germans closing in. Stalin sent him there on 8 September, and in less than a month, forceful and brutal as ever, he had got things under control.[31] The Germans helped by diverting Hoth's Third Panzer Group to the Moscow front to strengthen the forthcoming attack on the capital. Instead of taking Leningrad by storm, the Germans now intended to starve it to death. They nearly succeeded. Over the next nine hundred days nearly a million people died in the city.

The Battle of Smolensk lasted from 10 July to 10 September. Once again the Russians suffered far heavier losses than the Germans.[32] Historians disagree about the importance of the battle. At the time Shaposhnikov, who had now replaced Zhukov as Chief of Staff, had little doubt. He told Stalin in early August that the Russians had lost the opening period of the war outright. The strategic initiative lay entirely with the enemy. The Russians were still uncertain in defence, their frontline divisions were well under strength, and their reserves were inadequate or non-existent. But resistance to the Germans before Leningrad was becoming more determined by the day. Above all, said Shaposhnikov, the fighting around Smolensk had enabled the Russians to stop the German armies on the most dangerous axis of all, the axis which led to Moscow.[33]

Certainly the Germans had good reason to pause for thought. In the first four weeks of the war the Wehrmacht had secured stunning victories on the frontiers, and had pushed hundreds of miles into the interior towards the Soviet Union's three main cities, Leningrad, Kiev and Moscow. They had wiped out whole Soviet armies. They had destroyed thousands of Soviet aircraft and tanks. They had captured hundreds of thousands of dazed, shocked, and leaderless Soviet soldiers. This was what blitzkrieg was intended to achieve. Surely Hitler had been right in his original judgement that one short sharp blow against the rotten colossus of the Soviet system would bring it down? On 3 July, the same day as Stalin broadcast to the Soviet people, General Halder, the Chief of Staff of the Army, noted in his diary that it was 'probably no understatement to say that the Russian campaign has been won in the space of two weeks'.[34]

He soon started to change his mind. A month later he wrote:

> The whole situation makes it increasingly plain that we have underestimated the Russian colossus ... [Soviet divisions] are not armed and equipped according to our standards, and their tactical leadership is often poor. But there they are, and if we smash a dozen of them the Russians simply put up another dozen. The time factor favours them, as they are near their own resources, while we are moving farther and farther away from ours. And so our troops, sprawled over an immense front line, without any depth, are subjected to the incessant attacks of the enemy.[35]

Halder had put his finger on the nub of the problem, the inescapable fact which would eventually lead the Germans to defeat: the Russian ability – unsuspected by German intelligence – to reconstitute divisions as fast as they were destroyed, and the inability of the Germans to sustain a long campaign over the vast territory of Russia. The Wehrmacht's planning and resources had been designed for a rapid blitzkrieg leading to early victory and the destruction of the Red Army West of the Dvina and Dnieper rivers. Now the Germans were across those rivers. But the Russians were still fighting, and they had reduced the German rate of advance from twenty to five miles a day.[36]

The Germans were no longer in a position to pursue all three of their original lines of advance, towards Leningrad, towards Moscow, and deep into the heart of the Ukraine. Now they would have to choose. Could they quickly destroy the Soviet will to resist by capturing Moscow, thus depriving the Soviet Union of its political and administrative centre? Or should they concentrate instead on the destruction of the Soviet armies in the field, and on capturing the rich resources of Ukraine and the oil fields to the Southeast?

The ambiguity had been there from the start. On the eve of the war the German General Staff had asked itself, 'Is Moscow the decisive objective of the war?' And it had answered:

> The occupation or destruction of Moscow will cripple the military, political and economic leadership as well as much of the basis of Soviet power. But it will not decide the war. Our main opponent remains space, which East of Moscow stretches without limit. But whether the troops available to the Soviet leadership to the east will remain firmly in the hand of the leadership is a political matter, not a military one.[37]

Now the very success of Army Group Centre on the road to Moscow risked being its undoing. The further Army Group Centre advanced, the more it would expose its southern flank to Kirponos' armies still fighting West of Kiev in the Ukraine. There were more practical worries as well. Army Group Centre had lost many men, and some Panzer divisions had only ten tanks left. The Germans' railheads were now far behind, and they were having to bring ammunition, new equipment and spare parts for hundreds of miles over bad roads already under attack by partisans. One German tank commander commented, 'If this goes on we shall win ourselves to death.'[38]

Hitler and his generals argued for nearly a month, and eventually decided that Army Group Centre should go onto the defensive to rest and refit before it resumed its march on Moscow. Army Group South would carry out yet another vast encircling manoeuvre to surround and destroy Kirponos' Southwestern Front. Guderian would divert his tanks southwards, away from Moscow, to close the trap. It was a reasonable decision, later much debated by revisionist historians who, with the benefit of hindsight, argued that the delay before Moscow cost the Germans the war.[39]

Guderian moved almost immediately. The Bryansk Front under Yerëmenko was ordered to stop him, but it was insufficiently agile, insufficiently organised, and insufficiently equipped to do so. By 11 September the threat to General Kirponos was serious. Budënny, the overall commander of the Southwestern theatre, and Khrushchëv, who was a member of his Military Council, recommended that Kiev should be evacuated. Stalin believed that the political cost of abandoning the capital of the Ukraine was too great. He rejected the advice and replaced Budënny with Timoshenko.

On 16 September Guderian linked up with Kleist's First Panzer Group and the trap was closed. Timoshenko and Khrushchëv authorised the Southwestern Front to withdraw while they still had a chance. But Kirponos, mindful of what had happened to his colleagues who had withdrawn without direct orders from the Kremlin, demanded confirmation from Moscow. It arrived at midnight on 17 September: too late. Budënny, Timoshenko, and Khrushchëv escaped. But Kirponos died, together with his Chief of Staff, General Tupikov, the man who had sent such useful intelligence from Berlin before the war. Four Soviet armies ceased to exist. Some 665,000 men were taken prisoner. Only fifteen thousand got back to the Soviet lines.[40]

Stalin was beside himself with rage. He told Khrushchëv that he ought to be shot. When Timoshenko rang from the South to explain what was being done to extract the remains of Kirponos' forces from the German trap, Stalin warned him, 'Don't go in for meaningless heroics. You do too much of that as it is.'

'I don't understand,' replied Timoshenko.

'There's nothing to understand. You're always going in for meaningless heroics. Heroics are useless unless you use your head as well.'

'You think I'm just stupid? [...] I see you're dissatisfied with me.'

'And I see that you're too worked up and losing control of yourself.'

'If you think I'm no good, then I resign.'

Stalin held the receiver away from his ear and muttered, 'This idiot bawls at me at the top of his voice, and doesn't seem to realise he's literally deafening me.' And then he went on, 'What? You want to resign? People don't ask to resign around here, they get sacked.'

'If that's what you think, then sack me.'

'I'll sack you when I need to, but for now I suggest you get a grip on yourself.'[41]

The usual search for scapegoats could not hide the fact that, for the second time in the year, Stalin's strategic misjudgements had cost his people very dear.

It was during these August weeks, when the direct danger to Moscow had turned aside, that Dr Ye. Sakharova decided to keep a diary once again. She had lived through the hardships of the revolution and the Civil War in Moscow, she had known hunger, poverty and fear, and she had lost two children. By now she was fifty-three years old and working as a doctor in a polyclinic, where she had been living on a 'barracks regime' since the beginning of the war. She attended and spoke at Party meetings when it was demanded of her, but without much enthusiasm. She was respected and liked by her colleagues and her many friends. And she had a lover, Sergo. He was called into the army on 20 August. As they said goodbye, he asked her what she would do if the Germans got as far as Moscow. 'I would join the partisans,' she replied. He left, cheerful, sanguine, in the highest spirits. Thereafter she heard nothing. Like Lidia Smirnova, she went to the VoenKomat to find out where he had been sent. They could not tell her: the soldiers had gone to be trained, or perhaps to the front. Several of them had been so drunk that they would have been unable to tell which was which. A month later she still had no news of Sergo, and began to fear that he was dead.

As August turned to September the rain began to fall, mixed with sleet, and it started to get colder. Sakharova and her colleagues at the polyclinic scuffled with their neighbours for scarce supplies of wood and coal. As an air-raid precaution, people had to put out the fires in their apartments at nightfall, and Sakharova took to sleeping in her clothes to keep warm and to be ready for emergencies.

Those few weeks at the end of summer were the last before the storm. After their shattering victory in Ukraine, the Germans were once again able to turn their attention to Moscow.

– TEN –

FIRE OVER MOSCOW

The people of Moscow had their first direct brush with the war early in the morning of 24 June 1941. Unidentified aircraft appeared on the approaches to the capital. The sirens went off and the dogs howled in the streets.[1] Some people went dutifully to the shelters. Others came out to see what was going on. Colonel Klimov's fighters took off to intercept the intruders. The sky was already light, and when the anti-aircraft guns opened up it was covered with the puff of bursting shells, like thousands of little white clouds. The guns continued firing for more than an hour.[2] Nobody explained what had happened. The public were left to speculate. Had someone panicked? Was it an exercise for the air defences? Were there really German bombers in the vicinity?

The official line was that it had been a practice exercise for the PVO (Protivo-Vozdushnaya Oborona), Moscow's military air defence system.[3] In fact it seems as if, once again, the Soviet air defences had been unable to distinguish their own aircraft from the enemy's. General Gromadin, who had taken over Moscow's air defences after Pumpur's arrest, had alerted his forces when unidentified aircraft appeared on the approaches to the city. Colonel Klimov's pilots had found four aircraft and forced them to land at a Moscow airfield. They turned out to be Russian DC-3s flown by pilots of the civil airline. The planes had been severely punctured by bullets, but the pilots were safe. Klimov was ordered to land his aircraft, and Gromadin told his guns to cease fire.[4] Gromadin was summoned to Stalin that evening to be hauled over the coals. But he was let off with a warning, and his career continued to prosper. As the air campaign against Moscow developed, Stalin regularly visited his headquarters during raids, and invited him and Klimov back to the Kremlin or to his battle headquarters deep in the safety of the Kirov Metro station for a post-mortem.

Major Lapirov, the Chief of Staff of Moscow's Local Air Defence Organisation (Mestnaya Protivo-Vozdushnaya Oborona, MPVO or civil defence organisation), was in his office on the evening of 21 June when Pronin rang from the Kremlin to say that the situation could 'become very serious at any moment' and ordered him to bring all his people in at once. Lapirov sat down straight away to write out instructions for an immediate state of heightened alert. All public and private buildings were to be blacked out. All air-raid shelters were to be brought to readiness. Those in charge of factories, offices and apartment blocks were to appoint and train air-raid wardens. Air-raid warnings would be given by siren and over the ubiquitous public address system thus: 'Citizens, air-raid warning. Citizens, air-raid warning.' Buses and trams would stop, and the passengers would have to get out and go to the nearest shelter. The underground trains would drive to the next station and stop there, in case the power stations were bombed and people got stuck in the tunnels. In apartment blocks, people were to turn off their gas and kerosene stoves. Building administrators were to turn off the gas at the mains.[5] The measures would be enforced by the police and the local air defence authority. Any violation would be punished by court martial.[6] The order was posted all over Moscow immediately.

Preparations for an air attack on the capital had begun nine years earlier, when the MPVO was first set up in 1932.[7] The construction of air-raid shelters started the next year. From 1938 a proportion of all new buildings and offices were designed with shelters incorporated. Cellars began to be converted into shelters. In December 1939 Stalin told Pronin to go to Leningrad to see how the city was defending itself against aerial attack by the Finns: a remarkable compliment to the tiny Finnish Air Force. There was not much to be learned there, and Pronin suggested that the government should also look at the measures being taken by Germany, France, and Britain. Nobody knew what these were, so the Soviet intelligence services were told to find out. By the beginning of the war there were said to be sufficient shelters in Moscow for about four hundred thousand people. That was not enough for the peacetime population of four million, but the numbers needing shelter were much reduced by evacuation once the war began.

Despite all this work, Moscow's air defences remained inadequate. Colonel Sbytov's inspection in March 1941 and the fiasco over the flight to Moscow by the German Ju 52 in May, showed that much remained to be done. Stalin had made Shcherbakov responsible for sorting things out, and at the meeting in the Kremlin on the first day of the war Shcherbakov reported that Moscow's air defences had been organised in a series of defensive rings.[8] The outer ring was more than 125 miles from Moscow, and consisted of the men and women of the VNOS, the Air Observation, Warning and Communications Service, the equivalent of the British Observer Corps. Their task was to observe all aircraft passing overhead by day and night; identify their type, course and height; and convey that information to Moscow. Their job was made harder by a serious lack of binoculars, and by the observers' initial difficulty in distinguishing between their own aircraft and the enemy's.[9]

The squadrons of the 6th Air Defence Corps under Colonel Klimov were deployed about seventy-five miles from the city. They had six hundred fighter aircraft, of which more than half were of the latest type. The twin-engined Pe-2 bomber was also particularly effective as a night fighter, stalking the raiders back to their bases and shooting them down as they landed.

The approaches to Moscow were defended by nearly eight hundred medium anti-aircraft guns. Over six hundred large searchlights were deployed in a ring forty miles from the city to enable the guns and the fighters to operate at night. There were smaller searchlights inside the city itself. An inner ring of over a hundred barrage balloons was intended to force the Germans to fly high, and to confuse their aim. Anti-aircraft and machine guns were placed in the city itself, many of them on the tops of buildings. There were 'listeners' (*slukhachi*) all over town: acoustic devices to listen to the German bombers shaped like gramophone horns, only bigger. It was of course difficult for the fighters in the dark; and the guns could do little more than send up a curtain of fire to deter aircraft they could not see unless the searchlights picked them out. The expenditure of ammunition was very high in consequence: an average of more than 20,000 shells were fired for each aircraft shot down.[10] In the absence of effective radar tracking equipment, there was little else the gunners could do. The British had adopted the same rough and ready methods the previous year, though they claimed that they only needed to fire 2,000 shells to hit a German plane. Both in London and in Moscow the noise was good for morale, though the falling shrapnel was a hazard to life and property.[11]

Moscow was in any case peculiarly hard to defend from aerial attack. Despite the massive building programme of the 1930s, 70 per cent of the residential buildings in Moscow in 1941 were still made of wood. Factory workshops were roofed with inflammable rubberised material and tarred paper. Even in the centre of the city, even in places like Gorky Street, there were piles of firewood, wooden storehouses, and other combustible buildings. Moscow was a tinderbox.

It was therefore a primary objective of Moscow's air defence organisations to ensure that fires did not take hold. Significantly, the very first decision which the GKO took when it was set up on 1 July was to order an increase in the production of fire engines for the city's fire services.[12] Fire-fighters, both in uniform and out, were given canvas gloves and metal pincers to pick up the incendiaries, and buckets of water and sand to dowse them in. Observers were stationed on the top of every high building. Just before the first serious German raid on Moscow, Colonel Croad and Colonel Symonds of the British Home Office came out to advise on the experience gained during the Blitz. As an example of what the British could do, Colonel Symonds brought a stirrup pump with him, a simple and ineffective device that he himself had invented.[13] The visitors advised that rescue and fire-fighting operations should begin only after the 'All Clear' had been sounded. The Moscow authorities ignored the advice. The observers were left at their exposed posts even as the bombs were falling. They took higher casualties, but many people and buildings were saved that would otherwise have been lost.

The civil defence organisation (MPVO) was quickly fleshed out once war began. Schools were turned into field hospitals. Separate air defence battalions were formed in each of the twenty-five Raions, to rescue casualties from bombed buildings and to clear rubble after the raids.

Each consisted of five to eight companies, depending on the size of the Raion. They trained in parks, in the boulevards, in squares and on the courtyards of their own apartment buildings.[14] They were commanded by senior engineers, architects, and other specialists, most from among the city's own peacetime construction teams. Thus one regiment was formed from the Moscow City Directorate for Housing Construction; another from the Directorate of Roads and Highways; a third from the Directorate of Water Mains and Sewage; a fourth from the Directorate for Culture and Services. Thirty architects from the Moscow Architectural Planning Department were formed into an Engineering Observation Company. As soon as news of an incident came through, one of the architects went with a motorcyclist to see whether anyone was trapped or hurt, and to give technical advice to the rescue services.

Self-defence teams were organised in apartment blocks to preserve public order during raids and afterwards. They wore red armbands with 'MPVO' written on them. Section commanders wore red armbands with one blue stripe, group commanders had two blue stripes. The building administrators were responsible for the state of the shelters. Building Administrator Noskov failed to keep his shelter locked and clean. He was arrested and sentenced to two years in prison.[15]

The newspapers were full of helpful advice. *Vechernyaya Moskva* carried a series of articles on how to build a shelter, and a piece by Professor Pokrovski, who explained that the sound of a falling bomb preceded it by two to four seconds – enough time to jump into a ditch, a hole, or simply to lie down. The chances of surviving were then twice as great. The most important thing was to be able to distinguish between anti-aircraft shells going up and bombs coming down: the sound of a falling bomb went up in pitch, while the sound of a shell went down.[16]

By the time the German raids began in earnest, more than six hundred thousand Muscovites were serving in air defence squads. The overall responsibility for managing these very large numbers of people fell to the Moscow Party and the Moscow City Council. They passed their orders down through the organisations in the Raions: the Raion Party Committee, the Raion Council, and the Raion Komsomol organisation. The Party Secretary was the link in individual factories, offices, and apartment buildings. At the lowest level of all was, as usual, the building administrator.

*

In the centre of Moscow it was possible to use cellars as shelters. Further out few of the buildings had cellars and most of them were made of wood. Barns and sheds which could cause a fire hazard were pulled down. Where it was impossible to build proper shelters, foxholes and dugouts were constructed: by August there were enough of these to accommodate nearly a quarter of a million people. By the end of 1941 there were enough shelters for most of the people still left in the city.[17]

The most obvious places for people to shelter in during a raid were the underground railways stations. In London, the authorities feared that this would impede their primary purpose: to allow people to get to work. At first the staff at London Underground stations were ordered to admit only genuine travellers, and soldiers were used to keep others out. During the devastating raid of 7 September 1940, people took things into their own hands and forced their way into Liverpool Street Station. The government gave in, but continued to insist that people could only shelter in the Underground as a privilege, not as a right.[18] By contrast the Moscow Metro was designed from the start to provide shelter in war. Once the raids started, a routine rapidly built up. At night the services were suspended. During the day, when the Metro operated normally, the trains stopped at the nearest station when the alarm went. The MPVO troops put wooden duckboards on the rails, and closed off all apertures through which a bomb blast might penetrate. The whole process was supposed to take a couple of minutes only. Invalids, children, and the elderly were accommodated in the trains and in the stations, where there were first aid points and duty medical staff. The remainder went into the tunnels themselves for shelter. The stations were comparatively well lit. Water was available from drinking fountains on the platforms and from taps in the tunnels.[19]

Libraries and radio loudspeakers were set up in the stations. The RaiKoms drew on their local activists to form brigades of 'agitators', who organised lectures by local Communist officials and soldiers from the front, and laid on exhibitions and cinema shows, performances by concert brigades, mobile libraries, and kiosks for the sale of books and magazines. For the children they organised special readings and classes in drawing, model-making, and sewing.[20] More than two hundred babies were born in the Metro during air raids.[21]

On 5 August a German aircraft dropped a heavy bomb on the

Arbat Square, close by the General Staff building. There had been no preliminary alarm. People panicked, and rushed for the entrance to the nearest Metro station. Someone slipped on the stairs, others fell on top of them, and many people died in the crush. A similar tragedy occurred at Bethnal Green Station in London in March 1943, when 173 people seeking shelter were crushed to death. The official enquiry established after both incidents that a prime cause was the inadequate design and control of the station entrance.[22]

Moscow was blacked out on the first day of the war, and the blackout remained in force until April 1945. Before the war there were 26,000 street lights in Moscow (there are now 260,000). They were operated from so many different places that it could take an hour and a half to turn them on or off. The municipality therefore introduced a centralised system which made it possible to turn off all the city's street lights from one point. Special paper was produced to make blinds for the glass roofs and walls of the city's factories. The roof of GUM, the department store on Red Square, was painted black, so effectively that the glass had to be replaced after the war. All this cut off the natural ventilation, which greatly worsened working conditions. Special dampers were devised for blast furnaces which could not be closed down and which normally emitted a vivid glow at night. Traffic lights were masked so that they could only be seen from a short distance. Traffic moved very slowly and came to a halt whenever the air-raid alarm was sounded at night. All street lighting was shut off at the same time. The blackout was policed by duty officers in the factories, by PVO and self-defence units, and by mounted police and military patrols.[23] The sound of horses' hooves on the deserted streets at night stuck in people's memories.

The authorities made a determined effort to camouflage the city and confuse the German bomb aimers. The operation was headed by Boris Iofan, the architect who had designed the ill-fated Palace of the Soviets. Architects and students were mobilised to paint trees and the roofs of buildings on the streets and squares of the city. The golden cupolas of the Kremlin churches were painted in camouflage colours, and the red stars on the towers were covered in canvas. The buildings were disguised with camouflage netting. The Kremlin walls were painted in contrasting stripes to look like apartment buildings. Other major buildings – the Central Telegraph Office, the Moscow Hotel, the Bolshoi Theatre, the Theatre of the Soviet Army – were treated in similar fashion. But the painted buildings cast no shadow when they were lit by the flares dropped by the German raiders. So the artists and architects set out to change the silhouettes of the buildings themselves by adding outlines built out of plywood. Lenin's Mausoleum on Red Square was covered over to look like a two-storey building. Platforms with mock buildings on them were moored in the river. Nine fake aerodromes, a fake oil tank farm, seven fake factory complexes were built on the outskirts of the city to decoy the German airmen away from their real targets.[24]

The NKVD were unhappily surprised when they sent up observers in an aeroplane to check the results. The Kremlin could still be too easily identified by the configuration of the Moscow River which runs along its walls.[25] The distinctive shape of the Moscow River, and the concentric layout of the city could not in the end be hidden from the German navigators. Of course the German bomb aimers often missed their targets. But that was a function more of the primitive aiming technology of the day, and had little to do with the Russian attempts to disguise the city.[26]

In the first weeks of the war the Germans flew a large number of reconnaissance flights over Moscow. One of them, a Heinkel 111, was brought down when Lieutenant Goshko rammed it with his own aeroplane on 2 July. But the first blow against the city – long expected, and for Alexander Werth surprisingly long delayed – fell on 22 July. On that night, in accordance with Hitler's Directive No. 33 to reduce Moscow to ruins from the air, Kesselring's bombers attacked the capital. It was the beginning of an air campaign which lasted until April the following year – as long as the Blitz on London, which had been conducted by many of the same aircraft and many of the same crews less than a year earlier. Nearly two hundred aircraft attacked in four waves: 127 reached the target and dropped 104 tons of high explosive and 46,000 incendiary bombs. The Germans attacked by night because their fighters did not have the range to escort them all the way to the target. The anti-aircraft defences were much stronger than anything the German crews had faced over London the previous year. Ten bombers were shot down by gunfire and twelve by night fighters working with searchlights. For the Germans it was a disappointing result.[27]

Captain Timoshkov and his searchlight battery were stationed in Mozhaisk, sixty miles West of Moscow. For a whole month they saw no action. Other soldiers moving to and from the front would jeer at them, punning on the Russian acronym for 'Anti-aircraft defence', PVO: 'We will laze about as long as the war goes on' (*'Poka voina – otdokhnëm'*). On the evening of that first raid Timoshkov and his people were already manning their four searchlights and their two batteries of anti-aircraft guns when, at about 9.45, they saw the first German aircraft silhouetted against the setting sun. They were flying in tight formation, straight down the Mozhaisk Highway on their way to Moscow. Timoshkov and his men blazed away for most of the night. But they made no noticeable impact on the waves of bombers.[28]

As news of the German approach came into the MPVO headquarters in Moscow, Major Lapirov turned on the municipal broadcasting system. The announcer's voice blared through the loudspeakers on every street corner and in every factory: 'Citizens! Air-raid alarm!' The sirens started to wail, followed by the whistles of the locomotives in the station, and the hooters of the city's factories and workshops. People hurried towards the Metro, carrying bundles and suitcases. On the Western outskirts of the city, where the sky was still quite bright, hundreds of little sparks flared up and died away, looking like an invisible net between heaven and earth. As the incendiary bombs began to fall in clusters, they fizzed and spluttered until the defenders covered them with sand or grabbed them with their pincers and threw them into barrels of water.

The Knizhnaya Palata, the official bibliographical centre located in a nineteenth-century building on the river opposite the House on the Embankment, was set on fire. Major catalogues and other invaluable bibliographical material were lost. But the centre soon resumed work: it was in 1941 that it started publishing its flagship bibliography of Soviet bibliographies. Serious fires were started at the Belorussia Station, in the Trëkhgorka, in the Japanese embassy.[29] Four high-explosive bombs fell around the Kremlin. One bomb penetrated the roof of the Great Kremlin Palace and passed right through to the St George's Hall. It did not explode but left a big hole in the floor.

Seventy-six incendiary bombs fell in and around the Kremlin but were successfully extinguished.[30] Incendiary bombs also fell on the Moscow Zoo, and the lions, tigers, leopards and jaguars had to be moved to more secure cages while the bombardment was still in progress.

The Vakhtangov Theatre was seriously damaged. Its civil defence team, whose members slept in the building, was commanded by Vasili Kuza, the chief producer and head of the theatre's Party cell, who had devised a uniform for his team consisting of overalls, German boots from one of the current shows, and French helmets from another. The team was at full stretch during the raid of 22 July, extinguishing the incendiary bombs that fell on to the highly inflammable roof above the stage. And then a large bomb demolished the outer wall of the theatre. No one was hurt and the actors and staff gathered in the street, laughing and joking. The barrage started up again. Kuza shouted at everyone to get back into the shelter, pushing and shoving to make sure that no one was left outside. The next bomb blew him against one of the columns on the front of the theatre and he was killed.[31] For a while the company continued its performances in the second house of the Moscow Art Theatre. But repairs to their theatre began very quickly, and by the end of August they were already getting ready to return home.[32]

The Krasnaya Presnya Raion Council was chaired at this time by Nina Popova, who later made a good career and ended up as Chairman of the Soviet Society for Friendship with Foreign Countries. Her deputy was Mikhail Nemirovski, whose twin brother Semën ran Zhukov's intelligence organisation and got to Berlin.[33] Mikhail trained as an engineer, but was later transferred to the Krasnaya Presnya Raion Council when Khrushchëv was still the Raion Party secretary. In 1939 Mikhail was appointed to command the local air defence organisation, the 309th Independent Battalion of the MPVO, whose headquarters was housed in School No. 95. The backbone of his little force consisted of men of military age drafted in by the local recruiting office, each with an appropriate skill: firemen, engineers, doctors, carpenters, stonemasons, plasterers, decorators, plumbers, electricians, mechanics, roofers, blacksmiths. The men were organised into eight specialist companies, but did not start to train together properly until two months before the war began.

On the night of 21 June Nemirovski was summoned to his

command post. When he telephoned his colleagues in the neighbouring Raions, he discovered that they too had no idea why they had been called in. Then the lamp began to flash on the special telephone on his desk. It was Lapirov, who said, 'Open Package No. 1', the secret instructions for the event of war. Nemirovski immediately put his men on a war footing. For the first month, before the German air attacks began, he used them to convert existing cellars into bomb and gas shelters, put reinforced doors on the entrances, and brick up the windows to protect the shelters against blast.

One of his companies was quartered in a former stables on Vorovski Street. During the first raid on 21/22 July the stables were set alight. The fire spread quickly through the straw which still littered the place. There were not enough extinguishers, so the men did what they could to put out the fire with buckets and spades. They moved their equipment and personal belongings to battalion headquarters, only to find that the headquarters building had also been hit and partially destroyed, though there had been no casualties. Later they were called to rescue survivors from a nearby apartment building. One part of the building had been totally destroyed and the front of the other had been stripped off, so that you could see into individual apartments with their furniture. Fire had taken hold on the upper floors of the building. The entry to the cellar was blocked with rubble. When the fire-fighters turned their hoses onto the fire, the water heated up to boiling point, and began to trickle down into the shelter, endangering the survivors. It took several hours before the rescuers could work through to the shelter. They brought out 150 people, many of whom were hurt.

That first raid went on for five hours. The MPVO Command reported:

> From 22.25 hours on 21 July to 03.25 hours on 22 July, 1941 the enemy's air force carried out an attack on the city of Moscow in four successive waves. Some 200 aircraft took part. The first wave broke up on the approaches to Moscow in order to drop its bombs, but was dispersed by our fighters and anti-aircraft fire. Only a few aircraft were able to break through to the city. The attacks of the second and third waves were carried out [...] by individual aircraft and in small groups, both conventionally and by dive bombing, using

> incendiary and high-explosive bombs. Our fighter aircraft flew 173 sorties. According to pilots' reports, two enemy aircraft were shot down. The anti-aircraft units report that they shot down 17 enemy aircraft. This requires further confirmation.[34]

That night 130 people were killed, 241 were severely injured, 421 were lightly injured, thirty-seven buildings were destroyed, and1,166 fires were started.[35] Three incendiary bombs fell on the British embassy and were extinguished by the fire brigade.[36] By the standards of the London Blitz it was a flea bite. Alexander Werth had lived through the great raids on London. Now he heard once again the familiar *woo-woo* of the German bombers, and saw 'a fantastic piece of fireworks – tracer bullets, and flares, and flaming onions, and all sorts of rockets, white and green and red; ... the din was terrific; never saw anything like it in London. And searchlights and more searchlights, all over the place'. But he heard very few bombs, and the next day he saw almost no signs of devastation. A big crater north of the Kremlin had been filled in by 2 o'clock in the afternoon. It was a sunny day, the trams were running, and everyone looked cheerful. 'They should have seen Fleet Street on May 10th!'[37] His colleague, the American journalist Henry Cassidy, was equally surprised that there were so few signs of damage. 'What had seemed to be a withering raid had turned out to be a light one. Most of the impression of intensity ... came from the violence not of the bombing, but of the anti-aircraft defences.'[38]

Between 22 July and 17 August there were seventeen more raids. The toll may not have matched the destruction in London. But it was continuous and it told on the nerves of the people. MosGES, one of the main power stations in Moscow, was a prime target for the bombers, and the area around it was heavily damaged. The nearby Zatsepski Market was destroyed by incendiary bombs, and many apartment buildings round about were left damaged for months, their windows hanging loose, their interiors open to the public eye, the home of sparrows and stray cats.[39] On 27 July a high-explosive bomb scored a direct hit on a newly built school in Zemskoi Lane, which was almost completely destroyed. More than three hundred people were buried in the shelter beneath it. Despite the flames, the rescuers managed to get them out. A building opposite the Lenin Library was hit by a bomb which penetrated all four storeys and exploded on the roof of the cellar. Those sheltering inside were trapped by rubble as a fire broke out in the ruins above. With great difficulty the rescuers found a way through. It took them thirteen hours to free the thirty survivors.[40]

On 5 August a thousand-kilo bomb landed opposite the monument to the distinguished agricultural scientist Timiryazev by the Nikitski Gates. It blew a crater thirty yards across and ten yards deep, severely damaging the tramlines, the underground services and the nearby buildings. The statue was knocked down and shattered. A tram carrying sacks of flour had halted on the square when the alarm sounded. The flour was spread by the blast all over the square, which looked as if it was covered with snow. An emergency engineer team arrived almost immediately. They re-erected the statue, mended the underground services, filled in the crater, repaired the tramlines, and removed all the broken glass. Within a day the trams were running again past the Nikitski Gates, and vehicles were travelling along the new asphalt on the roadway. Shortly thereafter the same team was called on to re-erect the monument to Lomonosov just outside the old building of Moscow University in the centre of the city.[41]

The staff and vehicles of Moscow's Central Ambulance Service were called out nearly four hundred times during the raids in July, over a hundred times in August and over two hundred times in October.[42] Their first encounter with the war was at the end of June, when Shredov, the deputy head of the service, went with nurses and ambulances to the Belorussia Station to cope with the sick and wounded on a train of evacuees from the Baltic States. The windows of the carriages were broken, and the train had clearly been machine-gunned and bombed. The carriages were so crowded with sleeping people that the doctors found it impossible to board in the dark. They were told that there were about a dozen sick people among the passengers, so they decided to wait until morning, when the passengers could be unloaded. Instead, the train was sent on its way, with the passengers still on board and before any medical assistance could be given.[43]

Base No. 10 of the Central Ambulance Service was in the Filatov Hospital. A young woman called Russkikh was on duty in the Transport Office there during the first raid on 21/22 July.

> The warning went off at 10 p.m. I was told to sit by the phone and not move. Several incendiary bombs fell on the hospital grounds. [...] A fire started in the children's section. An order was given for them to be moved to the shelter. Workers from the Ambulance Service volunteered to take them. As they left the building to go to the vehicles, a high-explosive bomb fell nearby. One driver was killed by a splinter, another was knocked down by the blast, but the children were evacuated safely. The blast blew out the windows of my office. I turned out all the lights because of the blackout, and spent the rest of the raid sitting in the dark and holding on to my telephone to keep in contact with the staff. Wounded people started to come in, and I had to treat them. When the raid was over, I went out to see what had happened. There were bloodstained prints of hands on the walls, and patches of blood on the ground. The polyclinic building was destroyed. The whole yard was covered with broken glass, broken doors, and broken window frames.[44]

On 16 October, the day of the great Moscow panic, Giatsintova, a nurse from the Central Ambulance Service, was sent off to collect wounded men from a hospital at Naro-Fominsk, Southwest of Moscow and in the direct line of the German advance. 'I had five buses, each with twenty places. We arrived at the hospital at 7 o'clock in the morning and rapidly set to work. We hadn't managed to load up more than two vehicles, when a mounted messenger galloped up to say that the Germans were five miles away. We got a move on [...] and loaded up all the wounded.'[45]

Not everyone was so heroic. On 29 October Zenkov, one of the Ambulance Service's male staff, was sent with a team to load stretcher cases onto a train at the Savëlov Station. 'A German plane machine-gunned the train as it was being loaded,' Zenkov remembered. 'The bullets produced an unpleasant sensation as they struck the asphalt. The medical staff took shelter under the train. I phoned Fëdorov, the head of the Ambulance Service, to sort things out. He arrived quickly, and brought the situation under control. The shooting died away by midnight. Even so, the loading of stretcher cases was not resumed until the following morning.'[46]

The raids increased in frequency as the Germans got closer to

Moscow. Sergeant Roguliak's gun crew on Danilovski Square was wiped out by a direct hit. Two more crews were killed on Repin Square just behind the British embassy. A bomb fell on the Moscow Post Office building without exploding. The local defence team decided not to wait for the bomb disposal experts, but wrapped the bomb in sacking, tied it up with string, and dragged it to a place where it could do no harm. A bomb fell on a house in Protochny Lane, near where the offices of the British embassy now stand.[47] The people sheltering in the cellar were all killed. The cellar was not opened up, and the bodies were not discovered, until well after the war was over. Another bomb landed a little further up the road. A third hit the kerosene shop round the corner, which went up in flames.[48]

People concluded – as they had done in London – that it was just as dangerous to go to the shelter as to remain in bed. As time passed they no longer bothered to leave their homes at night. At first Raisa Labas and her son Yuli Labas sheltered in the Kirov Metro station. Later they preferred to remain at home, though they did go downstairs to the studio apartment of the sculptor Beatrice Sandomirskaya, who used to carve huge wooden statues of women: women pilots, and muscular peasants who looked like Valkyries. Yuli slept under the statue of a naked woman carved out of mahogany. Once, when the alarm had gone off during the day, the people simply gathered at the entrance to the apartment block. An exotic figure approached them, wearing a white jacket, white shorts which revealed hairy knees, great boots, and a flat cap on his head with a crest on it. He said in broken Russian, 'Ladies and gentlemen, go to the shelter. Our experience in England shows that the most dangerous thing you can do in a raid is to gather where you are gathering now. The shelter is just round the corner.'[49] Then a man in civilian clothes popped up and chased everyone into a nearby cellar.

Some of the worst damage was done on 28 October 1941. The Central Committee building on Old Square was struck by a heavy bomb: one of those killed was the popular writer Afinogenov. Another bomb destroyed a row of buildings on the embankment of the Moscow River, and killed the self-defence team. A young dancer called Yelena Vanke was just around the corner when the Bolshoi Theatre was hit that day. She came from a family of dancers, lived on Kuznetski Most behind the theatre itself, and was in her final year at the Bolshoi ballet school when the war began. She was too young to go as a full member of the company when it was evacuated, and too old to be evacuated with the ballet school. So she stayed in Moscow with the rest of her class. As the bomb came down, a passer-by shoved her into the space between sandbags covering a nearby shop front, and she was unhurt. She heard the explosion and saw a column of smoke rising over the theatre. It had hit the foyer, just behind the great quadriga over the entrance, and a woman had been killed. Vanke's reaction was to thank God that the bomb had not landed on the stage, which would have been a catastrophe.[50] Dr Sakharova described that day's raid in her diary: 'The Bolshoi Theatre was destroyed yesterday. A bomb fell on Gorky Street next to the Central Telegraph Office. There were many dead and wounded in a queue outside a food shop. It all happened before the alarm was sounded ... People are going about with their goods, with rucksacks, as if they were going away somewhere or moving from one place to another.'[51]

The next day a bomb exploded just outside Shcherbakov's office while he was holding a meeting. Fragments of glass and plaster rained down on the participants, who were knocked over by the blast. No one was hurt, but Shcherbakov was concussed. The doors were jammed shut, but the firemen were able to break one down and get everyone out. Shcherbakov went straight to the Kremlin. As he was approaching the Armoury, a column of cadets and instructors from the Military School of the Supreme Soviet passed him on the way to the shelter. Another bomb went off nearby. Shcherbakov was once again concussed, though only slightly. But forty-one soldiers were killed, four were missing, fifty-four were seriously wounded, forty-seven were lightly wounded. By the end of the air assault on Moscow the Kremlin had been hit by sixteen high-explosive bombs and a large number of incendiary bombs. Ninety-six members of the garrison had been killed. The monument to them in the Kremlin is the only memorial devoted to those who died in the bombing of Moscow.[52]

Other major buildings that were hit at various times included Moscow University, the Pushkin Art Gallery, the Lenin Library, the Conservatoire, the editorial buildings and print houses of *Pravda*, *Izvestia, Moskovski Bolshevik* and *Ogonëk*. Leo Tolstoy's house at Khamovniki was only saved by the efforts of the fire-fighters.[53]

*

The Germans were now so close that they could send fighters to escort their bombers, and raid by day as well as by night. On 14 November 180 aircraft raided the city by day: the Russians claimed forty-eight shot down.[54] The warning time for getting people into the shelters was sometimes reduced to as little as five minutes. Casualties started to go up, and the city's morgues had to work overtime. The cemeteries began to run out of space. People were buried three deep, and graves were dug closer together.[55]

This new development was not entirely unfavourable to the defence. Where the Germans had to improvise bases and supplies, the Soviet pilots were operating from well-equipped pre-war airfields around Moscow. The Central Aerodrome was the oldest in Moscow. It was situated on the Leningrad Highway, just past the Belorussia Station and opposite the Petrovski Palace, where Napoleon had stayed when he was driven out of the Kremlin by fire. All the main aircraft designers – Yakovlev, Artem Mikoyan and the others – had their offices and factories in the area, and they used the Central Aerodrome for test flying.

Before the war it was not a military airfield. But in 1941 two fighter regiments were stationed there: the 12th Guards Regiment and the 11th Fighter Regiment. The regimental headquarters were in dugouts. So were the pilots' ready rooms, the canteen, and the men's quarters. The aircraft were dispersed along the edge of the wood. The pilots themselves lived in two red-brick buildings by the road coming in from Moscow airport. They are still there. The concrete runways are still there too, and there is a small exhibition of about twenty aircraft. A scheme to set up a proper museum fell through, and the Moscow authorities are now building apartment blocks on the site. Except when they were on stand-by, the pilots took their meals at the Zhukovski Air Force Academy in the Petrovski Palace. At the end of November, when the Germans were at the gates, the two regiments were used chiefly for strafing enemy ground forces. Missions took less than twenty minutes from take-off to landing, and pilots could fly several sorties a day. Stepan Mikoyan served in the 11th Fighter and then in the 12th Guards Regiment. He joined his unit on 17 December, and flew eleven combat missions from the Central Aerodrome until, on 16 January, his Yak-1 was accidentally shot down by a pilot from another regiment; his aircraft crashed in flames, his leg was broken and he was badly burned.[56]

By November the sirens were sounding several times a day. Lessons in the schools, which had in practice already ceased, were now officially stopped. 'Things are getting more unsettled every day,' wrote Dr Sakharova in her diary.

> It is impossible to get used to the sirens. People's psychology is changing in a strange fashion. People tell you of the death of their closest relatives quite calmly, they register the fact, but the real reaction comes later [...] Our nights are dark, if it were not for the torches which we have managed to get hold of by hook or by crook, we would have broken arms and legs more than once [...] I do not doubt for a minute that victory will be ours, but will it be here, in Moscow? People coming from the front say that it is more frightening here than at the front, because here everything is unexpected, and you do not know where the next bomb will fall [...] The front is getting closer to us. Barricades are being built on the streets of Moscow – 'hedgehogs' from rails. I very much don't want to allow myself to believe that there could be street fighting here. But the fascist beast is strong and one must be prepared for that.

But there were good moments as well as bad. At the beginning of December Dr Sakharova learned to dance: 'It was rather strange and inappropriate. What happened was that the captain [an officer acquaintance] temporally gave us his gramophone, and Natalia Semënovna likes dancing and dances well. She decided to teach me too. And I turned out not to be bad at it. I already dance freely, even with the captain, who praised my success. Today all three of us practised.'[57]

The task of Moscow's civil defence forces was further compounded when they had to give up the equivalent of six battalions to send to the front. Three hundred men from Nemirovski's 309th Battalion went off to the front: only three of them survived the war. The reduced numbers were partially made up by teenagers, especially girls, who acted as runners and observers. The men remaining in the air defence units prepared, if it came to it, to fight it out on the ground, and formed mortar and anti-tank companies equipped with machine guns, armoured cars, and light tanks.[58]

As if that was not enough Nina Popova, the Chairman of the Raion Council, was transferred, and Nemirovski was promoted to fill her place in addition to his own. It was a huge added burden. The Council was responsible for almost every detail of people's lives in Krasnaya Presnya. They fought to keep the apartment buildings heated: by November 1941 only ninety-five of the boilers in the Raion were still working.[59] They monitored the production plan of the local hairdressers' cooperative, and plans for sowing and harvesting crops on the Raion's arable land.[60] They found accommodation for people who had been bombed out, and for cooperatives (*artels*) of shoemakers and dressmakers who needed new workshops. They allocated ration cards, set up kindergartens and crèches, and provided distance learning for children whose schools were still closed. They registered new marriages, authorised special allowances to a woman called Tatiana Arakcheeva and others with large families, arranged adoption for abandoned children, and found foster parents for one small girl whose father was at the front and whose mother was in prison.[61] And they spent an inordinate amount of time appointing minor officials: a bookkeeper for the Laundry Trust, the Head of the 2nd Raion Repair Office, the Chief Engineer of the 1st Raion Housing Directorate, a People's Judge in the Second Precinct. They devoted particular attention to the appointment of new building administrators, the basic level of local authority, and sent one building administrator, a man called Yeroshkin, before a military tribunal for failing to maintain the heating equipment in his apartment block.[62]

It was some compensation that Nemirovski's salary went up from 1,200 to 1,400 roubles a month, a respectable amount at a time when the average wage was about 420 roubles, especially when supplemented by the special rations to which Raion officials were entitled.[63]

An exhibition of German military trophies was set up next to the Bolshoi Theatre and then moved to Gorky Park. The items on show included a collection of unexploded bombs and the remains of a German bomber which flew into the cable of a barrage balloon and crashed into the Moscow River. A covered building was later constructed to the designs of the architect Shchusev, who had designed Lenin's mausoleum and the 'Moskva' Hotel, as well as the opera house in Novosibirsk, the largest in the world.

In January bombs fell once again on the Moscow Zoo, killing the director and wounding a night watchman. The lion house, the elephant house, the mammal house, the parrot house, and the monkey house were all hit, and the windows were blown out. The animals were terrified, especially an ape called Paris and a donkey called Emir, who had been left behind by his owners during the evacuation. Surprisingly, apart from a couple of parrots none of them was killed. But the outside temperature was now minus thirty degrees. The staff wrapped the animals in blankets and in their own clothes. The Raion engineers arrived and repaired the glass before any of the animals died of cold.[64]

By now the German air assault on Moscow was beginning to peter out. There were some substantial attacks both before and after the official end of the Battle of Moscow on 20 April 1942. The final mass raid on Moscow took place on 16 June 1942. Another attempt was made by a small group of aircraft in August and again in October.[65] But by 1943 only the occasional high-altitude Ju 88-R reconnaissance aircraft was still flying over the capital.

In 1949 the distinguished Soviet director Chiaureli made a film called *The Fall of Berlin*. It is dramatic, well put together, and very long. Its reputation has suffered because of its absurdly exaggerated praise of Stalin: that of course now adds to its historical interest. One scene depicts an armada of German bombers approaching Moscow. A swarm of fighters rises up to thwart them. The Germans are sent packing. A title passes across the screen: 'Not a single German aircraft ever broke through to Moscow.' Even though hundreds of thousands of Muscovites knew from their own experience that this claim was wholly untrue, it continued to figure in school textbooks and official propaganda for decades thereafter.

Even during the war, exact information about the damage was scarce and indirect, and filtered onto the pages of the newspapers only with difficulty. The claim, which still persists, that all traces of the night raids had usually been cleared away by morning is difficult to accept. The bombing of the Vakhtangov Theatre was reported only when the repair work was already well under way. Even today one can see the gaps left by the war in the heavily built-up centre of Moscow. The four-storey building opposite the Lenin Library was never fully rebuilt. There is now a little square on the corner of Bogoyavlenski

Lane and Nikolskaya where once was a three-storey building on which a German bomber crashed.[66]

Russian and German historians differ considerably in their view of the campaign. The standard German history says that in all Moscow was attacked seventy-six times by night and eleven times by day. Only the first three attacks deployed more than a hundred bombers; on fifty-nine occasions less than ten bombers were involved. The German losses, the German historian claims, were negligible.[67] The Russians say that between the first raid on 21 July 1941 and 20 April 1942 the Germans launched one hundred and forty-one major raids against the city.[68] They claim that the Germans lost nearly fourteen hundred aircraft, 10 per cent to Soviet fighters, the rest to the anti-aircraft guns.[69] This figure is impossible to reconcile with the German figures, and would represent an improbable and surely unsustainable rate of casualties among the attackers.

According to Russian figures published after the war, more than two thousand people were killed during the raids on Moscow, and nearly three times as many were injured; 5,584 domestic buildings were damaged or destroyed. So were ninety hospitals, 253 schools and nineteen theatres or palaces of cultures.[70] Complete figures for buildings destroyed and damaged remain unclear, because information about damage to military targets and official buildings has still not been released.

Although the German air campaign against Moscow lasted as long as the London Blitz a year earlier, the results were much less impressive. Between 7 September 1940 and 10 May 1941, German aircraft raided London seventy-one times and dropped over 18,000 tons of high explosive. During 7 September alone, London was attacked during the day by 348 bombers escorted by fighters. Thirty-three bombers were lost; 250 bombers came back that night. Fires in the docks ran out of control. By the morning of 8 September 430 people had been killed. On 19 April 712 aircraft attacked London in the heaviest raid of the war. The last raid of the Blitz took place on 10 May 1941 and killed 1,436 people. By then one Londoner in six had been bombed out of their homes. The bombardment of London continued, by piloted and pilotless aircraft and by rockets, until the last month of the war. Altogether nearly thirty thousand people were killed during the London

Blitz and over 50,000 wounded.[71] Three and a half million homes were damaged. In the borough of Stepney near the docks 85 per cent of the houses were destroyed.[72]

There were a number of reasons why Moscow suffered less than London. First, the Germans used their air force quite differently in the two campaigns. During the Battle of Britain and the Blitz the Luftwaffe was engaged in an undistracted strategic campaign against the British heartland. But in Russia the men and machines which Kesselring had used against Britain were primarily involved in giving tactical support to the German army on the ground. At the height of the Battle of Moscow the Luftwaffe was using most of its bombers to attack the railway lines bringing reinforcements, rather than against the city itself.[73] The Luftwaffe was never able to deploy the forces against Moscow which it had directed against London.

Second, the Germans suffered a number of practical disadvantages. At this stage in the war, their aircraft were superior, and their crews were much more experienced. But in the campaign against Britain they had operated from good airfields in France which were comparatively close to their targets and could be easily supplied with ammunition and replacement aircraft from Germany. In Russia the German aircraft were operating up to six hundred miles away from their targets, from bases less sophisticated and far less securely attached to the German industry on which they relied. They brought their bases forward as the front moved closer to Moscow. But this compounded their difficulties, especially once the autumn and winter weather set in. Aircraft had to be dug out of the overnight snow before they could fly, and often it was too cold for them to operate at all from the battered and ill-equipped airstrips which the Germans had captured. By December the Red Air Force was beginning to establish the solid presence over the battlefield which it had so painfully lacked in the first months of the war. But once they began to advance in their turn at the end of 1941, and to move into the improvised bases which had until recently been used by the Germans, the Russians too began to experience increasing difficulties.

Third, Stalin chose to deploy a very much larger force to defend his capital. During the Battle of Britain, the British had less than eight hundred fighters available to defend the whole country. By contrast

General Gromadin had nearly six hundred fighters for the defence of Moscow alone. In addition he could call on twenty-nine fighter regiments from the neighbouring Fronts. Between July 1941 and January 1942 nearly two thousand fighters had flown in the defence of Moscow.[74] By the end of the campaign most of the fighters were of the modern types which had been coming into production over the previous year. In addition there were American Airacobras, which the Soviet pilots liked; and two squadrons of Hawker Hurricanes which they did not.[75] These were figures the RAF could not match. Moreover far more guns were deployed around Moscow than around London. On the first day of the Blitz there were less than three hundred guns in London. The rest were still spread around the country to defend the ports, factories and airfields which had hitherto been the main German target. Even though the number of guns in London was doubled within forty-eight hours, the forces available to defend the city never matched those in Moscow.[76]

A fourth factor in the successful defence of Moscow against air attack was the ability of the authorities to mobilise, train, and deploy the population. Very many Muscovites volunteered to help defend their capital against attacks from the air. Those who did not volunteer were shamed or coerced by the formidable machinery of the Party, the Government, and the NKVD. No other belligerent was so ruthlessly able to harness its man- and womanpower to civil defence – or indeed to any other branch of the war effort. By contrast the training of the people of London was haphazard, and relied to a considerable extent on genuine volunteers. These were forthcoming in large numbers: by June 1940 well over one million civilians had joined the civil defence and fire-fighting forces deployed in London and other British cities.[77] But few of them had received even the minimal training which their Moscow equivalents had undergone. Mass Observation, which monitored popular attitudes in Britain throughout the war, reported in May 1940 – a mere two months before the Blitz began – that people 'do not know what they ought to do or how they ought to do it ... they still fail in many respects to conform with what might well be regarded and easily framed as minimum requirements for civilian knowledge and co-operation – e.g. knowledge of how to deal with an incendiary bomb, in its earliest stage.'[78] However ill-prepared the Russian civil defence system was before the war, it was somewhat better than that.

Soviet success in the air battle over Moscow was achieved at a cost. The defence of the capital drew strength away from the rest of the front line. Sevastopol in the Crimea was almost wiped out from the air in the first week of June. The first devastating daylight raid on Stalingrad, on 23 August 1942, was practically unopposed. Tens of thousands of people were killed in both cities in a matter of hours or days.[79] But in the end the Red Air Force overwhelmed the Germans in the air as comprehensively as the Red Army overwhelmed them on the ground.[80] The airmen and aircraft designers who suffered such injustice under Stalin were vindicated by the final result.

PART III

TYPHOON

– ELEVEN –

THE GERMANS BREAK THROUGH

On 16 September 1941 von Bock, the Commander of Army Group Centre, issued his operational directive for the capture of Moscow and gave it the codename 'Typhoon'. Three Panzer Groups were to spearhead the attack. The Third, which had been withdrawn from the drive on Leningrad, would lead in the North. The Fourth would make the push in the centre; and Guderian's Second Panzer Group would thrust up from the South after its victory in the Ukraine. Von Bock had assembled nearly two million men: three armies, three Panzer groups, and seventy-eight divisions. Facing them were 1,250,000 Soviet soldiers organised in three Fronts, the Bryansk Front under Yerëmenko; the Western Front, which Koniev had taken over from Timoshenko in the middle of September; and a new Reserve Front under Budënny – a total of eighty-four rifle divisions, a tank division, two motorised rifle divisions, nine cavalry divisions and a number of lesser formations (see map 3).[1]

On 30 September the Germans made their move, initially against the Bryansk and Southwest Fronts further to the South. Guderian's tanks broke straight through the defences of the Bryansk Front and pushed on towards Orël.[2] Vasili Grossman, the novelist and journalist, had been sent down there by his newspaper, *Krasnaya Zvezda*. He was enjoying the ordinary, almost pre-war, comfort of the local hotel when a photojournalist called Redkin burst in: 'The Germans are rushing straight for Orël, hundreds of tanks. I barely escaped from the firing, we must leave straight away, otherwise we'll be caught here.' The town was rapidly gripped by panic. After trying to get a pass from the local military office ('We issue passes at ten, wait for an hour, our superiors won't be here until eleven. Oh, how well I know that immovable calm which comes from ignorance, mixed with hysterical fear and panic.'), Grossman and his party took refuge in the forest with the headquarters of the Bryansk Front. The Germans entered Orël two hours after he had left it, at 6 o'clock in the evening.

Grossman had barely settled down before he and his colleagues were told to leave again by 4 o'clock sharp: the Germans were closing the trap around the Bryansk Front. They set off through the cold starlit night in their small truck and a lorry which they had christened 'Noah's Ark' because of the number of refugees they had already carried away from the advancing German flood. The road was clogged:

> I thought that I'd already seen a retreat, but I had never seen anything like this before, nor even imagined it. It was a Biblical Exodus! The vehicles were travelling in eight lines, engines screaming hysterically as dozens of lorries tried to get themselves out of the mud. People were driving huge flocks of sheep and cows over the fields, further off horse-drawn carts creaked along, thousands of carts, covered with coloured sackcloth, plywood, tin, carrying refugees from the Ukraine, still further ahead there were crowds of pedestrians with sacks, bundles, suitcases. It was not a stream, not a river, it was the slow movement of a flowing ocean, hundreds of yards wide from side to side. There were the black and white heads of children looking out from the covered carts, the biblical beards of Jewish elders, the headscarves of peasant women, older men in Ukrainian caps, black-haired girls and women. And what calmness there was in the eyes, what wise grief, what a sense of Fate, of universal catastrophe! In the evening the sun appeared from behind blue and black and grey clouds piled one upon the other. Its rays were broad, immense, they stretched down from heaven to earth, like a picture by Doré of one of those terrible biblical scenes when the wrath of the heavenly powers comes down upon the earth. In

> those broad, yellow rays the movement of the elders, the women with babies in their arms, the flocks of sheep, the soldiers, seemed so majestic and so tragic, that for minutes on end I felt that we really had been transported into a time of Biblical catastrophe.
>
> Everyone looked at the sky – not because they expected the Messiah, but because they were watching out for German bombers. Suddenly people started shouting: 'There they are, they're coming, they're coming this way!' High up in the sky a dozen aerial shapes sailed slowly towards us in a triangular formation. Tens, hundreds of people poured out of the lorries, jumped out of the cabs and ran towards the forest. Like an outbreak of plague, panic overtook everyone, the crowd of fugitives grew with every second. And then above the crowd a woman's voice rang out: 'Cowards, cowards, they're cranes flying!' Confusion.

Near Tula, Grossman's party stayed in a peasant house. The only inhabitant was an old woman whose son was at the front and whose daughter was in Moscow. She welcomed them warmly, fed them as generously as she could and offered to sing to them. Instead of the traditional folk songs which Grossman expected, she sang the latest hits from Moscow to appeal to the city folk. She told Grossman, 'The Devil came to me last night, and sunk his claws into my hand. I started to pray: "May God rise again and may his enemies be scattered", but the Devil took no notice. So I told him to — off, and then he did disappear.'[3]

Grossman was deeply moved:

> If we are to be victorious in this terrible, brutal war, it will be because deep in our nation we have people with these great hearts and souls, people who spare themselves nothing, like these old women, the mothers of these sons, who in their great simplicity 'lay down their lives for their friends', as simply, as generously, as that poverty-stricken old woman of Tula, who gave us her food, her light, her firewood, her salt. They are like the righteous of the Bible. They illuminate all our people with a miraculous light. They are a handful, but they will be victorious.

He was just as moved when he called the next day at Leo Tolstoy's family estate at Yasnaya Polyana. He was overwhelmed by the parallel between what was now happening and the scene in *War and Peace* when the old Prince Bolkonski dies and his daughter, Princess Maria, is forced from the family estate on the approach of the French. Tolstoy's granddaughter Sofia Andreevna was there, packing his treasures for evacuation. They walked through the garden for the last time, as Princess Maria had done before them, and stood by Tolstoy's grave. As they did so, a flight of German bombers passed overhead to pound Tula.

On Grossman's return to Moscow, David Ortenberg, the editor of *Krasnaya Zvezda*, asked him sharply why he had produced no copy about the heroic defence of Orël. He replied, 'Because Orël was not defended.' Ortenberg sent him straight back to the front.[4]

Stalin demanded an immediate counterattack. It was impossible. Like Pavlov before them, Yerëmenko and his headquarters had lost contact with their subordinates. Once again messages had to be passed through other units or by liaison officers making their perilous way over the German lines in fragile U-2 biplanes. The Bryansk Front was cooped up by the Germans in two large pockets. Yerëmenko was badly wounded. He and his staff were brought out by U-2. The rest of his troops had to escape as best they could, surrender, or die. The fighting in the Bryansk pockets did not finally die out until 16–17 October.

Next it was the turn of the Western Front and the Reserve Front behind it. It was in the 24th and the 32nd Armies of the Reserve Front that most of the volunteer divisions found themselves when the fighting began. Whatever the volunteers had originally expected, once they had been incorporated into the regular army, they were employed in battle just like everyone else. The blow was struck by the Third and Fourth Panzer Groups. They smashed through both Fronts to link up East of Vyazma, trapping four armies, including the 24th and the 32nd.[5]

The Krasnaya Presnya Division went into action for the first and only time in its brief history on 4 October. Its first two commanders had already moved on, and from the end of September it had been under the command of Colonel Zveriev, who had been captured by the Germans in the fighting on the frontier, escaped, and, after being given a clean bill by the NKVD investigators, restored to active service.

The Germans attacked in force with tanks, guns, and aircraft.

By the end of that first day the Division's regiments had practically run out of ammunition, their staffs had been decimated, and their numbers had been so reduced that the Division had ceased to exist as an effective fighting force. Twelve hundred men were wounded on the first day alone. As the Germans closed the trap around them, Lev Mishchenko was separated from his comrades and attached himself to a small remnant of the divisional staff which was still defending itself until it was abandoned by its commanders, ran out of ammunition, and fell apart. Mishchenko then wandered through the forests for a couple of days on his own, until he was surprised and taken prisoner while he was asleep. The remaining survivors of the Division were split into two detachments and ordered to find their own way out. One detachment was attacked and crushed two days later by German tanks. Many of the soldiers were killed, some hid in the woods, others were taken prisoner. The second detachment struggled through the forests to the Southeast for over sixty miles, evading the Germans as best it could, and eventually reached the Soviet lines near Tula.

Moisei Ginzburg and the other graduates of the Historical Faculty shared in the disaster. Yakov Pinus later wrote to Sasha Ospovat's girlfriend, Vera Kuteishchikovskaya, to describe what happened:

> The war has been going on for more than a year, so much time has passed since that day when – excited and joyful – we went to that school in Krasnaya Presnya, in order to begin a new and unknown life. And although out of those sixteen months we were together only for three, I cannot forget those days for a single hour, when we lived in our battery – Sasha [Ospovat], Musya [Ginzburg], Ilya, Boris, many other splendid boys. I will never forget my crew, where Sasha was the gun-layer. Those months brought us together. In the Historical Faculty we often quarrelled, swore at one another, were angry with one another, but in the battery, on the contrary, Sasha and I were in complete accord ...
>
> During the retreat we were side by side the whole time. But one evening our commander (whom we all liked) selected some people [including me] to find a way out of the encirclement ... Sasha stayed with the majority. I never thought I would not see him again. When we broke through to our people, others started to

> come out in ones and twos, including Musya, who had a fever ... When we got to Vyazma (I was with a small group of our regiment) we were surrounded again. It took me two weeks to work my way out. I covered nearly two hundred miles behind the German lines, and on 19 October I got out to Dorokhovo. As I learned later, few of our boys managed to get out.[6]

Neither Musya Ginzburg nor Sasha Ospovat was among them. Igor Savkov was taken prisoner, and was not heard of again.

Abram Gordon of the 5th (Frunze) Division was no longer on a horse: he had been transferred to one of the rifle regiments guarding the Warsaw Highway by the time the Germans attacked. The Division was subjected to very heavy artillery and aerial bombardment. There were no Soviet aircraft to be seen. They beat off the first attacks, but the German tanks and motorised infantry continued to advance up the Warsaw Highway. The survivors of the division – about two thousand, including the commander General Presnyakov and the divisional commissar Antropov – assembled in a wood. The general reorganised the survivors into groups, and ordered them to make their way to the East. Surprised by another German column, they panicked briefly, but then rallied, stopped the Germans and destroyed a number of tanks. By then there were only three hundred men left from the original two thousand. They had lost all their vehicles, their remaining guns, and their horses. Presnyakov and Antropov were captured and died in captivity.

The survivors killed the handful of German prisoners they had taken, and continued to feel their way to the East. Near Yukhnov they ran into the Germans again. They had no ammunition left to defend themselves, so they were rounded up and placed in a slaughterhouse in Yukhnov which the Germans were using as a prisoner of war camp. One of the Germans asked Gordon if he were a Jew: under the notorious 'Commissar Order' issued to the German troops at the beginning of the campaign, Jews in uniform were to be shot out of hand. But Gordon's comrades said he came from the Caucasus and he was saved. He and Lieutenant Smirnov managed to escape, and finally reached the Russian lines on 16 December. They were sent by an NKVD Special Detachment to Moscow for interrogation. Gordon was returned to the army, but Smirnov was sent off to a Soviet camp where he died.[7]

Small groups of officers and men from the 6th (Dzerzhinski) Division emerged from encirclement with their divisional flag intact, and were sent to the rear. The Division recovered in time to take part in the December counteroffensive before Moscow, and finished the war in Berlin. The 17th (Moskvorechie) Division tried to fight their way out of encirclement but were heavily bombed and lost most of their vehicles. They destroyed the remainder when they ran out of fuel and ammunition. Their commander, Colonel Kozlov, ordered them to make their way back to the Soviet lines in small groups. Those who survived emerged with their battle flag, 123 rifles, two sub-machine guns, and a machine gun. Only seventeen of their officers were left. By the middle of October they still numbered under three thousand even after they had been refitted and reinforced. But the Division was reconstituted as a fighting force in time to take part in the defence of Moscow, and ended the war in eastern Prussia. The 18th (Leningrad) Division also managed to escape encirclement with its equipment. It was assigned to the 16th Army under Rokossovski, took part in the counteroffensive in December, and in January was the first of the former volunteer divisions to become a Guards division. It finished the war in Germany.[8]

General Lukin, who had already fought his way out of Smolensk, took command of the forces encircled in the Vyazma pocket. They continued to fight desperately, and with some success. On the night of 12/13 October two rifle divisions broke out to the East through a swampy sector where German armour could not manoeuvre. Lukin then destroyed his heavy weapons and equipment, and the survivors escaped in small groups. Some made it to the next planned defensive line near Mozhaisk and Kaluga. Others joined the partisans and reinforced the threat to German communications and air bases.[9] Lukin himself was badly wounded and captured, and after the war had a hard time proving his good name.

Among those who made their way to safety was Colonel Zveriev, the third commander of the 8th (Krasnaya Presnya) Division. He was sent to the rear to form a new 8th Rifle Division to replace the disbanded Volunteer Division. In 1942 his new Division was also surrounded. He was once again captured by the Germans, but this time he did not escape. Instead he joined the Russian Liberation Army set up under General Vlasov by the Germans, and with Vlasov and others was sentenced to death by a Soviet court martial after the war.[10]

Not all the Soviet counterattacks failed. Guderian's tanks suffered an unprecedented setback as they approached Mtsensk on 6 October. Colonel Katukov concealed his T-34s in the woods while the Germans rolled by and then ambushed them from the flanks. The undergunned, underarmoured German tanks were unable to break out. By the end of the day most of them had been reduced to smoking hulks. 'This was the first occasion on which the vast superiority of the Russian T-34 to our tanks became plainly apparent,' Guderian later wrote. 'The [4th Panzer] division suffered grievous casualties. The rapid advance on Tula which we had planned had to be abandoned for the time being.'[11] It was not until 29 October that his lead tanks finally got to within a couple of miles of Tula, a key point on the approaches to Moscow from the south.[12] Tula was practically undefended. A local volunteer battalion was cobbled together from factory workers, teenagers and pensioners and put to defend a railway station and a grain elevator just outside the town. They and the few regular units available held long enough to stop the Germans taking Tula on the run. Guderian was never able to crack the nut, and his attempt to envelop Moscow from the south-east was permanently frustrated.[13]

About seventy thousand volunteers were trapped in the cauldrons at Bryansk and Vyazma, and five volunteer divisions – the 2nd (Stalin), the 7th (Bauman), the 8th (Krasnaya Presnya), the 9th (Kirov) and the 13th (Rostokino) – were so badly wrecked that the Red Army Command had to disband them. The fate of very many of the prisoners taken at Vyazma and Bryansk was in the end even worse than the fate of those who had fallen on the battlefield. The survivors of the volunteer divisions, factory workers, university professors, musicians, ballet dancers, schoolboys and their teachers were herded into improvised prison camps, such as DuLag-130 which the Germans had constructed for thirty thousand prisoners on the outskirts of Roslavl. Those who fell out on the march to scrounge food or from sheer exhaustion were shot down. Those who made it to DuLag-130 and the other camps were crammed together in leaking and unheated barracks with little food and almost no medicine.

Like the men who had surrendered on the frontier battles and in the South, they soon began to succumb to disease, exposure, and starvation. Their wounds became gangrenous, their limbs went black from frostbite. Few of the survivors ever forgot the greasy, insinuating smell of flesh rotting on the bodies of living men. The death rate rose to 4 per cent a day. By early December 8,500 men had died in DuLag-130 alone. Another 16,500 died there over Christmas and the New Year.

Two who survived both the fighting around Vyazma and their subsequent imprisonment by the Germans were Lev Mishchenko and Yelena Okuneva, a nurse. Yelena Okuneva's father was Polish, a leather worker, and the family was Catholic. Before the war they lived with six other families in a *kommunalka* on Sretenka in the centre of Moscow. 'As a member of the Komsomol,' Yelena remembered, 'I did military and nursing training in the evenings. When the war began we were staying in the country. I was subject to military service, so I went straight back into Moscow and found my call-up papers waiting for me at home. I went to the VoenKomat, and they posted me to the 13th (Rostokino) Volunteer Division. At the beginning of August I went to the school where the Division was being formed, wearing a short skirt and high heels. They told me there was no time to go home and change, so I walked with the volunteers in my bare feet all the way to their training ground outside Moscow. Two people died on the way, and the commander of the Division sent me home in a truck with the corpses so that I could get some more suitable clothes. There was no one at home, so I just left a message and went back to the Division to work as a nurse.

'When the fighting started around Vyazma in October I was in a lorry with a medical orderly and a doctor, looking after a number of wounded soldiers. We got lost, but were sure we were still well behind the lines. Then we heard Germans speaking. They stopped the lorry, made those of us who could walk get out, marched us off to a station, and sent us by train to a prisoner of war camp in Belorussia. Here the doctor, the orderly and I were employed and decently fed in the camp clinic, which was commanded by a young German doctor. There had been many eminent Russian doctors in the volunteer divisions. Several of them – the most distinguished was called Sergei Petrovich – were employed in the clinic: the young German consulted them in order to improve his own professional skills.

'There were four hundred women in the camp. Many of them were civilians, who were captured while they were digging trenches. Things began to get worse. Typhus began to spread among the prisoners in the main camp. The doctors, both German and Russian, did their best, but they did not have the medicines or the facilities to stem the epidemic. I was young and blonde. The German doctor tried to take me under his "protection", but the Russian doctors dissuaded him. Meanwhile the Germans discovered that some of the Russian doctors had developed links with the partisans. Brutal interrogations began: Sergei Petrovich was later hanged. It looked as if I would soon be in trouble too. I was saved when the German doctor arranged for me to be smuggled into a group of women being sent off to work in Germany. After the war the son of Sergei Petrovich sent me a photo of the camp and the monument which now stands there. I still have it today.

'I had learned a fair amount of German from my mother, and this was a great help when I got to Germany. The woman in the first family I worked with near Nuremberg was called Margarete. She was very kind to me. She had six boys and one girl, and I helped to look after them. But the family business was a bakery, and I discovered I was allergic to flour. I went to work with a new family, who were much less pleasant. The eldest boy was at the front, and they did not like Russians. They denounced me for giving food to the Russian prisoners in a nearby camp, and I was in a German prison for a couple of months. After I was let out, Margarete helped me again.'[14]

Yelena was liberated by the British, worked for a while in a Soviet military hospital, and returned to Moscow. She continued to work as a nurse, got married, took her new husband to live with her parents in the family *kommunalka*, and moved when the babies started to come. Her daughter married Rokossovski's grandson, like her a Catholic. When it became possible under perestroika, the two families were among those who led the agitation to reopen the old Polish church in Moscow. Yelena remained in touch first with Margarete and then, after Margarete died, with her daughter into the new millennium.

One group of prisoners – several thousand of them, including Lev Mishchenko – was marched for several days until they found themselves in DuLag-127 on the outskirts of Smolensk. Hunger, cold, squalor, and typhus soon began to reduce their numbers. The sick were sent to the camp hospital outside the wire, where they died like flies. In

December Mishchenko and other prisoners from Moscow were transferred to another camp in the village of Katyn.[15] They were well fed and housed: the Germans were hoping to recruit them as agents to cross the lines and report back on Russian plans and dispositions. Mishchenko and one of his comrades refused. To their surprise they were not shot, but transferred to Germany. In the years that followed Mishchenko was moved from camp to camp, worked in a number of German factories and in outside work parties, acted from time to time as an interpreter, resisted attempts to recruit him into the German-sponsored 'Russian Liberation Army', escaped from imprisonment and was recaptured after three weeks, spent a month in a German civilian prison, was sent to the concentration camp at Buchenwald for a while, was in Leipzig when it was bombed by the RAF, escaped again in spring as he and the other prisoners were being marched away ahead of the advancing Russians, fell in with the Americans, refused their offer to go to the United States, and was handed back to the Russians. Like hundreds of thousands of his fellow prisoners, he was then arrested, interrogated by the NKVD, and sent to the Gulag, from which he did not emerge until 1956. Thereafter he rejoined his wife Svetlana, returned to Moscow University, and worked for thirty-four years in the Scientific Research Institute for Nuclear Physics. Like Yelena Okuneva, he was kindly treated by civilians in Germany, and resumed contact with them once he was free to do so.[16]

The number of volunteers who died, either in battle or in German camps, has never been properly established. If any detailed figures or information about the fates of individual soldiers from the volunteer divisions survived the chaos of the fighting, they remain for the most part secreted in the archives.[17] At a small village called Korobets fourteen hundred volunteers from the Krasnaya Presnya Division were killed in their abortive attempt to break through the German encirclement. Over the next few weeks they were buried in a mass grave by the people of the village.[18] The bodies of many of them lay where they died, without proper burial. Six decades later good people were still digging up the remains of those who died on the battlefields of Vyazma and Bryansk. At that stage in the war the soldiers carried a tube about two inches long, in which they were supposed to place their personal details written on bits of paper. But the superstition was that this would bring you bad luck. Many of the tubes that the searchers found were empty, and their owners could no longer be identified.[19] Ninety bodies were reburied with military honours on the Vyazma battlefield on 2 October 2004, on the day which is celebrated as the anniversary of their first and last battle by the few survivors of the 8th (Krasnaya Presnya) Volunteer Division.

The Western, Reserve and Bryansk fronts were practically destroyed during the Vyazma and Bryansk battles. A quarter of a million soldiers were dead or wounded. Nearly seven hundred thousand were captured. Though the figures were comparable, it was a disaster even greater than the one which had overwhelmed Kirponos in the Ukraine three weeks earlier. In less than a week the Germans had blasted a hole in the Soviet defences over three hundred miles wide.[20] Now Moscow itself seemed to be there for the taking.

From Zhukov onwards, Russians have argued – perhaps rightly – that the sacrifice of the divisions encircled at Bryansk and Vyazma was not in vain. The Germans had to employ twenty-eight divisions to liquidate the pockets of resistance and to secure the prisoners they had taken. The Russians gained a little more time to strengthen their defences.

At first Stalin and his generals were unable to believe what was happening. On the morning of 5 October – when the three Fronts on the approach to Moscow were all on the verge of encirclement – the General Staff's early-morning round-up merely reported that they were engaged with the enemy. Some units had fallen back, the report admitted. But others had counterattacked, and most had held their ground. Nothing very unusual had happened during the previous night.[21]

The first sign of trouble came at 9 o'clock in the morning. Stragglers from the forward armies detained near Maloyaroslavets, eighty miles from Moscow, claimed that the Germans had mounted heavy attacks with tanks and aircraft. Several divisions were already surrounded. Colonel Sbytov, the man who had blown the whistle on Pumpur, was now commanding the air forces in the Moscow Military District. He had set up a standing air patrol to watch the approach roads to Moscow. At dawn that morning two of his fighter pilots saw a column of German armoured vehicles some fifteen miles long, moving along the Warsaw Highway from Roslavl towards Yukhnov, no more than one hundred and twenty miles away from Moscow. The pilots flew low enough to take a careful look, and came back to base with their aircraft peppered with machine-gun fire. Another pilot came back with the same message. Sbytov told his superior General Telegin the bad news.

Telegin immediately telephoned Shaposhnikov, the Chief of the General Staff. At first he was greeted with disbelief, but when a third pilot brought back the same news, Shaposhnikov passed it to Stalin. Stalin's first reaction was to tell Telegin that he should not believe every first bit of information he received. The air commander who had delivered the news should be arrested and handed over to the NKVD. Sbytov was summoned by Beria's deputy, Abakumov. The NKVD, said Abakumov, had no news of enemy tanks. Sbytov's pilots were panic-mongers and cowards. He threatened Sbytov with court martial.

When Stalin finally realised that the Germans had indeed broken through, and that they were on their way to encircle Moscow from the South, he immediately ordered them to be held on the Warsaw Highway for long enough to bring up reserves. The only forces available were the cadets of the military colleges in Podolsk, two or three regiments of artillery, and some air defence units. The Podolsk cadets and their teachers were ordered forward to hold the Germans at a river crossing. They slowed the Germans down, but at a very heavy cost. Their exploit entered into legend.

Stalin now summoned an emergency session of the GKO.[22] He ordered Zhukov back from Leningrad for consultations. The three Front commanders – Yerëmenko, Budënny, and Koniev – were authorised to pull their forces back to a better defensive line. Reinforcements were summoned from the strategic reserve, from the Far East and Central Asia, and from neighbouring Fronts, and sent to man the new and still incomplete Mozhaisk Defence Line, the next fortified position to the East. The Chief of the Air Staff telephoned Sbytov to tell him that the GKO had decided to approve his actions. Instead of being court-martialled, he was rapidly promoted.[23]

Despite the absence of official news, ordinary people managed to form a good idea of what was going on. Dr Peter Miller, a well-known historian of Moscow, had persuaded the Academy of Sciences to set up a group in the Institute of History to record the way everyday life in Moscow was changing under the impact of war. When the institute was evacuated, he remained behind and continued the work in the form of a detailed diary, in which he meticulously noted down weather conditions, air-raid damage, rumours even if they were improbable, his judgement of people and events. On 7 October, he wrote in his diary:

> The silence of the SovInformBuro is irritating, although people no longer read [its] communiqués ... There is a mood of catastrophe and fatalism. The shops are empty, even coffee has disappeared, which no one was buying anyway because there was no milk; they are selling kumyss [fermented mare's milk] in the cheese shop. No fats are available. Pressure is increasing to evacuate children, even though children's ration cards for milk were issued three days ago, which meant that they were assuming that the children would remain in the city. There is a feeling of approaching catastrophe in the air and endless rumours: Orël has been surrendered, Vyazma has been surrendered, the Germans have got to Maloyaroslavets [...]. The mood is particularly bad today.[24]

The foreign military observers and journalists in Moscow took some time to catch up with the extent of the catastrophe. On 3 October, the day the Germans captured Orël, the British Military Mission gave their Soviet opposite numbers their latest intelligence: the Germans were preparing an assault. Stalin's scepticism about the value of British intelligence was merely accentuated.[25] The British were not entirely to blame. As they noted desperately in their War Diary: 'It may be unbelievable but we are getting literally no information from the Russians and depend almost entirely upon the BBC.'[26] Werth and the other foreign journalists were still hoping that Moscow could look forward confidently to a moderately quiet winter. The concert season began on 5 October. Werth was unable to get a ticket, so he made do with a lively performance of *The School for Scandal* at the Moscow Art Theatre.[27]

On 8 October Moscow Dinamo beat Spartak 7–1.[28] But it was on that day that the authorities finally admitted that Orël was in German hands. Zhukov arrived in the evening from Leningrad, and went straight to see Stalin, who had flu but was working in his apartment. Stalin drew a gloomy parallel with the situation in 1918 when Lenin was forced to negotiate a peace with the advancing Germans at Brest Litovsk. He told Zhukov to take a car, find Koniev and Budënny, and discover what on earth was going on. The two Front commanders were warned by telegram that Zhukov, as the representative of the Stavka, had full powers to deploy their forces as he saw fit.

At 2.30 the next morning Zhukov reported to Stalin from Koniev's headquarters that there were not nearly enough troops at Mozhaisk to prevent a German breakthrough. The Mozhaisk Defence Line needed to be reinforced as rapidly as possible. Stalin ordered the wreckage of the Reserve and Western Fronts to be combined into a single Western Front under Zhukov, who commanded it until August 1942. It was on this Front that the main brunt of the German assault on Moscow was now to fall.

There was a bad moment when Stalin seemed to be all for shooting Koniev for failing to stem the German advance. According to his own account, Zhukov – himself ruthless in the application of the death penalty – objected.

'Shooting Koniev will not improve anything or encourage anyone. It will only produce a bad impression in the army. Shooting Pavlov was no use at all. Everyone knew that Pavlov should never have been put in charge of anything larger than a division ... But Koniev is not Pavlov – he is an intelligent man. He can still be serviceable.'

'What do you suggest?' asked Stalin. Zhukov recommended that Koniev should stay on as his deputy. Stalin asked suspiciously: 'Why are you defending Koniev? Is he some pal of yours?' But he agreed to the appointment.[29] A couple of days later Koniev was sent to get a grip on the situation around Kalinin [Tver], a hundred miles Northwest of Moscow on the Leningrad Highway, where the locals had panicked and another gaping hole had been left in the defences. On 17 October he was appointed to command a new Front there.[30] He performed successfully for the rest of the war, and his troops were the first to enter Berlin in April 1945.

The Mozhaisk Defence Line stretched for more than one hundred and twenty miles in an arc from the Moscow reservoir to the North of the city, around the small city of Volokolamsk, across the 1812 battlefield of Borodino just to the West of Mozhaisk itself, and down to the confluence of the Ugra and the Oka rivers. It was still incomplete when Zhukov rushed forward everything he could to man it: six divisions, six armoured brigades, ten artillery regiments and machine-gun battalions. One of the divisions was the 316th Rifle Division under General Panfilov. It came in ten trains, and settled in around Volokolamsk, on the highway of that name. From its first days in action, the 316th Division won the respect of the enemy: '[It] contains many well-trained soldiers and is conducting a strikingly obstinate defence,' wrote the commander of the opposing German corps.[31] Both the Highway and the Division were to become famous.

It was still not enough. Cities and villages continued to fall – Kaluga, Borodino, Kalinin, Maloyaroslavets, Mozhaisk itself. On 12 October the GKO set up the 'Moscow Defence Zone', stretching sixty miles out from the city, under General Artemiev, the commander of the Moscow Military District. They also ordered the construction of yet another line of defence, this time around Moscow itself.[32] This was to consist of an outer belt, running from the Moscow–Volga Canal in the North to Serpukhov in the South, and three separate lines of defence inside the city: one along the Circular Railway Ring, and two along the ancient defensive lines of the Garden Ring, and the Boulevard Ring. People living on the embankment of the Moscow River were ordered to move out so that their apartment buildings could be turned into strongpoints.[33] The detailed planning was done by Artemiev's staff and a troika from each Raion consisting of the Raion Party Committee Secretary, the deputy chairman of the Raion Executive Committee, and the head of the local MPVO engineering department. To construct these works, the Moscow Regional Soviet was told to mobilise 250,000 workers and peasants for twenty days, to provide for their food and equipment and to commandeer building materials and transport as necessary. Pronin, the Chairman of the Moscow City Council, mobilised another 200,000 from among Moscow's office workers and from among workers from factories not producing weapons. Altogether 600,000 Muscovites were involved in these construction projects. All those aged eighteen and over who were capable of physical work were ordered to appear with spades and if possible axes, picks and crowbars, dressed appropriately for the season, equipped with warm underwear, working shoes, and food for two weeks. This time there was no call for volunteers: it was forced labour, and only those in the defence industry were exempted. The Moscow City Council requisitioned the necessary transport and building materials. Each Raion was given its own sector, and detailed instructions of what to build where. The works were carried out at breakneck speed. Bridges and roads were mined along the main roads into the city. Barricades, obstacles, and firing points were erected along the three inner lines of defence.[34] Those working outside the city were accommodated by local villagers, and their food was brought in containers from the city.[35] It consisted, for the most part, of '*balanda*', boiling water with some flour and salt in it. This was an impressive turnout, but a lack of engineers and equipment prevented Artemiev from completing the work by his deadline of 20 October.

On 13 October Shcherbakov set out to raise more volunteer divisions. Most suitable men had already gone to the war, and this time each Raion was ordered to raise only a battalion. Stanislav Iofin was a student at the Moscow Institute of Non-Ferrous Metals. Now he and his fellow students were called together in the main hall of the Institute by the Komsomol Party Committee, and asked to volunteer. The audience split. Some decided to go with the Institute, which was being evacuated to Alma Ata. Iofin and some others decided to stay. The battalion was formed in three days – it contained twenty-five men only. Battalions of a sort were raised in each Raion. At first they were equipped with old French, Polish, Canadian, German and other rifles: an average of one rifle for every two men.[36] Not surprisingly, the October *opolchenie* produced no more than some ten thousand volunteers, a scraping of the barrel.[37]

Full divisions were, however, created by combining the volunteer battalions with sub-units from the regular army, conscripts recruited by the VoenKomats and members of the 'Destroyer Battalions' (Istrebitelnye Bataliony) set up in June. The five Moscow Rifle Divisions which resulted were given specialist units of engineers, signallers, medical staff and others, and eventually numbered nearly forty thousand people.[38] Though not of the quality of the volunteer divisions raised in the summer, several subsequently acquitted themselves quite well.

Among this new round of volunteers, despite the attempts of the authorities to dissuade them, were six hundred women. Two of them, Masha Polivanova and Natasha Kovshova, became famous as snipers and set up a sniper school within the division. On 14 August 1942 they entered into legend when they were surrounded by the Germans, ran out of ammunition, and blew themselves up with grenades rather than let themselves be captured.[39]

Yegor Rusakov, a sixteen-year-old postal worker, went off to volunteer as soon as he heard the call. In an office on the ground floor of the post office stood a queue of elderly men. A man in a thick jacket with a soldier's belt sat at a table and wrote the names of the volunteers into a notebook.

'That's it, Sokolov. Report with your things to the Raion Party Committee office at 12 o'clock. You'll get your weapon on the spot. Next!'

When Yegor got to the head of the queue, he gave his name. The man in the jacket began to write without even looking at him.

'Go on!'

'Born in 1926, Komsomol member, I've not served in the army, but …'

'1926?' The man looked at him and said, 'It won't do.'

'But I'm in the Komsomol and I can shoot!'

'It still won't do. I've no instructions to recruit people born in 1926. Next!'

Yegor went off to dig trenches instead.[40]

In addition to these scratch forces, regular divisions from the reserve were at last beginning to pass through Moscow to the front. A journalist from *Krasnaya Zvezda* saw some of them on the Garden Ring, and wrote an inspirational piece:

> As they march their pace rings out with disciplined precision. The sun shines on their bayonets, on their helmets, on their mess cans. They march with sunburned faces, the warriors of the Red Army, and as they march they smile at Moscow, the heart of the country. Everything has stopped for them – trams, buses, pedestrians. Make way for the soldiers! The people of Moscow line the pavements to welcome them … A song rings out about our Soviet Motherland. Company after company, battalion after battalion takes up the song. And the people of the capital take up the song as well.

Shcherbakov rang Ortenberg grumpily to protest at this apparent breach of security: the movement of reserves was a vital military secret. Ortenberg managed to persuade him that the story was just what people needed to sustain their morale.[41]

Daniel Mitlyanski, the sculptor who had been a classmate of Vladimir Kantovski at School No. 110, had a memory of a quite different kind: of a regiment going off to the front in complete silence – no band, no singing, gloomy faces, the faces of people who knew they would not be coming back. Decades later he still broke down in tears when he recalled the scene.[42]

Rokossovski was very nearly caught in the trap at Vyazma. On the evening of 5 October, as the German breakthrough was accelerating, Koniev ordered him by telephone to hand over his sector of the line, and 'proceed with your staff and the necessary support to Vyazma by forced march, arriving not later than the morning of 6 October ... Your task is to stop the enemy, who are advancing on Vyazma from Spas-Demensk.' Rokossovski was given a vague promise that he would find five divisions waiting for him. Malinin, his Chief of Staff, advised him to insist on getting the order in writing, lest he be made a scapegoat if things went wrong. He did so, and set off with Malinin and the other members of his immediate staff to discover what was going on. On the way they once again found bits and pieces of shattered armies, soldiers who claimed that German parachutists had disrupted their formations, groups of refugees with all their belongings on carts. But at Vyazma itself he found none of the divisions he had been promised: they had been trapped in the encirclement. General Nikitin, the garrison commander, told him that all he had available was the local police. The town's authorities were meeting in the town's cathedral, which was on a hill overlooking the city. Nikitin introduced Rokossovski to them as the new commander – a commander, Rokossovski thought to himself, with nothing to command. As they were talking a man rushed into the meeting room. He had been up on the bell tower. German tanks were entering the town.

Rokossovski and his people just managed to escape. They ran into a German tank on the outskirts, but managed to nip into a side alley before it could open fire. Rokossovski decided there was no point waiting any further for his missing divisions. He set off to find the Soviet front line with such troops as he managed to collect on the way: a few medium tanks and armoured cars, a squadron of NKVD cavalry and elements of the 18th (Leningrad) Volunteer Division which had escaped encirclement. These he organised into three columns, and pressed forward, screened by the troopers and supported by the tanks and armoured cars. It was a strong enough force to brush aside the occasional small groups of German soldiers that they encountered.

They made a brief stop in a village to eat and rest. Some Germans had passed through hours before. In the cottage where Rokossovski and his staff were eating, a grey-bearded old man spoke bitterly from a bed in the corner of the darkened room: 'Comrade Commander, what are you doing? You are leaving and abandoning us to the enemy. We did everything we could do for the Red Army. We would have given them the last shirt off our backs. I'm an old soldier. I've fought against the Germans. We never allowed the enemy onto Russian soil. What do you think you're doing?' The old man's reproaches were like a slap in the face.[43]

Rokossovski finally managed to disentangle his little force from the encroaching Germans and struggle through to the headquarters of the Western Front. Zhukov had just arrived as its new commander, and he ordered Rokossovski to set up his defences along the Northern part of the Mozhaisk Defence Line. On 13 October Rokossovski began to put together a scratch force, including the remnants of Lukin's 16th Army, Dovator's cavalry, the 316th Division under General Panfilov, a regiment of cadets from the School of the Supreme Soviet, what was left of the 18th (Leningrad) Volunteer Division, and a number of artillery and other units. The new formation took the name of the 16th Army, under which it entered history. They were spread painfully thin: no more than two or three hundred riflemen to cover each of the sixty miles they were supposed to hold. And they had nothing in reserve.[44]

At this critical moment Lieutenant Galina Talanova was posted to the 16th Army as the headquarters doctor. She was a regular officer of the medical corps. In spring 1941 she was serving in Bialystok in recently occupied Poland. A prescient senior officer sent her on leave at the beginning of June, and she was thus spared the fate of her colleagues in the frontier forces. She became Rokossovski's mistress, stayed with him throughout the war, and bore him a daughter, Nadezhda, in January 1945, when he and his 1st Belorussian Front were already in Poland. After the war Rokossovski returned to his wife, but remained in contact with Talanova and Nadezhda until he died.[45]

Vladimir Gurkin and his battalion of howitzers from the Krasin Artillery School were among the reinforcements who were rushed to man the Mozhaisk Defence Line. They travelled very slowly – the tractors that pulled the howitzers could only move at five miles an hour – but after three days they dug in on the estate near Volokolamsk which had belonged to Pushkin's parents-in-law. Their task was to support Panfilov's 316th Division, Dovator's cavalry, and the cadets from the School of the Supreme Soviet. Gurkin and his comrades were still wearing their cadet greatcoats. They looked very smart and in theory they were well trained. But they had never actually fired their guns before they went into action. Because there was so little artillery available, they continually had to move to plug gaps. At first they had no ear protectors. On one occasion the Germans were practically upon them and they were firing over open sights. Barbutian, the Armenian gun-layer panicked ('Like all Armenians,' Gurkin said) and pulled the trigger without warning. Gurkin had no time to turn his head away, and his hearing was permanently affected. Neither he nor his wife noticed his disability until he failed to pass the medical for staff college. He was unable to distinguish sibilants, a real problem when he was later posted to Poland and had to decipher that remarkably sibilant language. The Krasin cadets remained in the line until 15 November, when they handed their guns over to the 16th Army and were sent back to finish their training in the Artillery Academy, which by now had been evacuated to the Urals.[46] Remarkably they had lost only four people – through accidents, not enemy action. In February 1942 Gurkin passed out with the rank of Junior Lieutenant, and was posted to the General Staff.

Panfilov's 316th Rifle Division was on the left flank of the 16th Army, covering Volokolamsk from the West and the Southwest. The Division had been raised in Kazakhstan during the summer. It was up to full establishment, and unusually well trained and equipped. Rokossovski warmed to Panfilov immediately. He was a commander after Rokossovski's own heart: intelligent, highly professional, with a great deal of practical experience, a man of bubbling energy and powerful will under his misleadingly shy exterior. His command style was like Rokossovski's own: he knew each of his subordinates well, and spoke of them with respect. Rokossovski particularly liked his quiet sense of humour. Along one section of his front the 'fortifications' consisted merely of stakes driven into the ground to mark where the line would eventually run. 'Yes,' Panfilov grinned, 'we've been staked out good and proper.'[47]

On 15 October the Germans attacked with overwhelming force. The 316th Division resisted stubbornly, but on 28 October – despite a direct order from Stalin – they abandoned Volokolamsk in some disorder.[48] Morale began to fail. Soldiers complained that they were being treated like dogs, that they had been betrayed by their generals, that there was no point in fighting because the Germans were bound to win. After all, one of them said, at least half the peasants were against the regime. The commissar of the 16th Army told his colleague in the 316th Division to get a grip. Rokossovski and Panfilov were both criticised for their conduct of the battle.[49] But the Division recovered its composure, and the seeds of a legend were sown, a legend much distorted in detail but true enough in its broad outline, the legend of Panfilov and his Division, and their heroic defence of the Volokolamsk Highway.

Another legend was born some thirty miles to the South, at Borodino in the very centre of the Mozhaisk Defence Line. On 11 October elements of the 5th Army under General Leliushenko – three tank brigades, cadets from a Moscow military college, and the 32nd Division under Colonel Polosukhin – took up their positions on the very ground where Kutuzov had faced Napoleon in 1812. A concrete pillbox is still there, at the foot of the Raevski Redoubt where Tolstoy's Pierre Bezukhov watched some of the bloodiest fighting of that earlier battle. Polosukhin looked in on the old Borodino Museum, the last visitor before it was destroyed. The exhibits were being hurriedly packed in boxes for evacuation. In the visitors' book, under 'Purpose of Visit?', Polosukhin wrote, 'I have come to defend the battlefield.' As the fighting began, Polosukhin quoted Lermontov's poem about the earlier battle to his commanders. Both officers and men felt that their ancestors, the men who had fought and died in just that place a century before them, were looking down in the expectation that they too would fight and die where they stood.

On 13 October, as Napoleon had done before them, the Germans moved against the Shevardino Redoubt, in front of the Russian line. The next day they broke into the Russian positions. Leliushenko was wounded in the hand-to-hand fighting. But Polosukhin held out for five days. Then, like Kutuzov, he and his men were forced to abandon Mozhaisk and retreat, still unbeaten, along the road towards Moscow. They had gained more time for Zhukov to plug the huge gap that had been torn from Moscow's outer defences. Zhukov's reaction was to order Leliushenko and his fellow commanders of the 5th Army to shoot each and if necessary every soldier who had abandoned the battlefield without orders.[50] Much later people noticed that the start of the battle had coincided with the Feast of the Protection of the Holy Mother of God. Metropolitan Sergi had invoked her on that very day. Had it perhaps been a miracle?[51]

The Russians were retreating again. But now they were retreating in good order, a few miles at a time. The German advance slowed to a halt. The weather was already beginning to bear heavily on the fighting. It was not at first the snow of General Winter, but the far more intractable mud of the *rasputitsa*. The first snow had already fallen on 7 October – even earlier than it had done in 1812. But it soon thawed, making the mud still worse. Hitler's armies were in serious trouble long before the snow finally settled.

The *rasputitsa* spared the Russians no more than it spared the Germans. Their vehicles and their wagons sank into the mud just as quickly. They too had to manhandle food and ammunition through the mud when even horses failed. Their wounded faced the same nightmare journey to the rear. But for the time being the German offensive was literally bogged down. At the end of October the Germans paused to lick their wounds, sort out their lines of communication, now stretched to breaking point, and bring up new men, new weapons, new ammunition, and new supplies for what they believed, with increasing desperation, would be the final assault on the capital of Bolshevism.

– TWELVE –

PANIC

As autumn drew in, the people of Moscow started to get very cold indeed. The mines of the Ukraine and Western Russia were in the hands of the enemy. What little coal reached Moscow went primarily to factories producing for the war. The electricity supply began to break down. The Moscow City Council announced in the press that it was halving the amount of electricity for lighting purposes. In late November, as the Germans approached the Kashira power station South of the city, the local authorities asked for permission to blow it up. Stalin ordered instead that it be defended at all costs and sent General Belov and his Second Cavalry Corps down to help.[1]

Office buildings were practically unheated. Apartment blocks became uninhabitable as heating failed and bombs blew out the windows. Buildings were closed down – 'conserved' – by the local authorities, and the remaining inhabitants were moved into apartments left empty by people who had gone to the front or into evacuation. The original inhabitants were assured that they would get their apartments back when they returned. But the guarantees were not always honoured. Disputes were still going through the courts years later. Yuri Krotkov, a minor literary figure and NKVD informer, did not bother to go to the courts at all when he got back to Moscow in 1943. He simply used his connections with 'them', and got his friends in the secret police to evict the squatters.[2]

As conditions got harder, people experimented with ways of saving electricity, heating their food and finding substitutes for the delicacies they were used to in peacetime. One newspaper told housewives how to make oven boxes lined with straw:

> A thermos can be made out of a wooden box with double walls: the gap between should be filled with sawdust, straw, paper, or cotton wool. Soup can be simmered in such a thermos, instead of leaving it on the kerosene stove for a couple of hours. As soon as the soup has boiled, put it in the thermos to simmer, and in two to three hours it will be ready.[3]

Other advisers suggested ways of prolonging the life of carbon paper and typewriter ribbons. One young scientist devised a substitute for window glass blown out by the bombs. People baked fritters from potato peelings they would previously have thrown away. You put the peelings through the mincer, and added water, flour and salt. Or you grated the peelings, steamed them in water in a frying pan, and added crushed dried birch leaves instead of flour. You could make coffee from acorns. You cut the acorns in two, dried them on the stove, peeled them, boiled them in a saucepan with the lid on, and waited until the water was cold. Then you poured off the water, dried the acorns again, ground them in a coffee grinder, and added chicory or a bit of real coffee to give the taste. A spoonful of acorns was sufficient for one glass of coffee. In their window boxes people grew cucumbers and onions instead of flowers. All open spaces were turned into allotments. People started to keep chickens in the yards of their apartment blocks.[4] For people with longer memories, it was all too reminiscent of the time of famine during the Civil War.

In the summer Konstantin Simonov had watched the peasants evacuating their cattle from the countryside around Smolensk. Now, hundreds of miles and many weeks later, endless herds of cows, sheep, and goats plodded along the Moscow boulevards. They were emaciated and exhausted, and the women who herded them were in scarcely better shape. They were driven in their thousands right through the centre of the city and out to the East. They were dogged by sinister figures, who raided the columns and carried pigs off into the side streets and courtyards to be slaughtered and sold. Animals that collapsed with exhaustion had their throats cut, and their bodies were thrown on the carts which brought up the rear.[5]

Because most of the major factories had been evacuated, smaller factories were increasingly turned over to the production of arms. By the end of November their share of weapons production in Moscow had grown from less than a quarter to 94 per cent. Most of the workers were now women and teenagers. Nearly four hundred thousand Moscow housewives went to work in the factories. They repaired aircraft and tanks, filled shells, experimented with new kinds of explosive, made trench mortars and Molotov cocktails, welded tank traps and produced a whole variety of small arms. Some of the younger children needed special stools to be able to reach the lathes on which they were working. Factories switched from peacetime production to making goods for the front. A children's bicycle factory began making flamethrowers, eight die-stamping works which formerly made teaspoons and paperclips switched to making entrenching tools and parts for anti-tank grenades. A woodworking shop producing abacuses and screens changed over to making pistol cartridges. A furniture factory started turning out anti-tank mines, cartridge boxes and stretchers. A typewriter works began making automatic rifles and ammunition.[6]

Before the war Russian generals had had little time for sub-machine guns. Then they discovered from bitter experience in the Winter War against the Finns that sub-machine guns were just what you needed for close-quarter fighting. In 1941 the Russians designed and produced the PPSh-41. Like the T-34 tank, the PPSh was highly effective in action and very simple to make. Shcherbakov organised its mass production in a network of Moscow factories. The Secretaries of the Raion Party Committees were made personally responsible for seeing that the targets were met. A few hundred PPSh only were produced in November. But more than 155,000 guns were produced over the next five months, and by the spring production was running at up to three thousand a day.[7] The PPSh became the badge of the Soviet infantry for the rest of the war.

*

German policy in the occupied territories, at least to start with, was contradictory, and many Russians had still not rid themselves of their illusions of what lay in store for them if the Germans arrived. The Germans were determined to exploit the material resources in the occupied areas. Many did not care what the consequences might be for the inferior races who happened to be living there. But some believed that it would be more profitable to get the locals to cooperate. Russians were in any case needed for low-level administrative and guard duties. It might even be possible to recruit an army of Russians to fight alongside the Wehrmacht to overthrow the hated Soviet regime. Rather like the French in Algeria and the Americans in Vietnam, the Germans made sporadic and ultimately unsuccessful attempts to win the hearts and minds of those they had conquered. They appealed to three sentiments in particular: the ambition to run a private business, the desire of the peasants for their own land, and the innate streak of Russian anti-Semitism. Their appeals fell on fertile ground. In many places the ordinary German soldiers behaved well enough. They were greeted with the traditional gifts of bread and salt in parts of Ukraine which had suffered particularly badly from collectivisation. Such scenes were at first repeated even as they approached Moscow.[23]

Some people were beginning to hedge their bets in anticipation of the Germans' arrival. One small boy delivering call-up papers found people polishing their parquet floors and baking welcoming cakes 'just in case'.[24] The painter Alexander Osmërkin, who lived in the same artists' building as Raisa Labas, called on her as the Germans approached. 'Raya,' he said,

> 'I hear you're preparing to leave Moscow. Have you gone off your head? Excuse my crudeness, but who are you running to, and who are you running from? Do you really believe our cheap propaganda? In Kiev the Germans have set up a Social Revolutionary government. They are giving great support to the arts. They are after all the most cultured people in Europe. I'm sure that they won't persecute people like you and me. On the contrary, I'm waiting for them impatiently, although, as you know, my wife is Jewish. Well, I tell her, you'll have to wear a Star of David on your sleeve for a while. But there'll be no Cheka, and we will have free contact with Europe.

> I've burned my certificates, cleared out all compromising material from my apartment – the Marxist classics and the portraits and the rest of the filthy Bolshevik rubbish. Good Lord, I think, is it really all coming to an end?'[25]

If there was ever an opportunity for the Germans to win over the disaffected, they missed it entirely. The brutal indoctrination of the German troops, the order to shoot military commissars and Party officials, and the operations of the SS, had already resulted in the beginnings of mass murder. In September, in what was only the largest such massacre to date, thirty thousand Jews – including Vasili Grossman's mother – were shot in Berdichev in Ukraine by the SS and their local collaborators.[26] News of these atrocities filtered through to the population in Moscow, and they were played up for all they were worth in the Soviet press.

Since the summer, entry to Moscow had been severely restricted. You had to have a residence permit; if you lived outside the city limits you had to have a document from your employer or your collective farm to come to Moscow to work or sell your produce there. Those who had been evacuated were forbidden to return. Those who returned without permission got no ration cards, and their residence permit was not restored.[27]

But some slipped through the net. Maria Kiselëva had hired a dacha to the East of Moscow for the whole of the summer holiday. The dacha was not far from a military airfield and from the camp in which Anufriev, Teleguev, and the Spanish republican refugees were training with the special forces of the OMSBON. The Kiselëvs were an old established Moscow intelligentsia family. Maria's father had founded two museums (one, the toy museum, that still exists). Her husband Andrei was a professor. Her stepmother was painted by Serov, one of Russia's finest painters at the end of the nineteenth century, and the portrait still hangs in Moscow's Tretyakov Gallery.

When the Germans started bombing the airfield near her dacha Maria Kiselëva decided to go back to the city with her thirteen-year-old son Nikolai. She found that their house on Protochny Lane had been 'conserved': the people had left, the electricity and water had been turned off, and it was impossible to live there. She managed to get an empty apartment at 52 Vorovski Street, where the Rostov family lived in Tolstoy's *War and Peace*. The main part of the building was used by the Writers' Union, but the wings – the former stables – had been turned into flats. Opposite the house was a cinema – the First Picture-house (Pervy Kinoteatr). On its roof there was an anti-aircraft machine gun. The cinema remained open throughout the war: for months it showed a British film, *George's Dinky Jazz Band* (the English title is *Let George Do It*), in which George Formby finds himself accidentally broadcasting secret messages to German U-boats on his ukulele.[28]

The heating was not working in the Rostov house either, and it was very cold. Maria Kiselëva cooked on a *burzhuika*, a cheap wood-fired stove which had kept the bourgeoisie warm during the bad days of the Civil War. People fixed pipes out through their windows to lead off the fumes. There would be dozens of these pipes in the big apartment blocks, and on frosty days the smoke would hang in a picturesque curtain of every possible colour – blue-grey, black, yellow, and even crimson – depending on the fuel being used. This could be a dangerous business if you got it wrong. A growing number of people died from carbon monoxide poisoning. Not all the deaths were accidental. Dr Dreitser noted in her diary that one ingenious couple murdered a young man and tried to claim that he had been killed by the fumes from his *burzhuika*.[29]

The Moscow schools should have reopened on 1 September, but what with the general disruption and the departure of so many school-children they mostly stayed closed. Nikolai Kiselëv got a job in a small workshop along Povarskaya Street, making papier-mâché heads for dolls. This meant that he qualified for a larger ration as a worker, rather than a dependant. Because there was no street lighting, he had to feel his way home along the walls of the houses in the pitch blackness. That became even harder after the snow fell: it was cleared only along the middle of the street, to make way for the mounted patrols.

The Kiselëvs' main food was bran, and potatoes which tasted sweet because they had been frozen in the ground. At first Maria was able to fry the potatoes with castor oil bought at the chemist's. Later this was forbidden. There was of course no soap. As food got shorter, peasants from the surrounding countryside brought their produce to sell in the city. To trade in the official markets you had to pay a fee to the city authorities. Many traders operated on the side streets instead, and got in the way of the traffic. Even the official markets overflowed their boundaries. The Central Market took over the whole of Tsvetnoi Boulevard. A grey mass of people bought and sold padded jackets, greatcoats, headgear for tank crews, airmen and sailors. Cigarettes had been rationed since August. Now children and invalids specialised in the black market trade in tobacco, dealing in cigarettes collected from non-smokers who did not need their ration.[30] The journalist and writer Nikolai Verzhbitski carefully noted in his diary the occasions on which he had to line up for potatoes, kerosene, bread. The back of his hand was marked in indelible ink with numbers – 31, 62, 341, 5004 – to signify his place in various queues.[31]

The prices charged in the markets were beyond the means of ordinary people. By the end of the first year of the war prices had gone up eight times. Like many others, Maria Kiselëva started making the dangerous journey into the countryside to bargain directly with the peasants for food in exchange for warm clothing and other goods. On one occasion she reappeared at their apartment with a hulking great peasant, who was pulling her purchases on a sledge. Nikolai was wearing two pairs of trousers to keep warm. She made him take one pair off and hand it to the peasant. It was part of the price.[32]

Had the Germans actually taken Moscow, they would have found a desert. On 8 October Stalin and the GKO gave orders to prepare for the destruction of industrial enterprises in Moscow and the surrounding Region. A committee of five under General Serov, a Deputy Commissar from the NKVD, was put in charge.[8] In each Raion troikas were set up consisting of the Secretary of the Raion Party Committee as chairman, the head of the local NKVD, and a sapper from the Red Army. Serov produced a list of over a thousand factories to be destroyed. They were divided into two categories. Those producing defence equipment were to be blown up. The others were to be destroyed by smashing the machinery and by fire. Food or consumer goods in factory stores were to be distributed to the population.[9]

The list of buildings to be destroyed included bakeries, refrigerated stores, meat-processing plants, stations and other railway buildings, tram and trolleybus parks, lorry parks, power stations, bridges, the

Bolshoi Theatre, the Mint (GoZnak), the TASS building, the Central Telegraph Office and the telephone exchanges. The commandant of the Kremlin was supplied with explosive and detonators to destroy the service buildings there. The NKVD made its own arrangements for destroying its offices.[10]

The Trëkhgorka, like other factories, trained its own demolition team. They practised with real fuses, though not of course with real explosives. The trick was to light the fuse, and then see if you could get out of the building before the fuse had burned through and the notional demolition charge had blown up. Twenty seconds was the time allotted for people to make their escape. Some of the trainees were so enthusiastic that they jumped out of windows on the upper floor – and apparently survived.[11]

On 5 October Major Zhuravlëv of the NKVD was called by Shcherbakov to his office, the walls of which were covered with maps like a military headquarters. Shcherbakov told him that it had been decided to set up resistance groups to operate in Moscow 'if the very worst should happen'. The stay-behind groups would consist of party members. They would of course be volunteers, but Shcherbakov expected no shortage of these. Major Zhuravlëv pointed out the dangers of this scheme: the core of the underground network would be just those Raion Party Committee secretaries and chairmen of Raion Councils who were best known to their local communities. Shcherbakov answered sharply, 'There are plenty of ways of disguising them; it's your job to devise the methods and train people to use them.'[12]

Shcherbakov subsequently interviewed some of the candidates personally. One of them was the Komsomol Secretary of the Komintern Raion. Straightening his glasses, without taking his eyes off him, Shcherbakov asked, 'How old are you?', 'How are your relations?' (they were in occupied Belorussia), 'What about your health?'

The work, he said, was on the orders of Comrade Stalin himself.

'Do you realise how serious it is?'

'Yes I do, Alexander Sergeevich.'

'Do you understand the danger?'

'Yes, if I get it wrong, I'll end up on a German scaffold.'

Shcherbakov wished him luck.[13]

Mikhail Nemirovski was one of those who volunteered to stay

behind. He and Nina Popova were to lead the underground resistance committee for Krasnaya Presnya. Nina Popova is said to have prepared herself for torture by sticking needles under her nails. Nemirovski's wife Polina and his small daughter Lena were evacuated with the other families of the stay-behind team to a city on the Volga. But when Polina heard a rumour that Mikhail was having an affair with Popova, she rushed straight back to Moscow. The authorities turned a blind eye, because Polina resumed her work in one of Moscow's aviation factories which was still producing weapons for the front.[14]

The stay-behind teams never had to be used in Moscow itself. But by the end of November fifteen hundred partisans were operating in the parts of the Moscow Region which had been occupied by the Germans. Most of their commanders were NKVD officers chosen by Shcherbakov and Zhuravlëv. Pamphlets were printed for circulation to the people in the occupied areas, with titles like 'Living in Snow', 'Partisan Bands and Their Tactics' and 'How to Feed Yourself in Exceptional Circumstances'.[15]

The frenzy of preparation culminated on 15 October. Anastas Mikoyan's family were at the dacha and he was alone in Moscow when his bodyguard awoke him at an unusually early hour to tell him that Stalin had called a meeting in his office. When the meeting assembled, Stalin set out the situation calmly. The Germans might break through at any minute, he said, and the necessary preparations had to be made. After discussion he dictated a short decision sheet. Molotov was to arrange for the Presidium of the Supreme Soviet, the Government, and foreign diplomats to leave that day for Kuibyshev [Samara] on the Volga, and he was to go with them as deputy head of the Government. The Commissariats for Defence and the Navy would also go to Kuibyshev, but the General Staff would go to Arzamas, a secluded city near Gorki [Nizhni Novgorod] on the Volga where Sakharov later worked on the Soviet Union's first nuclear weapons. Moscow's research laboratories, its institutions of higher education, and its theatres were to be evacuated immediately to a variety of destinations.[16] General Artemiev, the Commander of the Moscow Defence Zone, would prepare a last-ditch defence. If the enemy reached Moscow, Beria and Shcherbakov would be responsible for destroying the factories and other objects listed for demolition. Water mains and the sewage system would be left unharmed.[17]

The meeting also decided that Stalin should leave Moscow the following day or later, depending on the situation; but within hours he resolved to remain in the capital.[18] Arrangements were in any case made for him in Kuibyshev. Nikolai Glebov, a young peasant from the Moscow countryside, had worked on the construction of the Moscow Metro almost from the beginning. Now he and some colleagues were sent to Kuibyshev to begin work on a special underground bunker for Stalin. It took them sixteen days to get there by train, and nobody told them what they were to do until they had actually arrived. When the job was done they went back to work in Moscow. The bunker was never used, and Glebov did not see it again until he went to Kuibyshev as a tourist in the 1970s. He looked for the opening to the bunker, which had been close to the riverside restaurant which he and his colleagues had shared with the evacuated artists from the Bolshoi Theatre. The entrance was now disguised as a public lavatory. Glebov poked around and found a locked oak door. The woman attendant did not know where it led, but she said that a couple of men came in once a month, opened the door, went through and locked it from the other side. Glebov retired from the Moscow Metro in 1965, when he turned fifty. He roared with laughter when he was told more than sixty years after his first visit to Kuibyshev that the bunker has now been restored as a tourist attraction where they hand out picture postcards of the meeting room designed for Stalin, and that people there firmly believe that in the name of secrecy all the workers were shot after it was finished.[19]

Instructions for evacuation were passed to factory managers and to Party, Government and municipal officials throughout the city. They began to carry them out immediately. They collected and burned all the sensitive papers they held. They loaded lorries with indispensable records and office equipment. They told their staff who was to leave and who was to stay. They arranged to give their workers two weeks' pay in lieu of notice. They ordered surplus stores of consumer goods to be distributed to the population. Not all the decisions made sense. One of the departmental heads of the Metro panicked and ordered the pumps to be dismantled. This threatened a flood, but the head of the Metro countermanded the order in time.[20]

Ortenberg was told to send half the editorial staff of *Krasnaya Zvezda* to Kuibyshev. They grumbled, but acquiesced. One who had been chosen to stay in Moscow – a man who had fought bravely in the Civil War – was sent off in a jeep to report on the fighting on the Mozhaisk Highway. He disappeared without trace, and Ortenberg feared the worst. But three weeks later the man finally sent in a report – on the situation in a small town far behind the lines. The local NKVD arrested him as a deserter, and sent him to serve in a punishment battalion. Ortenberg got him assigned to a frontline newspaper instead. He was wounded at Stalingrad, and after a decent interval *Krasnaya Zvezda* started to publish his pieces again.[21]

None of this was explained to the ordinary people. The bland and evasive communiqués of the SovInformBuro still began in the same way: 'In the course of the day, our forces have engaged in bitter fighting with the enemy along the whole front.' The day after the German break-through on 5 October the communiqués said only that Soviet forces had had a number of minor successes on land and in the air.[22] As one town fell after another, the same message was repeated day after day and word for word: 'After fighting obstinately for many days, our forces have pulled out of Bryansk ... Vyazma ...' As usual, rumour took the place of fact, and the nearer the fighting came, the quicker rumour found its way backwards and forwards between the front and the people of the city. Wounded men, nurses, journalists, returned to Moscow and told their version of the story. By the middle of the month the distant cannonade could be heard even in the centre of the city. It was rumoured that German tanks would appear at any moment on Gorky Street.

In order to raise morale as the Germans got closer to the capital, the authorities pasted notices all over the city to advertise forthcoming concerts by Liubov Orlova, Stalin's favourite film star. They calculated that people would conclude that as long as Orlova and Stalin remained in the city, it would not be surrendered. In fact Orlova was by then on her way to the safety of Baku in the Caucasus.

The morning of 16 October began in an ominous fashion. The night had been quiet enough. There had been no air-raid alarms: once again the German bombers had been grounded by low cloud and occasional rain mixed with flakes of wet snow.[33] At 6 o'clock precisely the loudspeakers crackled into life, as they did every day, with the morning's news from Levitan: 'This is the communiqué of the SovInformBuro for the morning of 16 October. For ...' And then his voice broke off. The listeners heard instead what they thought at first was the well-known Soviet patriotic song 'The March of the Airmen'. But as they listened more carefully, they began to realise that the familiar tune was somehow going wrong. Some of them recognised that it was not 'The March of the Airmen' at all. It was the 'Horst Wessel Lied', the marching song of Hitler's storm troopers. Were the Germans now so close that they had been able to plug into the Moscow radio network? Then the 'Horst Wessel Lied' broke off in its turn and Levitan said, as if nothing had happened, 'The situation around Moscow has sharply deteriorated!' The incident remained a mystery.[34]

When they went out into the streets that morning, people found a city transformed. There were no newspapers in their mailboxes: the post office workers who usually distributed the newspapers had been laid off the previous day. There were no buses running, no trams, no trolley-buses. The Metro had ground to a halt. And there were no policemen. In their place were people in civilian clothes with red bands on the sleeves of their soaking overcoats: members of the 'Destroyer Battalions' raised from among the city's Communists.

Everywhere a sinister snow was falling. But the flakes that fluttered down were black, not white. They were the ashes of papers being burned in one office after another. People burned their documents on bonfires in the courtyards. They burned archives, official files, personal notebooks, the labour books of the workers, the files held by building administrators, even the telephone directories. The Moscow authorities had already sent off two wagonloads of Party documents on 12 October. They now decided that the remainder would have to be destroyed outright: anonymous letters and denunciations; personal files; material about the purges, the expulsion of the kulaks and the situation in the collective farms; records of Party meetings. Documents due for destruction were marked 'No. 3'. They burned them in the boilerhouse of the public bath next to the Party archive building.[35]

The *dvornik* in Raisa Labas' apartment building came to ask her for advice: 'Raisa Veniaminovna,' he said, 'tell me what to do. The rubbish dump is cluttered with portraits and busts of the leaders, certificates of various kinds, fragments of documents of some sort. I even,' he whispered, 'saw a Party card all filthy and torn to shreds.'

'Don't do anything yourself,' Raisa advised him. 'Go to the building administrator for advice.' Then she thought again, and said: 'No, perhaps after all it would be better to take it all as far off as you can – at night so no one sees you.'

People were dragging large paper sacks out of the courtyard next to the ornate Chinese teashop just down Kirov Street from Raisa's apartment building, and loading them onto a barrow. The heavy smell of burning hung over the streets. Gusts of wind blew the black ashes off the roads and up into the air. The rubbish dumps in the courtyards of the houses were piled high with the detritus of Communism: classics of Marxism-Leninism, diplomas, badges and scraps of party and trade union identity cards. There were feathers from torn mattresses everywhere. It looked, one observer thought, like the aftermath of a pogrom against the Jews.[36] During those two days more than a thousand people destroyed their Party cards – a crime at the best of times, a sign in the eyes of the NKVD of outright treachery at this moment of crisis.[37]

The backlash was inevitable. People went to work and found the factory gates barred against them. They were told that they had been laid off. They were promised an advance of pay in lieu of notice, but the factories could get no cash from the banks. They went to the RaiKoms and the VoenKomats to ask for weapons to fight the Germans and were told that only members of the Party were being given guns.[38]

In the Komsomol offices of one Raion some officials were storing boxes of grenades and Molotov cocktails in the cellar. Others were trying out their weapons and practising taking grenades to pieces in the local shooting gallery. Squads of young people were going off to convert school buildings into barracks, to dig slit trenches and shelters, and to help load factory equipment onto the trains now leaving for the East. A local NKVD driver brought in one individual who had foolishly offered him 3,000 roubles for a lift to Gorki. The Komsomol leaders in the local drama school left Moscow without permission: they were expelled from the Komsomol for cowardice. Two militiamen were expelled for panicking and tearing off their badges of rank: they were sent straight to the front with no time to go home first. The Secretary of the Raion

Party Committee was cracking up and refusing to give clear orders: he was arrested that night.[39]

The wildest rumours began to spread: there had been a coup d'état, Stalin had been arrested, the Germans had reached Fili, just where the Mozhaisk Highway enters Moscow.[40] Romanchenko, the head of the Moscow militia, reported that both Party and militia officials had lost their heads and given up managing their Raions. It was hardly surprising, he said, that the workers were furious.[41] Andrei Sakharov made his way to the university, where a crowd of students had gathered, eager to make themselves useful. He and some others went to the office of the Party Committee. When they asked the Party Secretary what they could do to help, he stared wildly and blurted out, 'It's every man for himself!'[42] The number of marriages escalated as people tried to find themselves a spouse whose office or factory was being evacuated.[43]

Along the escape roads to the East, past the checkpoints at the city limits, onto the Highway of the Enthusiasts, a dense column of vehicles was moving out of the city. Cars loaded down with middle-level bureaucrats and their domestic treasures splashed past their fellow citizens who were struggling towards safety on foot.

The director of Factory No. 468 commandeered a factory lorry to take his personal property to the station: an upright piano, a grand piano, mirrors, cupboards, sideboards, beds, mattresses, bicycles, a goat and a dog. Arranging this took so long that he himself missed the train. He tried to commandeer an aeroplane instead. When that didn't work, he ordered one of the official drivers to catch up with the train. The Party officials in the factory not only failed to stop the director, but followed his example and took to their heels. The workers were furious and demanded that the whole lot should be punished under military law.[44]

When they saw their bosses setting off with their families for the safety of the East, ordinary people began to take matters into their own hands: Major Zhuravlëv, the head of the Moscow NKVD, called it 'anarchy' in his report two days later. They began to block the escape routes. Workers from Factory No. 219 attacked a group of six cars travelling along the Highway of the Enthusiasts, dragged out the passengers, beat them up, threw their possessions into the road and hurled their vehicles into a nearby ravine.[45] The deputy director of the Lenin

Library was caught trying to get out of Moscow in the Library's car. He was lucky: the mob simply sent him back into the city.[46]

Workers armed themselves with hammers and spades, and set on their bosses and on NKVD officials, militiamen, local Communist leaders and anyone who tried to reason with them. The director of the Molotov Precision Instrument Factory fled, together with his chief engineer and the deputy head of the canteen. Their workers, who had been promised a months' pay in advance, fell upon officials of the Commissariat of the Aviation Industry instead, dragged them from their vehicles, scattered their luggage, and faced down the NKVD officials who came to sort things out. At Ball Bearing Factory No. 2 the workers threatened to smash the machinery. At the Burevestnik Shoe Factory they broke down the factory gates and stole the shoes. At the Hammer and Sickle Factory an 'orgy of looting' broke out, encouraged by some members of the management.[47] Soon the looters were fighting among themselves. In one factory after another workers broke into canteens and liquor stores, stole the food and drank themselves silly. In Noginsk Factory No. 12 a group of about a hundred workers demanded that the director hand over the thirty-eight tons of industrial alcohol that he had in store. He poured it into the sewers instead. When they discovered their director making off, workers in a milk factory confiscated his car and threw him head first into a barrel of sour cream. On 17 October a crowd assembled outside the massive Stalin Car Factory, and demanded that they be allowed in to receive their pay. They hit a security guard over the head and beat up two militiamen who tried to restore order. The students at the factory's training college trashed the college buildings, tore up their textbooks, broke into the store cupboards, and stole warm clothes and food. The rumour quickly spread around the city that workers coming off duty had looted five tons of sausage from the Mikoyan Meat Kombinat.

Not everyone took the law into their own hands. The women at the Trëkhgorka came to work as usual and found the factory closed. They assembled at the factory's House of Culture – the atmosphere was calm, even though nobody had told them what was going on. They were given their pay and told that they had been dismissed. For three days they hung around with nothing to do. Then they were called back to the factory and started working as before.[48]

Long queues formed outside all the food shops. People fought in the queues, trampled on old women, and began to cry the age-old cry of the Russian mob: 'Beat the Jews.' For the most part the militia looked on in groups, wandered along the pavements, smoked, and said, 'We have no instructions.'[49] Aleksei Koptev, a carpenter in a railway depot, got drunk and started a fight when he tried to jump a bread queue. On the way to the police station, he shouted, 'Citizens, we are being robbed, they won't give us any bread!' At the station itself, he threw himself on the ground, and cried out with many oaths, 'The Jews have sold Russia, there is nothing with which to defend Moscow, there are no rifles, no cartridges, no shells. The Jews have stolen everything!'

Instead of giving out the daily ration, as he usually did, the baker at the shop on Sretenka was handing out three whole days' ration in advance; and a whole *pood* – more than thirty-five pounds – of flour on each coupon. The people in the queue were swapping rumours, drawing their own conclusions, working themselves up.

'Things must be bad if they've started handing out flour.'

'They say that two looters were shot yesterday on the Taganka, right by the shop ...'

'You'll see, the Germans want to surround Moscow ...'

'To hell with this flour! Better starve than let the Germans in ...'

One skinny old lady shouted indignantly, 'All those people who were running away with their rubber plants and their chests of drawers – they were dragged straight off their lorries! There was no time to evacuate the children, but those people thought they could get away with their rubber plants!'[50]

Dr Miller, the historian, described the scene in his diary:

> Everything has changed at once. (*Izvestia* has not come out and people say it has been evacuated.) The SovInformBuro has got close to the truth for the first time: it says that the situation on the Western Front has seriously deteriorated. The centre is broken through. That is why today Moscow is like an ant heap. But the 'ants' seem like strangers. People loaded down with goods are going in all directions. The *dvorniks* are not clearing the frozen pavements. The Metro is closed and people are saying it is to be blown up or flooded. People say the Garden Ring is also to be destroyed because it is the main

> artery (that is what it was built for). So are any factories which have not been evacuated or dismantled. Most of the crowd is gloomy and silent, but some people are as light-hearted as if they were going to the fair. There are huge queues, because the evacuation is being used as an excuse to distribute food products for a long time in advance. In addition it seems as if there has been a decision to sell off the contents of the remaining food stores (flour and sugar are being sold at market prices. A *pood* of flour is being given out for each worker's ration card). The trams are overcrowded and there are fewer of them. Buses too. Many of them have been taken out of service. People are even sitting on the roofs of the trolleybuses. In the crowds, people are saying that the Germans will arrive tonight, that Moscow, like Paris, should be declared an open city, that the air defences have been removed (although at 6 in the evening the guns were already firing and one could see the shells exploding).[51]

Even the journalist Nikolai Verzhbitski was driven to uncharacteristic fury by the mismanagement of the authorities and wrote in his diary on 18 October:

> Who gave the order to close the factories? To pay off the workers? Who was behind the whole muddle, the mass flight, the looting, the confusion in everyone's minds? [...] Everyone is boiling with indignation, talking out loud, shouting that they have been betrayed, that 'the captains were the first to abandon ship' and took their valuables with them into the bargain. People are saying things out loud that three days ago would have brought them before a military tribunal. There are queues, endless, unlimited queues: noisy, emotional, quarrelsome, agonising. The hysteria at the top has transmitted itself to the masses. People are beginning to remember and to count up all the humiliations, the oppression, the injustices, the clampdowns, the bureaucratic arrogance of the officials, the conceit and the self-confidence of the party bureaucrats, the draconian decrees, the shortages, the systematic deception of the masses, the lying and flattery of the toadies in the newspapers [...] People are speaking from their hearts. Will it be possible to defend a city where such moods prevail?[52]

Some began to shout anti-Communist slogans. Tank crews on their way to get replacements for their destroyed vehicles were jeered in the streets: 'So you tankists have had enough of fighting!'[53] An NKVD agent in the Manometr Factory found Polenov, a metalworker whom he had been cultivating, organising a drinking session in the laboratory and haranguing his fellow workers on the iniquities of the Soviet regime. When the agent warned him that his NKVD connections would get him into trouble when the Germans arrived, Polenov boasted that he could look after himself: the NKVD would need him to protect them, not the other way round. Workers from the Kommunarka State Farm outside Moscow tried to loot the NKVD's own barracks next door, even as the NKVD were still disposing of their victims there. In collective farms around the city, people hoisted white flags and tried to prevent the evacuation of the livestock.

For Moscow's underworld, the chaos was too good an opportunity to miss. Looters stripped the shops and apartments that had been abandoned, arguing that if they didn't take the stuff, the Germans would. Stolen sweets and chocolate were openly sold in the street.[54] One scruffy man was arrested when he attempted to walk off with two suitcases of diamonds and gold hidden in a child's pram.[55]

The unrest was not confined to Moscow. The traditionally unruly textile town of Ivanovo was nearly two hundred miles to the Northeast and well away from the Germans.[56] Here too the authorities made preparations to evacuate the machinery in the factories. Here too people were not told what was going on. Unlike their sisters at the Trëkhgorka, the women textile workers in Ivanovo were not prepared to take things lying down. When they came in to work on 18 October, they found that some of the machinery had already been packed. Rumours began to spread immediately. The machinery would be evacuated, people said, and the workers left to their fate. The bosses had already sent their families away. The local branch of the State Bank had gone too, and the workers would not be paid. All the bread in the town was being taken into the interior.

The workers in one factory began to unpack the crates to prevent any further attempt to remove the machinery. Their boss, Chastukhin, told them that they were wasting their time: the factories were to be blown up anyway to keep them from the enemy. At that, groups of workers ran round the factory shouting: 'They're going to blow up the factory with us in it. The charges are already in place. Chastukhin's given the order.' Managers fled when workers burst into their offices demanding their pay. Party officials ordered some of the machinery to be reassembled. One woman shouted at them, 'Leave the machinery where it is, so then we can work for Hitler if he turns up!' Others said that they would tear their managers to pieces if they tried to make them go back to work, and throw the bits into the cesspit. Most refused the summons to dig trenches around the city. One shouted, 'Don't listen to them [the Party bosses], they know nothing, and they've been deceiving us for twenty-three years. They've sent their own families away, and now they're trying to send us off to dig ditches'. One of the men shouted, 'Down with Soviet power! Long live good old Hitler!'

The Regional Party Secretary reported to Moscow that he had sacked the Party officials and managers responsible. He had improved the food in the factory canteens. He had suspended the evacuation. But the real blame lay with German agents and the ringleaders among the workers who came from politically unreliable backgrounds: peasant families ruined by collectivisation, relatives of people who had been sent to the camps, a woman who had been in prison for running an illegal abortion clinic. The military tribunal had sentenced one woman to be shot and five others to ten years in prison.[57]

Government, Party and police strove to bring the situation in Moscow under control. Senior members of the government went off to talk to the workers and calm them down. Anastas Mikoyan himself went to the Stalin Car Factory, where several thousand workers were holding an impromptu meeting. The factory director, Likhachëv, was shouting at them. Beside him a union leader was swearing at the workers in the most colourful language and telling them to go home. Likhachëv told Mikoyan that the workers wanted to go into the factory to work. But this was impossible because the factory was being got ready for demolition. The crowd asked Mikoyan, 'Why has the government run away, along with the secretary of the Party Committee and the Komsomol Committee? Why won't anyone explain why we're not allowed into the factory?' Mikoyan explained, 'Stalin and Molotov are both here. The ministries have left because the front line has come close to Moscow. Now you must be calm. You've been given your pay, so why are you making a fuss? Please stop attacking the director and go home.' The workers gradually began to disperse.[58]

Shakhurin, the Commissar for the Aviation Industry, found most of his factories empty, the doors open, the walls bare. Most of the equipment had already been removed. Only a few lathes and a few aircraft awaiting final assembly were left in the workshops. The workers had been promised their pay, but once again the local branches of the State Bank had no cash. Shakhurin assured them that immediate steps would be taken. Workers due for evacuation to the East asked, 'How will we live when we get there? Will there be any schools for our children?' Shakhurin was frank. There would be great difficulties with housing to start with, and with food, and with schooling. But construction teams would be sent to the evacuation destinations. Houses and schools would be built. The main thing was to start building aeroplanes – from components to start with, and then from scratch. Everyone nodded.

One woman came to him in tears: 'We thought everyone had left, and you'd abandoned us. But it turns out you are still here!' Shakhurin answered loudly enough for everyone to hear: 'If you mean the government and the military, then no one has left. Everyone is here. Everyone is at his post, but we are sending the factories to places where they will be able to go on producing modern aeroplanes for our army.' The workers began to calm down.

Later that morning Shakhurin and other Commissars joined Stalin in his apartment in the Kremlin. Shakhurin was one of the first to arrive. Stalin emerged from the bedroom, greeted him, lit his pipe, and started walking up and down. Molotov, Malenkov, Shcherbakov, Kosygin and others came in. Suddenly Stalin stopped and asked, 'How are things in Moscow?'

No one answered. They looked silently at one another, until Shakhurin described how his workers had not been paid and had thought themselves abandoned.

Stalin asked Molotov, 'Where's Zveriev?'

Molotov explained that the Commissar for Finance was in Gorki on the Volga.

'Fly the money in immediately,' said Stalin.

Shakhurin reported that the trams and the Metro were not working. The bread shops and other shops were closed. There was talk of looting in the city. Stalin thought for a bit, and said, 'Well, that's not so bad. I thought things would have been worse.'

Then he turned to Shcherbakov and added, 'We need to sort out the trams and the Metro immediately. Open the bread shops, the stores, the canteens and get the clinics going with whatever doctors are still in the city. You and Pronin must speak on the radio today, appeal for calm, and tell people that you will make sure that all the public services work normally.'[59]

Pronin issued the necessary orders that evening.[60]

Shcherbakov did speak over the radio on 17 October but his language was stilted and conventional. Pronin spoke the next day to greater effect. In calm and measured tones, he said that irresponsible elements had raised panic in the capital. Some managers of big factories had run away without permission. People had been stealing socialist property. Those who had abandoned their posts would be severely punished. Canteens, shops and services would resume work, city transport would run as normal, and theatres and cinemas would open to the public. People believed him, and the sense of panic began to ebb.

Although these measures began to take immediate effect, the mood in the Kremlin was still uncertain when Pronin was summoned there on the evening of 19 October. The place was dark and empty, and on the way into Stalin's office he heard Beria say to Molotov, 'We should abandon Moscow. Otherwise they will wring our necks like chickens.' Molotov prudently kept his mouth shut. Inside Stalin was walking up and down gloomily. 'What should we do about Moscow?' he asked. Everyone was silent. Then he said, 'I think that we should not abandon Moscow.' Beria was the first to speak: 'Of course, Comrade Stalin, there can be no question of that.' The others chimed their agreement.

Stalin turned to Malenkov. 'Draft a decree introducing a state of siege in Moscow.' When Malenkov read out what he had written, Stalin reacted irritably: 'That's childish. You'd do better as a village letterwriter. Here, Shcherbakov, write what I dictate.' The decree was published in the Moscow papers the following day. It began with old-fashioned pomp: 'By these presents it is decreed . . .' a deliberate archaism by Stalin.[61] No movement was to be permitted on the streets between midnight and 5 a.m. without a special pass from the Moscow garrison commander, General Sinilov. The only exception was to allow people to get to the shelters during air raids. Sinilov was to be made responsible for maintaining the strictest order in the city, and the militia, NKVD troops and volunteer workers groups were assigned to him for the purpose. Violators of public order were to be arrested and court-martialled. Provocateurs, spies and anyone fomenting unrest were to be shot on the spot.[62]

The next day everything in the city changed. Military and police patrols appeared on the streets again. The panicky flight ceased. The evacuation of the population and the factories took on an orderly rhythm. Even the taxis began to work again.[63] Twenty-two field bakeries started operating straight away. The Moscow City Council announced through *Vechernyaya Moskva* that there was enough food in the city. Seventy-six shops had already been opened to sell bread and flour. Two hundred shops and kiosks would be opened in the next few days. Those who were leaving the city would be given supplies for ten days. Industrial workers and officials who remained would get an extra sixteen kilos of flour. Potatoes would be handed out not only in the shops, but also at railway and river stations.[64]

The Moscow City Court and the People's Courts in each of the twenty-five Raions were now given the powers of military tribunals. The judges were empowered to conclude their sentences with the words: 'This sentence is definitive and not subject to appeal.'[65] By August 1942 General Sinilov was able to report that 830,000 people had been detained. Thirteen had been shot on the spot: for example, a man called Vlasov was shot by the Commandant of the Proletarian Raion for spreading anti-revolutionary rumours, and an unknown man was shot for the same reason by Malakhov, a soldier in the Red Army. Altogether more than nine hundred people had been arrested for spreading anti-revolutionary rumours: praising Hitler and his regime, speaking ill of Stalin, criticising the policies of the Soviet government, especially collectivisation, the labour discipline laws, and the low living standards of the workers.[66] The forces of law and order had caught over ten thousand deserters and nearly twenty-five thousand people who had tried to evade military service. More than forty-four thousand people had been sentenced to various terms of imprisonment and nearly nine hundred had been sentenced to death. It is said that some executions were carried out by a woman in a shed in the courtyard of the Moscow City Court.

The crackdown on subversive talk was unremitting. In November 1941 the head of the Heating and Power Department of the Moscow City Council, Vorotnikov, was arrested together with his deputy, the director of the MosGas trust, and the trust's engineer. They had sat around in Vorotnikov's office, criticising life in the Soviet Union, expressing doubts about victory and praising Hitler's army. Each was sentenced to ten years' imprisonment. Two people were imprisoned for calling for a pogrom of the Jews. A disabled lathe worker, Grechichkin, picked up a German leaflet by a vending machine on the corner of Dzerzhinski Square (not a good place, since it was opposite the Lubyanka) and read it aloud. He too was sentenced to ten years.[67]

Party members who had failed the test were rapidly sorted out. Many of them had received confusing orders on the eve of the panic, and believed that they had been authorised to leave. Others simply cut and ran. On 19 October the Party Secretary of the Volga town of Gorki telephoned to ask what he should do with the trainloads of Moscow Party officials who had turned up there. He was told to send them straight back to Moscow. The First Secretaries of the Komintern, Leningrad and Shakhovskoi Raions were sacked from their jobs and expelled from the Party for 'irresolution while the Soviet people is conducting a struggle against the Hitlerites, and deserting their posts'. By December the Moscow Party had expelled nearly three hundred of its members.[68]

The NKVD moved to clear up the detritus of panic. Thirteen packages were found in a tunnel in the Kursk Station addressed to the Moscow Party Committee. They contained Party cards, personal files and a host of other Party documents.[69] In the main building of the Central Committee itself there was no one left to keep the basic services running – heating, telephones, refrigerators, and electrical equipment. The fire-fighting team had taken itself off, and its equipment was in disarray. More than a hundred gas masks were lying around on the floor. Hundreds of typewriters, felt boots, tons of food, had been abandoned. Locks on desks were broken, and documents – including top-secret documents – were scattered everywhere. Five top-secret packages were discovered in the office of Andrei Zhdanov, the Politburo member who had been evacuated earlier on grounds of ill-health.[70] On 23 October more secret documents were discovered abandoned in buildings previously occupied by military intelligence.[71] These incidents were reported to Stalin personally.

Elements of the Dzerzhinski Division – which after all had been created for just that purpose – were already in the capital to maintain order. Frolov, Markov, Teleguev and their comrades were sent to the escape routes to the East along the Highway of Enthusiasts to impose control. Among those they stopped from leaving was the Rector of Moscow University, Butyagin. Some of the men in the Destroyer Battalions had orders to open fire on any windows that were lit up at night in defiance of the blackout, and on any cars being driven away from Moscow by officials. It was easy enough, they thought, to tell which cars were being driven by officials: no one else in Moscow had a car anyway.

Once order had been restored, the soldiers from the Dzerzhinski Division were sent to help build the inner line of the Moscow defences. Frolov built fortifications on Gorky Street, near the Belorussia Station, and was then sent out along the Leningrad Highway to mine bridges and roads. The ground was frozen solid, and it was not at all easy to bury the charges.[72] Teleguev met the woman who became his wife digging trenches along the Moscow River. Later he and his comrades marched several times through the centre of Moscow to the sound of a military band. It was an obvious device to raise the morale of the citizens, though the soldiers complained that they were wasting their time when they should have been fighting.[73] Then he was sent to fortify a third-floor apartment on Gorky Street. He and a colleague were supplied with anti-tank grenades, Molotov cocktails, and iron rations, and told that their task was to stop German tanks. Their superiors simply forgot about them and they were stuck there until the end of October.[74]

Although the panic was over, no one could yet be sure that the city would hold out. Preparations for its abandonment continued. On 23 October Pronin made a proposal to Stalin which a few months later was to have serious consequences for the people of Moscow. The food stocks in the city, he said, were sufficient for three to four months. But, he went on, with the approach of the Germans they might fall into the hands of the enemy. He therefore asked for permission to sell off perishable goods to the population, and send the grain to the East. For this he would need one hundred barges. His proposal was approved, and the goods were moved out at the end of the month.[75]

Beria was meanwhile taking his own measures to impose discipline. Bliuma Gamarnik, Yekaterina Kork, Nina Uborevich and Nina Tukhachevskaya, the wives of the senior officers who had been killed in 1937 and 1938, had been brought back to Moscow from exile in the summer of 1939. They were interrogated on and off for two years, and eventually driven to accuse one another of setting up a terrorist group to assassinate leading members of the Party. Bliuma Gamarnik and Yekaterina Kork were shot in July 1941. Nina Uborevich, the idol of the young Stepan Mikoyan, and Nina Tukhachevskaya were shot on 16 October, the day of the great panic. Their bodies were tumbled into the NKVD's burial pits at the Kommunarka State Farm.[76] On 16 October more than two hundred people were shot in Moscow by the NKVD, the biggest figure for a single day since 1938.

On 17 October Yakov Smushkevich, the hero of the wars in Spain and Mongolia, and a number of other 'especially dangerous state criminals' were taken from the Lubyanka and sent by train to Kuibyshev, the place of refuge for the Soviet government and the foreign diplomats. On 18 October Beria issued an order to the 'officer for special missions' in the NKVD's 'Special Group'. It read: 'On receipt of this order you will proceed to Kuibyshev and carry out the sentence of the highest measure of punishment (shooting) in respect of the following prisoners.' There followed a list of twenty-eight people. Among them were seven air force officers, including Proskurov, Golikov's predecessor as head of military intelligence and three former commanders of the Red Air Force – Loktionov, Smushkevich and Rychagov. Four were senior army officers. Four were senior officials from the defence industry. Seven were civilian officials. One was a 'literary worker'. There were four women including Rychagov's wife, the airwoman Maria Nesterenko, and the wives of two other officers. Four of the officers had served together in Spain. Seven of those on the list had lived in the House on the Embankment.

On 28 October the NKVD team – it consisted of Major (later Major-General) Bashtekov, who had already distinguished himself during the execution of the Polish officers at Katyn, Major Rodos and Senior Lieutenant Semenikhin – reported that they had carried out the sentence on twenty prisoners, including Smushkevich and all the other officers and their wives. The remainder were killed over the next ten days. Pumpur and others were shot, with Stalin's written approval, on Red Army Day, 23 February 1942.[77]

For a year and a half Smushkevich's wife Basya and his daughter Rosa were left alone. Then Rosa turned eighteen, and the NKVD took notice of them once again. They were arrested and sent to a camp in Petropavlovsk in Kazakhstan. Beria showed an uncharacteristic benevolence and wrote on their file: 'Mother and daughter are to be kept together.' This was exceptional, since family members were usually spit up immediately they were arrested. Young women on their own were subject to particular abuse. But Basya and Rosa remained together throughout their imprisonment and exile.[78]

There is a graveyard outside Moscow at Monino, where today there is one of the most fascinating aviation museums in the world. One of the gravestones says that General Proskurov and his wife are buried there. Another marks the grave of Yakov and Basya Smushkevich. But the graves contain the bodies only of the wives. It is not known for sure where Bashtekov and his accomplices buried the men. But one story has it that they lie, unmarked, in a disused sand quarry near Kuibyshev. The quarry was blown up to conceal the crime. Some small boys who used to play in the quarry heard the explosions and later found the spent cartridge cases.[79]

They still smelled of powder.

– THIRTEEN –

EVACUATION

Preparations for evacuation were made even before the war began. In the spring of 1941 the General Staff told the commanders of the Military Districts in the West to make plans for the immediate evacuation of military objects and the most important industrial plants, agricultural machinery, animals and grain.[1] Pronin put forward a plan for the evacuation of Moscow as early as 3 June, but Stalin rejected it as inopportune.[2] On the third day of the war Stalin called in Malyshev, the Commissar responsible for tank production, and ordered him to move the factories in Leningrad and Kharkov making the new KV and T-34 tanks to Siberia and the Urals immediately.[3] On 16 July the GKO set up an Evacuation Committee to oversee the process.[4]

Kaganovich was the Politburo member responsible for the massive transport operation. The two million workers in the Soviet railroad system were put on to a war footing from the first day of the war. 'Locomotive Columns', with their own mobile engineering and supplies units, were used to travel the very large distances involved. Both tracks of the line would be used for one-way traffic towards the front. Somehow or other, the evacuation trains carrying equipment and people struggled through in the opposite direction. The Luftwaffe attacked the trains. But their main task was to support the German ground forces, and they were never able to disrupt the flow significantly.[5]

It was vital to get troops, their supplies and their weapons to the front. But it was no less vital to get the arms factories going again as quickly as possible. Most of the aircraft and aero-engine factories in Western Russia were successfully evacuated in the summer and autumn of 1941, sometimes already under fire from the Germans. Some of them had to be evacuated a second time in 1942, when the Germans swept towards the Volga.[6] The trains often took weeks to reach their destinations and arrived to find that there were no buildings ready to house the machinery or the workers. Until these could be built, the workers were billeted in local schools, theatres, and hospitals. In Novosibirsk they were accommodated to begin with in a cinema, where they slept in the seats which had just been vacated by the audience. Once production had started, workers often slept in their factories. In some places the first aircraft came off the production line even before the factory buildings had roofs on them.[7] Aircraft often could not be completed for lack of components from other factories labouring under equal difficulties. In Novosibirsk uncompleted aircraft were parked on a nearby airfield. They disappeared under the snow and some were not found again until the spring thaw. But most factories restarted production six or eight weeks after arriving at their destinations.[8]

Over two and a half million people were evacuated from the Western parts of the country in the first forty days of the war: a huge figure, though comparable in proportion to the one and a half million people who were evacuated in Britain in the first three days of September 1939.[9] Several hundred thousand horses and millions of cattle, sheep, goats and pigs went with them. Special arrangements were made to get pedigree animals to safety.[10] Inevitably there was a great deal of panic, incompetence and confusion. Peasants and animals were abandoned by the leaders of the collective farms. Considerable stocks of military and industrial equipment were neither evacuated nor destroyed, but fell into the hands of the advancing Germans. But a million wagonloads of industrial equipment were moved from Ukraine, Belorussia and the Baltic States between 10 June and 20 November; and in the course of the whole war about ten million people were evacuated by train, and another two million by water.[11]

The evacuation of Moscow started within weeks of the outbreak of war, and continued until December 1941. The man primarily responsible for organising it was Aleksei Kosygin, the deputy chairman of the Evacuation Committee. At first children were sent to places in the Moscow Region, and then from mid-July to the regions of Ryazan and Tula. This was not far enough, and some were later trapped by the German advance or lost their lives when their trains were bombed as they were evacuated for a second time. Others were sent from the start to places of greater safety on the Volga, in the Urals, and in Central Asia, where new schoolrooms had to be built and equipped for them.

Some people left Moscow in the early days on their own initiative. Anna Nepomnyashchaya was eighteen and had just begun to study German at the Institute of Foreign Languages when the war began. In the middle of August she and her mother were loaded into empty goods wagons and travelled for a whole month to the East, living as best they could on the food they had brought with them and exchanging ration coupons for hot water, bread and food whenever the train stopped. If anyone fell ill on the way, they and their relatives were simply unloaded at the next station. Anna and her mother were eventually turfed out well beyond the Volga, at a village near Ufa. No arrangements had been made to feed or house them. They found their way to Ufa, where the two of them lived in one room. Anna's mother took in sewing, and Anna herself took up her German at the local university. In the summer vacation she was sent with a group of students to help out on a collective farm fifty miles from Ufa. When the vacation was over, the farm chairman tried to force the girls to stay. They deserted him and simply walked back to Ufa, staying overnight in a Tatar village on the way. Anna and her mother returned to Moscow in 1943. They were lucky enough to find that their apartment had not been taken over by squatters, and Anna went back to the Institute of Foreign Languages.[12]

The evacuation accelerated rapidly once the German assault on Moscow began. On 7 October Pronin ordered the urgent evacuation of women who were not in employment, together with their children. The Moscow militia was responsible for enforcing the order. Those who refused to go were to be prosecuted. On 11 October plans were made to evacuate 300,000 more women and children from the Moscow Region. On 13 October Moscow's scientific institutes were ordered to leave the city within two days: twenty-four wagons were made available for the scientists and their families, and another thirty-nine for their equipment.

Most people were evacuated from Moscow by train. By now there were no longer any orderly timetables. The few passenger trains still coming from the East quickly disgorged their passengers and left just as quickly to avoid the German bombers. Whole trains disappeared to distant parts of the country and were lost. The system was on the verge of collapse.[13] Kaganovich nevertheless managed to muster enough trains to carry the operation through.

Once again the building administrator was a key figure in the process. People leaving Moscow had to inform the building administrator. Those evacuated remained responsible for the rent of their apartments. They had to pay in advance, or send the rent to the building administrator from their place of evacuation. One lawyer called Mirabeau lost his right to his apartment in Moscow because in July 1941 he disappeared from Moscow for eight months, without showing the building administrator any authorisation for his evacuation, or paying his rent in advance, or giving a forwarding address.[14]

The British ambassador reported to London on 12 October that the Foreign Ministry had told him that he need not worry: 'There was no question of anyone being sent away at present.'[15] But Molotov summoned him at lunchtime on 15 October, and said that the embassy was to leave that night. They burned their papers, lost their provisions, crammed themselves onto a slow train with no heating or food, and scavenged their way to Kuibyshev for the next four days. They were luckier than most.[16]

Ordinary Muscovites, with no access to official transport, with their necessities tied up in bundles or stuffed into suitcases, began to flee from the city like a tidal surge. Struggling along on foot, they clogged the streets with their carts, their household possessions, their baggage, and their young children. The street outside the Academy of the Fine Arts where Raisa Labas lived was packed tight with vehicles loaded with people and goods. In one lorry a group of officers was sitting with some half-dressed women, in floods of tears. A soldier watching them suddenly started to swear, raised his carbine, and aimed it at one of the officers. But he did not shoot, and quickly hid among his comrades. Yuli Labas was desperately embarrassed when his mother caught sight of an official from the Union of Artists right outside their apartment block, publicly went down on her knees, and pleaded with the man – unsuccessfully – to take her son with him out of the city.[17]

Komsomol Square lies just to the North of the Garden Ring. It is bounded by three of the capital's main railway stations. The Leningrad Station is the oldest, built in 1849 in the style of Imperial St Petersburg: it was here that Anna Karenina saw the railway worker run over by a train the day when she met her future lover Vronski. By the late autumn of 1941 the Leningrad Station served only the immediate outskirts of Moscow: the Germans had occupied the rest of the line. The Yaroslavl Station, in the Russian neo-medieval style, served the Northern ports of Archangel and Murmansk, where the Allied convoys landed weapons and supplies for the Red Army and Russia's industries of war. The third station is the Kazan Station, built between 1913 and 1926 in an exuberant style of Russian medieval pastiche, and still one of the sights of the city.

The trainloads of evacuees left from every station and goods yard, carrying the best part of the Government, most of the Central Committee, more than seventy ministries, and the foreign embassies. But it was from the Kazan Station that most of the trains left for the cities on the Volga and beyond. In these panic days, Komsomol Square was packed with old men, women, children, adolescents, all hoping to get out of Moscow by hook or by crook. In the waiting rooms of the station itself thousands more people sat, stood, or lay on the floor on newspapers, waiting to hear their fate. Each time the station loudspeakers crackled, the crowd fell into the greatest excitement, trying to decipher the announcer's distorted voice: 'What did he say? What did he say?' Some had permits for the journey, some did not. All were determined to get away, if necessary by storming the waiting trains.

After the trains had left, the streets were filled with the howling of dogs abandoned by their masters.[18]

Conditions on the journey were hard even for the most privileged. The journey often took many days, sometimes under bombardment from the air, continually punctuated by long waits in sidings as the troop trains were hurried to the West. The evacuees sat, often with little or no food and water, in overcrowded, unheated carriages, or in '*teplushki*', goods wagons fitted with wooden bunks for forty people and a stove, for which there might or might not be fuel.

When the evacuees eventually arrived at their final destinations, they found – if they were lucky – accommodation even more primitive than what they had left in Moscow. The unlucky ones had to live in tents or earthen dugouts until something better could be devised. Those who travelled with their institutions or their factories were assured of work. Those who travelled as individuals had to find a place among unfamiliar surroundings, where people were often resentful of the influx of outsiders and the burden that this put on their already straitened circumstances. Evacuated officials arriving in Arzamas discovered that most of the accommodation was already occupied by earlier evacuees, who had taken over houses, clubs, schools, dormitories.

Irina Antonova came from a comparatively privileged background (her father had worked in the Soviet Embassy in Berlin) and was studying classical art when the war began. She and her mother were evacuated to Kuibyshev on 16 October. Their train was heavily bombed just outside Moscow. Everyone rushed for shelter into the surrounding woods. She herself remained in the train comforting a heavily pregnant woman who was unable to run away: she thought that would be no more dangerous than taking shelter elsewhere. At one stop her mother got out and the train started without her. She ran after it, but she was a very heavy woman and the other passengers were barely able to drag her aboard.

No accommodation had been prepared for them in Kuibyshev, so Antonova and her mother had to live in a grossly overcrowded railway carriage in the sidings. Because they had to cook in the carriage, it was always very hot. There was nowhere to wash and those with children had nowhere to clean them properly. The lavatory in the station was a dirty, cold, open sewer; but at least there was always hot water available. Every morning, while it was still dark, the women queued up at the station store for rolls of heavy, clay-like bread. By 10 o'clock the bread had run out. The women's nerves cracked under the intolerable living conditions, the overcrowding, the children's illnesses, and conflicts flared up between them.[19]

Irina and her mother decided to return to Moscow as soon as they could. Since Irina was not considered an essential worker, she was unable to get a permit. So in January 1942 she smuggled herself back by hiding in the luggage rack when the patrols came round the train. Her mother had locked their flat when they left. It had since been broken into, but all that was missing was the fourth volume of a complete Shakespeare, ten records of performances by Toscanini, a teapot, and a carpet. Irina returned to the university. There was no heating and it was so cold that the ink froze in the inkwells. She and another girl used to take their ration of food to the university: each looked after the other's portion to lessen the temptation of eating it too soon. She attended lectures during the day and studied nursing in the evenings. It was equally cold at home: the heating had been turned off, and Irina and her mother lived in the kitchen and used the gas stove to warm themselves. Her mother took family treasures into the country to trade with the peasants for food. Irina eventually became the Director of the Pushkin Fine Arts Museum, and one of the most influential women in the city both before and after the collapse of the Soviet Union.[20]

Irina Golyamina, the sculptor Daniel Mitlyanski's classmate from School No. 110, was also evacuated with her mother on 16 October. 'We travelled in the train carrying the workers from the Ball Bearing Factory. It took us seven days to get to Saratov on the Volga. A girl died of TB on the train. In Saratov we lived in a dormitory with no heating. My mother went off to work early in the morning and came back very late. My friend Dina and I decided we wouldn't continue with our education: it seemed wrong to be going to school while the boys from our class were fighting at the front, and we decided to work in a factory or learn to be nurses. But when they learned from our letters what we were going to do, the boys told us not to be so silly. So we did take evening classes, finished our 10th class, and went to Leningrad University, which had been evacuated to Saratov. Nevertheless, I did go to work in a hospital. At first I read letters to the soldiers and helped them write to their people. Many of them came from places occupied by the Germans, and had no news from their families at all. So we went on writing to them once they were sent back to the front, so that they should know that there was someone thinking of them. Later we were sent to Stalingrad, where I washed bloody clothes, blankets and bandages.'[21]

The roads to the East were as packed as the trains. Mr Baggalay of the British embassy struggled to get through to his boss in Kuibyshev with a column of a dozen embassy cars, with their drivers and the drivers' wives and children:

> The traffic consisted mainly of cars and lorries [...] of every kind – private cars, lorries with soldiers, a few lorries with military equipment such as searchlights and AA guns, a great many more with miscellaneous loads such as tyres, machinery, etc. lorries carrying civilians with every kind of bag and baggage. [...] In addition to this the roads were crowded with people on the march. Some were clearly organised bodies, from factories and so on, being evacuated en masse. Others were going singly or in groups of two or three families. One large lot consisted of technical schoolboys in their uniforms. Numbers of people were resting on the snow by the wayside. Later on, in the small hours of the morning, we passed quantities of men and women being marched under some sort of guard. These may have been people evacuated from areas now occupied by the Germans or they may have been people under some sort of arrest, but whatever they were they were being marshalled along and some must have been in the last stages of fatigue, as we saw many fallen or falling by the wayside. It was reminiscent of the gangs marching to Siberia in Tsarist days. The stream of traffic was continuous both through the night and the next day [...] with cars hooting and chauffeurs cursing in every direction. But apart from this there was no sign of excitement, still less of panic, or indeed of any emotion at all.[22]

Some people were evacuated by boat through the Volga canal system and down the river. Three hundred and fifty-seven psychiatric patients from the Kashchenko Hospital and fifty-six staff were embarked on a little old barge, which was to take them to Ryazan. The barge was so crowded that, as one woman remarked, there was 'no room to drop an apple or even a pin'. The sexes were formally divided, but the distinction soon broke down. The interior of the barge smelt foul, because the sanitation consisted of buckets. There were mattresses, blankets and sheets for only one-third of the patients. They were not allowed on deck for fear they would jump into the river and drown. There were only ten orderlies to guard the patients; they worked in two shifts, so they were always exhausted. The patients started to panic and to hammer on the sides of the barge. Two of them did indeed try to escape by jumping in the river. The medical supplies began to run out, but when the barge got to Ryazan the hospital there said it could take fifty patients only. They managed to land some more patients at Gorki, but finally completed their journey only in Kazan on the Volga, far down the river from their starting point.[23]

When Moscow University was evacuated in October, Andrei Sakharov travelled with the other students and teachers from the Department of Physics. Their first stop was Murom, a provincial town some two hundred miles to the East. Here they were billeted with a woman who supplemented her earnings by pilfering food from the grocery store where she worked during the day and entertaining a succession of soldiers at night. Trains carrying wounded soldiers arrived early every morning. Despite the advanced season, stretcher cases were left in the open, waiting for the next connection. Women from the surrounding villages came to the station to bring gifts of food and tobacco for the soldiers and to ask for news of their loved ones.

From Murom Sakharov's party continued on their way to Ashkhabad, the capital of the Turkmen republic, where the Department of Physics was to be reconstituted. Forty of them were crowded into each railway car, equipped with double bunks and a stove. 'During the month-long journey', wrote Sakharov,

> the cars became separate communities, as it were, with their own leaders, their talkative and silent types, their panic-mongers, go-getters, big eaters, the slothful and the hardworking. The trains moving east with us carried evacuees, damaged equipment, and wounded men; those racing toward the West carried combat troops: their faces were tense as they peered out from the train windows, and they all looked somehow alike.

The temperature dropped to twenty degrees below zero and lower. The students stole coal for their stove from the stocks kept at the stations to supply the locomotives. Once Sakharov found a piece of gingerbread in the snow near a water tower and swallowed it on the spot. On the Kazakh steppe they ran into a blizzard and the chimney pipe for the stove blew off. A first-year student named Markov, wearing only a vest, climbed up onto the roof to repair it. Some of the students traded their clothing for food brought to the train by peasants along the way. To while away the time, they played a trivia quiz game based on the comic novels of Ilf and Petrov, *The Twelve Chairs* and *The Golden Calf*. The champion was Iosif Shklovsky, who was later to become a distinguished astrophysicist.

At one point Sakharov got left behind. He caught up by travelling on an open coal wagon. The special carriage of the Commissar for Higher Education had been hitched to the coal train. The Commissar's people took pity on Sakharov, and allowed him to move in. One of them told him that his home in Moscow had been destroyed by a German bomb on 23 October, the very day he had left the city. Several people had been killed, but Sakharov's family survived and moved into an abandoned nursery school in the next street.[24] The students and their teachers finally arrived in Ashkhabad on 6 December.[25]

Sakharov graduated in July 1942 and was offered a teaching post. He preferred to contribute to the war effort by working in a defence factory. After another exhausting train journey across wartime Russia, which included a brief visit to Moscow to see his parents, he was posted to a munitions factory in Ulyanovsk [Simbirsk], Lenin's birthplace on the Volga. Instead of working in the factory, he was immediately sent off to cut firewood. He was billeted in a little village deep in the forest, inhabited only by women, children and old men. Neighbours begged his landlady for milk for their children or a handful of flour. Kerosene was so short that the villagers lit their lamps only during dinner and sat for the rest of the evening in darkness. For the first time in his life, Sakharov heard Stalin criticised openly: a worker whose son had just been killed at the front said, 'If he were a Russian, he'd feel more pity for the people.' Sakharov never forgot 'the atmosphere of tragedy and anxiety that permeated every word spoken, weighed upon the women drawing water at the well, and made even the children unusually reticent ... Hard as life was, there was a foreboding that things would get even worse before they got better, and the horror of the war was always uppermost in people's minds.'[26]

After a couple of weeks cutting wood Sakharov injured his hand, and had to return to the munitions factory. The factory followed the uniform national schedule: two shifts of eleven hours each, seven days a week. Theoretically, workers got a day off when they switched from the night to the day shift, and vice versa. In practice, however, shifts were rotated only a few times a year. The big machines, noisy, dirty, and dangerous, were operated by women from the surrounding villages. They worried about the children they had left behind them, but got little sympathy from the personnel manager of the factory. Leaving without permission risked five years in a labour camp and often the only way to get back to the village was to become pregnant again. The workers were fed at lunch with powdered egg and porridge served on sheets of paper. They ate it by their machines, and washed it down with ersatz tea from a tin cup. One man went berserk after drinking industrial alcohol. Often there were no utensils to eat with. Sakharov organised the illicit production of spoons for the whole factory. All had been stolen within twenty-four hours.

Coupons entitled people to food, but the shops were often empty. Even bread was not always available. A worker on night shift might have to queue for most of the day before getting his ration. Since he had to be back at work by eight at night, he had practically no time to sleep. Sakharov and the other single workers lived in wooden barracks, up to twelve people in a room. They soon got lice. The toilet was some distance away in the courtyard. People didn't feel like walking that far in the dark, and in the morning there were puddles of frozen urine outside the huts.[27]

Sakharov stayed in Ulyanovsk until 1945, when he returned to Moscow with his new wife and daughter and began his career as one of the country's best physicists.

The authorities began a systematic evacuation of people from the arts quite early on. On 8 August the river steamer *Alexander Pirogov* left Moscow carrying writers and their families, including Pasternak's wife and son. Ill at ease and unsociable in the crowd was Marina Tsvetaeva, one of Russia's finest poets. Tsvetaeva had attended the girls' school which eventually became School No. 110, and had published her first book of verse at the age of eighteen. Her husband Sergei Efron had fought against the Bolsheviks in the Civil War and fled to France. Tsvetaeva had joined him there in 1922. After they returned to Moscow in the late 1930s, Efron – who had allegedly worked for the NKVD in Paris – was shot and their daughter sent to a camp. Tsvetaeva was now a marked woman, ostracised by the official literary establishment, her works out of print, a star no longer.

The passengers travelled down the Volga as far as Kazan, and then up the River Kama until they got to Chistopol, where most of them disembarked. Tsvetaeva and her sixteen-year-old son Georgi (known as Mur) continued with the remainder of the party on to the small riverside town of Yelabuga, which before the revolution had prospered mightily from the grain trade and boasted thirteen millionaires. The millionaires were killed or expelled at the time of the revolution, and what had once been a pretty little place became a badly rundown backwater. Tsvetaeva got there on 17 August and settled with her son in a tiny room in a tiny wooden house belonging to a poor local family, the Brodelshchikovs. What happened thereafter is unclear. She failed to find work in the town, and was harassed by the local NKVD. She briefly visited the other writers in Chistopol, who seem to have cold-shouldered her. She hanged herself on 31 August, leaving a fish in a frying pan for Mur to eat when he came home. She was buried in an unmarked grave. The frying pan is displayed in the little museum down the road from the place where she died. Mur joined the army and died of wounds in July 1944.[28]

When the Germans began to close in on Leningrad in the late summer, the Soviet authorities evacuated a number of eminent artists, writers and musicians, at first to the comparative safety of Moscow. The poet Anna Akhmatova and the writer Zoshchenko were flown out on 28 September. Shostakovich, who had been in Leningrad, examining composition students at the Conservatoire, flew with his family to Moscow on 1 October. He brought with him three completed movements of his new Seventh Symphony, which he had begun in the first days of the war.

As the German breakthrough towards Moscow gathered pace, the Soviet authorities decided that the evacuees from Leningrad and their artistic colleagues in Moscow should be moved further East. The Moscow Art Theatre had been on tour in Minsk when war broke out, and had barely escaped being rounded up by the Germans. Now it was sent to Saratov.[29] The Moscow Maly Theatre was sent to Chelyabinsk, and the Vakhtangov Theatre to Omsk. The Bolshoi Theatre went to Kuibyshev: it took more than forty carriages and thirty-five goods wagons to evacuate the artists, their families, their costumes and their props. The artists were told that they could take only one dependant with them. The veteran ballerina Ye. D. Vasilieva went to the theatre to ask if she could take her mother and her sick sister as well as her husband. One official told her to run away, to escape by whatever means she could. Another told her that he had no idea what she should do next: 'You're not an artist of the Bolshoi Theatre any more. The Bolshoi Theatre has ceased to exist.'

Sergei Lemeshev, the tenor whom Werth rated behind his rival Kozlovski, was also left in Moscow. When he arrived at the Kazan Station the weather was foul, he was lightly dressed, and he soon began to freeze as he sat on his suitcase, awaiting the order to entrain. The organisers advised him to go home to warm up, because the train would not be leaving any time soon. He went home, went to sleep and when he woke up the train had gone.[30]

On 16 October, the day of the panic, Shostakovich was evacuated once again, this time by train. 'The Kazan Station ... was chock-a-block with evacuees and the square in front of it was also black with people,' one of his acquaintances wrote many years later.

> Inside the station writers, painters, musicians and artists from the Bolshoi and the Vakhtangov Theatres were huddled beside their belongings, trying to make themselves comfortable. The loudspeakers continually blared announcements. At last we were informed that the train was ready to board. People put on their rucksacks, picked up their bundles and suitcases, and made for the platform, which was enveloped in terrible darkness. Underfoot the snow was wet and squelchy. Everybody pushed and shoved at each other with their belongings. We had a single ticket for a whole group of artists, which got torn in half in the crush. We had been designated carriage no. 7; a queue had formed outside it. Somebody stood guarding the door, blocking the entrance, shouting, 'This carriage is only for the Bolshoi Theatre.[31]

A bewildered Shostakovich was standing there with his wife and children, holding a sewing machine in one hand and a child's potty in the other. At last he was allowed into the carriage with the Bolshoi artists. Among the passengers were the composers Khachaturian,

Khrennikov, Kabalevski and Shebalin. Some of the women from the Bolshoi were in tears. The grossly overcrowded train started off, and Shostakovich discovered he had left his two suitcases behind on the platform: he had only the old suit he stood up in. The other passengers rallied round to give him socks, a spare shirt, and other odds and ends. He was beset with contradictory advice. Some told him he should stay on the train until it got to Siberia or Central Asia, where he would be safer and better fed. Others said that the additional journey would be a nightmare, and that he would do better to get off at Kuibyshev, where the government and the Bolshoi people would be able to look after him. He finally decided on Kuibyshev, which the train reached after seven long days and nights. He and his family were squashed into a school classroom with fourteen other people: everyone slept on the floor. Later they were given their own room and a grand piano.

At first Shostakovich felt unable to work on his new symphony: 'As soon as I got on that train, something snapped inside me ... I can't compose just now, knowing how many people are losing their lives.'[32] But when the news came through of the German defeat outside Moscow, he finished the symphony in a burst of exuberant energy in less than two weeks. It was completed on 27 December and first performed in Kuibyshev on 5 March 1942. Irina Antonova attended the first performance in Moscow at the end of the month. The performance took place during the day; an air raid began as it ended, and the audience were sent down to the shelters. The symphony was an immediate success around the world: Henry Wood performed it in London on the first anniversary of the German attack. On 9 August 1942 the symphony was performed in besieged Leningrad itself, by a scratch orchestra of emaciated players under their conductor Karl Eliasberg. Several of the musicians died of starvation while the rehearsals were still in progress.

Like the parade on Red Square on 7 November 1941, this performance has remained a symbol of Russian defiance. The Soviet authorities decided that the symphony was about the fascist invasion of the Soviet Union. It was immediately dubbed the 'Leningrad' symphony. Later critics argued, on the contrary, that the symphony was a coded criticism of the Communist regime. After playing the piano score to his fellow evacuees in Kuibyshev, Shostakovich himself said, 'Music, real music, can never be literally tied to a theme. National Socialism is not the only form of fascism; this music is about all forms of terror, slavery, the bondage of the spirit.'[33]

The film studios MosFilm and LenFilm were sent to Alma Ata in Kazakhstan, along with the main directors, the stars, and the technicians.[34] Lidia Smirnova went with the team who were filming Simonov's *A Boy from Our Town*, in which she was playing the female lead. Her husband Sergei had asked the director Stolper to keep a friendly eye on her; it was too friendly, and she spent much of the next weeks and months fending him off. Their train was attacked by German aircraft on the way and they had to take shelter in the woods alongside the track. The journey took so long that they began to run out of food. The weather in Moscow had been foul – cold and wet – when they left. In Alma Ata it was a glorious autumn. Living conditions were hard: most of the actors shared rooms in a hotel where there was one toilet on each floor. But at first there was enough food: there were plenty of shops and the apples for which the city is famous.

Other artists began to arrive as well: the scriptwriter Aleksei Kapler, who had been the lover of Stalin's daughter Svetlana and paid for his audacity with a spell in the Lubyanka;[35] Roman Karmen, the documentary film director who had worked in Spain and China and whose wife had been having an affair with Vasili Stalin until Stalin ordered her to be returned to her husband; the writer Zoshchenko; the actors and directors from LenFilm who had escaped from Leningrad just before the blockade was closed. The composer Sergei Prokofiev, his wife and two small sons lived in the same hotel as Smirnova. He was working on the score of *Cinderella*, endlessly playing the same two notes until Smirnova felt like hitting him over the head with a frying pan. It was only later, she confessed in her memoirs, that she learned that he was a genius.

The filming of *A Boy from Our Town* continued in Alma Ata. Pudovkin was there too, making another film. So was Eisenstein, who was working on *Ivan the Terrible*. The technical facilities were primitive. It was freezing cold, and there was only one studio, so the three teams had to work in shifts. It shows in the final versions of the films.

For months Smirnova heard nothing of her husband, whom she had last seen when she accompanied him to his volunteer regiment outside Moscow in the early autumn. Eventually the news filtered through that his regiment had retreated in a panic when they ran into serious opposition on the Mozhaisk Highway. He had turned back through the German barrage to collect some papers he had left in the trench and was posted missing. None of his postcards ever arrived and Smirnova never saw him again.

Because there was now even less space, people had to sleep in cinema foyers. Food too became scarce. The artists – the wife of the director Ermler and Smirnova herself – sold their possessions to buy provisions in the market. Pudovkin's wife sold his ties and her gilded shoes. Lice multiplied, typhus began to spread, and in due course Smirnova caught both. She remained in Alma Ata until the end of 1943.[36]

The painters and sculptors from the studio apartments opposite the old Post Office building were evacuated to Samarkand in Central Asia. They took six weeks to get there, and some thought that even that was not far enough away from the Germans. Among the passengers were Raisa Labas, her sister and young Yuli, and the painters Tatlin, Favorski, and Robert Falk, Raisa's first husband. During the journey the head of the Party office of the Union of Artists looked in on them. He said to Favorski, who was travelling with his wife, their twelve-year-old daughter Masha, and their younger son Vanya, 'You're not a Jew or a Bolshevik. The Germans are civilised people. Why are you leaving Moscow? What are you afraid of?'

Favorski replied, 'I fought as an artillery officer in the Japanese War and the First World War. I've just heard that my eldest son has been killed. I'm not a Bolshevik. But I am a Russian. You can get out of this compartment right away, you —' And he used words that the young Yuli had never heard before.

In Samarkand the Labas family stayed in a hotel. But Favorski and Falk, as two of the Soviet Union's most distinguished artists, lived in the medressah of Ulug Beg, the learned grandson of Tamerlane the Great, in the great square on the Registan.

Special arrangements were made for one particular category of people: Moscow's Germans. The German community had been respected, if not much liked, for nearly two centuries. Peter the Great and then Catherine the Great had encouraged them to bring their skills to Russia and settle there. But even someone less paranoid than Stalin would have worried about where their sympathies lay once the war began. When he learned that German troops in the Ukraine had been welcomed by German villagers there, he ordered Beria to deport any Soviet citizens of German origin on whom he could still lay his hands – much as Churchill dealt with Germans and Italians in Britain in 1940, or Roosevelt with the West Coast Japanese in 1942.[37]

Major Zhuravlëv was told to deport Moscow's Germans to Kazakhstan in Central Asia by 15 September. Each person would be allowed to take 440 pounds of luggage. Food and medical services would be made available for the journey. On arrival the deportees were to be accommodated in empty buildings in collective and state farms. Where these did not exist, the authorities would lend them money to build their own homes. Ten days later Major Zhuravlëv reported that the deportations had been carried out without incident. There had been more Germans living in Moscow than he had realised. He had arrested over a thousand people, and deported more than ten thousand. Forty per cent of the deportees were factory workers, nearly the same number were office workers, a thousand were peasants, and fifteen hundred were 'individuals not engaged in socially useful work'. He had not deported people whose fathers were not German, the elderly, the families of men in the army, and 'major specialists' of use to the regime. 'For operational reasons' he had not deported another 150 Germans, which probably meant that they were working for him as agents. There had been a handful of suicides. Ten people had evaded deportation and were being sought by the police.[38]

The Germans travelled in crowded railway wagons for many days before they arrived at their destinations. When they arrived they found, as usual, that no arrangements had been made for their reception, and they had to construct shelter for themselves as best they could. They were not on the whole treated much worse than the other evacuees who also travelled for weeks in uncomfortable trains and were dumped in inhospitable places. The Communists among them were allowed to keep their Party cards.[39]

By the time the evacuation of Moscow was over, five hundred factories and two million people had been moved from the city. It took over seventy thousand trains to shift them.[40] The operation was completed by 25 November.[41]

– FOURTEEN –

COMPRESSING THE SPRING

In ordinary times the little stations serving the dacha country around Moscow are practically closed by late autumn, and the green, blue and yellow kiosks which serve the weekenders in the summer have been boarded up.

In the late autumn of 1941 the kiosks on the country stations were boarded up as usual. But this year the platforms were crowded with soldiers coming and going from the front, and with civilians too, more women than men, wearing overcoats, padded jackets, boots, skiing trousers and mittens, and carrying spades and pickaxes, on their way to dig the defensive ditches around the city. The new electric locomotives which used to pull the suburban trains – the '*elektrichkas*' – had been sent off to the East. The overhead cable which had supplied their power had been stripped, rolled up on drums, and sent to the rear, so that the valuable copper could be used for weapons and munitions in the evacuated factories. Instead of the *elektrichkas*, there were ancient steam engines, wheezing with age and belching out clouds of black smoke.

Moscow itself was becoming a fortress. By November the three new defensive lines were taking shape: along the Outer Railway Ring, and along the lines of the ancient concentric fortifications of Moscow, the Garden Ring and the Boulevard Ring in the very centre of the city (see map 1). Yevgeni Anufriev, Vladimir Frolov, Yevgeni Teleguev, their comrades from the OMSBON and the Dzerzhinski Division, and tens of thousands of other soldiers and civilians had barricaded the roads into the city with sandbags which looked like bags of flour under their covering of light snow. There were firing slits in the barricades, protected by armoured shields, and no more than a narrow gap to allow vehicles through. The buildings at each street corner were turned into fortified machine-gun nests. Machine guns and anti-tank detachments were positioned behind bricked-up windows and on balconies.

Although the city transport was working again, many of the vehicles had been commandeered for military purposes. The buses on line No. 21 were taking reinforcements out along the Volokolamsk Highway as far as Krasnogorsk, only ten miles from the front itself. Other buses were being used as ambulances. Trams travelled, nose to tail, carrying volunteers, with guns, boxes of ammunition and field kitchens on their platforms. The back of each tram carried a white stripe, so that the driver of the following tram could see it in the dark; but the blackout was broken anyway by the flashes from the overhead lines.[1]

German prisoners taken during October cheekily told their captors that the victorious Wehrmacht would parade on Red Square on 7 November – the Anniversary of the Revolution. Hitler had said so.[2]

Stalin too was wondering how to mark the anniversary. In a normal year, the Moscow City Council organised a formal meeting on 6 November, and the next day there was a military parade on Red Square and a march-past of workers and peasants. Stalin asked General Artemiev and the air commanders if the parade should be held as usual. The generals were flabbergasted and raised a host of objections. The Germans might bomb the parade. It would be a poor affair anyway: the tanks and guns were all at the front and it would be possible to muster only a miserable contingent of infantry. Stalin berated them: did they not understand the immense political significance of a parade at this crucial moment? The generals gave in.[3] Asked for a second opinion, Zhukov told Stalin that the Germans were unlikely to launch an early ground offensive: they were regrouping after suffering heavy losses in the October fighting. The parade could be held if Moscow's air defences were reinforced by fighter aircraft brought in from neighbouring Fronts.[4] Armed with these guarantees, Stalin decided to go ahead with both the formal celebration and the parade.

Artemiev scraped together cadets and infantrymen, veterans of the revolution, soldiers and cavalrymen from the Dzerzhinski Division, two artillery regiments and two tank battalions: 28,000 men in all.[5] He saw Stalin again on 30 October, and asked what time the parade should begin. Stalin answered, 'Make sure that no one knows until the last minute. Don't tell even me until after the ceremony on 6 November.'[6]

That ceremony, Stalin decided, would be held at the Mayakovski Metro Station on Gorky Street, the deepest and most splendid in Moscow. He inspected it late on the evening of 5 November, surrounded by his generals and his political colleagues. Hectic preparation began immediately. No more trains were allowed to stop at the station. After 7 o'clock the next morning, the only people allowed in were those with passes from the NKVD. On one side of the station they put up a platform brought in from the Bolshoi Theatre, and draped it in carpets. A bust of Lenin stood behind. There were flowers and posters everywhere. Chairs for the audience were brought in from the theatres on Mayakovski Square. Above the escalator was the usual banner: 'Hail to the 24th anniversary of the October Revolution!' Shamshin, the chief engineer of Moscow City Radio, struggled with the appalling acoustics in the station to set up a public address system.[7] Three of the best singers from the Bolshoi Theatre – Kozlovski, Reizen, and Barsova – were flown from their places of evacuation to Moscow with a fighter escort. Nobody told them why.[8]

Invitations were sent out at the very last minute. V. A. Kolosova, the Party Secretary of the Trëkhgorka, was at a meeting with the Secretary of the Krasnaya Presnya Raion Party Committee, when she was given a ticket, put straight in a bus with her colleagues, and driven off with no idea where she was going until she arrived at the Mayakovski Station. Trains were parked along one platform. Some had been converted into cloakrooms, others into improvised buffet cars serving tea and sandwiches, and even mandarins – luxuries which ordinary people never saw even in peacetime. Levitan, the radio announcer, was sitting in a carriage reserved for the performing artists, guarding his equipment and preparing to broadcast the event across the Soviet Union. In the ceremonial guard behind the tribune there were tank crews, marines, mountain troops, and a girl, who took it in turns to stand for five minutes by the bust of Lenin.[9] Many of the audience were in uniform and had obviously come straight from the front.

At 7 o'clock a special train drew up on the other platform. The doors opened very quietly. The first person to step out was Stalin, followed by members of the Politburo, the Government, and the Moscow city authorities. The applause went on for nearly ten minutes. Kolosova thought Stalin looked thinner and greyer than when she had last seen him at the May Day Parade: the strain of the war was beginning to tell.

Since Moscow City Council was the host for the occasion, the proceedings were opened by Pronin. He then gave the word to Stalin. At that moment the early-warning observers reported that enemy aircraft were approaching the city. The guns opened up, the fighters were scrambled, but Colonel Lapirov, at his post in the MPVO, took the risky decision not to sound the air-raid alarm, since that would have meant breaking off the live broadcast from the ceremony. He brushed off all enquiries from the Mayakovski Station. Everything, he replied, was calm. The Russians later claimed that two hundred and fifty German aircraft had attacked the city. Thirty-four, they said, were shot down on the outskirts. Not one broke through to the centre.[10] These figures seem exaggerated. The Moscow Central Ambulance Service merely recorded that the raid lasted from 17.25 to 18.20, and that no one was called out that night. The standard German history passes over the affair in silence.[11]

The audience in the station sat in complete silence as Stalin spoke simply, deliberately, and with his habitual Georgian accent. Because of the poor acoustics, it was not always possible to distinguish individual words, which were in any case from time to time drowned out by applause. He spoke with his usual relentless logic – crude, forceful, and difficult to resist. He began by claiming that in four months of war the Germans had lost four and a half million people, against Soviet losses of 350,000 dead, 378,000 missing and just over one million wounded. These figures were of course wildly misleading, and even among his listeners there were sceptics who found them hard to believe.[12] But he went on to analyse – objectively enough – why the German blitzkrieg was doomed to eventual defeat in Russia. In 1940 the French had been robbed of their will to fight by the internal disintegration of their system. The Germans believed that similar forces of disintegration would operate in the Soviet Union. They assumed that the initial defeats of the Red Army would lead to a collapse in Soviet morale and to discord between the peoples of the Soviet Union. It was quite possible, said Stalin, that any other state which had lost so much territory would have collapsed. The fact that the Soviet Union had held together was a tribute to the regime.

The Germans, Stalin went on, had grossly overestimated their own strength and underestimated that of the Red Army. The Red Army lacked the experience of the battle-hardened Wehrmacht. The Germans had had the advantage of surprise and an overwhelming superiority in modern tanks and aircraft. But as they advanced further into the depths of Russia their lines of communication were becoming ever longer and increasingly vulnerable to attack by Soviet partisans.

Moreover the Soviet Union, Stalin emphasised, was not alone. The Germans had never thought that the Western democracies and the Soviet Union would be able to combine against them. But unlike Germany, Britain and the United States were democratic countries even though they were capitalist. The coalition between the Soviet Union and the Western democracies was a growing reality. The British and Americans were not doing any actual fighting in the West. But they were already supplying the Soviet Union with tanks and aeroplanes, aluminium, lead, nickel, and rubber. The Nazi defeat was inevitable because between them the three could outproduce Germany. Above all the Soviet Union and its allies enjoyed the moral advantage of fighting a war of defence, a war of liberation against an imperial power which had brought most of mainland Europe under its yoke.

Stalin concluded with winged words to feed the themes of Soviet propaganda: 'Let us fight to liberate the nations groaning under the yoke of Hitlerite tyranny! Long live our Red Army and our Red Fleet! Long live our glorious Motherland!' And yet again: 'Our cause is just. The enemy will be beaten. Victory will be ours.'

The applause went on for so long that the audience's hands began to ache. Kolosova, a small woman, was lifted up by her colleagues to get a better look. The rest of the audience climbed on to their chairs in defiance of the NKVD guards. An orchestra played the Internationale, and the concert began. In distant Kuibyshev, the evacuated diplomats listened to 'a relay of M[onsieur] Stalin's speech from Moscow, of which nobody in the theatre could make out a single word'. Once again the British decided that this was because the speech was meant to be read rather than heard, 'M[onsieur] Stalin's accent being somewhat distressing to Russian ears and his delivery halting and unimpressive'.[13]

After the concert was over, and despite the urging of the NKVD guards, the audience at the Mayakovski Station refused to depart until Stalin's train had gone: 'Who d'you think you're shoving? We'll leave when we feel like it.'

General Artemiev now reported to Stalin that next day's parade would begin at 8 o'clock – two hours earlier than usual to confuse the Germans. Stalin said that the parade was not to be halted even if the Germans did attack.[14] General Sinilov, who had only just taken over as Commandant of Moscow, was responsible for organising the details. In peacetime he would have had six weeks or more to prepare, and the soldiers would have been regulars with plenty of parade ground drill under their belts. Now he only had a matter of days. Many of the soldiers were recent conscripts, with the sketchiest idea of ceremonial drill. They needed time to practise. To ensure that they had no inkling of what was afoot, he invented a cover story. The morale of the people of Moscow needed a boost. There would be a public inspection of units going to the front some time in the middle of November. The soldiers were to be prepared accordingly.

Most of the soldiers saw through the cover story quickly enough. Yevgeni Teleguev and his OMSBON unit were taken off battle training at the beginning of November and began to do up to four hours' drill a day. The cover story made no operational sense. They drew their own conclusions: there was to be a parade, and they were to be part of it. They got hold of new overcoats, sewed on their insignia, cleaned their equipment and polished their boots until they could see their own faces in them. They practised their drill on the embankments of the Moscow River, so that they could shelter under the bridges if the German bombers attacked. The Dzerzhinski Division brought in their military band so they could practise marching to music.

Pavel Gudz, the young tank lieutenant, and his fellows had less opportunity to practise than most. After their mauling in the Ukraine, the survivors of his unit were moved by train to a training camp near Moscow, where they received new tanks and some woefully inexperienced replacement crews. They were not told they would be taking part in the parade until the evening of 6 November. Illuminated only by the moon, Gudz immediately took one company of tanks and a lorry loaded with fuel and oil through the deserted night streets into the centre of Moscow. He left one tank in reserve by the Central Telegraph Office at the bottom of Gorky Street and took the other four to their start-up positions on the edge of Red Square. He and his fellow officers then walked through Red Square to get some idea of what they would face. The Mausoleum was still covered by a camouflaged tarpaulin, though the sentries were there as usual, guarding Lenin in his tomb. Gudz did not of course know that the tomb was empty.

An air of suppressed activity hung over all. Firemen, diverted from their proper duties, were putting up banners and slogans and great portraits of Lenin and Stalin on the façade of GUM, the department store on Red Square. Praskovia Sergeeva and her colleagues from the 242nd Volunteer Division had been badly battered as they retreated before the German advance. When they reached Moscow they were given new equipment and new uniforms, and – to their surprise – two weeks' training in ceremonial drill. Now they were setting up a casualty station with an operating table inside GUM itself. Ambulances were stationed outside in the side streets and in nearby courtyards. Emergency wards were set up at the military hospital in Lefortovo, and arrangements made to get casualties to hospitals in the suburbs in case enemy aircraft broke through.[15]

For Gudz and his fellows the most important thing was that there was no treacherous ice under the light snow: that would make it easier to preserve the alignment of their tanks as they drove through Red Square the next day. They looked up and saw that the bombers' moon was becoming overcast. In good weather the German aircraft might penetrate even a determined defence. Now that anxiety could be all but laid to rest.

General Sinilov finally gave commanders their orders at 2 o'clock in the morning. Few of the soldiers had slept, and they were worn out with the incessant drilling. The Commandant of the Krasin Artillery School paraded his sleepy cadets and told them that once they got onto

Red Square, they were to continue marching at all costs. As they left their barracks in Krasnaya Presnya, anxious civilians shouted: 'Don't abandon us! Stay and defend Moscow.'

When General Sinilov himself set off it was still dark. Snow was falling and everything was covered with a freezing white mist. He was very nervous: this was the first big event in his new job, and it could easily go wrong. With the temperature down to an unseasonable minus six degrees, the ground was very slippery indeed.[16] The cobbled slope into Red Square had been sprinkled with sand during the night, but the sand had been covered again by the morning snow. There were numerous accidents as the parade went forward. Some of the tanks took the slope at a run and succeeded in getting to the top. The more cautious skidded and slid, and had to be brought under control with tractors. Sinilov was everywhere, bullying the soldiers, rushing up to the Mausoleum to report what was going on, until at last everything was in place. The soldiers were drawn up in their ranks on the Square. Needles of frost settled on their bayonets and the wind kicked gusts of powdery snow into the air. Shcherbakov had delivered invitations throughout the night to leaders of Raion Councils and Party Committees. The lucky few were sitting in the freezing cold in their seats along the Kremlin wall. Alongside them were the representatives of the foreign press, called in so that news of the parade could be flashed around the world as soon as it was over.

At five minutes to eight, Stalin came onto the Mausoleum, now freed from its camouflage. He was followed by Molotov, Kaganovich, Mikoyan, Shcherbakov, Pronin and the rest. The crowd broke out into applause, and the leaders clapped in reply. Stalin raised his arms in greeting. He pointed to the overcast sky and remarked to his companions, 'The Bolsheviks are lucky. God is on their side.'[17] The snow was falling more heavily, and the sky had turned the grey colour of an army greatcoat. It had been planned to broadcast Stalin's speech only to Moscow. But now Stalin told Pronin that it should be broadcast to the whole country.

Pronin called the duty officer at the Central Telegraph Office: 'Broadcast the speech nationwide.'

'I don't have the authority. I don't have permission from the NKVD.'

'General Serov is standing next to me. I'm handing him the phone.'

The man complied.[18]

As the Kremlin bells chimed eight times to mark the hour, Marshal Budënny rode out on his white horse from the Spasski Gate. The commander of the parade, General Artemiev, rode to meet him. Artemiev had not ridden for many years, and so he had chosen a calm bay horse for the occasion. When the moment came, the animal refused to walk straight but kept pulling to the right. It turned out to be blind in one eye. Somehow Artemiev managed to make his report, and together the two generals inspected the troops. Each unit greeted the generals with the traditional 'Ur-ra-a-a-a-a!' When the inspection was over, Budënny joined the other leaders on the Mausoleum.

Silence fell as Stalin began to speak. Teleguev, for one, could barely hear him. His words were muffled by the snow, and Teleguev had to read the speech in the newspaper the next day. In contrast to his measured and analytical speech in the Mayakovski Metro Station, Stalin's address was brief and rhetorical. 'Comrade soldiers and sailors,' he began, 'commanders and political officers, workers, collective farmers, workers of intellectual labour, brothers and sisters in occupied territory, who have temporarily fallen under the yoke of the German bandits, our glorious partisans, who are destroying the German invaders behind the lines!' The country, he admitted, was in a difficult situation. But the young Soviet state had been in an even more difficult position during the Civil War and the foreign intervention. The country had been victorious then, and it would be victorious again. The enemy was not as strong as some scared intellectuals seem to think (a phrase which Moscow's intellectuals resented deeply when they heard it). The Germans faced catastrophe. They had lost four and a half million soldiers in four months. The conquered peoples of Europe and the German people themselves were becoming restless. 'In a few months, in half a year, in little more than a year,' Stalin said, with misplaced optimism, 'Hitlerite Germany will collapse under the weight of its own crimes.'

H went on: 'The whole world is looking at you, for it is you who can destroy the marauding armies of the German invader. The enslaved peoples of Europe look upon you as their liberators. [...] Be worthy of your mission! The war that you are fighting is a war of liberation, a just war. May you be inspired in this war by the valiant image of our great ancestors – Alexander Nevsky, Dmitri Donskoi, Kuzma Minin, Dmitri Pozharski, Alexander Suvorov, Mikhail Kutuzov' – the victorious generals of Russia's earlier wars against the foreign enemy.[19]

His final words – 'Death to the German occupiers' – were met by another thunderous 'hurrah', which rolled over the great Square from one end to the other. The guns roared out their salute, the bands struck up the Internationale, the rattle of drums gave way to a military march, and the parade began.

First were the cadets of the Krasin Artillery School.[20] Anyone who has ever taken part in a ceremonial parade knows the emotional power of the shouted orders, the crash of the military music, the intoxication of being one of a body of men moved by a single will. But now every man and woman on Red Square was overwhelmed by the feeling that they were participating in a great drama of patriotism and defiance. Markov and Ogryzko marched with the Dzerzhinski Division, Teleguev and Anufriev with the OMSBON. All the soldiers were dressed for war, wearing battledress, carrying their weapons and their packs, each lightly dusted with snow. Many of them had never been on a great parade before. Most had never seen Stalin in person. But despite their lack of experience, even though the guiding marks on the Square were hidden under the snow, they marched past in immaculate files of twenty, keeping their dressing throughout, as if they had been practising for weeks in ideal conditions. It took them twenty minutes to pass the Mausoleum.

They were followed by detachments of armed workers, and men from the volunteer militia. These men wore civilian jackets of fleece or padding, boots in leather or felt, fur hats with and without earpieces, caps from the Civil War; and they carried a motley variety of rifles, carbines, and anti-tank weapons.

The bands changed their tempo as the cavalry came onto the Square, the horses matched in colour and breed, trotting in disciplined ranks, banners flying on the lances of the troopers. They were followed by the mobile machine-gun units, their weapons rattling along on little carts drawn by shaggy ponies. Next came the motorised infantry in orderly columns, and then the guns – the field artillery, howitzers, and the anti-aircraft guns fully armed in case the Germans struck.

The tanks rattled onto the Square at 9 o'clock. They were a motley collection, assembled by General Artemiev from whatever was available around Moscow: tankettes of little military value, T-34s, and the powerful KVs, each followed by a cloud of smoke and snow, two hundred in all. And then something disturbing happened. As the last of the KVs rolled past the Mausoleum where Stalin was standing with his colleagues, one of them turned right round and started off in the opposite direction. It was followed by another. General Sinilov was ordered to find out what had happened and to punish the culprit severely. A young tank commander emerged from the turret of the first tank and explained that he had received a signal that another tank was in trouble. In accordance with standing instructions, he had gone to help. The second tank had done likewise. In the confusion Sinilov was unable to identify the tank which had called for assistance, and the incident passed off amid laughter from Stalin and the others on the Mausoleum.

A fly-past had been planned as well and three hundred aircraft were standing by. But the weather made that impossible. The parade was over. The leaders left the Mausoleum.[21] Gudz refuelled his tanks and drove out along the Volokolamsk Highway, back to his position in the front line. So did the guns and the other armoured detachments. Most of the footsoldiers went back to their barracks, where each was given a hundred grams of vodka.

There was a sequel. Every year, the parade was filmed by the news studio, Moskinokhronika. The technicians always brought their equipment two hours in advance, so that it would be ready when the operators arrived half an hour before the parade actually began at 10 o'clock. This year, too, they arrived on Red Square as usual at 8 o'clock. They were appalled to see that the troops were already drawn up, and Stalin already on the podium. They kept their nerve and began filming. But they had had no time to set up the recording equipment. So they filmed the whole parade, including Stalin's speech, without the sound.

When Belyakov, the senior cameraman, arrived on Red Square, it was already empty. The parade was over, Stalin had gone, so had the troops. Belyakov and his colleagues stood around with depressed and gloomy faces. They had failed to record the historic event and they were thoroughly frightened. An NKVD general came up and said, 'The government knows that Comrade Stalin's speech was not recorded.' Belyakov went white with fear, and his legs turned to jelly. 'But,' the general continued, 'it wasn't your fault. The NKVD failed to warn you that the time for starting the parade had been altered.' Stalin was willing to be filmed again, this time with the sound. The operators built a mock-up of the Mausoleum in the great St George's Hall inside the Kremlin itself. It was an unconvincing expedient: the camera team forgot to brush Stalin's shoulders with snow or some substitute; and the hall was too warm for steam to come from his mouth as he spoke. Rumours eventually arose that Stalin had never attended the parade at all. The film, *The Defeat of the German-Fascist Forces outside Moscow*, was given its première in sixteen of the capital's best cinemas on Red Army Day, 23 February 1942.[22] From there it went around the world. A version was produced by the British Ministry of Information with a commentary by the celebrated radio announcer Wilfred Pickles, and music by Arthur Bliss.[23] The American Film Academy judged it the best foreign film of the year. Mikosha, who had filmed the destruction of the Cathedral of Christ the Saviour, and was now a cameraman in the Soviet Navy, took delivery of the award in Hollywood in the course of an epic voyage around the world, during which he was bombed in London, refused a visa in New York, and nearly captured by Japanese destroyers in the Pacific.[24]

To hold the parade Stalin had withdrawn the equivalent of two divisions from Moscow's defensive line a mere month after the Germans had punched a three hundred-mile hole in it. It was a remarkable, perhaps a foolhardy, gamble. But unlike some of Stalin's other gambles in 1941 and 1942, it paid off in spades. Civilians and soldiers alike were buoyed up by his confidence and courage. The parade was an immensely powerful symbol of defiance, and for many Soviet citizens it was a moral turning point. Those who took part in it never forgot it.

The frosts finally set in at last, and then the heavy snow began to settle. For the small boys the arrival of snow was a godsend: they straightway built a hill of snow and ice for their toboggans by the Central Telegraph Office in Gorky Street.[25] And to start with, the frosts had one great advantage for the Germans. Their tanks had been bogged down in the quagmires of October. Now, once the congealed mud had been chipped

Clockwise from top left: **Irina Golyamina**, who kept the letters of the boys from School No 110 who never returned from the war; **Yelena Okuneva**, who as a nurse with the 242nd Volunteer Division helped man the casualty station in the GUM department store during the parade on Red Square on 7 November 1941; **Antonina Savina**, who spent most of her life as a hospital orderly in the Misericordia Hospital; **Yelena Volkova**, who trained as a pilot but served as a nurse and was decorated for rescuing wounded men under fire.

18. Writers

Top: **Ilya Ehrenburg** (centre) and **Vasil Grossman** (right). Ehrenburg was star of Soviet literature when the wa began, a man of great sophisticatio who had lived abroad but nevertheles managed to retain Stalin's favour. As war correspondent Grossman was muc respected by the soldiers because he wa always willing to share their dangers His remarkable novel *Life and Fate*, no published in Russia until the Gorbache years, is a brilliant analysis of the wa decent people had to make appallin compromises during the Stalin years.

Bottom: **Konstantin Simonov** mad a brilliant career as a novelist, poet cultural bureaucrat and journalist fo the army newspaper *Krasnaya Zvezda* His novel *The Living and the Dead* is on of the best accounts of the early days o the war. In this picture from the chaoti summer of 1941 Simonov, normall elegant and well turned out, look scruffy but surprisingly cheerful.

19. Evacuating the Animals

In the summer and autumn of 1941 hundreds of thousands of animals were evacuated from Western parts of the Soviet Union. Many went through Moscow itself: the cows are passing in front of the camouflaged Bolshoi Theatre.

20. The 46th Guards Night Bomber Regiment

Nadezhda Popova and her colleagues off duty. All the personnel in the Regiment were women, including the armourers and mechanics. Most of them were volunteers from Moscow. Popova and many other members of the regiment completed over 800 missions in the course of the war, and were made Heroes of the Soviet Union. The U-2 bombers on which they flew were unarmed and had a maximum speed of little more than 80 miles an hour. The U-2 was also used as an ambulance and liaison aircraft.

1. 6 November 1941: Stalin addresses the people

)n 6 November 1941 Stalin spoke at Moscow's traditional celebration of the anniver-
ary of the Revolution. Because of the danger of German air raids, the ceremony was
ıeld in the Mayakovski Metro Station, the deepest in Moscow. The women and children
vho normally sheltered there were cleared out for the occasion and lavish refreshments
vere laid on for those fortunate enough to be invited. The diplomats who had been
vacuated to Kuibyshev on the Volga three weeks earlier were not impressed by what
hey heard on the radio: they thought Stalin's delivery boring and his Georgian accent
omic.

22. The Parade on Red Square, 7 November 1941

To the dismay of his generals Stalin ordered the annual parade to be held in 1941, eve
though the Germans were only a few dozen miles away. General Artemiev, the Mosco
garrison commander, managed to scrape together cadets and infantrymen, veterans o
the revolution, cavalrymen and two hundred tanks, many withdrawn from the front fo
the occasion. After a moonlit night the clouds closed in and it began to snow, whic
made a German attack from the air almost impossible: Stalin commented, 'God is o
the side of the Bolsheviks'. The parade was an act of defiance and a huge boost to morale
Those who took part remembered it to their dying day.

23. Pavel Gudz and his Tank

Pavel Gudz is on the left in the photograph at the top. As a 21 year old newly commissioned lieutenant Gudz fought in the first battles on the frontier. He took part in the parade on Red Square on 7 November 1941, and fought in the action which won him the Order of Lenin a month later. The lower picture shows his KV-1 tank after the parade by the statue of Pushkin which became the rallying point for protest meetings in the late Soviet period. The heavy KV-1 tank was just coming into service at the beginning of the war, and was superior to anything the Germans had at the time.

24. Mud and Snow

The mud of the rasputitsa, the spring and autumn thaw, was an even greater impediment to movement that the snow of winter. Cavalry and horses could operate over snow. So on the whole could the well-adapted Russian tanks and vehicles. The German vehicles bogged down and froze.

25. Building Moscow's Defences

During the autumn and winter of 1941 hundreds of thousands of citizens – mostly women – were drafted to build Moscow's defences and to procure firewood from the forests around the city.

26. The Panfilov Heroes

These gigantic figures, each armed with a PPSh submachine gun, commemorate the exploits of twenty-eight members of Panfilov's 316th Division, who – it was said – died holding the German tanks outside Volokolamsk in November 1941. The incident was immediately taken up by the press and became a legend, which recent historians have gone far to deconstruct.

27. Zoya Kosmodemyanskaya is led to execution

Zoya Kosmodemyanskaya was in her last year at School No 201 when she volunteered for training as a partisan. In mid-November 1941 she was sent in a small group on a mission to burn buildings in a village occupied by the Germans about fifty miles from Moscow. She was caught and hanged. Photographs of her execution were later found on the body of a German soldier, and she became a national heroine.

28. Winter in wartime Moscow

Top: These 'Hedgehogs' welded from three pieces of steel, were designed to impede the advance of tanks. Here they are placed in front of a barricade of sandbags with machine gun slits. Hedgehogs form the core of the monument which marks the limit of the German advance on the way into the city from Sheremetievo airport.

Left: This mounted patrol is on the bridge which leads to Red Square.

29. The Belorussia Station

Top: on 17 July 1944, ninety thousand German prisoners of war – many from the defeated Army Group Centre which nearly three years earlier had got so close to Moscow along this very road – were marshalled on the Leningrad Highway outside the Belorussia Station, and marched through the city before being sent off to the camps, from which many never returned.

Bottom: A year later the victorious Russians returned to the Belorussia Station, from which so many were rushed to the front in the first disastrous days of the war.

30. Requiem

Daniel Mitlyanski was a pupil at School No 110, and his sculpture *Requiem* commemorating the one hundred pupils of the school who never returned from the war. The five figures represent Igor Boguslavski (killed 1941)' Grisha Rodin (March 1942); Yuri Danilkovski (March 1944); Gabor Raab (March 1945); Igor Kuptsov 9April 1945). The school used to hold an annual ceremony on the anniversary of the Victory. But in later years the schoolchildren got increasingly tired of hearing about the exploits of their elders in a war which no longer seemed relevant to their everyday lives. The monument was repeatedly vandalised, and had to be put in a place of incongruous safety over the modest entrance to the school.

31. The Boys from School No 110

Clockwise from top left: **Grisha Rodin** was killed in March 1942; **Gabor Raab**, the son of a Hungarian official in the Comintern, was killed in March 1945; **Yuri Danilkovski** was killed in Western Ukraine in March 1944; **Yuri Shlykov** survived the war but lost a leg in the first battles.

32. Gorky Street – The End

The crowds disperse after the Victory Parade on 24 June 1945. At the bottom end of Gorky Street is a glimpse of the Kremlin – the same view as the people had on the first day of the war as they listened to Molotov over the loudspeakers.

away – no mean task in itself – they were free again, to advance across the frozen countryside as well as along the few viable roads that were available. But once the deep snow took hold, the nature of the fighting changed again. Both sides abandoned the attempt to hold a continuous line. Groups of men huddled for warmth in ruined villages, dreading the order to move out into the attack through waist-deep snow against an enemy dug in around just such a ruin as they were leaving.

The Russians had eventually learned from the débâcle in Finland. The fresh troops who were now beginning to arrive on the scene had fur caps, white camouflage capes, fur or padded jackets, and warm felt boots. Whole battalions were trained to fight on skis. And their equipment was superior too. Their tanks had wide tracks which bore their weight even in deep snow. Their automatic weapons were simple and used lubricants which did not freeze even when it was very cold. Even their shaggy ponies were better able to cope with winter than the horses the Germans had brought with them from Europe.

Buoyed up by their original belief that the war would be over in weeks, the Germans had prepared barely at all. Extreme cold froze their automatic weapons, their artillery and their vehicles, and the expedients they used to get them going again often damaged the mechanisms beyond repair. The engines of many aircraft froze solid overnight and could not be restarted. Special clothing was available in quantities intended only for the much-reduced occupation force which was all the Germans thought they would need by winter. Even this failed to get through to the troops in the front line. Von Bock reported at the end of November that his men still had not received winter coats even though the temperature was now around minus forty degrees. Guderian lost twice as many men from frost as from enemy action. The German soldiers robbed the Russian dead of their clothing, improvised clumsy winter boots from straw and rags, and were captured wearing an increasingly bizarre collection of stolen and often female garments.[26]

Von Bock's plan was still for Guderian and Rheinhart (who had taken over Third Panzer Group from Hoth) to outflank the city to South and North with their tanks. But von Bock had fewer resources than he would have liked. Many of his divisions had only just finished mopping up the Soviet armies surrounded at Vyazma and Bryansk, which even in defeat had severely disrupted the German timetable. His railways were struggling to cope with the weather and growing assaults from partisans, so that by mid-November only twenty-three trainloads of food and equipment were getting through, instead of the seventy which his troops needed every day to keep going. Even so he still had almost as many men as the Russians facing him, many more guns, and more than twice as many tanks. But for the first time since the catastrophe which overtook the Red Air Force at the frontier, Russian aircraft almost matched the Germans in numbers, and were able to achieve something like local superiority in the air.[27]

The Soviet High Command was also making its preparations. The much-battered Bryansk Front was dissolved on 10 November, and its remnants redistributed. Koniev's Kalinin Front was given the task of protecting the city to the north. Zhukov's Western Front was reinforced with formations from the Far East, Siberia, Central Asia and elsewhere. Those volunteer divisions which had survived the massacres at Vyazma and Bryansk were deployed immediately before the city. Nine new reserve armies were formed in the rear.[28]

The 16th Army under Rokossovski lay once again on the likely line of the enemy's main blow. Rokossovski built up his defences in depth, placing his anti-tank defences with particular care. These preparations were rudely interrupted when, on 14 November, Stalin ordered Zhukov to launch two spoiling attacks, one to the South of Moscow and one around Volokolamsk. Zhukov protested that these attacks were highly unlikely to succeed, and would simply use up scarce reserves. Stalin overruled him.

Rokossovski was forced to mount his attack just as the Germans were preparing their own. He was severely outnumbered in men, tanks and guns, and had no option but to throw into the battle untried units from the newly arrived reserve forces. For a gain of little more than a mile he suffered grievous losses, and was compelled to abandon much of his plan for defence in depth. Later he commented bitterly:

> The commander knew well enough what the situation was. What he was thinking of when he gave the order to attack, I do not understand even today. Our forces were very limited, and we were given no more than a single night to prepare for the attack. My arguments for postponing or cancelling the attack, or at least for extending the

> period of preparation, were ignored. Dovator's cavalrymen got into serious trouble and were nearly encircled. And almost simultaneously the enemy began his move against us.[29]

The higher command had once again failed to take account of reality. Senior officers found it easier, Rokossovski thought, to pass on impossible orders than to argue the toss with Stalin. If things went wrong, they could always blame their subordinates for the failure. He clearly had Zhukov in mind.

In the midst of this fighting, an attack by the 44th Cavalry Division, newly arrived from Tashkent, was wiped out to a man. A German eye witness described what happened:

> 'We could not believe that the enemy intended to attack us across this broad field, which lay open like a parade ground before us. But then three ranks of cavalry started moving towards us. Across the sunlit field the horseman rode into the attack bent over their horses' necks, their sabres shining. The first shells exploded in their midst and soon a thick black cloud hung over them. Torn scraps of men and horses flew into the air. It was difficult to distinguish one from the other. In this hell the maddened horses were running about wildly. The handful of survivors was finished off by artillery and machine gun. And then out of the wood a second wave of horsemen rode to the attack. It was impossible to imagine that after the annihilation of the first squadrons the nightmare sight would be repeated. But our guns were now zeroed in on the target, and the destruction of the second wave of cavalry took place even more quickly than the first.'

The German defenders did not suffer a single casualty.[30]

Army Group Centre resumed its offensive against Moscow on 15 November. The following day it began its attack on the left flank of the 16th Army, held by Panfilov's 316th Division and a cadet regiment. A heavy artillery barrage and bombing from the air were followed by tanks, now at last able to roll forward over the frozen ground. Panfilov's left flank rested on a small railway crossing called Dubosekovo.

He had placed an infantry regiment there, the 1075th, to block any attempt by German tanks to break through to the Volokolamsk Highway. It included an anti-tank platoon armed with one machine gun, two anti-tank rifles, and Molotov cocktails. After destroying a number of tanks and suffering significant casualties, the regiment was compelled to withdraw towards evening. For retreating without orders the commander and political commissar of the regiment were temporarily suspended from their posts. From these events a legend was later born.

The rest of the battered division moved slowly back as the Germans continued their attacks the following day. Stalin had been husbanding the fresh troops arriving from the East in his Stavka Reserve, deaf to the pleas of Zhukov and others that they should be thrown into the desperate battle. But at this critical moment he partially relented. Fifty trains moved General Beloborodov's 78th Siberian Rifle Division into the line. This division was equipped to pre-war standards: it had 15,000 men and a generous number of artillery and tanks. Beloborodov temporarily saved the situation. But after three days of ceaseless battle, the 16th Army was again forced back. General Panfilov was killed at his observation point by a random mortar shell, much mourned by his soldiers and by Rokossovski.

The Germans now brought up reinforcements, and drove more than ten miles into the Russian front. By 19 November Rokossovski was in danger of being outflanked on both sides. There were no reserves available to parry these attacks, because they had been consumed in the futile offensive four days earlier. The next obstacles to the German advance were the River Istra and the Volga reservoir, one of the last natural obstacles on the approaches to Moscow. The Germans were clearly determined to take them at a rush. Rokossovski decided to withdraw in good order and set up a proper defensive line along the Istra, against which the Germans would break their teeth. Zhukov disagreed and told Rokossovski to fight where he stood. Rokossovski knew that there were some times when such an order was justified. But this was not one of them. Without reserves the destruction of the 16th Army would leave the road to Moscow open. He appealed over Zhukov's head to Shaposhnikov, who agreed that he should carry out his original plan. Zhukov intervened with a furious telegram: 'I'm the commander here! Your order to withdraw your forces to the Istra reservoir is countermanded. You are ordered to defend yourself on your present positions, and not to retreat a single step. Army General Zhukov.'[31]

Rokossovski had no choice but to obey. As he had foreseen, the Germans crossed the river on the run, seized bridgeheads on the eastern bank, and occupied Istra itself, the little town with the seventeenth-century monastery of New Jerusalem that Alexander Werth had visited only a few months earlier.

In the last weeks of November the Germans captured Klin and Solnechnogorsk, and got astride the Leningrad Highway. The 16th Army was once again in danger of being outflanked. Once again Rokossovski was nearly captured. A troop of T-34 tanks guarding his headquarters disappeared. Rokossovski was told that they had gone to refuel at a nearby petrol station. He had to explain that in wartime you brought the fuel to the tanks and not the other way round. He got out just as the Germans broke in at the other end of the village. He had two more narrow escapes before the German offensive was halted.

The Germans continued to push forward from Solnechnogorsk against Beloborodov's Siberians and the 18th (Leningrad) Volunteer Division, and brought up two huge 300mm guns to bombard Moscow. Heavy fighting broke out at what is now the airport of Sheremetievo, closer to the centre of Moscow than Heathrow Airport is to central London. The Germans seized a bridge over the Moscow–Volga canal at Yakhroma and got as far as Krasnaya Polyana, a mere fifteen miles North of the city. Even Stalin's nerve was shaken.[32] A furious and abusive Zhukov called Rokossovski and threatened to have him shot for allowing his forces to pull back. Rokossovski answered acidly that the threat was absurd, since he was more likely to be killed at any moment by the shells falling around his headquarters. Later he was summoned to take a call from Stalin. He assumed he was about to be relieved or worse. Instead Stalin expressed support and promised reinforcements.[33] They included the 20th Army, which had been re-formed from fresh Siberian divisions after the débâcle before Vyazma, and was commanded by General Vlasov, who had so distinguished himself in the fighting on the frontier. Zhukov threw the fresh troops straight into the battle on Rokossovski's right flank.

The Germans were forced back across the Moscow–Volga Canal

and pinned down around Krasnaya Polyana. Among those opposing them there was a battery of heavy artillery under Lieutenant Lagushkin close to the Timiryazev Agricultural Academy. Because the ground was frozen, you could feel each salvo like a passing earthquake. The concussion broke the windows in the nearby houses, burst doors from their frames, and brought chimneys down. In their spare moments the gunners helped the housewives stuff their broken windows with pillows, blankets, mattresses and bits of plywood. The housewives brought them cups of tea in exchange.[34] That was the closest the Germans ever got to Moscow.

The Germans were also held in the South. On 19 November a whole German division panicked and ran under Russian attack, the first time such a thing had happened.[35] Guderian had continued his attempt to outflank Tula, and by late November the city was almost encircled. He commandeered Tolstoy's estate at nearby Yasnaya Polyana as his headquarters.[36] His remaining tanks were still edging northwards. But it was in these culminating weeks of the Battle of Moscow that the Soviet cavalry came into its own. Alone among the troops on either side, cavalry could retain a degree of mobility even in mud, even in snow.[37] Zhukov ordered General Belov and his Second Cavalry Corps to restore the situation at any cost. He gave Belov some tanks, some Katyusha rocket-launchers, and a bunch of cadets, and sent this motley force (now renamed the 1st Guards Cavalry Corps) to break through the German lines and relieve the pressure on Tula. Guderian, the master of the flanking movement, was himself outflanked and halted. Tula continued to resist, a thorn which Guderian was never able to pluck out of his side.

The days of panic and rout were over. Now the Russians fought and died where they stood, or retreated in good order to fight again. The German advance slowed and faltered, as the two sides swayed and tottered like two punch-drunk boxers.[38] Russian resistance stiffened, like a spring under compression waiting to uncoil. As the casualties mounted, von Bock muttered that the outcome of the battle would depend on which of the two sides was left with the last battalion: he was facing another Verdun, 'a brutish, chest-to-chest struggle of attrition'.[39] But the Germans had no more battalions to summon: they were at the end of their logistical tether. It was now that they began to learn the extent of their strategic miscalculation as the Russians brought up division after division, army after army, of whose existence German intelligence had not the remotest inkling.

Many individual acts of heroism were done in those November days. Most went unrecorded. But some became legends, and were exploited by the authorities to raise morale, as such legends are always exploited in wartime.[40] At the end of November, a fortnight after the event itself, *Krasnaya Zvezda* carried an inspirational piece by Krivitski, with colourful details suggested by Ortenberg, under the title 'The Testimony of the 28 Fallen Heroes'. It described how, in the first attack on Panfilov's old division, the 316th, an anti-tank platoon from the 1075th regiment – twenty-eight men under their political commissar, Vasili Klochkov – had held off fifty German tanks. Only one had blenched and he had been shot by his comrades. The rest had died to a man. The commissar's last words were: 'Russia is vast! But there is nowhere to retreat! For Moscow is behind us!' The paper concluded:

> We do not know what was in the mind of the heroes before they died, but by their courage, by their fearlessness, they have left a testament to us, the living. 'We sacrificed our lives on the altar of the Fatherland', their voice speaks to us and with a loud undying echo resounds in the hearts of the Soviet people. 'Do not shed tears over our lifeless bodies! Grit your teeth, be steadfast! We knew why we were going to our deaths, we fulfilled our soldier's duty, we barred the path to the enemy. Go into battle with the enemy and remember: Victory or death! You have no other choice, as we had no other choice. We died but we were victorious.'

Klochkov's regimental commander protested that he had heard nothing of the twenty-eight 'heroes' until he had been told about them by journalists. Krivitski ignored him and wrote a more substantial piece in January. Shcherbakov commented to Ortenberg that no one could know what the dying commissar had said, since all the witnesses were supposed to have died with him: but Klochkov's final words were certainly appropriate, and they made a good story. Six months later all twenty-eight men were posthumously made Heroes of the Soviet Union. Among them was the machine-gunner Ivan Shepetkov; he and his brother Semën had been two of the best-known high-wire artists in the circus in Alma Ata.[41]

Almost immediately a number of disconcerting facts emerged. Many of the twenty-eight men had indeed died during the fighting – but not all of them at Dubosekovo, and not all of them on the day in question. Several had survived the battle after all. One was severely wounded and died in a Soviet field hospital. Two were captured and spent the war in German camps. Two escaped. One attached himself to a group of Soviet soldiers operating behind the German lines, until he was picked up by the NKVD and interrogated as a deserter. The other went home to occupied Ukraine, became a village elder under the Germans and was arrested after the liberation as a collaborator. These embarrassing details were hushed up by the authorities, and the records were doctored as necessary.[42]

The legend of the twenty-eight Panfilov heroes endures. A massive monument – six heroic figures each forty feet high – was erected at the crossroads of Dubosekovo. It became a pious ritual for Young Communists to place votive offerings on what was said to be their common grave, now awkwardly defaced because the names listed on it have had to be changed as the tale was retold over the years. Attempts to question the legend are still deeply resented by Russian patriots and veterans.

A more convincing account of the fighting around Volokolamsk, disguised as a novel, was written in 1942 by Alexander Bek, who had served briefly in the 'Writers' Company' of the Krasnaya Presnya Division before being sent off to become a war correspondent. *The Volokolamsk Highway* traces the fate of one battalion of Panfilov's 316th Division, under its Kazakh commander Baurdzhan Momysh-Uly, who later wrote his own fascinating account of the affair.[43] Momysh-Uly begins by shooting one of his men for cowardice. But under the wise guidance of Panfilov – the presiding spirit of the book – he learns that you cannot rely on men always to be courageous in battle, that men may break one day and become heroes the next. They will perform best if you explain your orders and then let them carry them out according to their own best judgement. Baurdzhan Momysh-Uly holds his battalion together when it is surrounded, leads it safely back to the Russian lines, and commands it effectively in the desperate and eventually unsuccessful defence of Volokolamsk itself. It is a good story in its own right; and though the novel was first published in 1943, the final version mentions neither Stalin nor the Party. At times it reads like a tract against the massive executions in the Red Army. At other times it reads like a training manual for infantry commanders. And by a quirk of fate that is exactly what it later became. The novel was bedside reading among young Jews in Palestine in the 1940s and 1950s. It was especially popular among members of the Palmac'h brigades (one brigade was commanded by Rabin, later Prime Minister), who did some of the heaviest fighting in the Israeli war of independence in 1947–9. For a while in the 1950s Bek's book became a standard tactical handbook in the Israeli army.[44] In the late 1980s it was the inspiration for a misty verse drama by the East German writer Heiner Mueller about the collapse of the Socialist ideal.[45] It still comes back into print in Russia from time to time, but it is no longer widely read.

By now the spring was compressed to the limit. The Germans were coming very close to the end of their strength and stamina. For the first time since the beginning of the war Rokossovski saw Soviet aircraft hitting the Germans hard.[46] But the battle was not yet over. It was now that von Bock launched his final throw: a strike against Moscow not only from the North and South, but from the West as well. The Germans went over to the offensive along the whole front on 1 December. They were particularly successful in the centre, smashing through the defences on the Mozhaisk Highway until they got to Golitsyno, a mere seven miles from Zhukov's forward headquarters at Perkhushkovo.[47]

General Golovanov, the commander of Stalin's heavy bombers and a crony, was in Stalin's office when the telephone rang. As he told the story, Stalin picked up the telephone and held it, as usual, some distance from his ear, so Golovanov could hear both ends of the conversation. Stalin's envoy General Stepanov was reporting from the headquarters of the Western Front. Zhukov's staff were worried that the Germans were so close. They wanted to move the headquarters East of Moscow.

There was a long and very uncomfortable silence.

'Comrade Stepanov,' said Stalin, 'ask them whether they have any spades.' There was another uncomfortable silence.

'I'll find out straight away.' (Pause) 'What sort of spades, Comrade Stalin? Entrenching tools or some other kind?'

'It doesn't matter what sort.'

'I'll find out straight away.' (Pause) 'Yes, there are spades, Comrade Stalin. What should they do with them?'

'Comrade Stepanov, tell your comrades to take their spades,' said Stalin, 'and dig themselves some graves. The Stavka's not leaving Moscow. I'm not leaving Moscow. And they're not going anywhere from Perkhushkovo.'[48]

– FIFTEEN –

THE SPRING UNCOILS

After the great panic, the people of Moscow did what they could to restore not only order, but some semblance of a normal life. On 19 October, the same day as it published the decree on the state of emergency, *Vechernyaya Moskva* gave details of fifteen films currently in Moscow's cinemas, including a version of Lermontov's *Masquerade* and *The Little Hump-backed Horse,* a fairy-tale film which became very popular in wartime Britain. On 22 November, along with an announcement that several men had been shot for stealing vehicles, *Vechernyaya Moskva* carried a small notice on the back page: 'The Moscow chess section proposes to begin a competition in the next few days. The following chess masters are being invited to this most interesting event: Alatortsev, Duz-Khutimirski, Zubarev, Panov, Petrov, Yudovich, the top players of the capital. The contest will probably be held in the building of the Moscow Committee for Physical Culture and Sport.'

The first round of the championship began on 27 November. There were eight participants. They included some of the most eminent Soviet players of the day. One of the less well known was Lieutenant Mazel, a middle-aged eccentric who used to play for money before the war, and was now serving at the front just outside Moscow. He was allowed by his commander to come into the city to play his games. The players met three times a week, on Tuesdays, Thursdays, and Saturdays. The finals were on a Sunday. Some rounds were held in the editorial offices of *Vechernyaya Moskva*, others in the Central House of the Workers of Art, in the Writers' Union, or in the House of Journalists. The players also visited military units and hospitals to play multiple games against the inmates.

The blackout, the shortage of trams and trolleybuses, the closure of the Metro at 7 o'clock, all made it difficult for the contestants to get home after their matches. Like everyone else, they were on firewatching duty during the night. At first they stopped their games during air raids to go down to the shelter. But the complaints soon began. Those who were winning thought that their opponents would profit from the delay to work out their countermoves. Those who were losing hoped that their opponents would begin to make mistakes under stress. In the end all concerned decided that they would not allow the alarms to interrupt them, and went on playing whether the bombers were overhead or not. The competition was enthusiastically covered in the press and on the radio. People wrote to the participants from the front line, from factories evacuated to the rear, from all over the Soviet Union. The competition was won by Lieutenant Mazel. Panov came second, and Petrov third. It was the high-water mark of Mazel's career. He died of typhus in 1943.[1]

The Stanislavski Theatre opened its new season with a performance of Planquette's operetta *Les Cloches de Corneville*.[2] The performance began at 1 o'clock in the afternoon, when there was usually a break in the German raids. The theatre was packed. Among the audience were directors, actors, artists, composers and writers who had remained in Moscow; and many soldiers with their rifles in their hands. Halfway through the performance, Tumanov, the theatre's artistic director, pushed his way through the chorus on the stage to tell the audience that there was a raid on and that they must make for the nearest shelter in the Metro. His words produced no effect. Nobody got up from their seats. People shouted out, 'Go on with the show', 'We're not frightened.' Tumanov finally managed to get them to take shelter by promising that the performance would be resumed on the following day at exactly the point where it had been broken off. After that it became traditional to complete performances which had been interrupted by raids.[3]

Apart from the Stanislavski Theatre, only six performing companies now remained in Moscow: the Circus and some local companies from the Moscow Region camping out in empty theatres. Mikhail Gabovich, the dancer from the Bolshoi Theatre, was serving just outside Moscow in a 'Destroyer Battalion'. One day – it must have been in late October – Yelena Vanke, the young dancer from the Bolshoi ballet school who was left behind when the company was evacuated, was walking past the old university building when Gabovich pulled up beside her on his motorbike, all splendid in full uniform and a helmet. He told her that he was organising a ballet group to perform in the Bolshoi Theatre Annexe on Pushkin Street. He invited her and her classmates still in Moscow to join him.

Lemeshev, Susanna Zvyagina, Yelena Vanke and the other Bolshoi artists still in Moscow started to meet every day in the Annexe. There was no proper rehearsal room there. It was freezing cold and the dancers wore felt boots except, of course, when they were actually dancing. A Party official came along to tell them that their patriotic duty was now to dig trenches, to work on the 'Labour Front'. One of the artists, Petrova, objected. The soldiers, she said, needed art, music, and the theatre; the Bolshoi should be reopened, and the artists still in Moscow should begin working there. The Party official took her remarks very badly, and seemed to regard them as counter-revolutionary. But the artists persuaded Moscow City Council to allow them to put on performances in the Annexe. Hitherto Gabovich had been only a dancer, though a very distinguished one. Now he turned out to be a first-rate theatre director as well. Lemeshev remembered, 'He had an innate gift for organisation and management. He was delicate and friendly in his relations with the artists, but unshakeable in matters of principle. Everything lay on his shoulders: the repertoire, the artistic quality of the performances, the accommodation and the rations of the staff, even the fire wood.'

At the end of October things had advanced sufficiently for Gabovich to decide that performances would soon start up again. On 18 November – just as the German assault on Volokolamsk was getting under way – he announced that the first concert would take place the following day. Muscovites who heard him were hardly able to believe their ears. The next day the house was packed with soldiers from the front and people from all over the city. The front line was only half an hour's drive away and Pushkin Street was packed with military vehicles painted camouflage white. Rokossovski himself was there. So was the commander of Moscow's air defences.

Gabovich, in full uniform, stepped forward on the stage to announce the programme. It consisted of excerpts from Russian operas, Russian songs, the Bell Song from *Lakmé*, and a number of ballet divertissements. But only two numbers had been performed before Gabovich came back onto the stage, called for attention and said, 'Comrades, the air-raid warning has gone. Please keep calm and leave the auditorium. Those who wish may go to the Metro on Sverdlov Square. After the All Clear, the concert will continue.'

Everybody got up dutifully and left the auditorium. But hardly anyone went to the Metro. The foyer was light and warm, and the theatre buffet was still working. People took no notice of the anti-aircraft fire outside. They stood and gossiped, queued for food, and warmed themselves at the radiators until the All Clear sounded. It happened again, and then for a third time just after the second half of the concert had started. Both the audience and Gabovich burst out laughing. Somebody declaimed a satirical verse from the gallery. The audience was in uproar. They stamped their feet and shouted that the concert should go on: but of course there was not much that Gabovich could do about it, and they had to file out yet again. At the end of the concert the artists were showered, not with flowers – there were none – but with green branches. Rokossovski thanked the artists in the name of frontline soldiers both present and absent.

The cultural bureaucrat Gridaspov did not agree with Rokossovski or the Moscow public. In mid-November he sent a sour note to his boss in the Moscow City Council. The theatres still working in Moscow, he complained, were putting on far too few patriotic pieces. It was true that one theatre was performing Simonov's *A Boy from Our Town*. But the Stanislavski Theatre was putting on *The Barber of Seville*, *Eugene Onegin*, *Les Cloches de Corneville*, and a string of operettas. The Children's Theatre was performing *Little Red Riding Hood*, a collective farm theatre was doing Calderon's *The Invisible Lady*, and several others were putting on vapid and frivolous French comedies. Things were just as bad in the concert halls. The Conservatoire had put together a concert which was full of gypsy music, but contained not a single patriotic item. Things were even worse in the closed concerts being given in hospitals for the wounded and in Red Army units. The artists claimed that they did not have the resources, costumes and scenery to put on new productions of patriotic plays. Some even argued that, if they put on anti-fascist productions, they would be punished by the Germans when they entered the city. Gridaspov had taken a number of measures. He had forced the Theatre of Comedy to take off one French play, on the grounds that it was of no interest to the Soviet audience. He had ordered that no concerts should be given in hospitals or military units unless they had his prior approval. He now recommended that bureaucratic controls should be rigidly centralised; that all productions both current and future should be licensed only by central authority; and that 'All entertainments of a gypsy, sentimental or decadent kind should cease. Concerts of gypsy music should be banned.'[4]

Nobody seems to have taken much notice of him.

By now the Germans had advanced more than six hundred miles into the Soviet Union. They had occupied the most industrialised part of the country, home to nearly half of the Soviet population, a territory as large as Britain, Spain, Italy and France rolled together. They had blockaded Leningrad and captured Kiev. And in the course of their headlong retreat since June the Russians had lost nearly four million men dead and wounded, 20,000 tanks, some 17,000 aircraft, more than 60,000 guns and mortars – almost all the stocks of weapons that they had built up in the years before the war.[5]

But on the very outskirts of Moscow, the Germans had run out of steam. Von Bock's offensive along the Mozhaisk Highway was in serious trouble. Neither he nor the German High Command had any idea of the forces which the Russians were now about to bring to bear. Their assessment on 4 December was that 'The enemy facing Army Group Centre is at present incapable of mounting a counter-attack without bringing forward substantial reserves.'[6] Nevertheless, von Bock believed it would be prudent to move into more defensible positions, and on 5 December his staff began to plan for an orderly withdrawal. Von Rundstedt, commanding Army Group South, was already deploying similar arguments. But Hitler and the sycophantic staff officers around him opposed all talk of retreat. The argument between them and the generals at the front became increasingly bitter. On 1 December Hitler dismissed von Rundstedt from his command for withdrawing without his permission. In the succeeding weeks von Bock, Guderian and others went the same way.

Stalin had begun thinking of the possibility of a counterstroke in late November. The General Staff moved back from Arzamas to Moscow to start the planning. On 29 November Zhukov told Stalin, 'The enemy is exhausted. But if we do not now liquidate the dangerous wedges the Germans have driven into our defences, they could transfer substantial reserves from their Northern and Southern Army Groups to reinforce their troops before Moscow, and the situation would become much more difficult.'[7] The operation was to be carried out by Zhukov and Koniev, the commanders of the Western and Kalinin Fronts, and Cherevichenko whose operational group on the Southern flank of the attack became in mid-December the kernel of a resurrected Bryansk Front.[8] 'We had no clear idea,' Zhukov later admitted, 'that we were embarking on the grandiose counteroffensive that subsequently emerged. The initial aim was important but limited: to repel the enemy forces that threatened to break through to Moscow [...] As far as I remember, no special order or general directive for a counteroffensive was issued.'[9]

The initial task fell on Zhukov's Western Front. Its two flanks, now one hundred and twenty miles apart, were to attack the German forces threatening Moscow from the North and South and then to encircle them. In order to achieve surprise, the Russians went straight over to the attack, without any pause for preparation. The weather was against them, as it had been for the attacking Germans in previous weeks. The soldiers had to move into their start positions through blizzards and deep snow. To mask their positions they were forbidden to light fires.

The Russian attack began at dawn on Friday 5 December 1941 and developed over the next four days. The temperatures fluctuated between minus forty degrees and zero. The advance began slowly: little more than two miles a day at best. And even units which had done well in defence still had to learn how to conduct themselves in an advance. Instead of filtering through the gaps in the patchy front line held by the Germans or attacking from the flank, too many of them continued, as they had done since the beginning of the war, to make headlong attacks on prepared German positions. Zhukov categorically forbade the practice, and ordered his army commanders to manoeuvre intelligently instead.[10] They did not learn quickly.

The NKVD continued to harass the fighting generals. On the eve of the Russian counterattack General Serov visited the 282nd Rifle Regiment, part of Rokossovski's 16th Army, which occupied a crucial position in the line. One battalion commander, Lieutenant Butsin, accused his superiors – including Rokossovski – of ineptitude and indecisiveness, and his own officers and soldiers of incompetence. Serov reported to Stalin that neither the 282nd Regiment nor Butsin's battalion were capable of carrying out their tasks.[11] More critical reports followed, even after the counteroffensive had got under way. General Malinin, Rokossovski's Chief of Staff, was singled out for particular criticism.[12] These reports had no serious consequences: Rokossovski's position was by now sufficiently secure, though the NKVD continued to dog him and his staff for the rest of the war, a perpetual reminder of a viciously counterproductive system.

Since the parade on Red Square, Gudz and his tank battalion had once again been worn to the bone: they were down to one KV, a few light T-60s and a handful of crews. As the counteroffensive began, Gudz and his fellow officers were sitting in battalion headquarters outside Moscow, an *izba* full of iron-bound boxes containing the battalion's goods and chattels, listening to Levitan giving the late-night news as they waited the order to move forward with the rest of Rokossovski's 16th Army. The woman of the house was baking potatoes for the officers while her three children looked on. A despatch rider entered, shook off the snow, and handed an order to the battalion commander, Captain Khorin, under whom Gudz had served since the early battles on the frontier: 'There are eighteen enemy tanks in Nefedievo. You are to destroy them by 8.00 on 6 December.'

Khorin summoned Gudz, ordered him to attack the German tanks with the single remaining KV, and told him to pick his own crew for what was clearly a suicide mission. Gudz was embarrassed. The tank's normal commander was Lieutenant Starykh, one of the two other officers in the room. He too had taken part in the parade on Red Square. But he had subsequently been temporarily relieved of command by the brigade commander for having 'shown an excess of initiative'.

Starykh finished his potato, and said, 'You're going to need an experienced gun-layer tomorrow.' 'I've already got one,' replied Gudz. But Starykh argued that he had been the best gun-layer on his course at the academy. Gudz agreed to take him, so that he could redeem his reputation. The other members of the crew were Junior Sergeant Kirin, the driver, a former tractor mechanic; Totarchuk, the gunner-radio operator; and Sablin, the loader. Gudz had not fought with any of them before.

The crew unloaded everything superfluous from the tank to make room for 125 armour-piercing shells. Totarchuk managed to squeeze in fifty drums for his machine gun. Then they moved slowly up to the rifle pits on the front line, less than a mile away from Nefedievo. A sceptical infantry officer told Gudz that – if his tank did not get stuck, and if the Germans did not hear his approach – he just might be able cross the river which marked the front and get within range of the German tanks. Gudz reconnoitred the ground on foot, and then – under cover of a modest artillery barrage to hide the sound of his engine – moved his tank into position. In order to give themselves yet more room, his crew unloaded some of their spare fuel and ammunition. Gudz was struck by how carefully his new crewmen buried the stores in the bank of the river. These were responsible people on whom he could rely.

As the night wore on, the snow ceased falling, the temperature fell below freezing, and the tank became very cold. Nefedievo was well behind the front line, and the Germans were relaxing in its warm cottages. Gudz and his crew could hear their voices, the sound of an accordion, the smell of burned chicken feathers from the kitchens. It was long after midnight before the voices died away.

Gudz began his attack as dawn broke. He set eight enemy tanks on fire before the Germans could gather their wits. Then their shells started to hit the KV. As usual they failed to penetrate the tank's thick armour, but the tank filled with cordite fumes and loose cartridge cases, and Sablin was briefly knocked unconscious. The surviving German tanks sought shelter behind the buildings in the village. German infantry came forward to support them and were shot down by Totarchuk. The Russian infantrymen crossed the river and Russian artillery shelled the retreating Germans. Gudz and his crew ate snow to wet their dry mouths and pursued the Germans as long as their ammunition held out. For this action Gudz was awarded the Order of Lenin and the rest of the crew were also honoured.[13]

On 8 December, after heavy fighting, Rokossovski's 16th Army recaptured Kriukovo, where he had had to abandon his headquarters a couple of weeks earlier. The place was full of wrecked German equipment. In the nearby village of Kamenka Rokossovski's men found the two great guns which had been brought up to bombard Moscow. On the same day Vlasov and his 20th Army threw the Germans out of Krasnaya Polyana and pushed on to Solnechnogorsk. The Germans were never again to come within artillery range of the capital.

Rokossovski and his men continued to advance towards Istra. The Germans blew up the dam of the reservoir, and a huge wave of freezing water poured out, sweeping everything before it. Beloborodov's Siberians forced their way across the torrent of icy water under fire, using anything that would float: wooden rafters, fences, doorways, rafts made of straw, rubber boats.[14] The Siberians and the men of the 18th (Leningrad) Volunteer Division liberated Istra itself on 11 December. They found the great monastery in ruins. The civilian population had been deported by the retreating Germans.

General Dovator now led his Cossacks – recently honoured for their exploits under his command as the Second Guards Cavalry Corps – on a deep raid behind the lines to harry the retreating Germans from the North. By 19 December they were on the Ruza River, which the 16th Army had had to abandon in October. The Germans were holding the village of Palashkino in force. Dovator's headquarters was on the other side of the river on a high bank. In waist-deep snow, the general crawled forward to his men's positions to see for himself what was going on. He was cut down by a burst of machine-gun fire. He was posthumously made a Hero of the Soviet Union, and buried in the Novodevichie Cemetery in Moscow, in a place of honour next to Panfilov. He was universally mourned. It was, said Zhukov, a grievous loss.[15]

Anthony Eden, the British Foreign Minister, left London for talks with Stalin on 7 December, just as the news of Pearl Harbor was coming in (*Vechernyaya Moskva* relegated it to the third page). After an arduous trip by warship and train he was met by Molotov at the Yaroslavl Station in Moscow with full military ceremonial. The arc lights of the camera crews filming the scene were so blinding that Eden nearly fell over the honour guard.[16]

The commander of the honour guard was Vladimir Ogryzko of the Dzerzhinski Division. 'After taking part in the parade on 7 November we went straight to the front to join Rokossovski's 16th Army,' he remembered. 'Our task was to protect his supply base. It was bitterly cold, we were under constant air attack, and we were occasionally involved in hand-to-hand fighting as well. Rokossovski was so impressed with us that he wanted us to act as his headquarters company. But he was overruled by General Artemiev, the Moscow commander, who ordered us to return to Moscow for a special task.

'In Moscow I was told that I was to command the honour guard for Eden and his delegation. They asked if I could train my men in time. I said I could, even though we had already lost some of our smartest pre-war soldiers. I put together a guard whose average height was about six foot – many of them coalminers from the Donbass and the Kuzbass.'[17]

Eden's talks with Stalin nearly foundered on disputes over the future of Poland and the prospects for a Second Front in the West. A day's rest was called for tempers to settle. To fill the time, Stalin granted Eden's request to go to see something of the recent fighting.

'I and my men were woken at 3 a.m.,' continued Ogryzko, 'and told we had to accompany Eden to the front, where Kalinin [Tver] was about to be liberated. We travelled up the Leningrad Highway which had been cleared of mines and deep snow. I provided the advance and flanking guards. I had been ordered not to talk any more than was necessary. But at one point Eden stopped for a cup of tea and sandwiches, and offered me brandy from a hip flask. He was courteous and intelligent. He spoke German and a few words of Russian. When we got to Klin and saw how the Tchaikovsky museum had been vandalised by the Germans, Eden was furious. He wanted to go on to look at the fighting around Kalinin, but we wouldn't let him.'[18]

There were ruined villages to each side of the highway. In some only the brick chimney stacks were standing, like gaunt fingers pointing to the sky. In others two-thirds of the buildings had gone. But some were almost undamaged. In the fields by the side of the highway, Eden saw the corpses of large numbers of German soldiers, frozen solid in the attitudes that they had taken up in death.[19] On the way back to Moscow he stopped to talk to a group of German prisoners. They were freezing. Some were dressed in summer overcoats without gloves. Some were wearing civilian clothes, and had pulled women's underwear over their heads to keep warm. When he imagined the fate in store for them, Eden found himself feeling very sorry for them.[20]

Even some Russians felt compassion for their enemy in his miserable state. As another group of German prisoners stumbled into captivity, a young Russian lieutenant stepped forward, took off his sheepskin jacket and gave it to one particularly wretched-looking youngster.[21]

Ogryzko did not see Eden again after they had returned to Moscow.

Late on 5 December, a correspondent from *Krasnaya Zvezda* gave a detailed account of the successful Soviet attack at Naro-Fominsk, just to the Southwest of Moscow. The SovInformBuro had still not announced the beginning of the counterattack, and was not to do so for eight more days. Ignoring the warnings of his more cautious colleagues, Ortenberg ordered the story to be printed. Shcherbakov called him in, and demanded to know why he had tried to scoop the SovInformBuro. 'There was no reason,' he said, 'to give the Germans advance warning of our attack.' Ortenberg pretended he had not understood: 'You mean the Germans don't already know? My man saw the snow strewn with German corpses and abandoned tanks.' Shcherbakov was adamant. Ortenberg went back to his office, and pulled the story. All the SovInformBuro said that day was, 'In the course of 6 December our forces engaged the enemy on all fronts.'[22]

The SovInformBuro finally went to town on 13 December. On that day the front page of every paper carried the headline: 'The Collapse of the German Plan to Surround and Capture Moscow – Defeat of German forces on the approaches to Moscow'. There were portraits of the leading generals. Zhukov had pride of place in the centre, surrounded by Rokossovski and seven others, including Vlasov, the commander of the 20th Army, who was soon to play a different and notorious role. Stalin did not figure. It was not until the victories of the Red Army began to succeed one another with a comforting regularity in 1943 that the publicity surrounding him began to overshadow that of his generals.

The SovInformBuro communiqué drew a conclusion which stands the test of time:

> The Germans complain that it was the winter that prevented them from carrying out their plan to capture Moscow. But first of all, the real winter has not yet started around Moscow: the frosts are no more than 3–5 degrees. Secondly, complaints about the winter demonstrate that the Germans did not bother to equip their army with warm clothing, although they proclaimed to the whole world that they had long been prepared for a winter campaign. And the reason why they had not equipped their army with winter clothing was because they hoped to finish the war before winter began. That was a most serious and dangerous miscalculation ... It is not the winter that was to blame, but an organic defect in the way the German High Command planned for the war.[23]

Despite official reticence, the news of the Soviet offensive rapidly found its way through the rumour machine and was greeted with huge jubilation and relief. Sakharov heard the news almost as soon as he arrived in Ashkhabad on 6 December. 'The news of our counteroffensive made me realize as never before the anxieties of the recent months, and as I listened to the solemn enumeration of armies, divisions, and generals participating in the battles, I shuddered at the thought of the countless persons, dead and alive, who had been engaged in the defence of Moscow.'[24]

Before the tables were turned in December the Germans had occupied seventeen Raions in the Moscow Region. By now they were no longer trying very hard to win the hearts and minds of the people, and had decided that they could get more out of the land by forcing the peasants to continue working it collectively. The Germans' half-hearted policy of stick and carrot had shifted brutally in the direction of the stick.

In his speech of 3 July, Stalin had said, 'Conditions in the occupied territories must be made unbearable for the enemy and all those who support him. He must be pursued and destroyed at every step, and his every undertaking frustrated.'[25] Russian soldiers who had escaped capture melted into the woods and forests. Enterprising leaders – often officers trapped behind the lines – formed them into organised groups, at first for survival and self-defence; but later to attack and harass the Germans as well, often using abandoned weapons collected from the recent battlefields. As time passed the partisan effort was increasingly systematised and controlled from Moscow. The Stavka ordered each Front headquarters to create partisan detachments, to help them cross into enemy territory, and to support them thereafter. Officers and men from the Red Army and the NKVD were sent through the line to provide a professional stiffening. Party and Komsomol organisations were reconstituted underground in the occupied areas. Communication between Moscow and the partisan units in the field, and between the partisan units themselves, was hampered by a sad lack of radios. Instead the slow U-2 biplanes served as admirable couriers. Larger aircraft were used to drop men, weapons, and ammunition.

The number of partisans continued to grow until the Germans were finally expelled from Soviet territory. The partisans may not have significantly affected German military operations. But they helped to make life miserable for the ordinary German soldier, and they were a continual hazard to German communications. In one major anti-partisan operation the Germans deployed two Panzer divisions, four infantry divisions and two SS battalions.[26] The partisans set up liberated regions behind German lines where the Germans could not operate and where Soviet law governed everyday life with all its usual harshness. Since the front line was never continuous, large numbers of people moved between the occupied territories and territory held by the Soviets. They produced food for themselves, for the partisan bands, for the large flying columns led by cavalry commanders such as Belov and Dovator, and even for the besieged population of Leningrad.[27]

As the Germans approached Moscow, Stalin ordered the systematic destruction of villages in the occupied territories to deny them shelter. Zhukov ordered the inhabitants to be driven out of a zone three, later fifteen, miles wide behind the front line. These orders were rigidly enforced. On 25 November the 5th Army reported that they had partially or wholly destroyed fifty-three villages by fire or artillery bombardment. The commissar of the 53rd Cavalry Division apologised to his superior at the headquarters of the 16th Army for the 'unnecessary and damaging liberalism' with which his men had hitherto carried out their orders, and promised to do better in future.[28] In practice the Russian villagers suffered more than the German soldiers, who simply drove them out of any buildings that remained standing.

Major Zhuravlëv, the head of the Moscow NKVD, set up two schools for saboteurs and partisans, one in a former rest home South of Moscow, a second at Kuntsevo, near Stalin's Nearby Dacha on the western outskirts of the city.[29] Shelepin, the head of the Moscow Komsomol, told a group of young volunteers with brutal clarity, 'It's an excellent thing that you have volunteered to fight behind the German lines. But it's quite possible that most of you will be killed. The fascists treat partisans with the utmost brutality. If any of you feel that is more than you can face, just say so. No one will blame you. You can fight the fascists in the regular army instead.' No one held back, though some were rejected on medical grounds. About two thousand people were selected altogether. They were assigned to groups in the Coliseum Cinema (now the Sovremennik Theatre), and sent off to Kuntsevo by lorry.[30]

Among the first students in Kuntsevo was Zoya Kosmodemyanskaya, an eighteen-year-old in her last year at school. After five days' training in demolition, small arms and unarmed combat, she was assigned to Partisan-Reconnaissance Unit No. 9903. At the beginning of November she crossed the front on her first mission in a group of twelve, carrying incendiary material, a gun, rations and the regulation allocation of one hundred grams of vodka a day. The group was ambushed by a German patrol. Some of its members were killed. Others fled. Others, including Zoya, carried out their mission and returned safely to their base.

On 21 November several groups of Unit No. 9903 went back across the line with orders to burn down ten villages. Zoya's group consisted of herself, Boris Krainov and Vasili Klubkov.[31] Their target was the village of Petrishchevo, about fifty miles away towards Mozhaisk. Zoya was to burn buildings at the Southern end of the village, Klubkov at the Northern end and Krainov in the centre.

The details of what happened are still unclear. Krainov successfully set his targets on fire and got away to the agreed rendezvous. Zoya set fire to her targets, which included three houses and a stable: twenty horses and a deal of equipment were destroyed. But as she was making for the forest she was picked up by a German patrol. Klubkov failed to set fire to anything. He too was caught. It was now 28 November.

Zoya was questioned in one of the surviving *izbas*. She denied that she had been involved in the arson attack. She was then confronted with Klubkov, who had admitted that he was a member of the group of saboteurs and had named both Zoya and Krainov. Zoya was stripped and beaten so brutally that two German soldiers left the room in disgust. Despite Klubkov's evidence Zoya refused to give her real name, or any details of her mission or her previous training. Later that night Solina and Smirnova, two of the village women whose houses had been burned, came to abuse her. One of them threw a bowl of washing-up water over her.

The next morning she was taken to the centre of the village, where a gallows had been erected at the crossroads. The Germans hung round her neck a placard with the word 'Arsonist' in Russian and German. About a hundred German soldiers came to watch and photograph the scene. The villagers were ordered to attend, though some managed to slip away. Eyewitnesses later said that before she died, Zoya told the German watchers that they would do better to surrender while they still had the chance: 'You can't hang us all!' Her body was left on the gallows for six weeks, until it was buried on the orders of the retreating Germans just before the village was liberated on 12 January.

Zoya was known to the villagers as 'Tanya', the false name she had given to the Germans. It was under that name that her fate was publicised in *Pravda* at the end of January. Several women came forward to claim that the 'Tanya' pictured in the newspapers was their daughter: mothers of war heroes could hope for financial support as well as fame. A commission was sent to Petrishchevo to sort things out. Two witnesses soon turned up. One was Boris Krainov, who confirmed that Zoya had indeed been at Petrishchevo, but had failed to make the rendezvous. The other was Vasili Klubkov. Under threat of death, he said, he had been persuaded by the Germans to work for them. They trained him and other Russians at a spy school in Smolensk. They then sent him back to Moscow to report on the partisan training school at Kuntsevo. The NKVD picked him up almost immediately. They interrogated him at length, and he was shot on 16 April 1942. Smirnova and Solina were shot later in the year.

Zoya's body was identified to the satisfaction of the commission by her mother and her brother Sasha, who later died in a tank battle. Zoya was made a Hero of the Soviet Union: the first woman to be so honoured in the war. The citation added the piquant detail that her last words were: 'Death to the German occupiers! Long live the Socialist Motherland! Long live Comrade Stalin!' She immediately became one of the country's most potent symbols of heroism. Soldiers are said to have carried her picture into the battle for Berlin.[32] She was reburied in the Novodevichie Cemetery. Generations of Soviet schoolchildren were brought up to honour her memory. Klubkov's betrayal and the fate of Smirnova and Solina remained shrouded in official secrecy lest the myth of universal resistance to the invader be undermined.

Much later, as the Soviet Union guttered to its close, it became fashionable to debunk the myths which had helped to keep it going. The stories of wartime heroism were among the targets of the revisionists. Anti-Soviet politicians and a new generation of historical commentators pointed out that many other young men and women had died as gallantly as Zoya. Masha Bruskina, a seventeen-year-old Jewish nurse, was hanged in September 1941 in Minsk for helping wounded Soviet officers escape to the partisans. She was possibly the first woman so to suffer, but she got no posthumous medal. Zoya and Krainov had in any case done little damage to the Germans. Sceptics cast doubt on Zoya's mental stability, and claimed that there had never been any partisans in Petrishchevo anyway: the whole thing was nothing more than Soviet propaganda. Doubts were also cast on the treachery of Klubkov: perhaps he had been set up by the NKVD officers who interrogated him. A story began to circulate that the girl who had been hanged was not Zoya at all, but someone called Lilia Azolina. Zoya, they said, had been shipped to a concentration camp, survived the war, and returned to Moscow to be repudiated by her mother. In December 1991 a forensic scientist was asked to compare an unconvincing picture of Zoya with photographs of Lilia and the dead girl. He pronounced that the martyred heroine was indeed Zoya. In all the confusion and rumour-mongering, however, one thing remained beyond doubt. A young girl did die gallantly, though perhaps pointlessly, at the hands of the Germans; and the balance of probability is that it was Zoya Kosmodemyanskaya. Yevgeni Teleguev, the OMSBON special forces soldier who ended his career as a general in the KGB, summed it up. 'Zoya Kosmodemyanskaya was a brave girl. But her exploit was of no military value. Her life was wasted, like the lives of many other youngsters.'[33]

In 1943, as the tide of war finally turned, Zoya's life and death were turned into a film by the director Lev Arnshtam. In *Zoya*, he tells the story of her final days with reasonable accuracy, though with a pardonable touch of heroic exaggeration. But his version of her babyhood, her growing up into an intense young member of the Komsomol, and her ambitions for heroism, though portrayed with sensitivity and charm, is largely a myth. *Zoya* is nevertheless more than a mere piece of wartime propaganda. It stands independently as a better than average film. It does not mention Stalin, despite the final heroic words attributed to her in the official citation. It is a welcome contrast to the film epics produced in Stalin's last years – *The Fall of Berlin*, *Cavalier of the Gold Star*, *The Young Guard*. These still exercise a morbid fascination. But their bloated and fraudulent patriotism, their grovelling praise of The Leader, and their breathtaking disdain for historical truth, make them feel almost greasy to the touch.

Most partisan operations were more professional than the sad adventure of Zoya Kosmodemyanskaya and her colleagues. Operations behind the German lines multiplied, supported by the NKVD and the army. Now the OMSBON came into its own: Vladimir Frolov, Yevgeni Anufriev and Yevgeni Teleguev were at last deployed for the kind of operations for which they had been training since the summer.

Vladimir Frolov began operating even before the end of the Battle of Moscow, mining roads on the northern approaches to the capital. On one occasion, he was ordered to mine the main road just South of Klin, and to blow up the charge between the departure of the last Russian troops and the arrival of the Germans. He dug a large charge under a culvert near the village of Davydkovo and waited. The first night he was visited by his platoon commander. The man was killed immediately after when his truck was destroyed by Finnish special forces operating on skis. The next night Frolov heard German voices and saw tracer bullets crossing the road. He tried to ignite the fuse but it wouldn't work. So he went right up to the charge and improvised a new, very short fuse. It did work, and he ran for his life before the charge went off. He didn't hear the explosion or remember what happened: he must have been knocked out. He spent the night in a village, where a young couple were burying their possessions to hide them from the arriving Germans. He got to Solnechnogorsk by the evening, but was then concussed again when an ammunition dump exploded.

Thirty years later, when he was working at the Australian National University in Canberra, Frolov went to an academic conference in New Guinea. He was greeted in the conference by a fat German with a cropped head and wearing shorts, Dr Krug, originally from Latvia, born in 1923 and half Russian. Krug addressed him in Russian in a friendly manner, and with a stream of the choicest Russian swear-words. At dinner Krug proposed toasts in sake – to the Soviet Union, to Friendship, and to the village of Davydkovo. Krug, it turned out, had survived Frolov's explosion there, even though a number of his comrades had been killed.

After fighting in the defence of Moscow, Anufriev and his OMSBON unit made deep penetration raids into occupied territory. 'We always carried four grenades,' Anufriev recalled, 'two anti-tank grenades and two hand grenades. We were told to keep one grenade for ourselves, and use it if we were wounded and looked like falling into enemy hands. On one occasion my unit was ordered to hold up the movement of three German divisions. Twelve men survived out of eighty. We had to withdraw through deep snow and one of my comrades was hit by machine-gun fire. At first I thought he was dead. But then he began to move. It was a horrible moral dilemma: if I tried to rescue my comrade I would certainly fail and be killed as well. If I left him behind, I would never be able to live with myself. He solved the problem for me by blowing himself up.

'As we advanced, we found ourselves attacking and destroying villages which the Germans had taken over, but where there were still Russian civilians. We discovered that the Germans had detailed maps dating from the 1930s, and much better than our own. They had brought with them equipment from every country in Europe. In the brief period of their occupation, they had constructed elaborate defensive positions. They had also earned the absolute hostility of the population. But unlike the Russians, they took their dead as well as their wounded with them when they retreated.

'Fighting in our own country had a profound effect on us. A pilot might find himself bombing his own mother. A gunner might have to shell his own village. I didn't hear at the time of Stalin's order to the Red Army to destroy the villages as they retreated. It would have been difficult to carry out in practice: when a soldier is making a fighting retreat he doesn't think about subordinate matters. The fighting itself naturally resulted in the burning and destruction of many villages.'[34]

Yevgeni Teleguev was asked if he would like to volunteer for deep penetration operations and he agreed. 'I set off with twenty-nine others to cross the front on skis in March 1942. At the last minute one of my group said he had a bad stomach and returned to Moscow. The rest of us travelled to our operational base in Belorussia. The next chance I had to wash myself was four months later. Nineteen of my group had been killed by the end of the war.

'I was two years behind the lines, during which I only once heard from home. It was not until 1944 that I learned that my elder brother had been killed in the Moscow battle even before I crossed the line. To start with I commanded a group of half a dozen men from my original unit. But we recruited local peasants and soldiers who had escaped from prison camps or encirclement, and by October 1942 our group had swelled to over a thousand. One evening we entered a village to get provisions before undertaking a long night march across open country. The villagers told us that the only representative of the occupying forces was a Dutchman, who was the local village commandant. We took him prisoner and relieved him of the weapons stored in his office. Then we discussed with the villagers what we should do with him. In the end, instead of shooting him, we told him that he should go back to Holland, where he belonged, and take no further part in the German war. During the two years we were operating behind the lines, we destroyed sixteen trains and four bridges.

'At the beginning of the war I could not understand why our army had done so badly on the frontier. Why did people retreat, instead of fighting to the last bullet? But during the fighting before Moscow I saw a unit which had just come out of battle. The men were still carrying their wounded, and they were completely exhausted. I realised that there is a point at which soldiers are no longer able to function. I certainly don't believe that so many people surrendered in 1941 because they hated Stalin. Of course many of them had good reason to dislike the regime. Whole units did surrender in the early stages. But the reasons were usually understandable. I know of one artillery regiment on the frontier which was being re-equipped when the Germans attacked. Their ammunition did not match their guns, and their protecting infantry had retreated. They could not defend themselves, and had no sensible alternative to surrender.'[35]

Both inside Russia and in the West historians and military analysts have expressed doubts about the effectiveness of the partisan campaign. But as the German offensive against Moscow petered out, von Bock noted in his diary, 'The Russians, who have destroyed almost all facilities on the main roads, have been able to obstruct our transport arrangements to such an extent that the Army Group no longer has what it needs to survive and to fight ... Today we no longer have the possibility of significant manoeuvre.'[36]

On 14 December Stalin ordered the removal of the demolition charges in Moscow's factories, bridges, and public buildings.[37] A couple of weeks later he ended the construction of new defensive works around the city centre. The civilian labourers and transport that had been drafted began to be released.[38] The advertisements in *Vechernyaya Moskva* measured the change. The Ippolitov-Ivanov Music College started to advertise for new students.[39] Charcoal toothpaste would soon be back in the shops. In addition to tortoises and fishing gear, one pet shop had a consignment of Australian parrots for sale.[40] Professor Morozov contributed a lengthy article on 'Shakespeare's Heroics' to the paper's middle page. He picked out *Henry V*, *Hamlet*, *Othello*, *Romeo and Juliet*, *Much Ado About Nothing*, and *The Taming of the Shrew* as particularly appropriate for reading aloud. He suggested that Lamb's *Tales from Shakespeare* could provide a convenient short cut. The Pedagogical Institute ran a series of lectures on the War of 1812 and the 1825 rebellion of the Decembrists. On the darker side, the paper reported that a certain Boll, a notorious gambler and player of the billiard tables in the Moscow and Metropole hotels, had been sentenced to ten years for selling on the black market twenty litres of medical alcohol which he had obtained from the director of a dental cooperative. And a building administrator had been demoted to *dvornik* for failing to ensure that the pavements outside the building were properly cleared of snow and sanded.[41]

There was a momentary setback to morale in mid-December when General Sinilov ordered that all pigeons in private possession should be handed in to the police in order to prevent their use by 'hostile elements'. Pigeon owners who failed to comply would go before the military tribunal. The collection of pigeons was soon stopped, because no one knew what to do with them. British pigeons were less fortunate. In June 1941 a policeman visited the pacifist Frances Partridge, and told her 'that by order of the Government all domestic pigeons were to be executed. He didn't know why, but it was something to do with invasion. So ours were killed and eaten in a pie.'[42]

By late autumn there were still about a hundred thousand children of school age in Moscow. Most of their schools were closed and at first there was no provision for their education. With parents away at the front or working long hours in factories and offices, an increasing number of them got into trouble: more than 40 per cent of those sentenced for criminal offences in the autumn of 1941 were children.

Some system was needed to keep them off the streets, ensure that they did not fall behind their fellows who had been evacuated, and use their labour for the production of weapons in the undermanned factories. At first the authorities did nothing. Parents hired people to teach their children informally in the offices of the building administrator in their apartment blocks. This did not go down well with the bureaucrats, who reported to Stalin that 'The inactivity of the authorities has led to the setting up of private fee-paying schools. The teachers do not observe the state curricula, and set their own rules for the length of lessons and the material covered.' The bureaucrats requested permission to take over.[43] In mid-January 1942 the Moscow City Council authorised the creation of forty-two 'consultation points'. Qualified teachers taught the children on lines derived from the official curricula, but streamlined and adapted to the difficult circumstances of the time. Teachers of literature were encouraged to emphasise works such as Pushkin's *Poltava* and Tolstoy's *War and Peace*, which celebrated Russian victories. But they were also supposed to devote 15 per cent of the final-year course to foreign literature, including Goethe's *Faust* and the *Nibelungenlied*.[44] Specialised technical training was provided for children between twelve and fifteen years old: the children were paid at adult rates and received rations at the highest ('workers'') level. Some teaching was resumed on the premises of Moscow University, the Bauman Institute and elsewhere for those students who had not been able to follow their institutions into evacuation.[45]

The first stage of the Russian counterattack was almost totally successful. In the twenty days after resuming their offensive against Moscow in the middle of November, the Germans had advanced up to seventy miles to the very outskirts of the city.[46] Now, in thirty-four days, along six hundred miles of front, the Russians advanced in some places more than 150 miles. The Germans had lost the strategic initiative for the first time since 1939. The immediate threat to the capital had been averted. It was never to be renewed, despite a nervous moment in April 1942, when the barricades were briefly re-erected as the Germans began once again to bestir themselves for their summer offensive.[47]

Everyone knew that history had been made. The counteroffensive had barely started when the Academy of Sciences set up a Commission to study the history of the defence of Moscow. Subcommittees chaired by the local Party secretary were set up in each Raion to collect material. Konstantin Simonov was commissioned to write a full-page article on the defence of Moscow for *Krasnaya Zvezda*, which was published on the eve of the twenty-fifth anniversary of the revolution in November 1942. The materials collected – documents, diaries, eyewitness accounts, newspaper cutting and photographs – became the basis for a scholarly archive in what is now the Institute of Russian History of the Russian Academy of Sciences.[48]

In one liberated village near Tula the local Party officials – now restored to power – told the women to identify and bury the Russian dead, but not to bother about the Germans. But the women collected the Germans' identity documents and buried them as well. 'After all,' they said, 'they have mothers waiting for them too.'[49]

– SIXTEEN –

DEFEAT INTO VICTORY

As the New Year approached trees began to be sold in preparation for the holiday. New kinds of decorations appeared – shining glass balls, little flags, dolls, miniature electric lamps, the silhouettes of animals from gilded cardboard. There were the official New Year's Eve parties, just as there had been the year before: in the Frunze House of the Red Army, in the Stalin Palace of Culture, where soldiers told of their experiences. There were parties too for the children who were still in the town.[1] *Vechernyaya Moskva* announced that there would be an exhibition on 'The Heroic Past of the Russian People'. The cinemas were showing *The Swinemaiden and the Shepherd*, *The Circus*, *Boxers*, and other popular films. Sobolev, the Director of the Trëkhgorka, told his workers that they would have to take 28 December as a holiday without pay: the money saved would be used to buy presents for the soldiers.[2]

Zhukov's daughters Ira and Ella flew with their mother and their English governess in a very cold plane from Kuibyshev to Moscow to celebrate the New Year with their father at his headquarters in a two-storey wooden house at Perkhushkovo. The guns were still rumbling in the distance. Their food was brought out to the house from Moscow in sealed containers. It had already been checked for poison by the same NKVD department which tested and sealed the food that was sent to Stalin and other leaders. As they celebrated the

New Year and the victory, the five-year-old Ella ate so many sweets she was sick.[3]

On New Year's Day Dr Sakharova wrote in her diary: 'This is to be the year of victory [...] Yesterday I was in our hospital when presents were given out to the wounded soldiers [...] We got home at 11 o'clock in the evening. Three of us greeted the New Year together: Natalia Semënovna, and her sister Niura and me. Niura spent her time enthusiastically fortune-telling with Marusia, the fire-watcher. They burned paper, made a lot of smoke, and then gathered under the stairway to tell fortunes with a candle and a mirror. After tea and *zakuski* we started to dance. Today I spent four hours baking pies: pies with rice and eggs and with rice and onion. Very tasty.'[4]

But the eve of 1942 was of course a much grimmer affair than its predecessor. People greeted it in the trenches and on the snow-covered battlefields, in freezing factories in Moscow and deep in the rear, as food became increasingly scarce and expensive. For those who had been liberated from the German occupation of the Moscow Region things were particularly miserable. 'Ragged peasants are walking through the streets in single file, their hands in their sleeves, obviously not in their own clothes, unshaven, wild-eyed,' Nikolai Verzhbitski noted in his diary.

> I ask them: Who are you? – Prisoners, they answer (that's what peasants who have been under the Germans call themselves) [...] I spoke to a woman 'prisoner' (she was from a collective farm from the village of Krasnoe near Tarutino in the Maloyaroslavets Region). The Germans had been in their village. 'They slaughtered all the cattle and chickens. They ate every two hours. They didn't let us into our cottages. We had to sleep in the open and cook on bonfires. They did allow some of the mothers with small children to sleep under the beds or in the porches. They did their own cooking on our Russian stoves, but they didn't know how to [...] We were afraid they would burn our houses. They demanded to see the chairman of the collective farm. It was a woman, eight months pregnant. We brought her in, the officer saw her belly, roared with laughter, and sent her away in peace. They didn't touch anyone, they didn't dig up the ground to see if we had hidden our goods. Two days before

> they retreated, they told us to go into the woods, and allowed us to take our cows with us. They burned the village as they left. They left two houses at the request of the women, so that there would be somewhere to shelter the children. But three versts away the Germans were hanging and beating people [...] They hanged the woman teacher and the chairman of the collective farm and they raped the girls.[5]

As the Russian soldiers pushed forward, they came across enough evidence of what the Germans had done to convince even the most sceptical of the nature of the enemy they were fighting. In Volokolamsk they found a scaffold on which hung the corpses of eight of the local people. The Russian commander refused to allow the victims to be cut down for several days, to allow his men to see what the Germans were capable of.

But liberation did not bring an end to the problems of the people who had been under occupation. Their houses had been destroyed in the fighting or deliberately burned down by the German army, the Russian army, or the partisans. Mines had been sown over their fields by both sides. Their health was shattered: in one small town the mortality rate had increased three times by the spring. The NKVD fanned out to catch those who had collaborated with the enemy: by the end of January they had arrested nearly fourteen hundred people.[6] At the end of December Shcherbakov reported to a meeting of Raion Party Secretaries that units of the Red Army had been commandeering food, forage, vehicles, and horses without authority and sometimes under armed threat. Orders went out that a 'pitiless struggle be waged against all attempts at arbitrary behaviour and looting'. Looters were to be punished without mercy.[7]

By now, indeed, the soldiers were as hungry as the civilians. Despite Kaganovich's best efforts, the system of supply was breaking down all over the country. There were simply not enough trains to transport equipment, supplies, evacuees, whole factories, from one end of the country to the other. Even the troop trains were affected. A contingent of reinforcements – more than three thousand men – set out from Tbilisi in January 1942. Many of them were illiterate Georgians who spoke no Russian. The temperature was minus fifty degrees. The train was unheated and there was neither food nor medical assistance. It arrived at its destination twenty days late. By then 178 men had gone missing, twenty-one had suffered frostbite, and two had died. There were other examples as bad or worse.[8]

Things were no better at the front. In March Gekhman, a correspondent from *Krasnaya Zvezda*, reported from the Kalinin Front north of Moscow that the soldiers in one battalion were literally starving: half of them were in hospital suffering from malnutrition. Stalin sent Shcherbakov and General Khrulëv, the Quartermaster General, to investigate. At first furiously convinced that Gekhman was simply making trouble, they eventually concluded that he was right. There was not enough transport to bring up even the meagre supplies available, and the supply officers were fiddling the figures. Those responsible were sent off to punishment battalions. Gekhman was given the Order of the Red Star.[9]

Buoyed up by their success in repelling the Germans before Moscow, the Soviet leadership greeted the New Year with great optimism. Stalin called a meeting on 5 January 1942 to discuss plans for further offensive action. 'The Germans are in disarray as a result of their defeat before Moscow,' he told his listeners. 'They've prepared badly for the winter. This is the most favourable moment to go over to a general offensive. The Germans hope to hold our offensive until the spring, so that they can resume active operations when they have built up their strength.' He continued, pacing up and down his office in his usual fashion: 'Our task is therefore to give the Germans no time to draw breath, drive them to the West, and force them to use up all their reserves before spring comes (he paused and accented the word 'spring') because by then we will have new reserves and the German reserves will have run out.'

The thought had some substance, but Stalin's proposals for putting it into effect did not. The new offensive would be on a grandiose scale. It would be launched along the whole Eastern front from Leningrad to the Black Sea. The main blow would be directed against Army Group Centre. Two spearheads would encircle the Germans to North and South, meet West of Vyazma, the site of the Russian disaster three months earlier, and thus crush the armies which had so nearly taken Moscow. But that would not be the end of it. The Leningrad and Volkhov Fronts would open a second major offensive to liberate Leningrad and destroy Army Group North. In the South Timoshenko would liberate Kharkov, the Donbass, and the Crimea, where Sevastopol was still holding out against a German siege. Stalin asked for comments.

Zhukov pointed out that neither his own Western Front, nor the others, had the resources for such a broad offensive. The Russian formations had been decimated. The survivors were exhausted. There was a desperate shortage of armour, artillery, and ammunition: guns were being rationed to one shell a day each. He and Voznesenski, the Deputy Prime Minister responsible for economic planning, recommended that the available resources be concentrated for the offensive against Army Group Centre. Stalin listened, then asked if anyone else wanted to speak. No one did. His proposal was accepted without further discussion.[10] Once again Stalin had imposed a major strategic misjudgement on his generals.

Out in the field, Rokossovski was equally convinced that such a broad offensive could not succeed. The Germans had built formidable defensive positions in the villages and the forests. 'It was a paradox: the stronger was defending himself, and the weaker was attacking up to his waist in snow.' The Russians should go over to the defence, and build up strength for a major offensive in the future. Rokossovski put these thoughts together, backed by figures, in a substantial report to Zhukov. But by then the die was cast. Zhukov was terse: 'Carry out your orders!'[11]

The attack began on 10 January. Koniev, supported by Vlasov's 20th Army and Rokossovski's 16th Army, broke through the enemy defences on the Volokolamsk Highway. The 2nd Guards Cavalry Corps (commanded by Pliev since Dovator's death) went through the gap, accompanied by tanks and ski battalions. Zhukov pressed forward along the Mozhaisk Highway. Belov's cavalry and a strike force under General Yefremov succeeded in getting to the Southwest of Vyazma.

But the Germans were now being reinforced with new divisions from Western Europe. Belov and Yefremov were themselves cut off. Zhukov sent parachutists to support them, and they continued to pick away at the Germans. But they were no longer able to close the trap: the encirclers were themselves encircled. Yefremov was badly wounded in an attempt to break out, and committed suicide rather than be taken prisoner. Belov finally emerged from behind the German lines in the middle of July.[12]

In mid-January a crisis developed to the South, at the junction between the Western Front and Cherevichenko's Bryansk Front. As the Russians swept ahead in the initial days of their offensive, a German division newly arrived from France was bypassed and surrounded at Sukhinichi. Supplied by air, it held out stubbornly, and the Germans fought hard to relieve it. By 24 January they had created a narrow corridor between the Sukhinichi garrison and the German main force. Stalin ordered Rokossovski to hand over his command, go with his staff to carve a new 16th Army out of Zhukov's Southern divisions, and get a grip on things. He went off immediately, taking with him Malinin and the rest of his by now highly experienced staff. To mislead the Germans he put it about in the press and on the radio that the whole of the 16th Army was moving on Sukhinichi. In fact the only formation to have served in the old 16th Army was the 11th Guards Division – the renamed 18th (Leningrad) Volunteer Division, which Rokossovski had met for the first time as they were coming out of encirclement at Vyazma four months earlier.

Rokossovski and his people quickly put together a plan of attack. The forces took up their start positions and the artillery prepared to bombard the town. Suddenly the telephone rang: civilians from Sukhinichi had told the Russian troops that the Germans had left. There were only minutes left before the artillery barrage was due to begin. Rokossovski made a quick judgement and held his fire. Luckily the Germans had indeed gone, and next morning he was able to move his headquarters into Sukhinichi unopposed.

On 8 March it was International Women's Day, and Rokossovski planned to celebrate it at his headquarters that evening. He spent the day visiting his units by aero-sledge, a ramshackle device built in the Duks Aviation Works in Moscow which made it possible to move fast over thick snow. Back at his headquarters Rokossovski was working with Malinin when a shell exploded outside the window and a splinter hit him in the back. It was his third wound: this time, he reflected ruefully, he had been hit not in battle, but sitting in a room with a pen in his hand.

He was immediately flown back to the Timiryazev Hospital for senior officers in Moscow, where the patients had separate rooms and were fed most generously – by wartime standards. Theatrical life was picking up. Simonov's partner Valentina Serova was still in Moscow, acting at the Drama Theatre. The actors, cold and very hungry, appeared on stage wearing their overcoats and from time to time visited hospitals to give recitals to the wounded. One of the doctors asked Serova to call in on Rokossovski to give him a private performance. As she came into the room, he was having his dinner. He saw her hungry eyes, and gave the food to her. In return she recited a short story by Chekhov. Contrary to subsequent myth, she seems to have met him no more than a couple of times thereafter.[13]

Rokossovski's career continued to prosper. He was at last able to track down his wife and daughter, who had been evacuated to Siberia, and wangled a flat in Moscow so that they could join him there. He was discharged from hospital in the third week of May, and returned to the front, where Galina Talanova was waiting for him. At the beginning of July he was given a Front to command for the first time. He distinguished himself in all the great battles which followed – Stalingrad, Kursk, Belorussia, until he joined up with the British under Montgomery in North Germany in the very last days of the war.

Meanwhile another brilliant career was coming to a tragic end. The Northern prong of Stalin's great offensive, the thrust to relieve Leningrad, also had some initial success. The Russians succeeded in encircling six German divisions at Demyansk, near Novgorod, about four hundred miles from Moscow along the Leningrad Highway. The Germans defended themselves behind blockhouses and battlements of snow and ice, since it was impossible to dig trenches in the frozen ground. It was the beginning of what turned out to be the longest encirclement battle in the whole war; and in the end the Germans got away.[14]

The forces of the Volkhov Front under Meretskov pushed towards Leningrad itself. After hard fighting the 2nd Shock Army broke through the German defences. But they could only make slow progress.

> They moved only at night: during the day they took cover in the forest. The way forward was not easy. In order to beat a path

> through the deep snow, they had to draw up columns in ranks of fifteen. The first rank went forward, trampling the snow, which in places came up to their waists. After ten minutes the front rank was withdrawn and took up position at the rear of the column. The difficulty of movement was increased because from time to time they would come across half-frozen patches of bog and streams covered with a thin layer of ice. Their boots were wet through and freezing. There was no way they could be dried out, since it was forbidden to light fires when they rested. Their horses were at the end of their strength. Their fuel ran out and their vehicles came to a halt. They had to carry their supplies of ammunition, equipment, and food on their own backs.[15]

Many had not washed for months. They were dirty and starving and very cold. They scraped shelters for themselves in the snow, huddling together under their waterproof capes for warmth. Some of them took clothing from the dead. When they had the chance to light a fire, they cut the legs from frozen corpses and thawed them out to remove the boots.[16]

Stalin demanded more rapid progress. He promised the Volkhov Front essential reinforcements. He reorganised the command. He sent Vlasov, who had so distinguished himself before Moscow, to take over the 2nd Shock Army, to sort out the mess and to push forward to join up with the forces of the Leningrad Front. The task Vlasov now faced was beyond the skill of any general. The 2nd Shock Army continued to stagger forward. But it was now dependent for its supplies on a narrow corridor continually battered by the Germans. Stalin's promised reinforcements did not arrive. The corridor was cut by the Germans, temporarily at first and then for good. Meretskov told Stalin, 'Second Shock is completely played out: it can neither attack nor defend itself. Its communications are at the mercy of German thrusts. If nothing is done, catastrophe can't be staved off.'[17]

Nothing was done. Vlasov's army was finally surrounded. The thaw began in mid-March, the land turned into a quagmire, and what passed for roads disintegrated. The men's warm winter clothing now became a lice-infested nightmare. They ran out of food and ammunition, and they were destroyed piecemeal by the Germans in the swamps and the forest. As they died in the marshes their bodies sank without honour into unmarked graves.[18]

For some time Vlasov himself wandered aimlessly in the wilderness, until he was finally captured in July. He was by now entirely disillusioned with Stalin and the Soviet regime. He allowed the Germans to persuade him that he could best serve his country by raising and commanding a Russian Liberation Army. In December 1942 he issued his first appeal 'to the whole Russian nation, and to the other nations of the Soviet Union'. He blamed Stalin and the Anglo-Americans for involving Russia in an unnecessary war with its natural ally Germany. Russia was being defeated, he said, because the Russian people were unwilling to defend Bolshevik power except under coercion. He called for the elimination of Stalin's apparatus of terror, the overthrow of Stalin's regime and a return to the democratic freedoms promulgated during the February revolution of 1917. His motives may have been good, but he was politically naïve and the Germans never fully trusted him. His 'Army' numbered only 50,000 men and saw almost no effective action.[19] He was captured by the Red Army near Prague at the end of the war, and executed with the maximum of ignominy on 2 August 1946.

For most Russians today Vlasov remains, not surprisingly, the archetype of a traitor. A history of the Battle of Moscow published as late as 2001 not only failed to mention his name; it even omitted his 20th Army from the order of battle of the Soviet forces which took part in the victory before Moscow.[20] The front page of *Pravda* for 13 December 1941, with Vlasov's picture among those of the other victorious generals, soon became an embarrassment. The Rokossovski family have lovingly preserved a copy in their archives. But Vlasov's portrait has been painstakingly excised.

Vlasov was of course far from alone in his collaboration with the Germans. The prisoners they took in the first months of the war were starving, demoralised, and without hope. Many of them concluded that their only chance of survival was to serve in the armed units – ninety battalions altogether – which the Germans set up for anti-partisan and police work in Occupied Europe, especially Yugoslavia and Italy. Deliberately exploiting the anti-Soviet sentiments of the non-Russian peoples of the Soviet Union, the Germans formed military units of

Tatars, Cossacks, Chechens, Ukrainians, and Balts inside the Soviet Union itself. Nationalist partisan groups fought the Red Army and sometimes the Germans as well. Two to three hundred thousand 'volunteers' ('Hilfswillige' or 'HiWis') agreed to serve the Germans as doctors, nurses, cooks, cleaners, drivers, casual workers, village policemen and elders. By the end of 1943 each German division was allowed two thousand HiWis on its establishment: 6 per cent of its total established strength.[21] As the fortunes of Germany waned, many of these people switched sides. In one spectacular incident, a Wehrmacht battalion of Georgians on the Dutch island of Texel rose against the Germans in April 1945. After two weeks of bitter fighting they were suppressed by overwhelming force. By then 117 Dutch civilians, 550 Georgians, and 800 Germans were dead.[22]

Any government fighting a war of survival would have taken harsh measures against collaboration on such a scale, let alone a government as paranoid as Stalin's. In December 1941 he ordered the creation of special assembly points and camps to weed out traitors, spies and deserters from among the Soviet soldiers who had been in German PoW camps or in units surrounded by the Germans.[23] The figures rose as the Red Army liberated the camps in Central Europe and as the Western Allies handed over the Soviet citizens they themselves had liberated. By March 1946 over five million men and women, prisoners of war and civilians deported for forced labour, had been repatriated to the Soviet Union. Nearly two million former prisoners went through the system of 'filtration'. Some 993,000 returned to active service, 277,000 were sent home and 344,000 were sent to pioneer battalions ('working battalions'). Another 283,000 were arrested and handed over to the NKVD: many of these were assigned to punishment units, forced labour, or exile.[24]

Anatoli Chernyaev's first introduction to war was not far from the sector where the 2nd Shock Army suffered and died. After a roundabout journey by train, his ski battalion was unloaded in the spring of 1942 in an open field near Staraya Russa, not far from Novgorod. They were to take part in a grandiose operation to surround and annihilate the large German force in the Demyansk pocket, which had been trapped by the rapid Soviet counteroffensive outside Moscow. From the start the operation was a shambles.

In these parts there was no clear front line. The Germans occupied some villages, the Russians other villages, and each could penetrate with relative impunity behind the positions of the other. Chernyaev's battalion spent the first night in a deserted village. The houses were intact, but all the chimneys had holes in them. Chernyaev's peasant friend Chugunov explained that the inhabitants had done this to prevent passing soldiers from lighting fires which might burn the houses down if they ran out of control. The platoon commander immediately went off sick. Chernyaev took over, and discovered that his soldiers were incapable of skiing in fresh snow. In any case, most of the skis had been broken or abandoned by their owners. So they loaded the remaining skis on the sledges carrying the mortars, and trudged along the roads instead. The organisation began to break down. The battalion cooks got lost, and the soldiers had to beg or steal food from their neighbours. After their first operation Chernyaev's mortar platoon ran out of ammunition. It was not replaced, and the mortars were sent to the rear. The battalion's maps dated from 1914. There were not enough rifles to go round. The soldiers were told to scavenge for weapons on the battlefield. In one of their early billets, the housewife suggested to the inexperienced Chernyaev that he should post a sentry lest marauding Germans tossed a grenade through the window. The man had no rifle. Chernyaev had to lend him his own.

The battalion's first serious attack was against a German-held village. They were led by the junior lieutenant through snow which in places was up to their waists. Of the battalion commander – fat, stupid, coarse, a hopeless organiser and a coward – there was no sign. The operation was successful, and the battalion were at last able to feed themselves properly with captured German food and to arm themselves with captured German weapons.

The next morning, Chernyaev was called to battalion HQ to witness an execution. The fat battalion commander was surrounded by his officers. The man brought in was Chernyaev's fellow student Gaft – without his coat, his belt, or his hat. During the night, while on sentry duty, he had gone off to sleep. 'We don't need soldiers like that,' shouted the battalion commander. 'He's to be shot, and you're to tell all your men that the same thing will happen to them if they're not careful.'

Gaft threw himself on his knees in tears. There was an uneasy movement among the officers. Chernyaev rushed forward: Gaft was a good soldier, he said, a member of the Komsomol, a volunteer. It was in vain. Gaft was dragged into the yard. Behind him went the commander of the headquarters company, all dolled up in his polished belt, breeches and cavalry boots. A pistol shot followed. Chernyaev returned to his men in a fury.

After the war Chernyaev went to see Gaft's parents and sisters, who lived not far away from his home in Mariina Roshcha. He told them that he had lost sight of Gaft during the fighting, and had not seen him again. They did not believe him.[25]

Seventeen-year-old Petya Sagaidachny never had time to become disillusioned. He had always wanted to join the navy. He sailed whenever he could on the Klyazma reservoir outside Moscow, and read books on naval affairs, kept a diary, and mooned about Olga, a classmate to whom he never plucked up courage to declare himself.

He was out sailing on the day the war began. When he got back to Moscow he found that the boys in the top class at school had already volunteered. Olga had joined a course on nursing. He was still too young to join up, so he and his friend Yura Fedorenko signed on as apprentices in a machine-tool factory. He had mechanical talent and learned how to operate a lathe with unusual speed. But it was an exhausting life. He joined his fellow workers digging trenches and foxholes for two hours a day. He studied for his school leaving exam whenever he had a spare moment. When he was on night shift, he would come home at 5 a.m., sleep until 8, then go to school, return at 2, sleep until 3, get up to do his school homework and then go back to the factory. Once he worked non-stop from 7 a.m. on one day to 5 a.m. on the next, despite having flu. Whenever he got a day off, he went sailing, until the arrival of winter and the Germans made it impossible.

His diary shows that he had no illusions about the way the war was going. In early July he wrote, 'The Germans may get as far as Moscow, they may even temporarily wipe it off the face of the earth.' By August he was writing, 'We are being beaten, soundly and brutally.' But he was sure that the Russians would win in the end, and he worried that the war would be over before he got to it. On 16 October, the day of the great Moscow panic, his mother, his stepfather, and their two small boys were evacuated, and he remained in Moscow on his own. 'Moscow is feverishly preparing to receive its guests. In the evening I went to work as usual and was shocked. The factory had stopped working, they were dismantling the machinery, and the workers were rushing around the workshops like bees abandoning the hive.'

For the next three days he dug trenches outside Moscow. On his foreman's suggestion he then volunteered for one of Shcherbakov's new workers' battalions, and was sent off to learn how to destroy tanks. In the last entry in his diary, he recorded the encouraging words of his commissar: 'This detachment is an elite, each one should become a hero, because probably all of you are going to certain death.'

After two months' training Petya and his unit were sent to the front. They travelled by train through villages destroyed by the retreating Germans, and then on foot until they were far in the enemy rear. They saw action for the first time at the beginning of March, and Petya was rapidly promoted to command a reconnaissance section. On 17 April he wrote to his mother:

> Good morning, dear mummy! [...] Today is indescribably beautiful. There was some frost during the night, and the tender spring sun has not yet succeeded in driving the frost from the ground, from the snow, and from the trees [...] We are going out on patrol again today to carry out an important task we've been given by our commander, and when it's done I'll write to you in more detail [...] The boys have boiled some potatoes and bacon fat in the cooking pot and want me to join them. So I'll have to finish. I kiss you hard. I really need your letters and am looking forward to the next one.[26]

The next day, on 18 April, Petya Sagaidachny was killed, two weeks before his eighteenth birthday.

The crisis for Moscow did not end with the rollback of the German armies. It was now that the full implications of the earlier decision to evacuate the stocks of grain and other supplies from the city began to unfold.

Things were already very bad in December. One skilled worker told his boss, 'If I don't come in to work on Monday, you can assume that I am dead. I'll kill my wife and then myself. By the spring I won't be the only one: there'll be many others. I'm not the only one starving: thousands are. That's what the war and our [Government's] wise policy have done for us.'[27] In the first months of 1942 the inhabitants of Moscow suffered from the cold, from increasing ill-health, and from a shortage of food which brought them almost to the brink of starvation. The railways, overloaded with troops, munitions, supplies and equipment to feed the Soviet offensive, were unable to bring food for the civilian population as well. Office workers, dependants and children got no meat at all in January and February. Supplies of potatoes dried up in January. March was just as bad. Things were available on the free and black markets. But most people could not afford the prices. A rate of exchange built up: a pair of shoes bought you eighteen pounds of potatoes, a pair of trousers twenty-two pounds, a handkerchief just over two pounds.[28] Ordinary people ran out of things to trade. In the markets the cost of milk, potatoes, flour and carrots continued to rise. There was almost no meat. If it did appear, it cost around 80 roubles a pound: the monthly salary of a doctor at that time was about 600 roubles. Even the food to which people's ration cards entitled them was often held up for weeks at a time.[29] There was growing anger at the apparent ability of the peasants to get rich at everyone else's expense.

For fourteen-year-old Oksana Sobchuk all went reasonably well until January. Then the central heating in her apartment was cut off, her mother had to go into hospital, and she was left alone with her two-year-old brother Valeri, Barsik the family cat, and a bowlful of goldfish. When she went off in the morning to her informal lessons (her school had not yet reopened) she wrapped her brother in a blanket along with the cat. They ate their meagre rations together; no one froze to death (not even the goldfish), and when spring came Oksana passed her school exams to go up a class.[30]

The full extent of the crisis was set out in a furious anonymous letter addressed on 25 February to Nikolai Voznesenski, the Chairman of the State Planning Organisation, GosPlan:

> The GKO ought to deal urgently with the problem of feeding the people of Moscow. It's wholly clear that MosSoviet isn't up to doing

> it on its own, there is nobody there of any substance, starting with the colourless figure of Pronin. The sycophantic people in MosSoviet prefer to starve the people of Moscow rather than tell Comrade Stalin what is going on and ask for his help. The million-strong population of Moscow has been suffering severely from hunger for five months, and is worn out and demoralised. And the situation is getting worse from month to month [...] How long can the population of Moscow bear such a level of starvation without, it seems, any prospect of improvement, while continuing to work so hard producing armaments? Can it really be true, people wonder, that the Soviet Union is unable to feed its capital city? [...] We ask you, Comrade Voznesenski, to inform Comrade Stalin that the people of Moscow are starving. We are convinced that Comrade Stalin is unaware that Comrade Pronin and Co., together with Shcherbakov, are trying to starve the people of Moscow.[31]

This was unfair on Shcherbakov and Pronin. But the main thrust of the accusation was accurate enough. Dr Sakharova summed up the mood at the end of March:

> Life is the same as it was in 1919, 1920 and 1921, when we sat without electricity. But then at least there was kerosene and now there is none. They have not even issued the ration cards for kerosene for February and March. I went to the central market ... [T]here were many customers, but the stalls were completely empty and there were no sales people. The customers seemed to be waiting for something submissively and patiently [...] Everybody was silent and looking into the distance, pressing themselves against the walls. The only activity was in the milk pavilion, where one woman from a collective farm was selling milk at 20 roubles a litre. Suddenly a woman ordered her to stop selling her milk [...] It appeared that the other saleswomen were trying to sell their milk for 25 roubles, but no one wanted to buy from them at that price. Many people are beginning to show the signs of malnutrition in all its stages. And that's to say nothing of the lice. Not a single bathhouse [...] is working in our Raion. And in other Raions it's much the same. You have to queue for four or five hours to get into one of the

> working bathhouses. [...] There are also problems with the supply of rationed food. Only bread is issued regularly. We got the sugar for February only yesterday. There is no soap. But there is typhus. So far it is not an epidemic, but it would not be in the least surprising if an epidemic began. This kind of typhus is the product of hunger. The buildings in Moscow are not heated, in many of them the water and sewage pipes are frozen. The temperature in apartments is between one and ten degrees centigrade. The courtyards of Moscow are filthy in the extreme. What will happen in the spring is hard to imagine [...] Our invalids leave the polyclinic unwillingly: they can keep themselves warm there. Many people from the neighbouring houses simply come in and sit by the radiators to warm themselves [...] There are not many doctors left in the polyclinic and most of them are invalids. House visits are being delayed until the next day. Patients die without the doctor once having visited them. Old people have been dying recently in great numbers. They have to wait five–seven days for a funeral, because there is a shortage of coffins. The face of Moscow has changed greatly since the war began [...] Things may get even worse in future. How will we feel when it gets to spring and summer? What will we eat and how will we keep up our strength? Or will we die under the ruins of a house hit by a bomb, perhaps even in our own polyclinic? Or in our first aid post? Or will we die from poison gas? I so much want to live and see what it will be like after the war. Will I have enough strength for that? I'm getting very thin. Yesterday I had a frightful headache, such as I only had before when I had typhus in 1919.[32]

A few days later Dr Sakharova woke up in alarm to find a louse on herself. She burned it off with a match.

By April 1942 the mortality rate in Moscow was three times higher than the previous year. Deaths from tuberculosis had nearly doubled. So had deaths from heart failure and other stress-related diseases. During the Civil War similar conditions had led to major epidemics in the city. But Dr Sakharova's worst fears were not realised. The incidence of infectious disease actually went down, thanks to the efforts of the Moscow health authorities and to those who worked for them, such as Dr Sakharova and her colleagues.[33]

Keeping the factories of Moscow working throughout the winter became increasingly difficult as the bombs fell, workers departed for the front, and raw materials were in increasingly short supply. The fuel crisis got even worse. At the end of December Shcherbakov reported to Stalin that only a few of the factories in Moscow had even a minimum reserve of fuel. Hospitals had only enough for five or six days. Electric power to textile factories and to many blocks of apartments had been cut off entirely. Once again, Shcherbakov had to turn to the population at large. A hundred thousand people, including housewives and schoolchildren, were conscripted in the course of 1942 to cut firewood in the forests.[34]

Sobolev, the Director of the Trëkhgorka, issued one order after another in a constant battle to save energy. He reduced the lighting in lavatories, shower rooms, stairwells, canteens, even laboratories. He ordered all 200-watt bulbs to be replaced with weaker ones. He banned electric stoves and heaters. He allowed more generous standards of lighting only in the production shops and the typists' offices. He told the mechanics to readjust the carburettors of their vehicles to save fuel.[35]

As public health in Moscow became more precarious, Sobolev arranged for the disinfection of the factory workshops, dormitories, cupboards, shower rooms and toilets. Workers arriving from outside Moscow were to be medically examined and quarantined before they were allowed to sleep in the factory's dormitories.[36] These outsiders were, he thought, particularly prone to pilfering: he told his managers to keep an especial eye on them.[37] He reminded his workers of the penalties for late arrival and absenteeism. Those who failed to produce a satisfactory written excuse could be hauled before a military tribunal.[38] A night watchman who set his sentry box on fire was sacked and his manager formally reprimanded.[39]

Sobolev did his best to sustain his workers' morale. He sorted out the distribution of ration cards.[40] He organised a kindergarten for a hundred children in an air-raid shelter.[41] He handed out Red Banners to the deserving. He thanked all those who had participated in the burdensome scheme for universal basic military training out of working hours, the VseObuch.[42] But despite his best efforts, the Trëkhgorka failed to fulfil its plan for the first quarter of 1942. This was a serious matter, especially in wartime. Sobolev promulgated stern measures to ensure there would be no repetition.[43]

Despite all the difficulties, the city began to struggle back to a kind of normality. In January teaching started up again in the colleges. Some schools began to reopen, though even a year later others could still not be heated and had to remain closed.[44] Evacuees began to return. Many found their apartments either occupied or looted. Looters were put on trial. The guilty were sentenced to imprisonment with the confiscation of their goods, or to be shot.[45]

Dr Sakharova started to go to the theatre and the cinema again. The ballet *The Vain Precaution* (known to us as *La Fille Mal Gardée*)

> began at 11 o'clock in the morning. We overslept, left home late and were sure we would not arrive in time. Luckily the beginning had been delayed and we arrived as the second bell was going off. I had not been in the theatre for eight months and it gave me great pleasure. Since the Bolshoi Theatre has not yet been restored after it was bombed, the artists performed in the junior theatre. The ballet ended at 1.15 [...] There were a lot of English airmen in the theatre. They sat in the front rows. Their uniform was very modest and made of material of a very dark protective colouring.

In the Stanislavski Theatre she saw the opera *Suvorov*, about the eighteenth-century general. The tickets were already sold out, but at the door a railway worker sold her a ticket for a box. Sakharova was impressed with the sets, the costumes, the music, and especially the scene where Suvorov leads his soldiers across the Alps. The theatre was full of soldiers, especially political officers. On 15 March:

> there's been an unusually strong snowstorm. The wind was strong enough to blow you off your feet. The trams had stopped. In the evening Natalia Semënovna and I struggled through the weather to see the film *Engineer Kochin's Mistake*. We were unlucky. The electricity supply stopped at the most interesting part, and the audience was told to go home. On the way back the wind was even stronger,

> blew at us from behind and propelled us at a run across the bridge. It was a good test for our new fur coats.'[46]

The coming of spring brought its own problems. The snow and ice had disguised the breakdown of the city's normal cleaning services. The thaw revealed all the filth that had piled up over the winter. In April the Moscow City Council mobilised the population once again, this time to clear the city's streets and public places. Rubbish, dung and mud were to be removed immediately. The streets were to be washed by 7 o'clock every morning and to be brushed three times a day. Those who failed to participate in this mass action were to be fined up to 200 roubles for a first offence, and tried on a criminal charge for a second.[47]

After the Soviet counteroffensive ground to a halt at the end of April, supplies began to flow into the city as the railways gained some spare capacity. Nikolai Verzhbitski wrote in his diary: 'Vodka is being sold everywhere at 33 roubles a half-litre. People are queuing by the thousand. Products have reached the shops in considerable quantities. They are selling Siberian salmon, red caviar and lard. The March shortfalls have all been made up.'[48]

Although the fighting had receded, it took time for people's nerves to settle down. 'The broadcasts in the last two weeks,' wrote Dr Sakharova in her diary on 9 April, 'begin with the news: "For such and such a date nothing has occurred at the front." This produces a bad impression.'[49] And on the last day of the month she wrote in her diary:

> Last night was beautiful, warm, moonlit. The air raid warning went off again. But there was no gunfire and no bombs [...] Today I went with Natalia Semënovna to the Hermitage Garden [...] It felt almost like peacetime. But there were many military among the visitors [...] And the kiosks were not selling anything. The season of public gatherings, conferences, official meetings, has begun again, a kind of fever and inappropriate nervousness [...] Avitaminosis is on the increase, that threatening symptom of famine and exhaustion, but people are not taking it seriously and almost nothing has been done to prevent it. This illness attacks the elderly and young children in particular. Are we going to suffer the same fate as the

> people of Leningrad, where the corpses are still lying where they have been since the winter? Two days ago we brought home an upright piano from the kindergarten – admittedly a very miserable one: it was full of wooden toys, and it was probably those that had ruined it. I bought some music and began to remember how once upon a time I had played really well. The barricades in Moscow are being taken down. The Garden Ring is already completely clear. Gunfire is beginning again – it is 1 o'clock in the morning. There was no alarm even though the shrapnel was rattling down on our roof. It's difficult, very difficult. But one so much wants to overcome all that, to survive, to win victory and [...] to see what will happen then, after the war.[50]

That year the Orthodox Easter fell on 4 and 5 April. Seventy-five thousand people attended services in Moscow's thirty working churches.[51] As summer began Dr Sakharova and Natalia Semënovna cleared a space for a little garden in the courtyard of their apartment block, and planted tomatoes, radishes, red sugar beet, dill, onions, parsley, and potatoes.

In his May Day message to the troops, Stalin ordered, 'The whole Red Army is to make 1942 the year of the final defeat of the German-fascist forces and the liberation of Soviet soil from the Hitlerite villains.'[52] By then, that was already a forlorn aspiration. The overall results of the Soviet spring offensive were just what Zhukov, Rokossovski and Voznesenski had predicted. The offensive lasted from 8 January to 20 April. Zhukov advanced in some places as much as 155 miles, but he lost more than twice as many men as the Germans did.[53] The offensive in the North got nowhere. Timoshenko pushed the Germans back sixty miles in the South but failed to break their determined and professional defence. The spring *rasputitsa* turned the fighting once more into a nightmare struggle through glutinous mud. The Soviet offensive petered out as the diminished and exhausted troops ran out of weapons, ammunition, vehicles, and food. It was not quite a disaster. But it came pretty close.

As they peered into the future, the Soviet intelligence agencies concluded that 1941 had taught the Germans that they did not have the resources to advance across the whole Russian front. They would concentrate instead on a single thrust across the Ukraine towards the oilfields of the Caucasus. The Stavka believed that the Germans would resume their offensive against Moscow, and Zhukov massed his forces in a defensive ring around the capital. But Stalin hankered after action. He authorised Timoshenko to mount an offensive to capture Kharkov, the second city in the Ukraine. Like Kirponos at Kiev the previous year, Timoshenko ran into a catastrophe. He lost three rifle armies and a tank army: at least 170,000 men. Unlike Kirponos, Timoshenko himself managed to escape. But the débâcle seriously weakened the Russians' ability to withstand the Germans' next aggressive move.[54]

In the middle of June 1942 Major Reichel of the 23rd Panzer Division lost his way, and landed on a Soviet airfield with plans for the Germans' summer offensive, Operation Blau.[55] The plans were forwarded to Moscow, where they were interpreted as a plant designed to divert Russian attention from the forthcoming attack on the capital. The Germans struck on 28 June. They swept triumphantly across the Ukraine and into the Caucasus, where they planted their flag on the top of Mount Elbruz, Europe's highest peak, on the very boundary with Asia. Once again the Red Army retreated helter-skelter. Once again Stalin ordered that the fugitives should be halted at all costs. Once again he issued an order – Order No. 227 of 26 July 1942 – prescribing punishments as draconian as those that had figured in Order No. 270 the previous year for those who broke and ran. At first the rout continued. But the Germans were now compounding their own mistakes. Instead of concentrating on the thrust to the Caucasus, Hitler diverted his Sixth Army to Stalingrad. When it ran into an obdurate defence and was surrounded, he refused to allow it to withdraw. The Russians annihilated the Sixth Army and captured its commander – von Paulus, the man who had written the first draft of Barbarossa, the original German plan of attack. At Kursk in July 1943, in the biggest tank battle in history, the Russians demonstrated that they had mastered the art of armoured warfare and could beat the Germans at their own game.

The Russians had thus won three crushing victories against the Germans before the British and Americans made their first landing on the European continent in Salerno in September 1943. On the morning of 22 June 1944, three years to the day after the war had begun and three weeks after the Western Allies had landed in Normandy, they fired the first shots of Operation Bagration, named after a hero of the Battle of Borodino. It was the greatest defeat suffered by the Germans in the whole of the war, greater than Stalingrad, a Barbarossa in reverse, as the Germans were driven headlong over the battlefields of 1941 for hundreds of miles, all the way to the outskirts of Warsaw. Army Group Centre, which had got so close to Moscow two and a half years earlier, was at last surrounded and destroyed. The Russians took nearly sixty thousand German prisoners to Moscow and herded them into the Hippodrome by the Belorussia Station. Nearby was the 'Lace House', so called because of the intricate decoration on its façade. Konstantin Simonov had an apartment there at one end of a corridor. Discreetly at the other was his partner, Valentina Serova. The Nemirovskis lived there too. So did General Sinilov, the Commandant of the Moscow Garrison. On 17 July, Mikhail Nemirovski's small daughter Lena watched Sinilov ride out on a white horse to put himself at the head of a column of prisoners who had been marshalled outside the Hippodrome. Sinilov led the men through the streets of the city, followed by water carts to clean up the mess. Crowds stood on the pavements to watch, mostly in silence, some with sympathy. When the parade was over, the German prisoners were loaded onto trains and sent to the camps, from which many never returned.[56] From now on the Russians were in continual victorious motion until the final storming of Berlin.

Since the end of the war the scale of casualties on both sides has been almost continuously debated and revised. This is partly because the basic facts are still difficult or impossible to ascertain, and partly because politicians and apologists on both sides, especially during the Cold War, have not always resisted the temptation to manipulate the figures to make a polemical point. As for Russian losses, the chaos which ruled during the first year of the war, the headlong retreats, the hurried mobilisation of volunteers, the loss of millions of men as prisoners, would in any case have made it very hard for the Russians to keep track. In April 1942 Stalin admitted, 'The lists of soldiers killed in action contain no more than a third of the actual numbers. The data about soldiers not accounted for and PoWs are even further removed from reality.'[57] Even when they were advancing, the Russians often failed to record or bury their dead properly. The arrangements for issuing soldiers with identity cards or dog-tags were sporadic, and men were often killed carrying no means of identification. Two-thirds of the Soviet wartime dead have no known graves. Commanders were allowed to forward general figures for dead, missing and wounded, without lists of names. They were tempted to underestimate their losses so that they could go on receiving the rations of 'dead souls', men who had already been killed. Igor Sats, who commanded a reconnaissance company during the war and later became the Secretary of the literary journal *Novy Mir* when Alexander Tvardovski was editor, used to keep three lists of the men under his command: a short list to ward off demands to detach people to other units; a reasonably exact figure when he was indenting for uniforms or ammunition; and a long list when he was indenting for rations. He found the numbers for men missing in action the easiest to manipulate. The wounded, after all, could be counted.

One broad estimate is that nearly nine million Soviet soldiers and seventeen million Soviet civilians died in the course of the war, men and women of Russia and Belorussia, of Ukraine and Kazakhstan, of Georgia and Armenia and Azerbaijan, of all the nationalities of an empire which disappeared fifty years to the day after the German defeat before Moscow. A recent Russian historian believes that the margin of error could be five million either way.[58] The figures do not include the wounded, the millions who were permanently disabled in body and mind. The totals will never be known for sure.

The Germans kept better records, but they too were overwhelmed as they fought desperately and hopelessly to defend their homeland in the last bloody months of the war. One recent German study estimated that over five million German soldiers died in the war. Nearly four million of them died fighting the Russians or in Soviet prisoner of war camps. By contrast 340,000 Germans died in France and Belgium between 1939 and 1944; and another 151,000 in the secondary campaign in Italy from 1943 to 1945.[59]

One can look at it this way: for every Briton or American who died, the Japanese lost seven people, the Germans twenty, and the Soviets eighty-five.[60] Four-fifths of the fighting in the Second World War took place on the Eastern front. Two-thirds of the German army were in the East even after D-Day. Indeed, had they not been fighting the Russians, they would have been in France, and there would have been no D-Day.

Some would dispute the precise figures. About the order of magnitude there can be no doubt. No wonder the Russians believe that it was they who won the war.

– SEVENTEEN –

AFTERMATH

Although the Russians failed fully to exploit their success outside Moscow, it was – as Muscovites at least now claim – a turning point, perhaps *the* turning point in the war. The Battle of Moscow demonstrated what none of the Western armies had yet been able to demonstrate, that the German army, the finest and most experienced in the world, could be beaten, ground down, and comprehensively defeated. The myth of invincibility was dispersed. From now on the Germans knew, what they had already dimly begun to recognise within a month of their invasion, that the despised Russians with their disorganised army were in fact a formidable and possibly a fatal opponent.

For many years the Soviet authorities made little of the Battle of Moscow. Leningrad, Stalingrad, Odessa, Sevastopol, were honoured as 'Hero Cities' almost as soon as the war was over. For Stalin the Battle of Moscow was associated with the catastrophes of the first six months, his own misjudgements, and above all with the shameful panic in October. He saw no reason to magnify a victory which the rest of the world associated with Zhukov. Moscow had to wait until 1965 to become a 'Hero City'. The Museum of the Defence of Moscow was created only in 1995.

As the victorious Russian soldiers burst at last into the territory of their hated enemy, they were overwhelmed by bitter memories of what the Germans had done to their homes and families. For four appalling years they had been told that their highest duty was to kill Nazis. They exploded into a vengeful fury of rape, murder, and pillage whose scale and motivation is still disputed by historians. Rokossovski and other generals did something to restrain their men. For Stalin the mayhem was politically inconvenient, and he ordered it to cease. Ilya Ehrenburg was told to stop his passionately anti-German writings. Many of the perpetrators themselves soon felt ashamed of what they had done.[1]

Once Berlin had fallen and the guns had stopped firing, both the Western Allies and the Russians set out to consolidate their political grip on the bits of Germany they occupied. From the highest to the lowest, the soldiers of the victorious armies expended much ingenuity in looting their defeated enemy for their own private advantage. But for the Russians it was also a matter of policy. They stripped Eastern Germany systematically of raw materials, industrial equipment, works of art, and even food. None doubted that this was no more than a minimal recompense for the damage that the Germans had done to their own shattered and starving country.

After bringing Lenin's body back to Moscow from Siberia in March, Ilya Zbarski and his colleague Sergei Mardashëv were put into uniform, sent off to Berlin, given a car and a pistol, and told to search laboratories in the Western districts of Berlin for materials or instruments that might be useful for the great man's further preservation.[2] They got together enough to fill a railway wagon, though much of the equipment was so badly packed that it was ruined in transit. Zbarski also had a brief affair with a young German girl, Helga, whom he picked up in one of Berlin's parks. She had been raped by a Soviet soldier, and her fiancé from Dresden had disappeared.[3] She lived with her French mother at the other end of the city from Zbarski's barracks at Karlshorst, so he occasionally stayed overnight at her place. They used to discuss literature and when she told him what life was like in Nazi Germany, Zbarski was struck by the similarities between Hitler's regime and Stalin's. One evening they were stopped in the streets by a Soviet patrol, and Zbarski was told off for consorting with a German. When he left Berlin later in the year, he took back to Moscow a radio which he had 'liberated' in Berlin: needless to say, the radio confiscated from him in June 1941 was never returned.[4] Helga gave him her photo, with a poem on the back in German. He kept it religiously for years. But a photo from a German could have been used against him during Stalin's anti-Jewish terror in 1952. He destroyed the photo, and never saw Helga again.

Now hordes of soldiers, liberated prisoners of war, women who had been deported to Germany as slave labourers, all began to find their way back to their ruined homeland by whatever means they could, an Exodus like the one Vasili Grossman had witnessed outside Orël in October 1941, but this time an Exodus full of hope. Primo Levi, just liberated from Auschwitz, watched

> the extraordinary spectacle of the Red Army returning home; a spectacle as stately and solemn as a biblical migration, as colourful and vagabond as a troupe of strolling acrobats. Trains stopped at Katowice, interminably long, made up of goods trucks equipped to travel for months on end, perhaps as far as the Pacific, full to overflowing with thousands of soldiers and civilians, men and women, Russian ex-prisoners, Germans now prisoners themselves; and goods, furniture, animals, dismantled machine tools, provisions, military material, rubbish of all kinds. They were like whole villages on the move. Some wagons seemed to contain entire families, one or two double beds, a wardrobe with a mirror, a stove, a radio, chairs and tables. Electric wires were strung between one wagon and the next, carrying power from a generator at the front of the train; the wires gave light for illumination, and at the same time served to hang the washing out to dry (and to get dirty again from the soot). When the sliding doors opened in the morning, the sleepy broad faces of half-dressed men and women appeared from the depths of these domestic establishments. Bemused, unable to grasp where they were, they looked about them, then got down to wash themselves in the freezing water from the hydrants, and passed round tobacco and pages of *Pravda* in which to roll their cigarettes.[5]

By December 1953 five and a half million people had returned to the USSR.[6]

Among those who returned to the capital was Anatoli Chernyaev, who had finished the war outside Riga in Latvia. He went back to the

History Faculty of Moscow University, wrote a doctorate on the British Trade Union Movement, became a member of the International Department of the Central Committee Secretariat, and ended his career as Gorbachëv's foreign policy adviser.

Yevgeni Anufriev and Vladimir Frolov completed their move from the countryside to the city, and became professors at Moscow University. Semën Aria moved to Moscow after the war, studied law, and in 2003 was still practising at the age of eighty-one.

Pavel Gudz became a general, specialised in the handling of armour on the nuclear battlefield, and took part in the controversial nuclear test at the Totsk range in the South Urals Military District in September 1954 which exposed large numbers of soldiers to radiation and left many of them seriously ill. Yevgeni Ogryzko and Yevgeni Teleguev remained in the armed forces of the NKVD. They too became generals.

Irina Golyamina, Daniel Mitlyanski's classmate, was still working as a physicist in an institute for acoustical research at the age of eighty. Lidia Robel and Klavdia Leonova stayed for the rest of their working lives at the Trëkhgorka. The factory was still going strong at the end of the century, and as Russia became more prosperous it opened a shop to sell its more elegant products to the women from the new middle class.

Vladimir Zeldin, whose career took off with *The Swinemaiden and the Shepherd*, and Lidia Smirnova, the star of Simonov's *A Boy from Our Town*, continued to act into deep old age. Smirnova had to give up in her eighties, when she was incapacitated by an accident on the set. But she was still defiantly lively and elegant, still full of gossip about the past, still mourning the child she never had, when she and Zeldin were personally awarded the Order for Services to the Fatherland by President Putin in the Kremlin in February 2005 on the occasion of their ninetieth birthdays. Valentina Serova parted from Simonov, took to drink, and died in misery.

Nadezhda Popova was demobilised from the air force with the rank of major in 1942, and thereafter devoted herself to public work and raising her family. Rufina Gasheva married Mikhail Pliats, a bomber pilot, while she was still at the front. She was demobilised in 1956, taught English at the Academy of the Armoured Forces, worked for a while in the military publishing house, and retired in 1972.[7]

Antonina Savina gave up sewing and went back to work in the X-ray department of the 'Misericordia' Hospital. She did not move out of her cellar and into a small but comfortable modern apartment in the Moscow suburbs until she retired in 1970. She furnished her new home with the alimony from her divorce, and was sufficiently careful with her money to be able to support her son when he lost his job at the Praga Restaurant in the Arbat after it was sold off to a commercial firm in the 1990s. In her old age she continued to believe that she had been better off under Stalin.

Vladimir Kantovski was rearrested at the end of the war and sent off to the camps once again. He did not get back to Moscow until 1956. He then worked until retirement in a scientific institute, and from the 1980s as a member of the Memorial Society, helping to track the fate of those who had suffered under Stalin. Twenty-five years after the end of the war he too was given the Order of the Red Star for his part in his one battle.

Mikhail Nemirovski was also arrested after the war and sent to a camp. His wife Polina was thrown out of her job. For five years she took one menial position after another to keep body and soul together. Nemirovski was released under Khrushchëv's amnesty in 1957. But camp life had drained him of his energy and his career was shattered. He and Polina no longer believed in the promise of Communism. In his last years, increasingly taciturn, he became a regular churchgoer.[8]

Alexander Tvardovski, the author of *Vasili Tërkin*, became a distinguished and liberal editor of the literary journal *Novy Mir* and a champion of Solzhenitsyn and other unorthodox Soviet writers. But he was driven to drink and to an early grave by the strain of defending his journal against the mounting hostility of the authorities and by the burden of a secret which he nursed throughout his career: his whole family had been deported as kulaks and sent in cattle trucks to the Urals.[9] By the time they returned, in the last years of Soviet power, Tvardovski was already dead.

Shcherbakov did not survive the war. Grossly overworked, grossly overweight and increasingly sick, his heart gave out on 9 May 1945, Victory Day. He was buried in the Kremlin wall.

As for the city itself, Stalin left his stamp on it one last time just before he died: seven massive skyscrapers, an indelible mark of the old dictator's taste. They stand in yet another ring around the city, matching the ancient monasteries, as if they were the latest in Moscow's successive systems of concentric defence. In these immense buildings, built in the mid-1950s by convicts and German prisoners of war, Stalin's architects achieved a grotesque style which relates in feeling directly to that other symbol of authoritarian rule, Ivan the Terrible's Church of St Basil on Red Square. Like Ivan's church, the skyscrapers have become symbols of a city like no other.

Stalin's vision of a Socialist Moscow was never realised. Other plans were devised by his successors. They lacked the vaunting ambition of the 1935 Plan. But they continued the devastation of the old city. Many landmarks were replaced with the utilitarian apartment and office blocks of the 1960s and the cold and shoddy monumentalism of the 1970s. What was left of pre-revolutionary Moscow decayed quietly for nearly eight decades, until the trend was energetically reversed under the leadership of Yuri Luzhkov, Moscow's last mayor of the twentieth century, who did more than anyone to restore to Moscow its role as one of the world's great capital cities. Those of delicate sensibility find it hard to stomach many of the changes which have taken place under his aegis: the garish office blocks and apartment buildings which have sprung up at random to challenge Stalin's skyscrapers; the monument to Peter the Great, which rivals the Colossus of Rhodes in size, but not in elegance; the transformation of the Manege Square next to the Kremlin into a kitsch theme park of Russian folklore; perhaps above all the rebuilding of that ancient eyesore, the Cathedral of Christ the Saviour, which now once again glares down on the House on the Embankment on the other side of the river. But it was Luzhkov who restored whole areas of the city round the Arbat, in the Kitaigorod, across the river from the Kremlin. He regilded the domes of the churches. Where the churches no longer existed he rebuilt them from scratch. Inside the Garden Ring and along the Boulevard Ring, Moscow began to look much as it had done before 1914. In the end, the destruction of nineteenth-century Moscow was no greater, and may even be less, than the destruction of nineteenth-century London. What politics achieved in the one city, Hitler's Blitz achieved in the other. Rampant capitalism now shapes them both.

In the years that remained to him after the war, Stalin had four main problems to tackle. He had to consolidate his grip on Eastern Germany and Eastern Europe. He had to ensure that the Soviet Union remained capable of defending itself against America, and after Hiroshima this meant acquiring nuclear weapons as rapidly as possible. He had to rebuild the economy. And he had to deal firmly with the subversive yearning for political change.

Stalin was obsessed by the possibility that history would repeat itself, that the virus of enlightenment would be brought back from Europe by the soldiers of the victorious Red Army as it had been by the soldiers who beat Napoleon. What he heard from his secret policemen gave him no comfort at all. Disaffection persisted even after the Russians had seen just what the Germans were capable of doing to their country and their people, and even when the tide of war had turned.

In 1943 and 1944 the NKVD reported the unsettling views of a number of writers and journalists, some of them national figures. The themes were those that had preoccupied the peasants ten years earlier: the abolition of the collective farms and the possibility of a change in the regime. One journalist who was also a Party member remarked: 'The Russian peasant in the occupied areas is in two minds. On the one hand, he doesn't want the Germans to stay in Russia. On the other, he doesn't want the return of Soviet power with its collective farms and its insupportable demands for deliveries of farm produce. Our government should have liquidated the collective farms at the beginning of the war. If the peasants had believed that the change was serious and long term, they would really have gone out to fight the Germans. At present they fight unwillingly, because they are made to – and they are after all the mainstay of the army, on whom all else depends.' One writer looked forward to 'liberation from twenty-five years of slavery'. Others persuaded themselves that the Western Allies would impose change, whether the regime liked it or not: a surprising conclusion for sophisticated people. Kornei Chukovski, in public a comparatively loyal supporter of the system who was awarded the Lenin Prize in 1962, argued that there was no essential difference between the despotism of Hitler and the despotism of Stalin: the theme of Vasili Grossman's novel about the war, *Life and Fate*, banned in Russia until the Gorbachëv years. One writer, the NKVD reported, had even predicted that a popular general – Zhukov or Rokossovski – would return from the war and overthrow the regime.[10] It is difficult to imagine anything more likely to inflame Stalin's paranoia.

Stalin was determined to repress all hope that victory would bring relaxation. It was not too difficult to deal with the lesser people. Most of those who had borne arms against their fellow Russians were sent to the camps and some, including General Vlasov, were executed. The Germans had taken over four million Soviet prisoners in the course of the war. Only two-fifths of them survived to return home.[11] But many even of these were sent to labour camps. The millions of returning civilian forced labourers were treated little better. Those who fell into none of these categories suffered almost as much. The gigantic task of simultaneously rebuilding and rearming the country left no time or energy for political relaxation. Famine struck once again in the countryside. Most people were simply struggling to survive.

The generals were a harder nut to crack. Zhukov and Rokossovski, the architects of victory, were heroes to their soldiers and to the people at large. Stalin bided his time. He gave both men the honour of conducting the Victory Parade on Red Square on 24 June 1945. He then began a slow and painstaking campaign to cut them down to size.

Zhukov had stayed on in the Soviet Zone of Germany as its military commander. He was recalled from Berlin in March 1946, and at a meeting of the Supreme Military Council Stalin accused him of hogging the credit of victory and harbouring political ambitions beyond his station. This charge of Bonapartism, one of the most heinous crimes in the Bolshevik catalogue, was a very serious charge indeed. Zhukov was sent off to command ever more distant Military Districts and relieved of his title as Candidate Member of the Central Committee.[12]

He was accused in parallel of having used his position in Germany to pile up loot on an improbable scale. The NKVD found (or claimed to have found) gold, silver, diamonds, furs, rolls of cloth, carpets, eight accordions and several expensive English hunting rifles in his dacha.[13] He was formally rebuked for giving his friend, the singer Lidia Ruslanova, the Order of the Patriotic War First Class in the (possibly drunken) margins of a military parade in Berlin.[14] Lidia Ruslanova and her husband General Kriukov were arrested for corruption. Ruslanova pleaded that she was no richer than other Soviet stars, but it did her no good. Both she and Kriukov were sent to prison.[15] The corruption charges were kept hanging over Zhukov's head, but no further proceedings were taken against him, and after a couple of years Stalin allowed him to creep back from disgrace. Under Khrushchëv, Zhukov rose again. Once again the politicians decided he was getting too big for his boots, and he was sacked, this time for good.[16] He died in 1974.

Stalin was more subtle in his handling of Rokossovski. By an irony of fate, Rokossovski's sister Helena was trapped in Warsaw during the rising against the Germans in the autumn of 1944, while he was commanding the 1st Belorussian Front, which had halted on the other side of the Vistula. After Warsaw was liberated, Helena found her way to the brother she had not seen since 1915. He took her with him to Berlin, she attended the Victory Parade in Moscow in 1945, and she was introduced to Stalin.[17] These Polish connections may have suggested to Stalin a convenient way of neutralising any political attraction Rokossovski might have in Russia. In October 1949 he sent him into honourable exile in Warsaw as Minister of Defence and Commander of the Polish Armed Forces. It was of course a poisoned chalice. Rokossovski was expected to clamp the Soviet will on the Soviet Union's most troublesome satellite. Soviet 'advisers' were distributed throughout the Polish armed forces. Rokossovski did a good deal to reorganise the army and to improve the lot of the officers and men themselves. But he had little choice but to acquiesce, however reluctantly, in the execution of Polish officers suspected of Western connections in 1951. In 1956 the Poles came to the brink of armed defiance. Khrushchëv managed to strike a deal. The Soviet advisers were sent home. Rokossovski went with them. As he left Warsaw, he remarked sadly to a Polish colleague, General Cymbarewicz, 'The Russians regard me as a Pole, and the Poles regard me as a Russian.'[18] To General Jaruzelski, at that time his successor as Polish Defence Minister, he later said, 'I was, am, and always will be a Pole.'[19]

Helena attended Rokossovski's funeral in Moscow in 1968, died in 1983 and is buried with her father Ksawery and her uncle Roman Wysocki in a family vault in Brudno in Praga, a suburb of Warsaw.[20] Rokossovski's apartment in the prestigious building on Granovski Street, where he and so many of Stalin's other marshals and political colleagues had lived, was sold to an anonymous middle-aged couple in the autumn of 2003 for one and a half million dollars.

In the year 2004 the municipal authorities of the Polish seaport of Gdańsk stripped Rokossovski posthumously of his honorary citizenship of their town.[21]

While Stalin was still alive, it was impossible for Russians even to attempt to write serious history. All was flattery and myth until Khrushchëv made it fashionable to criticise the old dictator. The generals then began to write their memoirs. These accounts too were skewed. As the politics varied, so did the historiography. Successive editions of the generals' memoirs were modified by the historians in the Ministry of Defence to reflect the currently orthodox line.

The myth of the 'surprise attack' remained unchallenged for many years. This was not entirely surprising. The responsibility for the catastrophe on the frontier did not, after all, belong to Stalin alone. Generals and politicians still in power had failed in their professional duty to persuade the dictator to change his mind, and they were determined that the matter should not be reopened. In 1966 the historian Alexander Nekrich published a well-documented book, *22 June 1941*, which established the extent of their foreknowledge of the German attack, and their failure to act upon it. The book was banned. Nekrich was asked, 'What do you think is more important, political expediency or historical truth?' He gave the wrong answer, and was thrown out of the Party.[22]

In the late 1970s another thought began to establish itself, especially in military circles. The undisputed architect of the victory was not Stalin, but Marshal Zhukov, 'the general who had never suffered defeat'. In a stream of films and admiring books, the Marshal began to acquire the status of a national icon.

All these hallowed truths were disputed in the atmosphere of free debate which followed Gorbachëv's reforms. Hitherto secret documents were released in ever-greater numbers. Russian historians began to ask just those questions which quite ordinary people had asked in Moscow on the first day of the war. Why had Stalin failed to foresee the German attack? Was he himself perhaps preparing to attack when Hitler stole a march on him? Why did the Red Army perform so badly in the first days and months of the war, despite the huge sacrifices which the people had made to give it the best equipment in the world? Could Hitler have captured Moscow and won the war if he had not sent Guderian South into the Ukraine? Could, above all, the Victory have been won without such an appalling expenditure of blood? Were the millions of casualties – many, many times what the German enemy had suffered – the consequence of German efficiency or Soviet ruthlessness, brutality, and incompetence? Both in Russia and in the West people began to experiment enthusiastically with counterfactual history, to the fury of the orthodox and the elderly, who increasingly resented the attempts of intellectuals and liberal politicians to revise the history of the war, and saw them as a shameful slur on the glory of the Victory.

Above all, people asked why the Soviet people fought with such courage and at such a price in blood for a regime which had imposed such hardships on them in the years between the wars, when an inadvertent word or incautious action could lead to the loss of job, liberty, or life itself. Were they driven by patriotism or by fear of retribution from their own side? The writer Mikhail Prishvin posed the question in the summer of 1943, while the fighting was still going on: 'The people don't want war, they are dissatisfied with the system, but as soon as they get to the front they fight bravely without thought of themselves [...] I am wholly unable to understand this phenomenon.'[23]

There was an obvious contrast with what had happened in France in 1940. The distinguished historian Marc Bloch tried to analyse the reasons for the débâcle in France in his book *Strange Defeat*. The central reason for the French collapse, he believed, was that France's 'governors, both individually and as a class, did lack something of that ruthless heroism which becomes so necessary when the country is in danger'.[24] In a paroxysm of what Bloch called 'this timidity of the nation at large',[25] the French government declared that it would not defend cities of more than twenty thousand inhabitants, in the hope that the Germans would spare them from bombardment.

There was rarely any doubt of Stalin's heroic ruthlessness, or of the ability of the Party machine to impose his will at all levels. Stalin was personally, directly and inescapably responsible for the disasters which rained down on his country in the first year of the war. No amount of subsequent whitewashing by Russians nostalgic for the past can alter that record. And yet the army's subsequent recovery, its willingness to fight in encirclement, to retreat without breaking, to hold its ground and to counterattack were due in no small measure to Stalin's ruthless willpower. He may occasionally have despaired – in the hours and days after the German attack, and at the most dramatic moment of their approach to Moscow. He toyed once or twice with the possibility of a separate peace with Hitler. But on the whole he did not waver. He drove his commanders in the most brutal fashion. They knew that the penalty for failure might well be disgrace and death for themselves and perhaps for their families as well. Yet the toughest of them bore up under almost intolerable psychological pressure. As they learned their jobs – at the expense of their men, for most of them were as ruthless as their boss – Stalin came to trust them and to bow to their military judgement. By the end of 1942 he and they were working almost as a team – though no one ever dared to doubt who was ultimately in charge.

Nor, despite the doubts of the Moscow intellectuals, was there much timidity among the Russian people at large. There was cowardice, treachery, and confusion, and a bloody discipline ruthlessly applied. But the soldiers on the frontier and the volunteers in Moscow did not fight because they were driven to it by the NKVD. They fought heroically in actions unremarked by those who hand out the medals. For many of them the outbreak of war, however terrible, was a kind of relief. Andrei Sakharov's Aunt Valya, still mourning her husband murdered by the Bolsheviks, said, 'For the first time in years I feel that I am Russian.'[26] Tvardovski's Vasili Tërkin talks only of fighting for his comrades, for Russia, and for the Russian land. People were not always able to put their patriotism into convincing or measured words. So they drew on the heroic epics of the past, the heroes of their earlier wars against Tatars, Turks, Poles, Swedes, Frenchmen. They drew on the faith of the Orthodox, the passionate link which even agnostic Russians still feel between their nation and their religion, between themselves and their ancestors. They fought whatever their reservations about Stalin and his system. They fought with a stoicism and stamina forged, as Konstantin Simonov hinted, amidst the privation, the ordeal, and the struggle of their pre-war lives, and matched only by the disciplined ferocity of their enemies.

Stalin himself understood well enough that the people were fighting for Russia, not for the regime, as he told the American ambassador in 1941.[27] At the end of it all, what mattered to them most was that they had fought and won the greatest war in history. They had liberated Europe and planted the Red Flag in the heart of the enemy's capital. That seemed, in itself, a justification for all the sufferings, the purges, the murderous discipline, the unbearable losses in battle.

Every returning soldier was invited by Mikhail Nemirovski and his colleagues in the city administration to plant an apple tree where the Mozhaisk Highway entered Moscow.[28] A vast orchard grew up along both sides of the road down which so many invaders had passed over the centuries, around the hut in which Kutuzov took his fateful decision to abandon the city to Napoleon, and on the shallow hill, the Poklonnaya Gora, where Napoleon waited in vain to receive the homage of the City Fathers.

The trees flowered every spring, but the pain lived on. Every year, in the courtyard of School No. 110, the veterans and the schoolchildren would gather around Daniel Mitlyanski's statue *Requiem* to honour with flowers and speeches the hundred or more pupils who never returned from the war. The statue depicted five young soldiers, five boys whose letters and pictures were kept by Irina Golyamina so that they would live on in the memories of those who had known them: Igor Bogushevski, who was killed in the Moscow *opolchenie* of 1941; Grisha Rodin, who was killed in March 1942; Gabor Raab, Irina's last letter to whom was returned in March 1945 marked 'Addressee has left for an unknown destination'; Igor Kuptsov, who was killed in Berlin at the very end of the war.

Yuri Danilkovski was the youngest of the five, intelligent, intense and poetical. He was called up in May 1942, and killed in Western Ukraine in March 1944. Irina Golyamina preserved the *Testament* which he composed for his friends two years almost to the day before his death. It is full of passionate patriotism, of doubts about the Party line, of fear that his generation could not measure up to the revolutionary ideals of their parents, the confused and powerful emotions of a sceptical but ardent adolescent who believed that a brave new world would after all be built by those who survived the war.

'Respect what is human in everyone, seek it out and create it,' Yuri ended his *Testament*. 'The true citizen of the future is he who is free from prejudice and convention, who does not fear for himself and does not fear the misunderstanding of others, who places above all else in life the marvellous emotion of love and the happiness of untrammelled creativity. That is the humanity for which I died.'

As new generations arose, the memory of the war began to grow dim. New buildings ate their way into the orchards on the Mozhaisk Highway. People stopped reading Simonov and Tvardovski.[29] For the children at School No. 110, the annual ceremonies of remembrance began to seem increasingly pointless. Mitlyanski's *Requiem* was vandalised, and had to be removed from the courtyard to a precarious place of safety over the entrance to the school. The band of those who could recollect that bolt from out of a clear June sky began to fade away. Those who remained settled into a pattern of nostalgia: they remembered fire-watching on the roof, the sticky paper criss-crossing windows to protect them from blast, the barrage balloons in the sky, the steel hedgehogs barricading the streets, the tens of thousands of women digging the trenches, the hardship of the evacuation, the hunger and the fear. More than the martyrdom of Zoya Kosmodemyanskaya or the heroic legend of the twenty-eight Panfilov men who stopped the German tanks on the Volokolamsk Highway, they remembered the understated heroism of the peasant soldiers, people like Vasili Tërkin and Alyosha Skvortsov, people like themselves. And they knew the price of victory only too well. The guns had barely fallen silent before they began to sing – secretly at first, for the sentiment was subversive – the bitter song of the soldier, victorious and bemedalled, who returns to a home in ashes and a murdered wife, and drinks himself unconscious on her grave.[30]

For many of the people of Moscow the war years remained the most intense, the best, of their lives. To some the Victory became the only enduring monument to their otherwise wasted existence. 'I envy my friends who died in the war,' wrote one elderly woman as the Soviet Union fell about her ears in the autumn of 1991. 'I envy the fact that they left this life without having lost their faith, without becoming disillusioned.'[31] As Marina Ladynina, the star of *The Swinemaiden and the Shepherd* and *Six o'clock after the War*, put it at the end of her long life, 'The conditions were unbelievably bad, but no one ever complained, we were all in it together. We all believed in victory, we believed in one another, we never felt that bitterness and – alas – that loneliness one can feel today.'[32]

NOTES

New Year 1941

1 K. Simonov, *Zhivye i Mërtvye* (Moscow, 2004), p. 27. Simonov's novel about the first months of the war is not called *The Living and the Dead* for nothing. For him it is the dead, as well as the living, who share the glory of the victory. The phrase crops up elsewhere too, for example in *War and Peace*, where Tolstoy speaks of '... the line dividing the living from the dead [beyond which] lies uncertainty, suffering and death' ((Everyman edition, London, 1991), Vol. I, p. 178). My attention was drawn to this reference by Nina Tumarkin, who uses it as the epigraph to *The Living and the Dead* (New York, 1994). But there is an echo of the Bible too: 'I charge thee therefore before God, and the Lord Jesus Christ, who shall judge *the living and the dead* at his appearing and his kingdom' (Timothy 2, 4:1). In the King James version the phrase is translated 'the quick and the dead'.

2 Grandfather Frost can also be seen in a white or a blue robe.

3 On 20 December 1939 President Kalinin issued an Ukaz appointing Stalin Hero of Socialist Labour and describing him in these terms (quoted in M. Chegodaeva, *Dva Lika Vremeni: 1939 Odin God Stalinskoi Epokhy* (Moscow, 2001), p. 156).

4 G. Andreevski, *Zhizn Moskvy v stalinskuyu epokhu 1930–1940e gody* (Moscow, 2003), p. 9; L. Ivanits, *Russian Folk Belief* (Armonk, NY, 1992).

Chapter 1: The Shaping of the City

1 All figures for casualties in the fighting on the Eastern front in the Second World War, and even for the numbers involved on the two sides, need to be treated with circumspection. G. Krivosheev (ed.), *Rossia i SSSR v Voinakh XX*

Veka: Statisticheskoe Issledovanie (Moscow, 2001), gives figures for Russian losses of 926,244 dead and 897,879 wounded for the Battle of Moscow from 30 September 1941 to 20 April 1942 (pp. 273, 276, 277). The figures comparing the Battle of Moscow with other great battles of the war in the East combine information from Mikhail Myagkov (Kulkov et al., *Voina*) and Boris Nevzorov (see the latter's *Moskovskaya Bitva – Fenomen vtoroi mirovoi* (Moscow, 2001), p. 12). The official figure for British dead in the First World War is 744,702 (written answer in *Hansard*, 5 May 1921). British soldiers killed in the Second World War numbered 264,443; total British dead, including civilians, was 357,116 (W. Mellor (ed.), *Casualties and Medical Statistics* (London, 1972), pp. 829–39). The US Department of Defense gives a figure of 53,402 for battle deaths and 63,114 for 'other deaths' in the First World War. The figures for the Second World War are 292,000 battle casualties and 115,187 for 'other deaths' (DoD historical note at web1.whs.osd.mil/mmid/casualty/WCPRINCIPAL.pdf).

2 See, for example, the pallid reproductions in *Russian Landscape*, the catalogue of the National Gallery's exhibition *Russian Landscape in the Age of Tolstoy* (London, 2004).

3 C. Duffy, *Borodino and the War of 1812* (London, 1999), p. 59.

4 The population of greater London was about 50,000 in the middle of the sixteenth century: see Joseph P. Ward of the University of Mississippi (www.the-orb.net/encyclop/culture/urban/emessay). For Russian figures, see I. Gavrilova, *Naselenie Moskvy: Istoricheski Rakurs* (Moscow, 2001), p. 23; R.Hakluyt, *Voyages in Eight Volumes* (London, 1967), Vol. 1, p. 255. At fifteen feet, the Kremlin walls are quite close to what Chancellor was told.

5 The French observer seems to have been fooled by the stucco façades (quoted in K. Berton, *Moscow: An Architectural History* (New York, 1977), p. 150).

6 Quoted ibid.

7 Ibid., p. 152.

8 A. Palmer, *Napoleon in Russia* (London, 1967), p. 181.

9 Polenov's painting of a courtyard in the Arbat in 1902, almost in the centre of the city, shows a scene that you could find in almost any village in the Moscow region. See also C. Merridale, *Moscow Politics and the Rise of Stalin: The Communist Party in the Capital, 1925–32* (London, 1990), p. 11.

10 Berton, *Moscow*, p. 109.

11 B. Ruble, *Second Metropolis* (Washington, DC, 2001), p. 93.

12 P. Terentiev (ed.), *Prokhorovy* (reprinted Moscow, 1996).

13 T. Colton, *Moscow: Governing the Socialist Metropolis* (London, 1995), pp. 34–6.

14 Ibid., p. 47.

15 Ruble, *Second Metropolis*, p. 110, 175.

16 M. Baring, *What I Saw in Russia* (London, 1927), pp. 20–21. A provincial school-master confirmed to Baring that *Paradise Lost* was the most popular book in his village library, and at a fair at Moscow during Passion Week Baring found five

or six different translations of the poem. While he was looking at one of them a peasant came up and advised him to buy it. 'It's very interesting,' he said. 'It makes one laugh and cry.'

17 L. Tolstoy, *War and Peace* (Everyman edition, London, 1991), Vol. II, p. 404.

18 Blok's poem *The Twelve* ends with the image of Christ come to judge a chaotic and sinful world in wrath, leading the Red Guards through the torn streets of revolutionary Petrograd in January 1918. I am indebted to John Garrard for drawing my attention to his article '*The Twelve: Blok's* Apocalypse', *Religion and Literature*, No. 35(1), Spring, 2003, pp. 45–66; the text of the poem is in A. Blok, *Sobranie Sochinenii* (Moscow, 1960), Vol. 3, p. 347. See also J. Billington, *The Icon and the Axe* (London, 1966), p. 504.

19 Moscow City Archive, Fond P-425, Inventarnaya Opis 4.

20 R. Pipes, *The Russian Revolution 1899–1919* (London, 1990), p. 50.

21 B. Lincoln, *Armageddon* (Oxford, 1994), pp. 468–71.

22 K. Paustovski, *Povest o zhizni* (Moscow, 1965), Vol. I, pp. 659 et seq.

23 Pipes, *The Russian Revolution 1899–1919*, p. 595

Chapter 2: Forging Utopia

1 I have used 'Region' throughout to indicate the Soviet administrative division of the 'Oblast'.

2 N. Aleshchenko, *Moskovski Soviet v 1917–1941 gg.* (Moscow, 1976), p. 157.

3 Ibid., p. 146.

4 T. Colton, *Moscow: Governing the Socialist Metropolis* (London, 1995), p. 214.

5 Vladislav Mikosha, interview, 3 February 2002; Yu. Zakrevski, *Nashe Rodnoe Kino* (Moscow, 2004), p. 119.

6 Colton, *Moscow*, p. 270.

7 N. Khrushchev, *Khrushchev Remembers* (London, 1971), p. 62.

8 Valentin Bolotov, interview, 17 February 2003.

9 Colton, *Moscow*, p. 121.

10 Article 'Dom na Naberezhnoi' (museumdom.narod.ru/hist); E. Stevens (ed.), *Guide to the City of Moscow* (Moscow, 1937), p. 205.

11 A. Sakharov, *Memoirs* (London, 1990), pp. 9–11.

12 Sara Litvin, interview, 9 October 2004.

13 A. Chernyaev, *Moya Zhizn i Moë Vremya* (Moscow, 1995), pp. 5–7.

14 In 1933 Stalin said it was mere demagoguery to suggest that basement housing could be eliminated by 1945 (Colton, *Moscow*, p. 344).

15 S. Fitzpatrick, *Everyday Stalinism: Ordinary Life in Extraordinary Times – Soviet Russia in the 1930s* (New York, 1999), pp. 46–50.

16 Ibid., p. 41.

17 J. Brooks, *Thank You, Comrade Stalin!* (Princeton, 2000), p. 53.

18 Colton, *Moscow*, p. 206.

19 This passage draws heavily on Sheila Fitzpatrick's fascinating account of the views of the Russian peasantry between the wars, based on police reports, the rumours that circulated among the peasantry at the time and the letters of complaint which the peasants themselves wrote to the authorities (*Stalin's Peasants: Resistance and Survival in the Russian Village after Collectivization* (Oxford, 1994). See also L. Viola, 'The Peasant Nightmare: Visions of Apocalypse in the Soviet Countryside', *Journal of Modern History*, 62 (4), 1990, pp. 747–70. In *War and Peace* Tolstoy describes the unrest among the peasants as the French approach (Everyman edition, London, 1991), Vol. II, pp. 404 et seq.). On the views of the intelligentsia in 1943 and 1944, see A. Artizov and O. Naumov (eds.), *Vlast i Khudozhestvennaya Intelligentsia (Dokumenty 1917–1953)* (Moscow, 2002), pp. 492, 552.

20 A. Zamoyski, *1812: Napoleon's Final March on Moscow* (London, 2004), p. 201.

21 C. Merridale, *Moscow Politics and the Rise of Stalin: The Communist Party in the Capital, 1925–32* (London, 1990), p. 14.

22 Zinoviev gave a perversely contrarian interview to George Urban in *Encounter*, XII(4), April 1984. Though a dissident and a philosopher of history, he argued that the Soviet system had many merits, and that the Communist system would eventually prevail throughout the world. The passage quoted is on p. 21.

23 Antonina Naumova (née Savina), interview, 11 February 2003.

24 He was speaking to a meeting of farm machinery drivers (quoted in Fitzpatrick, *Everyday Stalinism*, p. 90).

25 Because the present school resulted from an amalgamation of School No. 100 and School No. 110, both names are occasionally used. I have stuck to the present-day name.

26 The list is kept in the Museum of School No. 110.

27 Irina Golyamina, interview, 9 December 2004.

28 Vladimir Kantovski, interview, 1 June 2002.

29 Vladimir Kantovski found the originals of his letters in the KGB archives in the 1990s and made copies.

30 M. Chegodaeva, *Dva Lika Vremeni: 1939 Odin God Stalinskoi Epokhy* (Moscow, 2001) p. 160.

31 Ibid., p. 159.

32 Biographical note at www.sovlit.com/bios/fadeev.

33 Grossman describes the dispiriting and humiliating workings of the Soviet system of control with particular insight. This passage is taken from Chapter 40 of *Life and Fate*, which is worth reading in full (*Zhizn i Sudba* (Moscow, 2004), pp. 526–8.

34 Aleksei Simonov, interview, 17 February 2003. See also his article (under pseudonym 'Kirillov') at www.krugosvet.ru/articles/101/1010183/1010183a1. *Zhivye i Mërtvye* was republished in Moscow in 2004.

35 B. Pankin, *Chetyre Ya Konstantina Simonova* (Moscow, 1999), p. 453. This book is a 'Biography-Novel' by a man who was active as a literary bureaucrat in Simonov's later years, and knew him and his entourage well.

36 V. Safoshkov, *Lidia Ruslanova: Zhizn v Pesne* (Moscow, 2003), p. 43; R. Stites, *Russian Popular Culture: Entertainment and Society since 1900* (Cambridge, 1992), pp. 74, 5.

37 A. Govokhovski, in *Fakty i Kommentarii*, 5 March 2002 (www.brazd.ru/addon/guestbook).

38 Trotsky thought that films could take the place of vodka in the villages (P. Kenez, *Cinema and Soviet Society: From the Revolution to the Death of Stalin* (London, 2001), p. 78).

39 The atmosphere of intimacy at the top is well illustrated in S. Sebag Montefiore, *Stalin: The Court of the Red Tsar* (London, 2003).

40 I am indebted to Julian Graffy for this reference, which comes from Ginzburg's chapter, 'I zaodno s pravoporiadkom', in *Tynianovski sbornik: Treti tynianovskie chteniia* (Riga, 1988), pp. 218–30.

41 Maria Chegodaeva thinks that the Russians were able to cope with the conflicting pressures of Stalinism in part because it reflected their apocalyptic view of the world in general (*Dva Lika Vremeni*, p. 313).

42 Quoted in A. Goldberg, *Ilya Ehrenburg: Writing, Politics and the Art of Survival* (London, 1984), introduction by Eric de Mauny, p. 6. I have slightly modified the translation. People like Ehrenburg had the excuse that they had to adapt to an impossible situation which they could not avoid. The people who had no excuse were those Western intellectuals, like Leon Feuchtwanger and Bernard Shaw, who visited the Soviet Union briefly, abandoned their critical faculties, and came home arguing that the great purges of the 1930s were understandable and justified.

43 Interview with George Urban, *Encounter*, May 1984, p. 34.

44 R. Thurston, *Life and Terror in Stalin's Russia 1934–1941* (New Haven, 1996), p. 196.

Chapter 3: Wars and Rumours of Wars

1 K. Rokossovski, *Soldatski Dolg* (Moscow, 2002), p. 21.

2 M. Sadykiewicz, *My Opinion on Marshal K. Rokossovski* (MS, London, 2004).

3 The poll was published on 28 December 1999 by the news agency RIA Novosti.

4 F. Chuev, *Soldaty Imperii* (Moscow, 1998), pp. 334, 374.

5 Marshal Bagramyan in his memoirs, quoted in H. Shukman (ed.), *Stalin's Generals* (London, 1997), p. 179.

6 I. Ehrenburg, *Liudi, Gody, Zhizn: Sobranie sochinenii v deviati tomakh* (Moscow, 1962–7), Vol. 9, p. 332.

7 Dr Galina Talanova, who was with Rokossovski at the front throughout the war, told her daughter that Rokossovski always spoke quietly and courteously even in the most extreme crises (Nadezhda Rokossovskaya, interview, 6 December 2004).

8 Crayfish often seem to figure in Russian proverbs. The sense here is 'He'll give them what for!' From an NKVD report, quoted in M. Gorinov, 'Budni Osazhdennoi Stolitsy', *Otechestvennaya Istoria*, 3, 1996, p. 23.

9 Konstantin Vilievich Rokossovski (grandson), interview, 12 December 2003. K.V. Rokossovski served, like his grandfather, in the Soviet army. He does not speak Polish and has lost track of his Polish relatives, but he is a Catholic – unusual in Russia and part of his Polish inheritance.

10 The official Russian version has it that Rokossovski was born in the Russian city of Velikie Luki. However, in his personal file in the Ministry of Defence there are two different CVs written by Rokossovski himself. The first says he was born in Warsaw and dates from before the war. The identity card issued after his release from prison in 1940 also describes him as a Pole by nationality. The second says he was born in Velikie Luki, where his father worked on the railways. That would make him a Russian citizen by birth. After the war, this was a more convenient version for the Soviet authorities, and Rokossovski did not repudiate it in public. The foregoing information is from Rokossovski's grandson.

11 Letter of 11 November 2004 from Colonel Janusz Pruszkowicz.

12 Chuev, *Soldaty Imperii*, pp. 360–61.

13 K.V. Rokossovski kindly gave me a copy of the letter to Voroshilov from Commissar Shestakov of the Transbaikal Military District, No. 19/a of 5 June 1937.

14 In the post-Soviet film *Zavtra Byla Voina* (*Tomorrow There Was a War*, 1987) the central event is the refusal of a schoolgirl to denounce her father, with tragic consequences.

15 I. Cherushev, *Udar po Svoim: Krasnaya Armia 1938–1941* (Moscow, 2003), p. 430.

16 Stalin expressed these views at a meeting which Golovanov attended on the eve of the Battle of Kursk in July 1943 (Chuev, *Soldaty Imperii*, p. 342).

17 Ibid., p. 340.

18 O. Chaney, *Zhukov* (Newton Abbot, 1972), p. 16, quoting from a German military document captured in May 1943.

19 B. Sokolov, Georgi *Zhukov: Triumfy i Padenie* (Moscow, 2003), p. 68.

20 This is a general view, confirmed by Nadezhda Rokossovskaya, who saw him and his daughters together from time to time (interview, 6 December 2004).

21 This too is a general view, supported by many anecdotes. See also Sokolov, *Georgi Zhukov*, p. 113.

22 Rokossovski, *Soldatski Dolg*, p. 122.

23 S. Fitzpatrick, *Everyday Stalinism: Ordinary Life in Extraordinary Times – Soviet Russia in the 1930s* (New York, 1999), p. 107.

24 N. Shunevich, 'Chelovek i Obshchestvo', in *Fakty i Komentarii*, 16 April 2002 (www.brazd.ru/books/stat/o_smusheviche).

25 R. Pennington, *Wings, Women and War: Soviet Airwomen in World War II Combat* (Lawrence, KS, 2001), pp. 13–17.

26 It may never be possible to establish the exact number of people who died in the purges. There is a careful analysis of the problem in A. Getty and O. Naumov, *The Road to Terror: Stalin and the Self-Destruction of the Bolsheviks, 1932–1939* (New Haven, 1999), pp. 587–94. Over 900,000 people were probably arrested in 1937 and more than 600,000 in 1938, most of them for 'counter-revolutionary' crimes and 'anti-Soviet agitation'. Nearly 700,000 people were shot in 1937–8. Many more were killed without a hearing, or died under interrogation, in prison or in the camps. After Khrushchëv's 1956 attack on Stalin, official Soviet enquiries concluded that the courts handed out 781,692 death sentences in 1937–8. See also R. Thurston, *Life and Terror in Stalin's Russia 1934–1941* (New Haven, 1996), pp. 62–3.

27 Much of the material in this paragraph was collected by the Memorial Society, Moscow, and is published on their website: www.memo.ru/memory/communarka.

28 T. Colton, *Moscow: Governing the Socialist Metropolis* (London, 1995), pp. 288–91.

29 The BBC's documentary *Gulag* (2000) contains eyewitness accounts of the killings in the Butovo 'zone'.

30 D. Rayfield, *Stalin and His Hangmen: An Authoritative Account of a Tyrant and Those Who Served him* (London, 2004), p. 353.

31 What is known as the Katyn massacre took place in Katyn and two other places. Blokhin himself was at Mednoe, North of Moscow, where there is now a museum and a memorial to the murdered Poles. See also Viktor Lozinski, 'Mozaika Doma Nashego' (www.hro.org /editions/karta/nr1/ lozinsk); A.T. Rybin, 'Stalin Predvidel' (zero.thewalls.ru/htdocs/tirani/itog/st_predv).

32 R. Service, *Stalin* (London, 2004), p. 279.

33 Yakir and Uborevich were Army Commanders First Rank, roughly equivalent to a five-star general; Kork was an Army Commander Second Rank. The title 'General' was not introduced into the Red Army until May 1940.

34 Though much work has been done by historians, the figures for officers purged are still disputed. Distinctions are not always drawn between those executed, those imprisoned and those dismissed the service. It is often said that half of the officers corps – 35,000 officers out of 70,000 – fell victim to the purges. David Glantz quotes a figure of 50,000 officers 'liquidated' (D. Glantz, *Colossus Reborn: The Red Army at War 1941–1943*) (Kansas, 2005), p. 446). According to the significantly lower figures collated by Reese, about 22,705 officers were purged

in all out of a much higher figure for the total officer corps of 206,000: 9,506 were arrested, and of these an unknown number died in prison or were shot; about 13,000 other officers were dismissed the service for non-political offences. (R. Reese, *The Soviet Military Experience* (London, 2000), pp. 86–7).

35 D. Glantz and J. House, *When Titans Clashed: How the Red Army Stopped Hitler* (Edinburgh, 2000), p. 18.

36 N. Khrushchëv, *Khrushchev Remembers* (London, 1971), p. 152.

37 W. Trotter, *The Winter War: The Russo-Finnish War of 1939–40* (London, 2002), pp. 187–93.

38 H. Shukman (ed.), *Stalin and the Soviet-Finnish War 1939–40* (London, 2002), p. 274.

39 A. Boyd, *The Soviet Air Force since 1918* (London, 1977), p. 98 .

40 G. Glantz and House, *When Titans Clashed*, pp. 39–41.

41 G. Gorodetsky, *Grand Delusion: Stalin and the German Invasion of Russia* (New Haven, 1999), pp. 128–30.

42 Report of 15 April, No. 92,307 s.s. from A. Zaporozhets to Stalin and others (Volkogonov papers, Box 4, Folder R11541).

43 Glantz and House, *When Titans Clashed*, p. 38; the analysis is in Volkogonov papers, Box 4, Folder 11544.

44 Gorodetsky, *Grand Delusion*, p. 115.

45 Thurston, *Life and Terror in Stalin's Russia 1934–1941*, p. 204–5.

46 Gorodetsky, *Grand Delusion*, p. 134.

47 The first chapter of the Butler Report on British intelligence during the run-up to the Iraq war of 2003 – 'The Nature and Use of Intelligence' – is a brief and elegant account of the problem (Lord Butler (chairman), *Review of Intelligence on Weapons of Mass Destruction* (London, 2004), pp. 7–16.

48 War diary of British Military Mission in Moscow for 28 June 1941 (PRO WO178/25).

49 Gorodetsky, *Grand Delusion*, p. 55

50 V. Naumov (ed.), *1941 God: Dokumenty* (Moscow, 1998), p. 466 .

51 In his memoirs Churchill attaches a quite improbable degree of importance to this scrap of information about German troop movements in the Balkans (*The Grand Alliance* (Boston, 1950), p. 361). The Russians were in any case receiving numerous reports through their very well-placed spies in London. Golikov and his masters continued to regard information from British sources as a provocation. See for example D. Murphy, *What Stalin Knew: The Enigma of Barbarossa* (New Haven, 2005), p. 149.

52 Naumov (ed.), *1941 God*, Vol. 1, p. 776; and Gorodetsky, *Grand Delusion*, p. 136.

53 MI14 minute of 25 April 1941 (PRO WO190/893/54c).

54 JIC (41) 218 (PRO WO208/1761).

55 Timoshenko to Military Commanders of Okrugs and Commanders of Mechanised Corps, 14 June 1941 (Volkogonov papers, Box 4, Folder R10729).

56 There are a number of accounts of the speech. This one comes from V.A. Nevezhin, 'Tak chto skazal Stalin 5 maya 1941 g.?' (gpw.tellur.ru/p..html?r=eve&s=5may). Nevezhin cites a number of published and unpublished accounts of the speech by people who were present.

57 Gorodetsky, *Grand Delusion*, p. 208.

58 The idea that Stalin's aggressive plans were thwarted by an unexpectedly rapid German attack is put forward by Viktor Suvorov in *Icebreaker: Who Started the Second World War?* (London, 1990) and by Albert Weeks in *Stalin's Other War: Soviet Grand Strategy 1939–1941* (London, 2003). Alexander Werth's account of Stalin's 5 May speech to the cadets (*Russia at War 1941–1945*) (London, 1964), p. 123) seems to reinforce this interpretation: 'Depending on the international situation,' he reports Stalin as saying, 'the Red Army will either wait for a German attack, or it may have to take the initiative.' Constantine Pleshakov takes it for granted that Stalin was intending an attack, though he adduces no new evidence (*Stalin's Folly: The Secret History of the German Invasion of Russia, June 1941* (Boston, 2005), passim). The thesis is opposed by David Glantz (*Stumbling Colossus: The Red Army on the Eve of World War* (Kansas, 1998) and Gorodetsky. See also Glantz and House, *When Titans Clashed*, p. 41. The arguments are summarised with merciful brevity and massive common sense by John Erickson ('Barbarossa June 1941: Who Attacked Whom?', *History Today*, July 2001), who supports the orthodox interpretation.

59 I. Naumov (ed.), *1941 God*, Vol. 2, p. 383.

60 G. Zhukov, *Vospominania i Razmyshlenia* (Moscow, 2002), Vol. I, p. 258.

61 There is a translation of the communiqué in A. Werth, *Russia at War 1941–1945*, p. 125.

62 S. Stepashin (ed.), *Organy Gosudarstvennoi Bezopasnosti SSSR*, Vol. 1, *Nakanune* (Moscow, 1995), pp. 286–96.

63 Gorodetsky, *Grand Delusion*, p. 299. The account is indirectly derived from Timoshenko himself.

64 Churchill, *The Grand Alliance*, pp. 367–8.

65 Gorodetsky, *Grand Delusion*, p. 306.

66 Yu. Labas, 'Chërny sneg *na Kuznetskom'*, *Rodina*, 6–7, 1999, pp. 36–7.

67 A. Chernyaev, *Moya Zhizn i Moë Vremya* (Moscow, 1995), pp. 88–9.

68 The film *If War Should Come Tomorrow* (*Esli Zavtra Voina*) was made in 1938 by Efim Dzigan. It is a barely two-dimensional pseudo-documentary which begins with scenes of the happy Soviet people attacked on a summer's dawn without warning or provocation. So far, so similar to what actually happened in June 1941. The rest of the film departs entirely from reality. It went into cold storage after the signature of the Molotov-Ribbentrop Pact, in 1939, but once the war started Dzigan received the Stalin Prize. The golden summer day polluted by the black

clouds of Nazi aggression has remained a cliché in most Soviet and Russian films about the war. A recent example is G. Sukhachëv's *Prazdnik* (*The Holiday*), 2001.

Chapter 4: 22 June 1941

1 L. Ginzburg, *Chelovek za Pismennym Stolom* (Leningrad, 1989), p. 517.

2 J. Gelder, in R. Stites (ed.), *Culture and Entertainment in Wartime Russia* (Bloomington, IN, 1995), p. 52.

3 As usual, different authorities give different figures. These are taken mainly from D. Glantz and J. House, *When Titans Clashed: How the Red Army Stopped Hitler* (Edinburgh, 2000), p. 31. According to W. Fowler, *Barbarossa: The First Seven Days* (London, 2004), p. 78, the Luftwaffe had 1,280 aircraft actually serviceable on the first day of the war. The figure for horses is from S. Sebag Montefiore, *Stalin: The Court of the Red Tsar* (London, 2003), p. 318. Horses represented 80 per cent of the motive power of the German army. In 1939 the British Army was the only completely mechanised army in the world: J. Lucas, *War on the Eastern Front: The German Soldier in Russia, 1941–1945* (London, 1998), p. 113.

4 Even here, different authorities give different figures. John Erickson says the Germans had seventy-six infantry divisions, seventeen Panzer divisions, three mountain divisions, and a cavalry division. In addition there were sixteen Finnish divisions with four German divisions attached, and two Romanian armies (*The Soviet High Command: A Military-Political History* (London, 2001), p. 588).

5 A. Boyd, *The Soviet Air Force since 1918* (London, 1977), p. 110.

6 Until the war began the Fronts were called 'Military Districts' or 'Special Military Districts'. They are here called 'Fronts' throughout for simplicity. The composition of military formations in the Soviet Army underwent numerous changes in the course of the war. A Front contained up to nine mixed ('*obshchevoiskovye*') armies, up to three tank armies, one or two air armies and various supporting formations. A mixed army contained five or six rifle divisions and supporting arms. At full strength a Soviet rifle division was supposed to contain 14,483 men, about two thousand less than a German division. In practice Soviet divisions were significantly smaller, especially if they had been involved in heavy fighting (D. Glantz, *Stumbling Colossus: The Red Army on the Eve of War* (Kansas, 1998), p. 152.

7 D. Glantz, *Barbarossa: Hitler's Invasion of Russia 1941* (Stroud, 2001), p. 242.

8 Glantz and House, *When Titans Clashed*, p. 44; D. Murphy, *What Stalin Knew: The Enigma of Barbarossa* (New Haven, 2005), p. 136.

9 E. Radzinski, *Stalin: Zhizn i Smert* (Moscow, 2003), p. 492.

10 G. Gorodetsky, *Grand Delusion: Stalin and the German Invasion of Russia* (New Haven, 1999), p. 311.

11 Glantz and House, *When Titans Clashed*, p. 49.

12 J. Erickson, *The Soviet High Command*, p. 587.

13 Ibid., p. xx.

14 G. Kumanëv, *Ryadom so Stalinym* (Smolensk, 2001), p. 476.

15 Gorodetsky, *Grand Delusion*, p. 313.

16 This account comes primarily from G. Zhukov, *Vospominania i Razmyshlenia* (Moscow, 2002), Vol. I, pp. 264–5. Ya. Chadaev, the chief administrative assistant to the Council of Ministers, kept notes of this and other meetings, but the full text of his memoir has not been published (it was placed after his death in the secret section of the Archive of the October Revolution). Extracts appeared in an article by Georgy Kumanëv in *Otechestvennaya Istoria*, 2, April 2005, pp. 6–26.

17 Chadaev was present at this meeting and took notes (ibid., p. 11).

18 Ibid., p. 13.

19 A translation is in Glantz, *Barbarossa*, p. 243.

20 Chadaev heard Voroshilov and Malenkov saying as much as they left Stalin's meeting (Kumanëv, *Otechestvennaya Istoria*, 2, 2005, p. 14).

21 Article at wwii-soldat.narod.ru/odon/odon, 4 June 2003.

22 A. Ponomarev, *Aleksandr Shcherbakov: Stranitsy Biografii* (Moscow, 2004), p. 98.

23 Sergei Markov, interview, 2 February 2002.

24 Vladislav Mikosha, interview, 3 February 2002.

25 I. Zbarski, *Obyekt No. 1* (Moscow, 2000), p. 116; and interview, 31 May 2002.

26 E. Khrutski, *Kriminalnaya Moskva* (Moscow, 2000), pp. 205–6.

27 Geldern, in Stites (ed.), *Culture and Entertainment in Wartime Russia*, p. 53.

28 In Russian, confusingly enough, you can speak of both 'Fatherland' (*Otechestvo*) and 'Motherland' (*Rodina*). Soldiers went into battle (allegedly) crying, 'Forward! For the Motherland!' Here I have translatated Molotov's '*Rodina*' as 'beloved country', which gives something of the same feeling.

29 Chadaev, quoted in Kumanëv, *Otechestvennaya Istoria, 2 April*, p. 7.

30 G. Andreevski, *Zhizn Moskvy v Stalinskuyu epokhu 1930–1940e gody* (Moscow, 2003), p. 95.

31 E. Vasilieva (ed.), 'Iz vospominania V. F. Krylova 'Moskva v Dni Velikoi Otechestvennoi Voiny', *Golosa Istorii*, 4, 2000, pp. 87–114.

32 J. Barber, 'Popular Reactions in Moscow to the German Invasion of June 22, 1941', in J. Wieczynski (ed.), *Operation Barbarossa: The German Attack on the Soviet Union, June 22, 1941* (Salt Lake City, 1993).

33 Moscow Embassy telegram No. 849 of 25 June 1941 (PRO FCO371/29499, p. 28). This strange thought is repeated in a later report of the Revolution Day celebrations in Kuibyshev, whither the Embassy was evacuated in October 1941.

34 Report by an official of the Leningrad Raion Party Committee, 22 June 1941 (I. Kovalchenko et al. (eds.), *Moskva Voennaya 1941/45: Memuary: Arkhivnye Dokumenty* (Moscow, 1995), p. 42).

35 Zhuravlëv's reports are dated between 23 June and 26 June 1941. They can be found ibid., pp. 49–55. The ranks of officers in the NKVD understated their

position. Zhuravlëv was roughly the equivalent of a brigade commander in the army.

36 M. Gorinov, 'Budni Osazhdennoi Stolitsy', *Otechestvennaya Istoria*, 3, 1996.

37 Andreevski, *Zhizn Moskvy v Stalinskuyu epokhu 1930–1940e gody*, p. 95.

38 The NKVD reports on popular attitudes in Moscow at the beginning of the war are taken from Kovalchenko et al. (eds.), *Moskva Voennaya 1941/45*, pp. 49–55.

39 I. Ehrenburg, *Liudi, Gody, Zhizn: Sobranie sochinenii v deviati tomakh* (Moscow, 1962–7), Vol. 9, p. 288.

40 Yu. Labas, 'Chërny sneg na Kuznetskom', *Rodina*, 6–7, 1999, pp. 36–7.

41 Stalin, Order No. 130, 1 May 1942, *Sochinenia*, Vol. 2 (XV) (Stanford, 1967), p. 53.

42 Yevgeni Anufriev, interview, 3 February 2002.

43 A. Chernyaev, *Moya Zhizn i Moë Vremya* (Moscow, 1995), pp. 88–91.

44 Service assessment by General Snegov, 11 April 1941 (Volkogonov papers, Box 4, Folder 9748).

45 Rokossovski, *Soldatski Dolg* (Moscow, 2002), p. 33.

46 Glantz and House, *When Titans Clashed*, p. 55.

47 Rokossovski, *Soldatski Dolg*, p. 44.

48 Glantz and House, *When Titans Clashed*, p. 55.

49 Ibid., p. 51.

50 Photocopy of original kindly supplied by K.V. Rokossovski.

51 A. Nekrich, *1941 22 iiunia* (Moscow, 1995), p. 205.

52 'Possible View of German Advance which might be made by German Armoured Divisions in Russia', 23 July 1941 (PRO WO190/893/82a).

53 Andreevski, *Zhizn Moskvy v stalinskuyu epokhu 1930–1940e gody*, p. 353.

Chapter 5: The Russians Fight Back

1 Joint decision of Council of People's Commissars and Politburo No. 825 (Yu. Gorkov, *Gosudarstvenny Komitet Oborony Postanovlaet* (Moscow, 2002), 494.

2 Ya. Chadaev, quoted in Georgy Kumanëv, *Otechestvennaya Istoria*, 2, 2005, p. 8.

3 I. Cherushev, *Udar po Svoim: Krasnaya Armia 1938–1941* (Moscow, 2003), p. 345.

4 V. Shunkov, *Krasnaya Armia* (Moscow, 2003), p. 246.

5 Confusingly the U-2 is also known in its military version as the Po-2, after Polikarpov, its designer. I have referred to it throughout as the U-2.

6 Cherushev, *Udar po Svoim*, pp. 347–8.

7 Ibid., p. 346.

8 Gorkov, *Gosudarstvenny Komitet Oborony Postanovlyaet*, pp. 22–4.

9 It is clear from his office diary that Stalin continued to work regularly from the first day of the war until after midnight on 28 June, and that he was back at his desk by the afternoon of 1 July. The diary has been widely published (ibid., pp. 223–469).

10 There are several accounts of the meetings in the Commissariat for Defence and the Nearby Dacha. Anastas Mikoyan was present on both occasions (see Mikoyan, A., *Tak Bylo: Razmyshlenia o Minuvshem* (Moscow, 1999), p. 391, and G. Kumanëv, *Ryadom so Stalinym* (Smolensk, 2001), p. 31). He records Zhukov bursting into tears and Stalin's outburst about Lenin's legacy (the Russian word Stalin used is scatological rather than sexual). He was convinced Stalin believed that the Politburo had come to the Nearby Dacha to arrest him. Radzinski has a more colourful version of the meeting in the Defence Commissariat (E. Radzinski, *Stalin: Zhizn i Smert* (Moscow, 2003), p. 501), which he attributes to Chadaev. However, Chadaev was not present at either meeting, and this part of his memoir has not been published.

11 I. Kovalchenko et al. (eds.), *Moskva Voennaya 1941/45: Memuary: Arkhivnye Dokumenty* (Moscow, 1995), p. 704.

12 Joint decision of Council of People's Commissars and Politburo No. 825 (Gorkov, *Gosudarstvenny Komitet Oborony Postanovlyaet*, p. 495).

13 Ibid., pp. 101, 102.

14 The GKO's decisions included No. 801 of 15 October 1941 on the evacuation of Moscow (ibid., p. 506); No. 8916 of 3 June 1945 on the planning for the war in the Far East (ibid., p. 540); and No. 9887 of 20 August 1945, which set up the Special Committee under Beria to develop a Soviet atom bomb (see *Voenno-Promyshlenny Kurier*, 31 (48), 18–24 August 2004 (at www.vpk-news.ru)).

15 Gorkov, *Gosudarstvenny Komitet Oborony Postanovlaet*, pp. 38–9.

16 Ibid., pp. 46, 57.

17 D. Glantz, *Barbarossa: Hitler's Invasion of Russia 1941* (Stroud, 2001), p. 40.

18 Altogether the BEF lost 68,111 men killed, wounded or missing in the whole of the campaign in France: about one-fifth of their total strength (J. Gardiner, *Wartime: Britain 1939–1945* (London, 2004), p. 175).

19 H. Plocher, *The German Airforce versus Russia, 1941* (USAF Historical Division, 1966), p. 321. For comparison, the number of British prisoners remaining in German and Japanese hands at the end of the war was less than two hundred thousand. Many had of course already been liberated by the advancing Allied armies (Gardiner, *Wartime*, p. 420).

20 M. Roseman, *The Villa, the Lake, the Meeting: Wannsee and the Final Solution* (London, 2002), pp. 29–30.

21 A. Werth, *Russia at War 1941–1945* (London, 1964), p. 91.

22 H. Guderian, *Panzer Leader* (Cambridge, 2002), p. 250.

23 I. Zbarski, *Obyekt No. 1* (Moscow, 2000), p. 118.

24 Yu. Kruglov et al. (eds.), *Veliki Podvig: Vuzy Moskvy v gody Velikoi Otechestvennoi Voiny* (Moscow, 2001), Vol. I, p. 42.

25 Kovalchenko et al. (eds.), *Moskva Voennaya 1941/45*, p. 66.

26 Konstantin Simonov describes his own reaction in *Sto Sutok Voiny* (Smolensk, 1999), pp. 48–50.

27 Kovalchenko et al. (eds.), *Moskva Voennaya 1941/45*, p. 67.
28 Ibid., p. 69.
29 A. Nekrich, *1941 22 iiunia* (Moscow, 2001), pp. 204–5.
30 D. Ortenberg, *Stalin, Shcherbakov, Mekhlis i Drugie* (Moscow, 1995), p. 160; R. Rothstein, 'Homeland, Home Town, and Battlefield' in R. Stites (ed.), *Culture and Entertainment in Wartime Russia* (Bloomington, IN, 1995), p. 79.
31 Ortenberg, *Stalin, Shcherbakov, Mekhlis i Drugie*, pp. 20–21.
32 Ibid., p. 100.
33 Memorandum of 25 June 1941 from Lieutenant-General Malinin to the commanders of the Northern, Northwestern, Western and Southwestern Fronts (Volkogonov papers, Box 4, Folder R11741, in the National Security Archive in Washington, DC).
34 Simonov, *Sto Sutok Voiny*, pp. 407–22.
35 Ibid., pp. 410–17.
36 Quoted Gardiner, *Wartime*, p. 135.
37 Simonov, *Sto Sutok Voiny*, p. 64.
38 K. Simonov, *Stikhi Voennykh Let* (Prague, 1946), p. 64. For those who live in the Russian village, the community still consists not only of its living members but of those who came before – parents, grandparents, ancestors. It is true of the cities too: anyone who has attended a wake in today's Moscow will have shared the feeling that the spirit of the departed is still present in a very real sense. Maggie Paxson deals at some length with the intimate relationship between the living and the dead in a modern Russian village (M. Paxon, *Solovyovo: The Story of Memory in a Russian Village* (Washington, DC, 2005), pp. 196 et seq., 316 et seq.). See also M. Lewin, 'Popular Religion in Twentieth-Century Russia', in *The Making of the Soviet System* (New York, 1994).

Chapter 6: The Volunteers

1 Yuri Averbakh, interview, 26 March 2002.
2 Viktor Merzhanov, interview, 2 February 2002.
3 A. Ponomarëv, *Aleksandr Shcherbakov: Stranitsy Biografii* (Moscow 2004), pp. 95–6.
4 J. O'Riordan, *Sport in Soviet Society* (Cambridge, 1977), p. 155.
5 E. Vorobiëv (in Yu. Kammerer et al., *Moskve – Vozdushnaya Trevoga* (Moscow, 2000), p. 107; B. Fischer, 'Preparing to Blow Up the Bolshoi Theatre', *International Intelligence History Association Newsletter*, 7 (2), Winter 1999 (www.intelligence-history.org/newsl-7-2).
6 Yevgeni Teleguev, interviews, 24 March 2002 and 11 February 2003.
7 A. Sella, *The Value of Life in Soviet Warfare* (London, 1992), p. 62.
8 Tatiana Milkova, interview, 26 May 2002.
9 Liubov Vostrosablina, interview, 26 May 2002.
10 Praskovia Sergeeva, Interview, 26 March 2002; Yuri Averbakh, interview, 26 March 2002.

11 Yelena Volkova, interview, 6 October 2004.

12 This account of Raskova's career and the wartime women's air regiments is based on R. Pennington, *Wings, Women and War: Soviet Airwomen in World War II Combat* (Lawrence, KS, 2001), p. 31.

13 Galina Dokutovich was killed on 1 August 1943, six weeks after writing this entry (Ye. Senyavskaya, *1941–1945 Frontovoe Pokolenie* (Moscow, 1995), p. 184.

14 I. Filatov, untitled article (region.utmn.ru/raz).

15 Article on Popova (www.3-millenium.ru/index.php?m1=2&cont=21&cer=11&page=popova).

16 Pennington, *Wings, Women and War*, p. 170.

17 *Nebesny Tikhokhod* (*Celestial Slowcoach*) in 1945 and *V Boi Idut Odni 'Stariki'* (*Only the Veterans Get the Action*) in 1973.

18 Pennington, *Wings, Women and War*, p. 88.

19 Filatov (region.utmn.ru/raz).

20 J. Erickson, 'Soviet Women at War', in J. and C. Garrard, (eds.), *World War 2 and the Soviet People* (London, 1993), pp. 50–76.

21 Galina Dokutovich, journal entry for 31 May 1943 (Senyavskaya, *1941–1945 Frontovoe Pokolenie*, p. 184).

22 B. Sokolov, *Georgi Zhukov: Triumfy i Padenic* (Moscow, 2003), p. 433 et seq.

23 Ibid., p. 432

24 K. Simonov, 'Syn', from *Stikhi 1954 goda* (Moscow, 1954), p. 84. I am grateful to Ludmila Matthews for her critique of the poem.

25 A. Chernyaev, *Moya Zhizn i Moë Vremya* (Moscow, 1995), p. 154.

26 N. Aleshchenko, *Moskovskoe Opolchenie* (Moscow, 1969), pp. 31, 33.

27 A. Kolesnik, *Opolchenskie Formirovania Rossiiskoi Federatsii v Gody Velikoi Otechestvennoi Voiny* (Moscow, 1988), p. 10.

28 V. Filatov (ed.), *Moskovskaya Bitva v Postanovleniakh Gosudarstvennogo Komiteta Oborony* (Moscow, 2001), pp. 24–6.

29 D. Bekkerman, 'Rasskazy o Pushechnom Myase' (www.pavlovskyposad.ru/p_article_canonmeat).

30 A. Gordon, 'Moskovskoe Narodnoe Opolchenie 1941 Goda Glazami Uchastnika', *Otechestvennaya Istoria*, 3, 2001; G. Popov, 'Gibel Moskovskogo Narodnogo Opolchenia', *Nezavisimy Almanakh 'Lebed'*, 248, 2 December 2001 (www.lebed.com/2001/art2743).

31 V. Korneev, *Ot Moskvy do Kenigsberga, ot Opolchenia do Gvardii* (Omsk, 1993), p. 58.

32 The exact figure was 1,065, according to an excellent article on the Internet, 'Vosmaya Strelkovaya Divizia i "Taifun"' (www.smol1941.narod.ru), whose author unfortunately does not give her name.

33 Ludmila Romanova and Klavdia Leonova, interviews, 6 October 2004.

34 Irina Golyamina, interview, 9 December 2004.

35 Vasili Ponomarëv, interview, 26 March 2002.

36 Aleshchenko, *Moskovskoe Opolchenie*, p. 36.
37 Ibid., p. 38.
38 B. Runin, 'Pisatelskaya Rota', *Novy Mir*, 3, March 1985, pp. 95–123.
39 T. Bek, '"Volokolamskoe chaussee" kak put Aleksandra Beka', in *Do Svidania, alfavit* (Moscow, 2005), pp. 140–62.
40 Runin, 'Pisatelskaya Rota', p. 102.
41 Bek, '"Volokolamskoe chaussee" kak put Aleksandra Beka'.
42 Vera Dëmina, interview, 6 October 2004.
43 Runin, 'Pisatelskaya Rota', pp. 95–123.
44 G. Popov, *Moskovsky Komsomolets*, 266, 26 November 2001.
45 M. Gefter (ed.), *Golosa iz mira, kotorogo uzhe net* (Moscow, 1995), p. 61.
46 GKO Postanovlenie No. 172 of 16 July (Yu. Gorkov, *Gosudarstvenny Komitet Oborony Postanovlyaet* (Moscow, 2002), p. 504).
47 K. Simonov, *Sto Sutok Voiny* (Smolensk, 1999), p. 131.
48 Aleshchenko, *Moskovskoe Opolchenie*, p. 45.
49 The figures were 6,345 rifles and carbines, 1,266 automatic rifles, 129 heavy machine guns, 164 hand machine guns, 160 PPD sub-machine guns, twenty-eight 76-mm guns, fourteen 37-mm anti-aircraft guns, eight 122-mm howitzers, eighteen 82-mm mortars and eighty-one 50-mm mortars. They come from V. Korneev, *Ot Moskvy do Kenigsberga, ot Opolchenia do Gvardii* (Omsk, 1993), p. 31.
50 Lev Mischenko, interview, 18 November 2004, and MS memoirs.
51 'Vosmaya Strelkovaya Divizia, "Taifun"'.
52 Alexander Sandrikov; interview, 26 March 2002.
53 Aleshchenko, *Moskovskoe Opolchenie*, p. 38.
54 Ibid., p. 43.

Chapter 7: Mobilising the Masses

1 Yu. Kruglov et al. (eds.), *Veliki Podvig: Vuzy Moskvy v gody Velikoi Otechestvennoi Voiny* (Moscow, 2001), p. 50 et seq.
2 A. Chernyaev, *Moya Zhizn i Moë Vremya* (Moscow, 1995), pp. 92–5.
3 Information from Valentin Gefter.
4 A. Ponomarev, *Aleksandr Shcherbakov: Stranitsy Biografii* (Moscow, 2004), p. 103.
5 Antonina Savina, interview, 11 February 2003.
6 Klavdia Leonova and Lidia Robel, interview, 6 October 2004.
7 Information from Ghia Sulkhanishvili.
8 Ponomarev, *Aleksandr Shcherbakov*, p. 130.
9 All London's theatres closed on the outbreak of war. Half a dozen were reopened in October 1939. The Windmill Theatre, by modern standards a not very risqué music hall, claimed, 'We Never Closed!' J. Gardiner, *Wartime: Britain 1939–1945* (London, 2004), p. 5).

10 H. Segal, 'Drama of Struggle', in R. Stites (ed.), *Culture and Entertainment in Wartime Russia* (Bloomington, IN, 1995), pp. 109, 128.
11 Ibid., p. 108.
12 R. Stites, 'Frontline Entertainment', ibid., p. 134.
13 Ibid., p. 106.
14 V. Safoshkov, *Lidia Ruslanova: Zhizn v Pesne* (Moscow, 2003), pp. 92, 97, 137.
15 Susanna Zvyagina, interview, 26 May 2002.
16 Ivan Petrov, interview, 26 May 2002.
17 His article on the visit appeared in *Krasnaya Zvezda*, 16 August 1941.
18 J. Brooks, *Thank You, Comrade Stalin!* (Princeton, 2000), p. 170.
19 V. Petelin, *Zhizn Alekseya Tolstogo, Krasny Graf* (Moscow, 2001), pp. 330, 879.
20 D. Ortenberg, *Stalin, Mekhlis, Shcherbakov i Drugie* (Moscow, 1995).
21 The biographical details are taken from J. and C. Garrard, *The Bones of Berdichev* (New York, 1996).
22 Ortenberg, *Stalin, Mekhlis, Shcherbakov i Drugie*, pp. 24–30. In 1959 Grigori Chukhrai's film *Ballad of a Soldier* was also criticised for showing a woman unfaithful to her husband at the front. But by then times were different and the film survived.
23 Ibid., pp. 31–9.
24 S. Aria, *Mozaika – Zapisi Advokata, Rechi* (Moscow, 2000), p. 27.
25 At least one war memorial of a Soviet soldier is nicknamed 'Alyosha', perhaps in honour of Skvortsov.
26 L. Polukhina, *Marina Ladynina i Ivan Pyriev* (Moscow, 2004); Vladimir Zeldin, interview, 3 February 2002; reportage by Radio Liberty, (www.svoboda.org/programs/Cicles/Cinema).
27 Yu. Gorkov, *Gosudarstvenny Komitet Oborony Postanovlyaet* (Moscow, 2002), p. 492.
28 D. Glantz and J. House, *When Titans Clashed: How the Red Army Stopped Hitler* (Edinburgh, 2000), p. 68.
29 Olga Trifonova, interview, 7 February 2003.
30 Report of 2 December 1941 to Abakumov, based on intercepted correspondence (V. Khristoforov et al. (eds.), *Lubyanka V dni bitvy za Moskvu* (Moscow, 2002), p. 279).
31 Chernyaev, *Moya Zhizn i Moë Vremya*, pp. 96–100.

Chapter 8: Stalin Takes a Grip

1 A. Boyd, *The Soviet Air Force since 1918* (London, 1977), p. 89.
2 Ibid., p. 99.
3 Stepan Mikoyan, interviews, April 2003 and 9 October 2004.
4 D. Glantz, and J. House, *When Titans Clashed: How the Red Army Stopped Hitler* (Edinburgh, 2000), p. 38.

5 Interviews with Stepan Mikoyan. There are several accounts of the confrontation between Stalin and Rychagov.
6 The text of this discussion is in I. Cherushev, *Udar po Svoim: Krasnya Armia 1938–1941* (Moscow, 2003), pp. 436–7.
7 Timoshenko to Commanders of Air Force Districts, 17 May 1941 (Volkogonov papers, Box 4, Folder R11744).
8 A. Ponomarëv, *Aleksandr Scherbakov: Stranitsy Biografii* (Moscow, 2004), p. 87.
9 See article by L. Ivashov, *Voenno-Istoricheski Zhurnal*, 6, 1990, pp. 43–5. David Murphy speculates that the Ju 52 was carrying a personal and secret letter to Stalin from Hitler, intended to reassure him that the German military build-up on the frontier was not a threat to the Soviet Union. (D. Murphy, *What Stalin Knew: The Enigma of Barbarossa* (New Haven, 2005), p. 189.
10 From the short note on her life issued by the Museum in the House on the Embankment. See also note on Rychagov at aces.boom.ru/spane/rychag.
11 Stalin had pressed for Proskurov's arrest as early as 12 April, in a manuscript note on a report by Zhukov and Timoshenko on aircraft accidents. But for some reason the final order for the arrest was not issued until 27 June (Volkogonov papers, Box 4, Folder 9699; Cherushev, *Udar po Svoim*, p. 327; Murphy, *What Stalin Knew*, p. 225).
12 D. Ortenberg, *Stalin, Mekhlis, Shcherbakov i Drugie* (Moscow, 1995), p. 54.
13 Olga Trifonova, interview, 7 February 2003.
14 V. Shevelëv, *Moskovskie Novosti*, 15, 2002 (www.mn.ru/issue.php?2002-15-36), interview with Rosa Smushkevich.
15 GKO order of 17 July 1941 (N. Patrushev (ed.), *Nachalo: Sbornik Dokumentov* (Moscow, 2000), Vol. 1, pp. 337–9).
16 Ibid., p. 366.
17 Ibid., pp. 371–2.
18 Ibid., pp. 411–12.
19 Stavka Directive 001919 of 12 September 1941 (ibid., Vol. 2, p. 85).
20 Alexander Yakovlev, interview, 5 October 2004.
21 A. Toptygin, *Neizvestny Beria* (Moscow and St Petersburg, 2002), p. 121. See also article by I. Pykhalov, 'Zagradotryady: Vymysel i realnost' (neostalinism.nasha-rodina.ru/mtr/zagrad).
22 Order of 17 September 1941 and Order No. 4976 of 28 September 1941, quoted in B. Sokolov, *Georgi Zhukov: Triumfy i Padenie* (Moscow, 2003), pp. 255, 578. It is not clear whether the latter order was put into practice; Zhukov left Leningrad soon afterwards.
23 V. Filatov et al. (eds.) *Moskovskaya Bitva v Postanovleniakh Gosudarstvennogo Komiteta Oborony* (Moscow, 2001), p. 39.
24 E. Radzinski, *Stalin: Zhizn i Smert* (Moscow, 2003), p. 462.
25 Pavlov's fate and the fighting on the frontier are well depicted in the film *Voina na Zapadnom Napravlenii* (*War in the Western Theatre*), 1990.
26 K. Simonov, *Sto Sutok Voiny* (Smolensk, 1999), p. 344.

27 Ibid.

28 In the first Session of Gorbachёv's newly elected People's Congress in April 1989, Andrei Sakharov accused the military of bombing their own soldiers who had been taken prisoner in Afghanistan. There was, of course, a furious row.

29 The text was not published for many years, and there were those in the Soviet Union who tried to deny it had ever existed. It is now widely available. For an English translation, see, for example, G. Roberts, *Victory at Stalingrad* (London, 2002), pp. 197 et seq.

30 This paragraph is based on I. Cherushev, *Udar po Svoim: Krasnaya Armia 1938–1941* (Moscow, 2003), pp. 334, 356, 359.

31 K. Meretskov, *Na Sluzhbe Narodu* (Moscow, 1968), beginning of chapter 'Severo-Zapad' (text at militera.lib.ru/memo/russian/meretskov/index).

32 Cherushev, *Udar po Svoim*, p. 440.

33 E. Dolmatovski, *Zelenaya Brama*, Vol. III of *Complete Works* (Moscow, 1990), pp. 558–9.

34 Alla Ponedelin, interview, 9 October 2004.

35 Zhukov is said to have introduced punishment battalions while commanding the Western Front in the Autumn of 1941; Vitali Moroz, interview, 19 February 2003.

36 A discussion of punishment units and blocking detachments is at G. Krivosheev (ed.), *Rossia i SSSR v Voinakh XX Veka: Statisticheskoe Issledovanie* (Moscow, 2001), pp. 436–42.

37 Order No. 227 of the People's Commissar for Defence (see www.klio.webservis.ru/ doc06/sta227). Rokossovski's order of 13 March 1943 is quoted in D. Glantz, *Colossus Reborn: The Red Army at War 1941–1943* (Kansas, 2005), p. 577.

38 Report of 25 August 1944 by Major-General Lobachev to Shcherbakov, who was by then head of the Main Political Directorate of the Armed Forces (*Voenno-Istoricheski Zhurnal*, 8, 1988, pp. 79–80.

39 Glantz, *Colossus Reborn*, p. 582.

40 A. Chernyaev, *Moya Zhizn i Moё Vremya* (Moscow, 1995), p. 141.

41 R. Reese, *The Societ Military Experience* (London, 2000), pp. 115–16.

42 Semёn Aria, interview, 14 May 2003; S. Aria, *Mozaika – Zapiski Advokata, Rechi* (Moscow, 2000).

43 S. Norilski (Shcheglov), *Stalinskaya Premia* (Tula, 1998), pp. 26–7.

44 Ibid., p. 108.

45 Ibid., p. 21.

46 Ibid., pp. 67–9.

47 Vladimir Kantovski, interviews and correspondence.

48 Based on correspondence with Alexander Pyltsyn, his book *Shtrafnoi Udar, ili Kak Ofitserski Shtrafbat doshёl do Berlina* (St Petersburg, 2003) and his interview at www.geocities.com/CapitolHill/Parliament/7231/shtrafbt.

49 Extracts from the colourful eighteenth-century version of the Royal Navy's Articles of War can be found in P. O'Brian, *Master and Commander* (London, 1998), p. 85. A full text is at www.io.com/gibbonsb/articles.
50 F. Crozier, *The Men I Killed* (London, 1937), pp. 49, 78, (italics in the original).
51 N. Patrushev (ed.), *Nachalo* (Moscow, 2000), Vol. 2, p. 164.
52 Sokolov, *Georgi Zhukov*, p. 274.
53 Krivosheev (ed.), *Rossia i SSSR v Voinakh XX Veka*, pp. 441, 246n; Alexander Yakovlev gives a higher figure for those shot of 157,000 (A. Yakovlev, *A Century of Violence in Soviet Russia* (New Haven, 2000), p. 174).
54 M. Hastings, *Armageddon* (London, 2004), p. 192.

Chapter 9: The Eye of the Storm

1 A. Werth, *Moscow War Diary* (New York, 1942), pp. 74, 106.
2 Ibid., p. 43; M. Gorinov, 'Budni Osazhdënnoi Stolitsy' *Otechestvennaya Istoria*, 3, 1996, p. 5).
3 Werth, *Moscow War Diary,* p. 94.
4 Report by P. Gridaspov and M. Smirnov of 9 January 1942 (I. Kovalchenko et al. (eds.), *Moskva Voennaya 1941/45: Memuary i Arkhivnye Dokumenty* (Moscow, 1995), pp. 575–83.
5 Werth, *Moscow War Diary*, pp. 112, 164.
6 Ibid., p. 145.
7 Ibid., p. 157.
8 Ibid., p. 43. The Germans had very good maps of Moscow in 1941. Two of them are in the British Library. Even in 1988 the only decent map of Moscow available to foreigners was published by the CIA.
9 G. Andreevski, *Zhizn Moskvy v stalinskuyu epokhu 1930–1940e gody* (Moscow, 2003), p. 105.
10 Report No. 1/1155 of 18 November by NKVD censorship for period 1–15 November (I. Kovalchenko et al. (eds.), *Moskvya Voennayo 1941/45*, pp. 158–60; J. Gardiner, *Wartime: Britain 1939–1945* (London, 2004), p. 132.
11 J. Barber and M. Harrison, *The Soviet Home Front 1941–1945* (London, 1991), p. 81; N. Ponikarpova, 'Moskva, Ispytanie Voinoi', *Moskovski Zhurnal*, May 1999 (www.mj.rusk.ru/99/5/index), pp. 33–8.
12 In Britain meat, sugar, dairy products, were all strictly rationed. You got one egg a week if you were lucky. Bread was not rationed in Britain until after the war (Gardiner, *Wartime*, p. 146; Barber and Harrison, *The Soviet Home Front 1941–1945*, p. 82.
13 Andreevski, *Zhizn Moskvy v Stalinskuyu epokhu 1930–1940e gody*, p. 213.
14 Diary of P.N. Miller (M. Gorinov (ed.), *Moskva Prifrontovaya* (Moscow, 2001), p. 289.
15 E. Khrutski, *Kriminalnaya Moskva* (Moscow, 2000), pp. 206–8.
16 Andreevski, *Zhizn Mosky v stalinskuyu epokhu 1930–1940e gody*, p. 132.

17 Nikolai Kiselëv, interview, 4 October 2002.
18 Kovalchenko (ed.), *Moskvya Voennaya 1941/45*, p. 69.
19 *Pravda*, 25 August 1941, p. 3.
20 Kovalchenko (ed.), *Moskvya Voennaya 1941/45* p. 74.
21 *Pravda*, 12 August 1941; Kovalchenko (ed.), *Moskvya Voennaya 1941/45*, p. 76.
22 *Krasnaya Zvezda*, 10, 14 and 16 August 1941.
23 *Vechernyaya Moskva*, 20 August 1941.
24 D. Ortenberg, *Stalin, Schcherbakov, Mekhlis i Drugie* (Moscow, 1995), p. 146.
25 Decision No. GKO-377 (V. Filator (ed.), *Moskovskaya Bitva v Postanovleniakh Gosudarstvennogo Komiteta Oborony* (Moscow, 2001), p. 52.
26 Werth, *Moscow War Diary,* pp. 129, 151, 154.
27 K. Rokossovski, *Soldatski Dolg* (Moscow, 2002), p. 70.
28 Report of 25 August by Military Jurist Rozenblatt (Volkogonov papers, Box 4, Folder R11261).
29 A. Yakovlev, *A Century of Violence in Soviet Russia* (New Haven, 2000), p. 174; Vitali Moroz, interview, 19 February 2003.
30 H. Cassidy, *Moscow Dateline, 1941–1943* (London, 1943), p. 82. See also accounts in Werth, *Moscow War Diary*, and M. Bourke-White, *Shooting the Russian War* (New York, 1942).
31 Zhukov says in his memoirs that Stalin sacked him as Chief of Staff because he favoured abandoning Kiev to save the Southwestern Front (G. Zhukov, *Vospominania i Razmyshlenia* (Moscow, 2002), Vol. I, p. 352). By all accounts he was much better on the battlefield than in the staff. Stalin regularly used him as a one-man fire brigade, and he was probably just the man to go to Leningrad at the moment of crisis there.
32 The figures for Russian losses are from G. Krivosheev (ed.), *Soviet Casualties and Combat Losses in the Twentieth Century* (London, 1997), p. 272.
33 D. Volkogonov, *I V Stalin: Triumf i Tragedia* (Moscow, 1990), Vol. 2, p. 201.
34 F. Halder, *The Halder War Diary 1939–1942* (Novato, 1988), p. 446.
35 Ibid., p. 506.
36 G. Jukes, *The Defence of Moscow* (London, 1969), p. 51.
37 J. Piekalkiewicz, *Die Schlacht um Moskau* (Bergisch Gladbach, 1981), p. 17.
38 D. Glantz and J. House, *When Titans Clashed: How the Red Army Stopped Hitler* (Edinburgh, 2000), p. 60.
39 Russell Stolfi's *Hitler's Panzers East* (Oklahoma, 1992) supports the proposition with a wealth of technical detail. For a more light-hearted version, see David Downing's *The Moscow Option* (London, 2001).
40 The figures for prisoners are German (see, for example, H. Plocher, *The German Airforce versus Russia, 1941* (USAF Historical Division, 1966), p. 321). Modern Russian research regards them as somewhat inflated but not incredible (Glantz and House, *When Titans Clashed*, pp. 74–7).

41 This story was told by Chadaev to Georgi Kumanëv (*Ryadom so Stalinym* (Smolensk, 2001), p. 482).

Chapter 10: Fire over Moscow

1 E. Khrutski, *Kriminalnaya Moskva* (Moscow, 2000), p. 209.
2 K. Simonov, *Sto Sutok Voiny* (Smolensk, 1999), p. 309.
3 A. Chernyaev, *Moya Zhizn i Moë Vremya* (Moscow, 1995), p. 91.
4 Simonov, *Sto Sutok Voiny*, p. 309. A similar incident happened in September 1939, when British fighters shot down a couple of British bombers over the Thames.
5 G. Andreevski, *Zhizn Moskvy v stalinsknyu epokhu 1930–1940e gody* (Moscow, 2003), p. 115.
6 Yu. Kammerer et al., *Moskve – Vozdushnaya Trevoga* (Moscow, 2000), p. 416.
7 Ibid., pp. 41–8.
8 Ya. Chadaev, *Otechestvennaya Istoria* 2, 2005, p. 11.
9 D. Glantz, *Stumbling Colossus: The Red Army on the Eve of World War* (Kansas, 1998), p. 172.
10 G. Timoshkov, in Kammerer et al., *Moskve – Vozdushnaya Trevoga*, pp. 60–69.
11 J. Gardiner, *Wartime: Britain 1939–1945* (London, 2004), p. 293.
12 GKO decision, London 1996, No. 1 of 1 July 1941 (V. Filatov et al. (eds.), *Moskovskaya Bitva v Postanovleniakh Gosudarstvennogo Komiteta Oborony* (Moscow, 2001), p. 13.
13 A. Werth, *Moscow War Diary* (New York, 1942), p. 20.
14 Yu. Kammerer, in Kammerer et al., *Moskve – Vozdushnaya Trevoga*, pp. 146–8.
15 Andreevski, *Zhizn Moskvy v stalinskuyu epokhu 1930–1940e gody*, pp. 122.
16 Ibid., p. 123.
17 Kammerer, in Kammerer et al., *Moskve – Vozdushnaya Trevoga*, pp. 131–6.
18 Gardiner, *Wartime*, p. 324.
19 One of those who sheltered there in the autumn of 1941 as a small boy was Valentin Bolotov, who later rose to a senior position in the Metro hierarchy, and on retirement became the Director of the Museum of the Moscow Metro (Valentin Bolotov, interview, 17 February 2003).
20 A. Soloviev, in Kammerer et al., *Moskve – Vozdushnaya Trevoga*, p. 153.
21 Kammerer, ibid., pp. 136–8 .
22 Gardiner, *Wartime*, p. 526.
23 Kammerer, in Kammerer et al., *Moskve – Vozdushnaya Trevoga*, pp. 126–131.
24 Ibid., pp. 122–6.
25 Report by Major Shpigov and others (V. Khristoforov et al. (eds.), *Lubyanka v dni bitvy za Moskvu* (Moscow, 2002), p. 52.
26 A. Boyd, *The Soviet Air Force Since 1918* (London, 1977), p. 129.
27 H. Boog (ed.), *Das Deutsche Reich und der Zweite Weltkrieg*, Vol. 4 (Stuttgart, 1983), p. 698. See also Boyd, *The Soviet Air Force since 1918*, p. 128.

28 Timoshkov, in Kammerer et al., *Moskve – Vozdushnaya Trevoga*, pp. 60–69.
29 'Moskva pod Bombami', *Pochtovye Vedomosti*, 4, 27 February 2001.
30 Khristoforov et al., *Lubyanka v dni bitvy za Moskvu*, p. 49.
31 A. Tolstoi, in Kammerer et al., *Moskve – Vozdushnaya Trevoga*, pp. 92–4.
32 B. Galich, 'Stolichny Den', *Moskovski Bolshevik*, 31 August 1941, reprinted ibid., pp. 99–100.
33 Yelena Nemirovskaya, interview 9 October 2004. She still has a picture of her uncle by the Brandenburg Gate on the day the war ended.
34 Simonov, *Sto Sutok Voiny*, pp. 423–5.
35 'Moskva pod Bombami', *Pochtovye Vedomosti*, 27 February 2001.
36 War diary of British Military Mission in Moscow for 21 July 1941 (PRO WO178/25).
37 Werth, *Moscow War Diary*, p. 82.
38 H. Cassidy, *Moscow Dateline 1941–1943* (London, 1943), p. 71.
39 *Iz vospominania V. F. Krylova 'Moskva v Dni Velikoi Otechestvennoi Voiny'*, ed. E. Vasilieva, *Golosa Istorii No. 4* (Moscow 2000), pp. 87–114.
40 F. Krutetski, in Kammerer et al., *Moskve – Vozdushnaya Trevoga*, p. 162.
41 Kammerer, ibid., p. 148.
42 The information about the activities of Moscow's Central Amubulance Service comes from a file put together at the end of 1944, consisting of drawings, diagrams, photographs, and personal accounts (Moscow City Archive Fond P-552, Opis 2, Delo 336, List 20).
43 Reminiscences of Shredov, Deputy Head of Moscow Central Ambulance Service (EvakPunkt) (Moscow City Archive Fond P-552, Opis 2, Delo 337, List 30).
44 Reminiscence of Russkikh (Moscow City Archive Fond P-552, Opis 2, Delo 337, List 30).
45 Description by Nurse Giatsintsova (Moscow City Archive Fond P-552, Opis 2, Delo 337, List 31).
46 Reminiscence of Zenkov (Moscow City Archive Fond P-552, Opis 2, Ed. Khr 339, List 8).
47 So called because the water runs down the street into the Moscow River.
48 Nikolai Kiselëv, interview, 4 October 2002.
49 The apparition was presumably a British officer in summer uniform (Yu. Labas, 'Chërny sneg na Kuznetskom', *Rodina*, 6–7, 1999, pp. 36–7, and interview on 2 August 2004).
50 Yelena Vanke, interview, 26 May 2002.
51 N. Ponikarpova, 'Moskva, Ispytanie Voinoi', *Moskovski Zhurnal*, May 1999, pp. 33–8.
52 Yu. Kammerer, in Kammerer et al., *Moskve – Vozdushnaya Trevoga*, pp. 41–48; A. Ponomarev, *Aleksandr Shcherbakov: Stranitsy Biografii* (Moscow, 2004), p. 133; V. Khristoforov et al (eds.), *Lubyanka v dni bitvy za Moskvu*, p. 93.
53 Ya. Pikalkevich, in Kammerer et al., *Moskve – Vozdushaaya Trevoga*, pp. 143–6.

54 Ibid., p. 67.

55 Andreevski, *Zhizn Moskvy v stalinskuyu epokhu 1930–1940e gody*, p. 119.

56 S. Mikoyan, *Memoirs* (Shrewsbury, 1999) p. 70, and interview, 9 October 2004.

57 I. Kovalchenko et al. (eds.), *Moskva Voennaya 1941/45: Memuary i Arkhivnye Dokumenty* (Moscow, 1995), pp. 657–87.

58 B. Kulumbekov, in Kammerer et al., *Moskve – Vozdushnaya Trevoga*, pp. 155–61.

59 Decision of 22 November 1941 (Moscow City Archive Fond P-399, Opis 1, Ed. Khr. 2, List 2).

60 Decisions of the IsPolKom of the Krasnopresnenski Soviet Deputatov Trudyashch-ichsya for January 1942 (Moscow City Archive Fond P-399, Opis 1, Ed. Khr. 6, List 1).

61 Decisions of Krasnaya Presnya Soviet, January–April 1942 (Moscow City Archive Fond P-399, Opis 1, Ed. Khr. 5, List 7 and List 8).

62 Decision of Krasnaya Presnya Soviet, October–December 1941, Decision of 22 November 1941 (Moscow City Archive Fond P-399, Opis 1, Ed. Khr. 2, List 2).

63 M. Nemirovski, in Kammerer et al., *Moskve – Vozdushnaya Trevoga*, pp. 56–60; Moscow City Archive P-399, Opis 1, Ed. Khr. 2, List 3.

64 Kovalchenko et al. (eds.), *Moskva Voennaya 1941/45*, pp. 463–7.

65 G. Timoshkov, in Kammerer et al., *Moskve – Vozdushnaya Trevoga*, pp. 60–69.

66 Ponikarpova, 'Moskva, Ispytanie Voinoi'.

67 Boog (ed.), *Das Deutsche Reich und der Zweite Weltkrieg,* p. 698.

68 Timoshkov, in Kammerer et al., *Moskve – Vozdushnaya Trevoga*, pp. 60–69.

69 S. Lapirov, ibid., pp. 25–41.

70 Kammerer, ibid., pp. 151–2.

71 J. Ray, *The Night Blitz 1940–1941* (London, 2000), pp. 13, 232; Gardiner, *Wartime*, pp. 338, 528.

72 Figures at Portcities London (www.portcities.org.uk/london/server/show/nav.001).

73 Boyd, *The Soviet Air Force since 1918*, p. 127.

74 Ibid., pp. 128–9.

75 The Russians wanted Spitfires, but the British would not release them.

76 Gardiner, *Wartime*, p. 293.

77 Ray, *The Night Blitz 1940–1941*, p. 265.

78 J. Lukacs, *Five Days in London – May 1940* (London, 1999), p. 164.

79 J. Hayward, *Stopped at Stalingrad: The Luftwaffe and Hitler's Defeat in the East, 1942–1943* (Kansas, 1998), says the number of lives lost in the first raid on Stalingrad is undocumented, but he believes a figure of some 24,000 is plausible (p. 188). A. Beevor, *Stalingrad* (London, 1998), repeats the estimate that 40,000 people died (p. 106). Either way the contrast with what happened in Moscow is very striking.

80 The Russians had gained strategic superiority over the Luftwaffe by midsummer 1943 (D. Glantz, *Colossus Reborn: The Red Army at War 1941–1943* (Kansas, 2005), p. 414).

Chapter 11: The Germans Break Through

1 D. Glantz, *Barbarossa: Hitler's Invasion of Russia 1941* (Stroud, 2001), p. 141; D. Glantz and J. House, *When Titans Clashed: How the Red Army Stopped Hitler* (Edinburgh, 2000), p. 79n.
2 Ibid., p. 79.
3 V. Grossman, *Gody Voiny* (Moscow, 1989), pp. 281–4. Grossman puts into the old woman's mouth a common Russian euphemism ('*Ya pokryla ego matom*') for very bad language indeed.
4 Ibid.
5 Glantz and House, *When Titans Clashed*, p. 79.
6 M. Gefter (ed.), *Golosa iz mira, kotorogo uzhe net* (Moscow, 1995), p. 83.
7 A. Gordon, 'Moskovskoe Narodnoe Opolchenie 1941 Goda Glazami Uchastnika', *Otechestvennaya Istoria*, 3, 2001).
8 D. Bekkerman, 'Rasskazy o Pushechnom Myase' (www.pavlovskyposad.ru/p_article_canonmeat).
9 H. Plocher, *The German Airforce versus Russia, 1941* (USAF Historical Division, 1966).
10 The sentence is reproduced in N. Konyaev, *Vlasov: Dva Litsa Generala* (Moscow, 2003), p. 309. Other details are from 'Vosmaya strelkovaya divizia i "Taifun"' (www.smol1941.narod.ru).
11 H. Guderian, *Panzer Leader* (Cambridge, 2002), p. 233.
12 Ibid., p. 242.
13 J. Erickson, *The Road to Stalingrad* (London, 1983), pp. 216–17; R. Reese, *The Soviet Military Experience* (London, 2000), p. 105; V. Karpov, '*Marshal Zhukov, ego soratniki* I *protivniki*', Vol. 1 (militera.lib.ru/bio/karpov/31).
14 Yelena Okuneva, interview, 18 November 2004.
15 None of the prisoners knew, of course, that this was where thousands of Polish officers had been murdered the previous year by the execution squads of the NKVD.
16 L. Mishchenko, interview, 18 November 2004, and MS memoir, passim.
17 Bekkerman, 'Rasskazy o Pushechnom Myase'.
18 'Vosmaya Strelkovaya Divizia i "Taifun"', quoting one of the Division's nurses, Aleksandra Riumina.
19 Boris Nevzorov and Kirill Dryannov, interview at Museum of the Defence of Moscow, 8 February 2003.
20 B. Nevzorov, *Moskovskaya Bitva – Fenomenon vtoroi mirovoi* (Moscow, 2001), p. 53.

21 From General Staff Operational Communiqué 211 of 5 October (V. Zhilin (ed.), *Bitva pod Moskvoi: Khronika, Fakty, Lyudi* (Moscow, 2001), Vol. I, p. 238).
22 Yu. Gorkov, *Gosudarstvenny Komitet Oborony Postanovlyaet* (Moscow, 2002), pp. 252–3: list of Stalin's visitors.
23 A. Boyd, *The Soviet Air Force since 1918* (London, 1977), p. 133.
24 M. Gorinov (ed.), *Moskva Prifrontovaya 1941–1942: Arkhivnye Dokumenty i Materialy* (Moscow, 2001), p. 289.
25 War diary of British Military Mission in Moscow for 3 and 4 October 1941 (PRO WO178/25).
26 War diary of British Military Mission in Moscow for 8 October 1941 (PRO WO178/25).
27 A. Werth, *Moscow War Diary* (New York, 1942), p. 252.
28 H. Cassidy, *Moscow Dateline, 1941–1943* (London, 1943), p. 108.
29 K. Simonov, *Glazami Cheloveka Moego Pokolenia* (Moscow, 1989), p. 363.
30 O. Chaney, *Zhukov* (Newton Abbot, 1972), pp. 141–7.
31 E. Kulkov, M. Myagkov and O. Rzheshevski, *Voina 1941–1945: Fakty i Dokumenty* (Moscow, 2004), p. 67.
32 GKO Order No. 768 of 12 October (V. Filatov et al. (eds.), *Moskovskaya Bitva v Postanovleniakh Gosudarstvennogo Komiteta Oborony* (Moscow, 2001), p. 67).
33 V. Fedotov, *My Vyshli iz Shineli i LitInstituta* (Moscow, 2001), p. 19.
34 GKO decision No. 678 of 12 October 1941 (Filatov et al. (eds.) *Moskovskaya Bitva v Postanovleniakh Gosudarstvennogo Komiteta Oborony*, p. 68); NKVD Directive No. 2685 of 1 October (N. Patrushev (ed.), *Nachalo: Sbornik Dokumentov* (Moscow, 2000), Vol. 2, p. 158); A. Ponomarëv, *Aleksandr Shcherbakov: Stranitsy Biografii* (Moscow, 2004), p. 118. Altogether ten million people throughout the country were employed in building defensive works in the summer and autumn of 1941.
35 V. Ivanov, 'Moskovskaya Zona Oborony v Zashchite Stolitsy', 2001 (www.novostroy.ru/html/points/moszona_6).
36 Ibid.
37 Bekkerman, 'Rasskazy o Pushechnom Myase'.
38 Ivanov, 'Moskovskaya Zona Oborony v Zashchite Stolitsy'.
39 Stanislav Iofin, interview, 28 March 2002. The story (or legend) is widely repeated.
40 *Pochtovye Vedomosti*, 5, 27 February 2001.
41 D. Ortenberg, *Stalin, Shcherbakov, Mekhlis i Drugie* (Moscow, 1995), p. 63.
42 Daniel Mitlyanski, interview, 27 July 2004.
43 K. Rokossovski, *Soldatski Dolg,*(Moscow, 2002), p. 88.
44 Ibid., pp. 82–92; Report by the Western Front on the operations of the 16th Army from 15 to 28 October (V. Knyshevski (ed.), *Skrytaya Pravda Voiny: 1941 god* (Moscow, 1992), pp. 175–80).
45 Nadezhda Rokossovskaya, interview, 6 December 2004.
46 One of Gurkin's howitzers is now in the Museum of the Russian Army.

47 Rokossovski, *Soldatski Dolg*, pp. 95–108.
48 Knyshevski (ed.), *Skrytaya Pravda Voiny*, p. 181.
49 Commissar Lobachev's Order of 27 October (ibid., p. 184).
50 Ibid., p. 185.
51 M. Gorinov, *Podvig Moskvy 1941–1945* (Moscow, 2003), pp. 88–91.

Chapter 12: Panic

1 A. Ponomarev, *Aleksandr Shcherbakov: Stranitsy Biografii* (Moscow, 2004), p. 146.
2 Krotkov was later used by the KGB to inform on the Moscow intelligentsia and as part of a notorious, but ultimately unproductive, plot to compromise the French ambassador, Maurice Dejean (J. Barron, *KGB: The Secret Work of Soviet Secret Agents* (New York, 1974), pp. 122–40). One of the best feature films made about Stalin, Jack Gold's black comedy *Red Monarch* (1983), is based on a series of stories by Krotkov.
3 Similar advice about 'straw boxes' was published in the British press at this time.
4 G. Andreevski, *Zhizn Moskvy v stalinskuyu epokhu 1930–1940e gody* (Moscow, 2003), pp. 124–5.
5 E. Vorobiëv, in Yu. Kammerer et al., *Moskve – Vozdushnaya Trevoga* (Moscow, 2000), p. 107.
6 J.D. Barber and M. Harrison, *The Soviet Home Front 1941–1945* (London, 1991), p. 135.
7 Ponomarëv, *Aleksandr Shcherbakov*, pp. 145–53.
8 GKO decision of 8 October 1941 (N. Patrushev (ed.), *Nachalo: Sbornik Dokumentov* (Moscow, 2000), Vol. 2, p. 185.)
9 Kotlyarov's notes on the draft instruction dated 11 October 1941 (V. Khristoforov et al. (eds.), *Lubyanka v dni bitvy za Moskvu* (Moscow, 2002), p. 77).
10 Request dated 10 October 1941 from Major General Spiridonov to Serov (ibid., pp. 77, 78). The detailed lists remained unpublished: sixty years later they were still a state secret.
11 N. Ponikarpova, 'Moskva, Ispytanie Voinoi', *Moskovski Zhurnal*, May 1999, pp. 33–8.
12 Ponomarëv, *Aleksandr Shcherbakov*, pp. 114–15.
13 Ibid., p. 117.
14 Yelena Nemirovskaya, interview, 9 October 2004.
15 Ponomarëv, *Aleksandr Shcherbakov*, pp. 142–3.
16 Texts of decisions in M. Gorinov (ed.), *Moskva Prifrontovaya 1941–1942: Arkhivnye Dokumenty i Materialy* (Moscow, 2001), pp. 259–60.
17 It is perhaps not surprising that those present at the time, dictating their memoirs many years later, often got the chronology muddled up. So it is in this case. The meeting to which Mikoyan refers took place on 15 October, not

16 October (see GKO decision No. 801 of 15 October, V. Filatov et al. (eds.), *Moskovskaya Bitva v Postanovleniakh Gosudarstvennogo Komiteta Oborony* (Moscow, 2001), p. 70).

18 General Vlasik, Stalin's bodyguard, and Molotov both told the historian Georgi Kumanëv that Stalin decided on the afternoon of 15 October that he would not leave Moscow (Kumanëv, interview, 25 July 2005).

19 Nikolai Glebov, interview, 1 June 2002.

20 Ponikarpova, 'Moskva, Ispytanie Voinoi': The deputy director of the Metro responsible for equipment, A.K. Shmit, described this incident in 1944.

21 D. Ortenberg, *Stalin, Shcherbakov, Mekhlis i Drugie* (Moscow, 2002), pp. 13–14.

22 V. Zhilin (ed.), *Bitva pod Moskvoi: Khronika, Fakty, Lyudi* (Moscow, 2001), Vol. I, p. 241.

23 M.M. Gorinov to author: his mother was a child in Shakhovskaya in 1941.

24 Olga Trifonova, interview, 7 February 2003.

25 Yu. Labas 'Chërny sneg na Kuznetskom', *Rodina*, 6–7, 1999, pp. 36–7.

26 J. and C. Garrard, *The Bones of Berdichev: The Life and Fate of Vasily Grossman* (New York, 1996), pp. 23–4.

27 Ponikarpova, 'Moskva, Ispytanie Voinoi'.

28 I am greatly indebted to Kathy Berton for identifying the George Formby film.

29 Dr A.G. Dreitser, diary entry for 14 October 1941 (M. Gorinov (ed.), *Moskva Prifrontovaya 1941–1942*, p. 284).

30 G. Andreevski, pp. 215–16.

31 M. Gorinov, 'Budni Osazhdënnoi Stolitsy', *Otechestvennaya Istoria*, 1996/3, p. 5.

32 Nikolai Kiselëv, interview, 4 October 2002.

33 *Pochtovye Vedomosti*, 5, 27 February 2001.

34 Ibid.; Labas, 'Chërny sneg na Kuznetskom'.

35 M. Gorinov, speech to conference organised by Moscow Mayor's office on 10 December 2004. One long-term consequence was that the Moscow archives for 1941 are very thin: it was not until the beginning of 1942 that papers began once again to be kept properly in the files of Moscow's municipal organisations and factories.

36 K. Simonov, *Zhivye i Mërtvye* (Moscow, 2004), p. 230.

37 Report by Moscow Party Committee of 15 November 1941 (Gorinov (ed.), *Moskva Prifrontovaya 1941–1942*, p. 264).

38 In October 1941 over 5,000 pistols were distributed to Party officials and activists, members of 'Destroyer Battalions' and special groups. The handover was not properly documented and by the spring of 1942 large numbers were still unaccounted for (report by the military department of the Moscow GorKom, 30 April 1942, M. Gorinov (ed.), *Moskva Prifrontovaya* (Moscow, 2001), p. 253.

39 From an account by F. Medvedev, head of the Moscow Underground Komsomol organisation, 23 March 1943 (ibid., p. 277).

40 V. Kravchenko, *I Chose Freedom* (London, n.d.), p. 179.
41 Romanenko's report No. 1/322 of 18 October (Gorinov (ed.), *Moskva Prifrontovaya 1941–1942*, pp. 265–6).
42 A. Sakharov, *Memoirs* (London, 1990), p. 43.
43 H. Cassidy, *Moscow Dateline, 1941–1943* (London, 1943), p. 123.
44 Extract from the workers' formal 'Act' of complaint (Gorinov (ed.), *Moskva Prifrontovaya 1941–1942*, p. 263).
45 Zhuravlëv report of 18 October (Patrushev (ed.), *Nachalo*, Vol. 2, pp. 222 et seq.).
46 Liubov Vostrosablina, interview, 26 May 2002.
47 Extract from report dated 17 October 1941 (Gorinov (ed.), *Moskva Prifrontovaya 1941–1942*, p. 261).
48 Klavdia Leonova, interview, 6 October 2004.
49 Andreevski, *Zhizn Moskvy v stalinskuyu epokhu 1930–1940e gody*, p. 144.
50 *Pochtovye Vedomosti* 5, 27 February 2001.
51 Gorinov (ed.), *Moskva Prifrontovaya 1941–1942*, p. 289.
52 I. Kovalchenko et al. (eds.), *Moskva Voennaya 1941/45: Memuary: Arkhivnye Dokumenty* (Moscow, 2001), p. 478.
53 Simonov, *Zhivye i Mërtvye*, p. 320.
54 Ponikarpova, 'Moskva, Ispytanie Voinoi'.
55 Andreevski, *Zhizn Moskvy v stalinskuyu epokhu 1930–1940e gody*, p. 145.
56 Textile workers in Ivanovo struck against the Tsars in 1905 and against the Communists in 1932 (R. Service, *Stalin* (London, 2004), p. 310.
57 Report of 21 November 1941 by Ivanovo ObKom Secretary Paltsev (A. Livshin (ed.), *Sovietskaya Povsednevnost i Massovoe Soznanie 1939–1945* (Moscow, 2003), pp. 43–53).
58 Yu. Gorkov, *Gosudarstvenny Komitet Oborony* (Moscow, 2002), p. 88, quoting note dictated by Mikoyan.
59 A. Shakhurin, *Krylya Pobedy* (Moscow, 1990), Chapter 4, 'To the East'.
60 Decision No. 40/12 of MosSoviet of 16 October (Gorinov (ed.), *Moskva Prifrontovaya 1941–1942*, p. 261).
61 Extract from Pronin's memoirs (ibid., p. 271).
62 GKO Order No. 813 of 19 October 1941 (Filatov et al. (eds.), *Moskovskaya Bitva v Postanovleniakh Gosudarstvennogo Komiteta Oborony*, p. 74).
63 Labas, 'Chërny sneg na Kuznetskom'.
64 *Vechernyaya Gazeta*, 18 October 1941.
65 Andreevski, *Zhizn Moskvy v stalinskuyu epokhu 1930–1940e gody*, p. 134.
66 Kovalchenko et al. (eds.), *Moskva Voennaya 1941/45*, pp. 550–61; M. Gorinov, 'Budni Osazhdënnoi Stolitsy', (*Otechestvennaya Istoria*, 3, 1996, p. 10).
67 These anecdotes come from Andreevski, *Zhizn Moskvy v stalinskuyu epokhu 1930–1940e gody*, p. 134–9.

68 Ponomarev, *Aleksandr Shcherbakov*, pp. 123, 128.
69 Note from Serov to Beria of 18 October 1941 (Gorinov (ed.), *Moskva Prifrontovaya 1941–1942*, p. 269).
70 Report of 20 October from D.N. Shadrin to the Deputy Commissar for Internal Affairs (Patrushev (ed.), *Nachalo*, Vol. 2, p. 231).
71 Report by Abakumov to the General Staff of 31 October 1941 (ibid., p. 256).
72 Vladimir Frolov, interview, 24 March 2002.
73 Sergei Markov, interview, 2 February 2002.
74 Yevgeni Teleguev, interview, 23 March 2002.
75 M. Gorinov, speech to conference organised by Moscow Mayor's office on 10 December 2004 (Gorinov (ed.), *Moskva Prifrontovaya 1941–1942*, p. 275).
76 Memorial website.
77 The documents are in Patrushev (ed.), *Nachalo*, Vol. 1, pp. 215, 248; see also D. Murphy, *What Stalin Knew: The Enigma of Barbarossa* (New Haven, 2005), pp. 236–9.
78 N. Shunevich, 'Chelovek i Obshchestvo', in *Fakty i Komentarii*, 16 April 2002 (www.brazd.ru/books/stat/o_smusheviche).
79 This generally accepted story is set out in Murphy, *What Stalin Knew*, p. 244.

Chapter 13: Evacuation

1 Yu. Gorkov, *Gosudarstvenny Komitet Oborony* (Moscow, 2002), p. 28.
2 G. Kumanëv, 'The Soviet Economy and the 1941 Evacuation', in J. Wieczynski (ed.), *Operation Barbarossa: The German Attack on the USSR* (Salt Lake City, 1993), p. 164.
3 List of Stalin's visitors for 24 June: I. Kovalchenko et al. (eds.), *Moskva Voennaya 1941/45: Memuary i Arkhivnye Dokumenty* (Moscow, 1995), p. 58.
4 GKO decision No. 173 (Gorkov, *Gosudarstvenny Komitet Oborony*, p. 33).
5 M. Sadykiewicz, *The Soviet Rail System* (2nd edition, Vienna, Virginia, 1990), pp. 88–93.
6 Figures in Gorkov, *Gosudarstvenny Komitet Oborony*, p. 166.
7 A. Boyd, *The Soviet Air Force since 1918* (London, 1977), pp. 189–90.
8 Ibid.
9 J. Gardiner, *Wartime: Britain 1939–1945* (London, 2004), p. 14.
10 GKO decision No. 165 (Gorkov, *Gosudarstvenny Komitet Oborony*, p. 162).
11 Ibid., p. 167.
12 Anna Nepomnyashchaya, interview, 12 March 2002.
13 'Proval na Transporte, Glava Pervaya', *Pochtovye Vedomosti*, 8, 17 April 2001.
14 G. Andreevski, *Zhizn Moskvy v stalinskuyu epokhu 1930–1940e gody* (Moscow, 2003), p. 135.
15 Moscow Embassy telegram No. 1282 of 12 October 1941 (PRO FCO371/29558, p. 6).

16 Kuibyshev Embassy despatch No. 1 of 22 October 1941 (PRO FCO371/29558, p. 31).
17 Yu. Labas, 'Chërny Sneg na Kuznetskom', *Rodina*, 6–7, 1999, pp. 36–7.
18 E. Wilson, *Shostakovich: A Life Remembered* (London, 1995), p. 149.
19 'Proval na Transporte, *Glava Vtoraya*', *Pochtovye Vedomosti*, 8, 17 April 2001.
20 Irina Antonova, interview, 19 February 2003.
21 Irina Golyamina, interview, 9 December 2004.
22 PRO FCO371/29558, pp. 46–55.
23 Andreevski, *Zhizn Moskvy v stalinskuyu epokhu 1930–1940e gody*, p. 128.
24 A. Sakharov, *Memoirs* (London, 1990), pp. 43–5.
25 Ibid., p. 45.
26 Ibid., p. 52.
27 Ibid., p. 54.
28 Article by Svetlana Makarenko at www.peoples.ru/family/children/efron/. Elaine Feinstein says Tsvetaeva's son was killed in the battle of Moscow (*A Captive Lion* (London, 1987), p. 270). But he would then have been still too young to join the army and he would have been hard put to get to Moscow from Yelabuga in the time available.
29 H. Segal, '*Drama of Struggle*', in R. Stites (ed.), *Culture and Entertainment in Wartime Russia* (Bloomington, IN, 1995), p. 108.
30 Essay by M. Gorinov on theatre in Moscow in November 1941 (M. Gorinov (ed.), *Moskua Prifrontovaya 1941–1942* (Moscow, 2001), p. 366.
31 Wilson, *Shostakovich*, p. 150.
32 Ibid., p. 153.
33 Ibid., p. 158.
34 Gorkov, *Gosudarstvenny Komitet Oborony*, p. 162.
35 Yu. Zakrevski, *Nashe Rodnoe Kino* (Moscow, 2004), p. 41.
36 Lidia Smirnova, interview, 19 April 2003, and Smirnova, *Moya Liubov* (Moscow, 2001).
37 Report No. 28 of 3 August 1941 by the Military Council of the Southern Front (Kovalchenko et al. (eds.), *Moskva Voennaya 1941/45*, p. 77.
38 GKO Order No. 636; Beria Order No. 1237 of 8 September 1941; Major Zhuravlëv's Report No. 1/732 of 19 September 1941 to Beria (ibid., pp. 77–9).
39 This is the somewhat counterintuitive conclusion of Robert Conquest, who is never inclined to give the Soviet authorities the benefit of the doubt (see *The Nation Killers* (London, 1970), p. 109).
40 Gorkov, *Gosudarstvenny Komitet Oborony*, pp. 163–4.
41 Record of conversation with a senior railway official, 6 January 1944 (Gorinov (ed.), *Moskva Prifrontovaya 1941–1942*, pp. 280–83).

Chapter 14: Compressing the Spring

1 E. Vorobiëv, in Yu. Kammerer et al., *Moskve – Vozdushnaya Trevoga* (Moscow, 2000), p. 107.

2 Z. Khiren, 'Parad sorok pervogo', *Ogonëk*, 45, 1960, pp. 3–6, quoted in S. Bialer, *Stalin and His Generals: Soviet Military Memoirs of World War II* (New York, 1969), p. 305.
3 A. Sbytov, in K. Bukov et al. (eds.), in *Bitva za Moskvu* (Moscow, 1985), p. 361.
4 G. Zhukov, *Vospominania i Razmyshlenia* (Moscow, 2002), Vol. 2, p. 26.
5 A. Ryazanov, 'The Front Line Parade Which Became a Legend', *Pravda KPRF*, 6 November 2001.
6 'Parad posle voskhoda solntsa', *Moskovski Komsomolets*, 6 November 2001.
7 I. Shamshin, chief engineer, Moscow City Radio Network, in Kammerer et al., *Moskve – Vozdushnaya Trevoga*, pp. 48–52.
8 'Parad posle voskhoda solntsa', *Moskovski Komsomolets*, 6 November 2001.
9 Note of conversation with V. Kolosova, dated 21 September 1942, in I. Kovalchenko et al. (eds.), *Moskva Voennaya 1941/45: Memuary; Arkhivnye Dokumenty*, (Moscow, 1995), p. 144.
10 Vorobiëv, in Kammerer et al., *Moskve – Vozdushnaya Trevoga*, pp. 102–13.
11 H. Boog (ed.), *Das Deutsche Reich und der Zweite Weltkrieg*, Vol. 4 (Stuttgart 1983), p. 698; Moscow City Archive, Fond P-552, Opis 2, Delo 337.
12 Diary of P. Miller (M. Gorinov (ed.), *Moskva Prifrontovaya 1941–1942: Arkhivnye Dokumenty i Materialy* (Moscow, 2001), p. 360.
13 Embassy despatch No. 15 (from Kuibyshev) of 8 November (PRO FO371/29499, p. 118).
14 Z. Khiren, quoted in Bialer, *Stalin and His Generals,* p. 306; 'Legendarny Parad', *Krasnaya Zvezda*, 8 November 2001.
15 Praskovia Sergeeva, interview, 26 March 2002.
16 P. Miller diary for 7 November (Gorinov (ed.), *Moskva Prifrontovaya 1941–1942*, p. 359.
17 V. Karpov, *Generalissimus* (Kaliningrad, 2002), p. 500.
18 Vorobiëv, in Kammerer et al., *Moskve – Vozdushnaya Trevoga,* p. 102–13.
19 Kuzma Minin (died 1616), a butcher from Nizhni Novgorod, and Prince Dmitri Pozharski (1578–1642) raised the army (*opolchenie*) which expelled the Poles and installed the first Romanov in 1613. Their statue is on Red Square. This defining moment in Russian history is the background to Glinka's opera *A Life for the Tsar*.
20 The honour is disputed. The men of the Dzerzhinski Division claim that they led the parade. So do the men of one of the volunteer divisions.
21 V. Zhilin (ed.), *Bitva pod Moskvoi: Khronika, Fakty, Lyndi* (Moscow, 2001), Vol. 1, pp. 528–32.
22 N. Ponikarpova, 'Moskva, Ispytanie Voinoi', *Moskovski Zhurnal*, May 1999, pp. 33–8.
23 The British version of the film is in the photographic archive of the Imperial War Museum. A film of the parade itself is randomly available, often attached as

additional material to DVDs of classic Soviet feature films about the war. It still has the power to move.

24 Vladislav Mikosha, interview, 3 February 2002, and *Ryadom s Soldatom* (Moscow, 1983).

25 Vorobiëv, in Kammerer et al., *Moskve – Vozdushnaya Trevoga,* p. 107.

26 A. Chew, *Fighting the Russians in Winter* (Leavenworth Paper No. 5, Combined Arms Research Library, Fort Leavenworth, Kansas, December 1981).

27 Russian historians tend to give the Germans a considerable edge in numbers at this point in the Moscow battle. The figures here are derived from those in D. Glantz, *Barbarossa: Hitler's Invasion of Russia 1941* (Stroud, 2001), p. 169.

28 Richard Sorge, the Soviet agent in Tokyo, had reported that the Japanese would not attack while the Russians were preoccupied by the threat to Moscow; and this is usually taken as the basis for Stalin's decision to move forces from the Far East, where they had been facing the Japanese. If so, Stalin had changed his view of Sorge's reliability since he had so brutally rejected his warning of the German attack in June. In any case, the Japanese were on the eve of launching a war in the Pacific and, unlike Hitler, they had more sense than to let themselves in for a war on two fronts.

29 K. Rokossovski, *Soldatski Dolg* (Moscow, 2002), p. 134.

30 B. Nevzorov, *Moskovskaya Bitva-Fenomen vtoroi mirovoi* (Moscow, 2001), p. 83, quoting a captured German report.

31 Rokossovski, *Soldatski Dolg*, p. 115.

32 G. Zhukov, *Vospominania i Razmyshlenia* (Moscow, 2002), Vol. II, p. 31.

33 Rokossovski reverted to the incident in his speech at the Party meeting which expelled Zhukov in October 1957 (V. Naumov (ed.), *Georgi Zhukov – Documenty* (Moscow, 2001), p. 359).

34 Vorobiëv, in Kammerer et al., *Moskve – Vozdushnaya Trevoga,* p. 107.

35 H. Guderian, *Panzer Leader* (Cambridge, 2002), p. 248.

36 He later furiously denied Russian claims that his men had desecrated the Tolstoy house (ibid., p. 257).

37 The Germans had reduced their cavalry to a shadow by the beginning of the war. They expanded it again under the conditions of the war in the East. At the beginning of the war in 1941 the Russians had nine cavalry divisions and four mountain cavalry divisions. By the end of that year they had developed a large number of smaller and more manoeuvrable light cavalry divisions (S. Zaloga and L. Ness, *Red Army Handbook 1939–1945* (Stroud, 2003), p. 107; 'Velikaya Voina, Kavaleriiskie Soedinenia' at velikvoy.narod.ru/voyska/voyskacccp/struktura/kaval).

38 The simile comes from D. Glantz and J. House, *When Titans Clashed: How the Red Army Stopped Hitler* (Edinburgh, 2000), p. 82.

39 F. Halder, *The Halder War Diary 1939–1942* (Novato, 1988), pp. 561, 569.

40 The case of Private Lynch, the American 'heroine' of the Iraq war, is one of the most recent examples.

41 R. Stites (ed), *Culture and Entertainment in Wartime Russia* (Bloomington, IN, 1995), p. 138.

42 See documentation in Gorinov (ed.), *Moskva Prifrontovaya 1941–1942*, pp. 533–40. See also Ye. Senyavskaya, *Psikhologia Voiny v XX-om Veke* (Moscow, 1999), pp. 214–37; B. Sokolov, *Georgi Zhukov: Triumfy i Padenie* (Moscow, 2003), p. 293. The subject of the twenty-eight Panfilovtsy has also been much debated in the press and in articles on the Internet. See, for example, V. Kardin, 'Legendy i Fakty' *Novy Mir*, 2, 1966, p. 237; G. Bregin, 'Podvig i Podlog' (gentrees.com/a20/books/podvig); A. Platonov, '28 Panfilovtsev – a byl li podvig?' 9 November 2003, (www.statya.ru/index.php?op=view&id=2213); 'Sovietski Geroicheski Mif', Radio Liberty (www.svoboda.org/programs/TD/2001/TD.111801.asp).

43 B. Momysh-Uly, *Psikhologia Voiny* (Alma Ata, 1990). Momysh-Uly's acount of the events as seen through his own eyes, and of the problems of collaborating with a non-military civilian to describe his own military methods, is elegant and perceptive.

44 Information from Edward Luttwak; Panfilov and the popularity of Bek's novel in the Israeli army figure in *Odessa-Mama* by Amos Keinan from *Flight to the Prison*, published in Tel Aviv, 2004, and briefly available in Russian on the Internet.

45 H. Mueller, *Die Schlacht, Wolokolamsker Chaussee* (Frankfurt am Main, 1988); G. Heeg, 'Der Weg der Panzer', in W. Storch (ed.), *Explosion of a Memory: Heiner Müller* (Berlin, 1988), p. 138; J.-C. Hauschild, *Heiner Mueller* (Berlin, 2001), pp. 422–34.

46 German air activity over the central front fell by two-thirds in January 1942 (C. Bergstrom and A. Mikhailov, *Black Cross, Red Star: The Air War over the Eastern Front*, Vol. 2 (Pacifica, 2001), p. 40.

47 Gorinov (ed.), *Moskva Prifrontovaya 1941–1942*, p. 297.

48 This story has been much repeated: see, for example, V. Karpov, *Generalissimo* (Kaliningrad, 2002), p. 494; S. Sebag Montefiore, *Stalin: The Court of the Red Tsar* (London, 2003) p. 355. G. Kumanëv (*Ryadom so Stalinym* (Smolensk, 2001), p. 312) claims that he was told the story by Golovanov himself. Golovanov remembered the conversation taking place in October. But the Germans did not get so near to Perkhushkovo until the end of November, which seems a more likely date. At least one Moscow historian, Anatoli Ponomarëv, wonders if the exchange took place at all (private conversation). But the story neatly illustrates two of Stalin's most important characteristics: his willpower and his black humour. Like other anecdotes about him, *se non è vero, è ben trovato*.

Chapter 15: The Spring Uncoils

1 *Vechernyaya Moskva*; Yuri Averbakh, interview, 26 March 2002; 'Pervenstvo Moskvy v 1941 godu', item on Club Kasparov website (www.clubkasparov.ru).

2 Now largely forgotten, the French composer Robert Planquette (1848–1903) specialised in comic opera. *Les Cloches de Corneville* was one of his most successful pieces.

3 Yu. Kammerer et al., *Moskve – Vozdushnaya Trevoga* (Moscow, 2000), pp. 90–92.
4 Gridaspov's report is dated 11 November. He was presumably referring to a forthcoming programme (M. Gorinov (ed.), *Moskva Prifrontovaya 1941–1942: Arkhivnye Dokumenty i Materialy* (Moscow, 2001), pp. 362–3.
5 G. Krivosheev (ed.) *Rossia i SSSR v Voinakh XX Veka: Statisticheskoe Issledovanie* (Moscow, 2001), p. 263; B. Nevzorov, *Moskovskaya Bitva – Fenomen vtoroi mirovoi* (Moscow, 2001), p. 95.
6 H. Boog (ed.), *Das Deutsche Reich und der Zweite Weltkrieg*, Vol. 4, (Stuttgart, 1983), p. 601, quoted ibid., p. 103.
7 G. Zhukov, *Vospominania i Razmyshlenia*, Vol. 2 (Moscow, 2002), p. 37 .
8 Cherevichenko commanded the Bryansk Front until April 1942.
9 Quoted in Nevzorov, *Moskovskaya Bitva*, p. 99.
10 Ibid., p. 110.
11 Note No. 2955/b of 3 December 1941 (Gorinov (ed.), *Moskva Prifrontovaya 1941–1942*, p. 322).
12 Report by Commissar Belyanov of 6 January 1942 (V. Kristoforov et al. (eds.), *Lubyanka v dni bitvy za Moskvu* (Moscow, 2002), p. 314. General Maslennikov's note of 28 November to Beria, criticising Koniev's dispositions on the Kalinin Front, is another example of the way in which the NKVD continued to second-guess the professional military (Volkogonov papers, Box 4, Folder 11599, 11.28.1941).
13 Pavel Gudz, interview, 1 June 2002; B. Yarotski, *Ne Odnazhdy Ispytav Sudbu* (Moscow, 1997), pp. 63–92.
14 K. Rokossovski, *Soldatski Dolg* (Moscow, 2002), p. 142.
15 Zhukov, *Vospominania i Razmyshlenia*, Vol. 2, p. 41.
16 A. Eden, *The Eden Memoirs: The Reckoning* (London, 1965), p. 289.
17 Vladimir Ogryzko, interview, 1 June 2002.
18 Vladimir Ogryzko, interview, 1 June 2002.
19 A. Eden, *Facing the Dictators* (London, 1962), p. 298.
20 Ibid., p. 299.
21 Information from Anatoli Ponomarëv, 6 December 2004.
22 D. Ortenberg, *Stalin, Shcherbakov, Mekhlis i Drugie* (Moscow, 1995), pp. 104–5.
23 *Pravda*, 13 December 1941.
24 A. Sakharov, *Memoirs* (London, 1990), p. 45.
25 I. Kovalchenko et al. (eds.), *Moskva Voennaya 1941/45: Memuary i Arkhivnye Dokumenty* (Moscow, 1995), p. 65.
26 J. Lucas, *War on the Eastern Front: The German Soldier in Russia, 1941–1945* (London, 1998), p. 64.
27 E. Kulkov, M. Myagkov and O. Rzheshevski, *Voina 1941–1945: Fakty y Dokumenty* (Moscow, 2004), p. 219.
28 V. Knyshevski (ed.), *Skrytaya Pravda Voiny: 1941 god* (Moscow, 1992), pp. 212–13.

29 Zhuravlëv order of 18 September (extracts) (N. Patrushev (ed.), *Nachalo: Sbornik Dokumentov* (Moscow, 2000), Vol. 2, p. 116.
30 The myths and facts surrounding the story of Zoya Kosmodemyanskaya are set out in Ye. Senyavskaya, *Psikhologia Voiny v XX-om veke* (Moscow, 1999), pp. 214–37; M. Gorinov, 'Zoya Kosmodemyanskaya: Pravda i Vymysel', *Otechestvennaya Istoria*, 1, 2003, p. 77; Gorinov (ed.), *Moskva Prifrontovaya 1941–1942*, p. 581.
31 This account is taken from the report of the NKVD's interrogation of Klubkov, dated 11–12 March 1942 (reproduced in Kristoforov et al. (eds.), *Lubyanka v dni bitvy za Moskvu*, pp. 182–90).
32 A. Beevor, *Berlin* (London, 2002) p. 212.
33 Yevgeni Teleguev, interview, 23 March 2002.
34 Yevgeni Anufriev, interview, 3 February 2002.
35 Yevgeni Teleguev, interview, 23 March 2002.
36 Quoted in Kulkov, Nyagkov and Rzheshevski, *Voina*, p. 218.
37 GKO Order No. 1025 of 14 December 1941 (V. Filatov et al. (eds.), *Moskovskaya Bitva v Postanovleniakh Gosudarstvennogo Komiteta Oborony* (Moscow, 2001), p. 91).
38 GKO Order No. 1068 of 27 December 1941 (ibid., p. 92).
39 *Vechernyaya Moskva*, 12 December 1941.
40 *Vechernyaya Moskva*, 16 December 1941.
41 *Vechernyaya Moskva*, 26 December 1941.
42 G. Andreevski, *Zhizn Moskvy v stalinskuyu epokhu 1930–1940e gody* (Moscow, 2003), p. 105; J. Gardiner, *Wartime: Britain 1939–1945* (London, 2004), p. 155.
43 A. Ponomarëv, *Aleksandr Shcherbakov: Stranitsy Biografii* (Moscow, 2004), pp. 180–81.
44 Dunstan, *Soviet Schooling in the Second World War* (London, 1997), p. 139.
45 M. Morukov, *Iz Istorii Obrazovania v Moskve Voennoi* (paper presented at conference in Moscow on 10 December 1944).
46 Kulkov, Myagkov and Rzheshevski, *Voina 1941–1945*, p. 86.
47 N. Aleshchenko, *Moskovski Soviet v 1941–1945 gg.* (Moscow, 1980), pp. 145–6.
48 Ponomarev, *Aleksandr Shcherbakov*, pp. 182–3.
49 Andreevski, *Zhizn Moskvy v stalinskuyu epokhu 1930–1940e gody*, p. 130.

Chapter 16: Defeat into Victory

1 N. Ponikarpova, 'Moskva, Ispytanie Voinoi', *Moskovski Zhurnal*, May 1999, pp. 33–8.
2 Order of 27 December 1941 (Fond No. P-425, Opis No. 4, Ed. Khr.12, List 3).
3 Ella and Era Zhukov, interview, 2 February 2002; interview with Zasypkin, whose father worked in the KGB department concerned.

4 Sakharova diary (I. Kovalchenko et al. (eds.), *Moskva Voennaya 1941/45: Memuary i Arkhivnye Dokumenty* (Moscow, 1995), pp. 657–87).
5 M. Gorinov, 'Budni Osazhdennoi Stolitsy', *Otechestvennaya Istoria*, 3, 1996, p. 13.
6 M. Gorinov (ed.), *Moskva Prifrontovaya 1941–1942: Arkhivnye Dokumenty i Materialy* (Moscow, 2001), p. 415.
7 A. Ponomarëv, *Aleksandr Shcherbakov: Stranitsy Biografii* (Moscow, 2004), pp. 168–9.
8 Yu. Gorkov, *Gosudarstvenny Komitet Oborony Postanovlyaet* (Moscow, 2002), p. 204, quoting a report by Zhukov, 'A Short Analysis of Operations during the Great Patriotic War 1941–45'.
9 D. Ortenberg, *Stalin, Shcherbakov, Mekhlis i Drugie* (Moscow, 1995), pp. 79–84.
10 G. Zhukov, *Vospominania i Razmyshlenia*, Vol. 2, (Moscow, 2002), pp. 42–3.
11 K. Rokossovski, *Soldatski Dolg* (Moscow, 2002), p. 153.
12 Zhukov, *Vospominania i Razmyshlenia*, Vol. 2, p. 51.
13 It is indelibly lodged in the popular mnind that Serova and Rokossovski had a long-lasting affair. Members of all three families – the Rokossovskis, the Simonovs, and Valentina Serova's daughter Maria – are firm that this was not so. The story that Rokossovski gave his dinner to Serova was passed on to me by his great-granddaughter Ariadna Rokossowska, who got it from Nina Grib, a nurse at the hospital.
14 J. Erickson, *The Road to Stalingrad*, (London, 1983), p. 305.
15 N. Konyaev, *Vlasov: Dva Litsa Generala* (Moscow, 2003), p. 60, quoting P. Gerasimov, *Voenno-Istoricheski Zhurnal*, 7, 1967.
16 Both sides seem to have adopted this practice. So did civilians. Grossman describes how, in the fighting around Moscow, one old man came back from the battlefield with a sackful of frozen legs. He thawed the legs out on the stove in his *izba* so as to get the boots off more easily. They weren't very good boots, commented Grossman: German boots were not designed for winter wear (J. and C. Garrard, *The Bones of Berdichev: The Life and Fate of Vasily Grossman* (New York, 1996), p. 155.
17 Quoted Erickson, *The Road to Stalingrad*, p. 332.
18 Altogether the 2nd Shock Army lost 66,000 men (J. Erickson, Foreword to G. Krivosheev (ed.), *Soviet Casualties and Combat Losses in the Twentieth Century* (London, 1997), p. viii).
19 E. Kulkov, M. Myagkov and O. Rzheshevski, *Voina 1941–1945: Fakty, Dokumenty* (Moscow, 2004), p. 236.
20 V. Zhilin (ed.), *Bitva pod Moskvoi: Khronika, Fakty, Lyudi* (Moscow, 2001), p. 39.
21 Kulkov, Myagkov and Rzhevshevski, *Voina 1941–1945*, p. 232.
22 M. Hastings, *Armageddon: The Battle for Germany, 1944–45* (London, 2004), pp. 479–80.

23 GKO Order No. 1069 of 27 December 1941 (V. Filatov et al. (eds.), *Moskovskaya Bitva v Postanovleniakh Gosudarstvennogo Komiteta Oborony* (Moscow, 2001), p. 93.
24 Kulkov, Myagkov and Rzheshevski, *Voina 1941–1945*, pp. 232–9; N. Ramanichev, 'Vlasov i Drugie', annexe to article in *Pervoe Sentyabrya*, No. 34, 2001. Not all the relevant documents are yet available.
25 A. Chernyaev, *Moya Zhizn i Moë Vremya* (Moscow, 1995), pp. 100–107.
26 P. Sagaidachny, *Dnevnik Peti Sagaidachnogo* (Moscow, 1963), p. 277.
27 Gorinov, 'Budni Osazhdënnoi Stolitsy', p. 24.
28 Verzhbitski diary for 26 March 1942 (I. Kovalchenko et al. (eds.), *Moskva Voennaya 1941/45: Memuary i Arkhivnyne Dokumenty* (Moscow, 1995), p. 502.
29 Ponikarpova, 'Moskva, Ispytanie Voinoi'.
30 Gorinov, 'Budni Osazhdennoi Stolitsy', p. 7.
31 Gorinov (ed.), *Moskva Prifrontovaya 1941–1942*, pp. 481–2.
32 Sakharova diary (Kovalchenko et al. (eds.), *Moskva Voennaya 1941/45*, pp. 657–87).
33 M. Gorinov, speech to conference organised by Moscow Mayor's office on 10 December 2004.
34 Ponomarëv, *Aleksandr Shcherbakov*, pp. 171–2.
35 Order No. 39/a of 10 December 1941 (Moscow City Archive, Fond No. P-425, Opis 4, Ed. Khr. 24, List 40).
36 Order of 26 February 1942 (Moscow City Archive, Fond No P-425, Opis 4, Ed. Khr. 24, List 22).
37 Order of 19 March 1942 (Moscow City Archive, Fond No. P-425, Opis 4, Ed. Khr. 24, List 28).
38 Order of 30 March 1942 (Moscow City Archive, Fond No. P-425, Opis 4, Ed. Khr. 24, List 34).
39 Order of 24 March 1942 (Moscow City Archive, Fond No. P-425, Opis 4, Ed. Khr. 24, List 30).
40 Order of 16 February 1942 (Moscow City Archive, Fond No. P-425, Opis 4, Ed. Khr. 24, List 9).
41 Order of 30 April 1942 (Moscow City Archive, Fond No. P-425, Opis 4, Ed. Khr. 24, List 55).
42 GKO decision No. 690 of 17 September 1941 (Filatov et al. (eds.), *Moskovskaya Bitva v Postanovleniakh Gosudarstvennogo Komiteta Oborony*, p. 61); Order of 12 January 1942 (Moscow City Archive, Fond No. P-425, Opis 4, Ed. Khr. 24, List 2).
43 Order of 15 April 1942 (Moscow City Archive, Fond No. P-425, Opis 4, Ed. Khr. 24, List 41).
44 J. Duncan, *Soviet Schooling in the Second World War* (London, 1997), p. 92.
45 N. Ponikarpova, 'Moskva, Ispytanie Voinoi'.
46 Sakharova diary (Kovalchenko et al. (eds.), *Moskva Voennaya 1941/45*, pp. 657–87). The opera is by Sergei Vasilenko (1872–1956) and was written in 1941. It

has not been published. Vasilenko taught for nearly fifty years at the Moscow Conservatoire until his death.

47 N. Ponikarpova, 'Moskva, Ispytanie Voinoi'.

48 Verzhbitski diary (Kovalchenko et al. (eds.), *Moskva Voennaya 1941/45*, p. 504).

49 N. Ponikarpova, 'Moskva, Ispytanie Voinoi'.

50 Sakharova diary (Kovalchenko et al. (eds.), *Moskva Voennaya 1941/45*, pp. 657–87).

51 NKVD report, quoted by Gorinov, 'Budni Osazhdënnoi Stolitsy', p. 25.

52 Quoted in B. Sokolov, *Georgi Zhukov: Triumfy i Padenie* (Moscow, 2003), p. 328.

53 G. Krivosheev (ed.), *Rossia i SSSR v Voinakh XX Veka: Statisticheskoe Issledovanie* (Moscow, 2001), p. 277; Sokolov, *Georgi Zhukov,* p. 328.

54 It is not clear where the responsibility for the decision-making lay. This account in based on D. Glantz and J. House, *When Titans Clashed: How the Red Army Stopped Hitler* (Edinburgh, 2000), p. 116, and D. Glantz, *Colossus Reborn* (Kansas, 2005), pp. 34–5. The figure for Russian losses comes from Kulkov, Myagkov and Rzhevshevski, *Voina 1941–1945*, p. 80.

55 B. Taylor, *Barbarossa to Berlin*, Vol 1 (Staplehurst 2003), p. 247.

56 S. Zaloga. *Bagration 1944: The Destruction of Army Group Center* (Westport, 2004); G. Andreevski *Zhizn Moskvy v stalinskuyu epokhu 1930–1940e gody* (Moscow, 2003), p. 196; Yelena Nemirovskaya, interview, 9 October 2004. Mikhail Nemirovski and his family had just moved into an apartment in the 'Lace House', and Lena remembers seeing the parade from her window as a very small girl.

57 Order of 12 April 1942 by People's Commissar for Defence (i.e. Stalin) (quoted in A. Ideimenov, 'Tsena Pobedy', *Voenno-Istoricheski Zhurnal*, 4, 1990, pp. 4–5; translation from A. Sella, *The Value of Life in Soviet Warfare* (London, 1992), p. 69).

58 The story about Igor Sats is in Sokolov, *Georgi Zhukov*, p. 244. The five million margin of error also comes from Sokolov.

59 R. Overmans, *Deutsche militaerische Verluste im letzten Weltkrieg* (Munich, 1999), p. 265.

60 J.D. Barber and M. Harrison, *The Soviet Home Front 1941–1945* (London, 1991), p. ix. Since all the figures that go to make up these ratios are disputed by one authority or another – even the totals for British and American dead vary from author to author – too much reliance should not be placed on the exact numbers. But whatever figures you choose, the broad picture remains the same.

Chapter 17: Aftermath

1 Rokossovski's restraining Order No. 006 was not immediately understood by some of his men, who thought it a break with previous policy, even a 'provocation by the Commissars' (A.V. Golubev (ed.), *Rossia i Zapad* (Moscow, 1998), p.

258). The late historian Nikolai Andreev was there at the time. When he asked a Russian soldier if he was not ashamed of what happened, the man replied, 'I am now, but I certainly wasn't then.'

2 I. Zbarski, *Obyekt No. 1* (Moscow, 2000), p. 196.

3 Western historians have written at length about the large-scale rape and violence committed by Russian soldiers in Germany at the end of the war. Russian historians, offended that the glory of the victorious Red Army should be so tarnished, have denied that anything of the kind happened at all, or at least on that scale. But throughout the centuries soldiers have behaved badly in the heat of victory. What happened in the Spanish city of Badajoz after it was stormed by Wellington's soldiers in 1812 was different only in degree from what happened in Berlin in 1945. The Russians could tell themselves that they were taking revenge on an enemy who had done unspeakable damage to their own people. The British soldiers did not have that excuse: the citizens of Badajoz were our allies at the time. That was not so long ago, and human nature does not change that much or that quickly.

4 Zbarski, *Obyekt No. 1*, p. 204.

5 P. Levi, *La Tregua* (Turin, 1967), p. 94.

6 M. Hastings, *Armageddon: The Battle for Germany, 1944–45* (London, 2004), p. 582.

7 Article on Popova at www.3-millenium.ru/index.php?m1=2&cont=21&cer=11&page=popova; article on Gasheva by I. Filatov (untitled) (region.utmn.ru/raz).

8 Yelena Nemirovskaya, interview, 9 October 2004.

9 Alexander's brother Ivan tells the story in his *Rodina i chuzhbina – kniga zhizni* (Smolensk, 1996) .

10 The reports from the security authorites date from 1943 and 1944. They are in A. Artizov and O. Naumov (eds.), *Vlast i Khudozhestvennaya Intelligentsia (Dokumenty 1917–1953)* (Moscow, 2002), pp. 492, 552.

11 Hastings, *Armageddon*.

12 Order of Minister of Defence (i.e. Stalin) of 9 June 1946 (V. Naumov (ed.), *Georgi Zhukov: Dokumenty* (Moscow, 2001) pp. 16, 19.

13 B. Sokolov, *Georgi Zhukov: Triumfy i Padenie* (Moscow, 2003), p. 496.

14 Politburo decision No. 58 of 27 June 1947 (Artizov and Naumov (eds.), *Vlast i Khudozhestvennaya Intelligentsia (Dokumenty 1917–1953)* (Moscow, 2002), p. 622.

15 Sokolov, *Georgi Zhukov*, p. 499.

16 Decision of the Central Committee, 29 October 1957 (Naumov, *Georgi Zhukov*, pp. 440–41).

17 Note by Helena Rokossowska in K. Rokossovski, *Soldatski Dolg* (Moscow, 2002), pp. 462–6.

18 Konstantin Vilievich Rokossovski, interview, 12 December 2003.

19 General Wojciech Jaruzelski, interview, 25 June 2004.

20 Nadezhda Rokossovskaya has visited the grave.

21 There are several accounts on the Internet about the sale of Rokossovski's apartment. See, for example, www.realprice.ru/SYSTEM/HTML/art_view.php4?ID=0762. On the honorary citizenship of Gdansk, see *Moskovski Komsomolets*, 11 October 2004, p. 11.

22 A. Nekrich, *1941 22 Iiunia* (Moscow, 1995), p. 263.

23 Artizov and Naumov (eds.), *Vlast i Khudozhestvennaya Intelligentsia (Dokumenty 1917–1953)*, p. 499.

24 M. Bloch, *Strange Defeat* (London, 1949), p. 134.

25 Ibid., p. 132.

26 A. Sakharov, *Memoirs* (London, 1990), p. 39.

27 J.D. Barber and M. Harrison, *The Soviet Home Front 1941–1945* (London, 1991), p. 70.

28 Yelena Nemirovskaya, interview, 9 October 2004.

29 Simonov's *The Living and the Dead* was, however, published more than ten times between 1959 and 2004.

30 The song – 'Vragi sozhgli rodnuyu khatu' – can still reduce a Russian audience to tears. It was written in 1945 by Mikhail Isakovski, who also composed 'Katyusha'. But the message of the song was so contrary to the official note of triumphalism that it was not freely performed for years.

31 J. Wieczynski (ed.), *Operation Barbarossa: The German Attack on the Soviet Union, June 22, 1941* (Salt Lake City, 1993), p. 276. Article by N. Tumarkin, 'The Invasion and War as Myth and Memory', quoting O. Golubeva, *Literaturnaya Gazeta*, 30 October 1991.

32 Interview on Radio Liberty (www.svoboda.org/programs/cicles/cinema/russian/6pm.asp).

SOURCES

Russian accounts of the war in the East have been overlaid and distorted by decades of pious legend, by the political correctness of officially approved historiography, and by the desire of the authorities – revived on the occasion of the sixtieth anniversary of the Victory – to emphasise the heroic achievements of the Soviet Union for their own political purposes. There is nevertheless a solid tradition of serious and professional historical writing in Russia. It can now flourish freely in the post-Soviet world, and much of the legend is being stripped away. But in recent years it has sometimes seemed as if everyone who could wield a pen felt that he (sometimes she) should produce some new and preferably sensational interpretation of the course of events and the motivations of the protagonists. Many of these new works are polemical in purpose, sloppily written, badly sourced, grossly biased and – worst of all – without an index.

The leading protagonists – generals like Rokossovski and Zhukov, Politburo members like Mikoyan and Khrushchëv, heads of government ministries like the Commissar for the Aviation Ministry, Shakhurin, writers and journalists like Ortenberg, Ehrenburg and Simonov – were unable to produce their memoirs until after Stalin died. Their works were then heavily censored on first publication, and were often rewritten many times as the demands of the political leadership changed. The lengthy and colourful passages of direct speech these memoirs contain are suspect for obvious reasons. Taken together, however, they give a human dimension to a story that risks otherwise becoming a dry chronicle of military and historical events.

I have also drawn heavily on the personal memories of men, women, children, civilians, workers, secret policemen, officials, doctors and nurses, artists, writers, musicians, who were there at the time. Of course they remember with advantages the things they did during those terrible days. But their voices – even when filtered through six decades of memory – are an essential part of the texture. Direct speech attributed to witnesses in the text is based on a combination of notes, the audio record, and in some cases published and unpublished memoirs. They are not necessarily literal transcriptions.

The figures for casualties in the battles and campaigns in the East, and even for the numbers of men involved, are vague or disputed, or were never available in the first place because of the nature of the fighting. The figures given by various authorities therefore vary, sometimes wildly. For the Russian figures I have relied especially on G. Krivosheev, *Rossia i SSSR v Voinakh XX Veka* (Moscow, 2001). His conclusions are not undisputed, but they are based on solid research in the archives. German record-keeping in the early stages of the war was more orderly. But it broke down in the chaotic fighting in Germany itself in the last months of the war. The problems of establishing German wartime losses are carefully set out in the introduction to R. Overmans, *Deutsche militaerische Verluste im letzten Weltkrieg* (Munich, 1999), pp. 1–8.

Films – even the most trivial or ideologically distorted – give a good feeling for a period. Those listed date from the 1930s to the present day. Those produced in the Soviet period reflected, of course, the ideology of the day. But some are excellent and many remain popular today. With the collapse of the Soviet Union, money has now replaced ideology as the limiting factor. Even so a wide variety of competent and interesting films about the war, expressing the full range of opinion for and against Stalin and the Soviet past, now regularly appears on the screen and on television. In 2004 three very popular block-buster television serials appeared of varying quality – *Shtrafbat*, *Deti Arbata*, *Moskovskaya Saga*. Contrary to a certain tendency in Russia today to glorify the Soviet past, these were highly critical of the Soviet regime, and emphasised that during the war the Russians fought for their country, not for Stalin.

I have not listed articles in the bibliography that follows. Their provenance is given in the notes. Many come from the Internet: the Russians have taken to the web with great enthusiasm, and there is a mass of useful material to be found as well, of course, as a great deal of rubbish.

Translations are by me except where indicated.

Archives, Museums and Libraries

RUSSIA

Krasnaya Zvezda Archive
Moscow Central Archive of Audiovisual Documents
Moscow City Central Archive
Moscow House of the Photograph
Museum of the Defence of Moscow
Museum of Contemporary Russian History
Museum of the Krasnaya Presnya Raion
Museum of School No. 110, Moscow

State Central Archive of Photography and the Cinema, Krasnogorsk
Vechernyaya Moskva Archive

UNITED KINGDOM
British Library
British Library Newspaper Library
Imperial War Museum Archive of Photographs and Film
London Library
National Archive

WASHINGTON
Library of Congress
Library of Congress Prints and Photographs Division
National Gallery of Art Photograph Collection
National Security Archive (Volkogonov Papers)

Published Documents

Access to Russian state archives varies from time to time, and the policy for opening them is erratic. But the archivists themselves are very helpful, knowledgeable and enthusiastic, and a great deal of useful material is available.

Since 1991 a large number of wartime documents have been systematically published in Russia. Many of them come from official sources, such as the Federal Security Service (FSB), the successor to the KGB, the Moscow City Authority, and others. Many others have been published by institutions such as Alexander Yakovlev's International Foundation for Democracy and the Memorial Society. The three collections of documents published under the auspices of the Moscow Mayor's Office between 1995 and 2001 (*Moskva Voennaya*, *Moskva Prifrontovaya* and *Moskva Poslevoennaya*) draw on the collections of documents and personal reminiscences which the Moscow authorities started to collect as early as 1942. They have been heavily mined by other authors and have been particularly useful for the present work.

Artizov, A., and Naumov, O. (eds.), *Vlast i Khudozhestvennaya Intelligentsia (Dokumenty 1917–1953)* (Moscow, 2002)
Filatov, V., et al. (eds.), *Moskovskaya Bitva v Postanovleniakh Gosudarstvennogo Komiteta Oborony* (Moscow, 2001)
Getty, A., and Naumov, O., *The Road to Terror: Stalin and the Self-Destruction of the Bolsheviks, 1932–1939* (New Haven, 1999)
Gorinov, M. (ed.), *Moskva Prifrontovaya 1941–1942: Arkhivnye Dokumenty i Materialy* (Moscow, 2001)
Khristoforov, V., et al. (eds.), *Lubyanka v dni bitvy za Moskvu* (Moscow, 2002)
Knyshevski, V. (ed.), *Skrytaya Pravda Voiny: 1941 god* (Moscow, 1992)

Kovalchenko, I., et al. (eds.), *Moskva Voennaya 1941/45: Memuary i Arkhivnye Dokumenty* (Moscow, 1995)
Naumov, V. (ed.), *1941 God: Dokumenty*, 2 vols (Moscow, 1998)
Patrushev, N. (ed.), *Krushenie 'Blitzkriga': Sbornik Dokumentov* (Moscow, 2003)
– *Ot Oborony k Nastupleniu: Sbornik Dokumentov* (Moscow, 2003)
– *Nachalo: Sbornik Dokumentov*, 2 vols. (Moscow, 2000)
Platonov, A., *Zapisnye Knigi, Materialy k Biografii* (Moscow, 2000)
Prokofiev, S., *Materialy, Dokumenty, Vospominania* (Moscow, 1961)
Stepashin, S. (ed.), *Organy Gosudarstvennoi Bezopasnosti SSSR*, Vol I, *Nakanune* (Moscow, 1995)
Zolotarev, V. (ed.), *Russki Arkhiv* 15/4(1): *Velikaya Otechestvennaya – Bitva pod Moskvoi, Sbornik Dokumentov* (Moscow, 1997)

Other Printed Material

Akhromeev, S. (ed.), *Voenny Entsiklopedicheski Slovar* (Moscow, 1986)
Aleshchenko, N., *Moskovskoe Opolchenie* (Moscow, 1969)
– *Moskovski Soviet v 1941–1945 gg.* (Moscow, 1976)
– *Moskovski Soviet v 1917–1941 gg.* (Moscow, 1980)
Andreevski, G., *Zhizn Moskvy v stalinskuyu epokhu 1930–1940e gody* (Moscow, 2003)
Andreyev, C., *Vlasov and the Russian Liberation Movement* (Cambridge, 1987)
Applebaum, A., *Gulag. A History of the Soviet Camps* (London, 2003)
Arapova, L. (ed.), *Golosa Istorii – Kniga Chetvertaya* (Moscow, 2000)
Aria, S., *Mozaika – Zapisi Advokata, Rechi* (Moscow, 2000)
Averbakh, Yu., *Shakhmaty za Kulisami* (Moscow, 2003)
Axell, A., *Marshal Zhukov* (London, 2003)
– *Russia's Heroes 1941–45* (London, 2002)
Baedeker, K. *Baedeker's Russia 1914* (London, 1971)
Barber, J.D., and Harrison, M., *The Soviet Home Front 1941–1945* (London, 1991)
Baring, M., *A Year in Russia* (London, 1907)
– *What I saw in Russia* (London, 1927)
Barron, J., *KGB: The Secret Work of Soviet Secret Agents* (New York, 1974)
Beevor, A., *A Writer at War: Vasily Grossman with the Red Army 1941–1945* (London, 2005)
– *Berlin: The Downfall 1945* (London, 2002)
– *Stalingrad* (London, 1998)
– *The Spanish Civil War* (London, 1999)
Bek, A., *Volokolamskoe Shosse* (Moscow, 1995)
Bek, T., *Do Svidania, alfavit* (Moscow, 2005)
Bergstrom, C., and Mikhailov, A., *Black Cross, Red Star: The Air War over the Eastern Front*, Vol. 2, *Resurgence January–June 1942* (Pacifica, 2001)
Berton, K., *The British Embassy Moscow* (Moscow, 1991)
– *Moscow: An Architectural History* (New York, 1977)

Beshanov, V., *Tankovy Pogrom 1941 goda* (Moscow, 1998)
Bezymenski, L., *Ukroshchenie 'Taifuna'* (Smolensk, 2001)
Bailer, S., *Stalin and his Generals: Soviet Military Memoirs of World War II* (New York, 1969)
Billington, J., *The Icon And The Axe* (London, 1966)
Bloch, M., *Strange Defeat* (London, 1949)
Blok, A., *Sobranie Sochinenii* (Moscow, 1960)
Boog, H. (ed.), *Das Deutsche Reich und der Zweite Weltkrieg*, Vol. 4 (Stuttgart, 1983)
Borodina, P., et al. (eds.), *Moskva: Entsiklopedia* (Moscow, 1980)
Bourke-White, M., *Shooting the Russian War* (New York, 1942)
Boyd, A., *The Soviet Air Force Since 1918* (London, 1977)
Brackman, R., *The Secret File of Joseph Stalin: A Hidden Life* (London, 2001)
Brent, A. and Naumov, V., *Stalin's Last Crime: The Doctors' Plot* (London, 2003)
Brett-James, A., *1812* (London, 1966)
Brooks, A., *Air war over Russia* (Hersham, 2003)
Brooks, J., *Thank you, Comrade Stalin!Soviet Public Culture from Revolution to Cold War* (Princeton, 2000)
Bukov, K., et al. (eds.) *Bitva za Moskvu* (Moscow, 1985)
Cassidy, H., *Moscow Dateline, 1941–1943* (London, 1943)
Central Statistical Office, *Statistical Digest of the War* (London, 1951)
Chaney, O., *Zhukov* (Newton Abbot, 1972)
Chegodaeva, M., *Dva Lika Vremeni: 1939 Odin God Stalinskoi Epokhy* (Moscow, 2001)
Chernyaev, A., *Moya Zhizn i Moë Vremya* (Moscow, 1995)
Cherushev, I., *Udar po Svoim: Krasnaya Armia 1938–1941* (Moscow, 2003)
– *1937 god: Elita Krasnoi Armii na Golgofe* (Moscow, 2000)
Chizhkov, A., *Podmoskovnye Usadby Segodnya* (Moscow, 2000)
Chuev, F., *Soldaty Imperii* (Moscow, 1998)
Churchill, W., *The Second World War,* Vol. 4, *The Grand Alliance* (Boston, 1950)
Clausewitz, C. von, *The Campaign of 1812 in Russia* (London, 1995)
Colton, T., *Moscow: Governing the Socialist Metropolis* (London, 1995)
Connor, W., *Accidental Proletariat: Workers, Politics and Crisis in Gorbachev's Russia* (Princeton, 1991)
Conquest, R., *The Great Terror* (London, 1971)
– *The Nation Killers* (London, 1970)
Craig, R., *Citadel: The Battle of Kursk* (London, 1993)
Crozier, F., *The Men I Killed* (London, 1937)
Dolmatovski, E., *Zelenaya Brama (Vol III: Works)* (Moscow, 1990)
Downing, D., *The Moscow Option: An Alternative Second World War* (London, 2001)
Druzhba, O., *Velikaya Otechestvennaya Voina v Soznanii Sovetskogo i Postsovietskogo Obshchestva* (Rostov, 2000)
Duffy, C., *Borodino and the War of 1812* (London, 1999)
Dunstan, J., *Soviet Schooling in the Second World War* (London, 1997)

Eden, A., *The Eden Memoirs: Facing the Dictators* (London, 1962)
– *The Eden Memoirs: The Reckoning* (London, 1965)
Ehrenburg, I., *Liudi, Gody, Zhizn: Sobranie sochinenii v deviati tomakh* (Moscow, 1962–7)
– *Men, Years, Life* (Vol. 6) (London, 1964)
Erickson, J., *The Road to Stalingrad* (London, 1983)
– *The Soviet High Command: A Military-Political History* (London, 2001)
Fedotov, V., *My Vyshli iz Shineli i Litinstituta* (Moscow, 2001)
Feinstein, E., *A Captive Lion* (London, 1987)
Feuchtwanger, L., *Moskva 1937* (Moscow, 2001)
Figes, O., *Natasha's Dance* (London, 2003)
Fischer, G., *Soviet Opposition to Stalin* (Harvard, 1952)
Fitzpatrick, S., *The Commissariat of Enlightenment* (Cambridge, 1970)
– *Education and Social Mobility in the Soviet Union 1931–34* (Cambridge, 1979)
– *Everyday Stalinism: Ordinary Life in Extraordinary Times – Soviet Russia in the 1930s* (New York, 1999)
– *Stalin's Peasants: Resistance and Survival in the Russian Village after Collectivization* (Oxford, 1994)
Fowler, W., *Barbarossa: The First Seven Days* (London, 2004)
Gardiner, J., *Wartime: Britain 1939–1945* (London, 2004)
Garrard, J. and C., *The Bones of Berdichev: The Life and Fate of Vasily Grossman* (New York, 1996)
– *Inside the Soviet Writers' Union* (London, 1990)
Garrard, J. and C. (eds.), *World War 2 and the Soviet People* (London, 1993)
Garros, V., et al. (eds.) *Intimacy and Terror: Soviet Diaries of the 1930s* (New York, 1995)
Gavrilova, I., *Naselenie Moskvy: Istoricheski Rakurs* (Moscow, 2001)
Gefter, M. (ed.), *Golosa iz mira, kotorogo uzhe net* (Moscow, 1995)
Ginzburg, L., *Chelovek za Pismennym Stolom* (Leningrad, 1989)
Glantz, D., *Barbarossa: Hitler's Invasion of Russia 1941* (Stroud, 2001)
– *Colossus Reborn: The Red Army at War 1941–1943* (Kansas, 2005)
– *The Initial Period of War on the Eastern Front 22 June–August 1941* (London, 1993)
– *Stumbling Colossus: The Red Army on the Eve of World War* (Kansas, 1998)
– *Zhukov's Greatest Defeat: the Red Army's epic disaster in Operation Mars, 1942* (Kansas, 1999)
Glantz, D., and House, J., *When Titans Clashed: How the Red Army Stopped Hitler* (Edinburgh, 2000)
Goldberg, A., *Ilya Ehrenburg: Writing, Politics and the Art of Survival* (London, 1984)
Golubev, A.V. (ed.), *Rossia i Zapad* (Moscow, 1998)
Gorinov, M., *Podvig Moskvy 1941–1945* (Moscow, 2003)
Gorkov, Yu., *Gosudarstvenny Komitet Oborony Postanovlyaet* (Moscow, 2002)

Gorodetsky, G., *Grand Delusion: Stalin and the German Invasion of Russia* (New Haven, 1999)
– *Stafford Cripps' Mission to Moscow 1940–42* (Cambridge, 1984)
Grant, N., *Soviet Education* (London, 1979)
Gröschner, A., *Dokumentation einer vorläufigen Erfahrung {Heiner Müller}* (Berlin, 1991)
Grossman, V., *Gody Voiny* (Moscow, 1989)
– *Zhizn i Sudba* (Moscow, 2004)
Guderian, H., *Panzer Leader* (Cambridge, 2002)
Hakluyt, R., *Voyages in Eight Volumes* (London, 1967)
Halder, F., *The Halder War Diary 1939–1942* (Novato, 1988)
Hanson, L. and E., *Prokofiev: The Prodigal Son* (London, 1964)
Hastings, M., *Armageddon: The Battle for Germany, 1944–45* (London, 2004)
Hauschild, J.-C., *Heiner Mueller* (Berlin, 2001)
Hayward, J., *Stopped at Stalingrad: The Luftwaffe and Hitler's Defeat in the East, 1942–1943* (Kansas, 1998)
Holmes, E.R., *Borodino 1812* (London, 1971)
Hylton, S., *Their Darkest Hour: The Hidden History of the Home Front 1939–1945* (London, 2003)
Ilyin, M., *Moskva* (Moscow, 1963)
Ivanits, L., *Russian Folk Belief* (Armonk, NY, 1992)
Jackson, D., and Wageman, P. (eds.) *Russian Landscape*, catalogue of National Gallery exhibition *Russian Landscape in the Age of Tolstoy*, 2004 (London and Groningen, 2004)
Jukes, G., *The Defence of Moscow* (London, 1969)
Kammerer, Yu., et al. *Moskve – Vozdushnaya Trevoga* (Moscow, 2000)
Karpov, V., *Generalissimus* (Kaliningrad, 2002)
Kenez, P., *Cinema and Soviet Society: From the Revolution to the Death of Stalin* (London, 2001)
Khrushchev, N., *Khrushchev Remembers* (London, 1971)
Khrutski, E., *Kriminalnaya Moskva* (Moscow, 2000)
Kiselëv, A. (ed.), *60 Let Moskovskoi Bitvy* (Moscow, 2003)
Kolesnik, A., *Opolchenskie Formirovania Rossiiskoi Federatsii v Gody Velikoi Otechestvennoi Voiny* (Moscow, 1988)
Kolodny, L., *Moskva v Ulitsakh i Litsakh – Kniga Pervaya* (Moscow, 2002)
Konecki, T., and Ruszkiewicz, I., *Marszałek Dwóch Narodów* (Warsaw, 1976)
Konyaev, N., *Vlasov: Dva Litsa Generala* (Moscow, 2003)
Korneev, V., *Ot Moskvy do Kenigsberga, ot Opolchenia do Gvardii* (Omsk, 1993)
Kovalëv, B., *Natsistskaya Okupatsia i Kollaboratsionizm v Rossii 1941–1945* (Moscow, 2004)
Kozlov, V. (ed.), *Moskovski Arkhiv 1996* (Moscow, 1996)
Kravchenko, V., *I Chose Freedom* (London, n.d.)

Krivosheev, G. (ed.), *Rossia i SSSR v Voinakh XX Veka: Statisticheskoe Issledovanie* (Moscow, 2001)

– *Soviet Casualties and Combat Losses in the Twentieth Century* (Foreword by John Erickson) (London, 1997)

Kruglov, Yu., et al. (eds.), *Veliki Podvig: Vuzy Moskvy v gody Velikoi Otechestvennoi Voiny* (Moscow, 2001)

Kulkov, E., Myagkov, M., and Rzheshevski, O. *Voina 1941–1945: Fakty i Dokumenty* (Moscow, 2004)

Kumanëv, G., *Ryadom so Stalinym* (Smokensk, 2001)

Lewin, M., *The Making of the Soviet System* (New York, 1994)

Lincoln, B., *Armageddon* (Oxford, 1994)

Livshin, A. (ed.), *Sovetskaya Povsednevnost i Massovoe Soznanie 1939–1945* (Moscow, 2003)

Longmate, N., *How We Lived Then: A History of Everyday Life during the Second World War* (London, 2002)

Lucas, J., *War on the Eastern Front: The German Soldier in Russia, 1941–1945* (London, 1998)

Lukacs, J., *Five Days in London – May 1940* (London, 1999)

Makedonov, A., *Tvorcheski Put Tvardovskogo* (Moscow, 1981)

Maslov, A., *Captured Soviet Generals: the Fate of Soviet Generals Captured by the Germans, 1941–1945* (London, 2001)

Mellor, W. (ed.), *Casualties and Medical Statistics* (London, 1972)

Meretskov, K., *Na Sluzhbe Narodu* (Moscow, 1968)

Merridale, C., *Ivan's War: The Red Army 1941–1945* (London, 2005)

– *Moscow Politics and the Rise of Stalin: The Communist Party in the Capital, 1925–32* (London, 1990)

– *Night of Stone: Death and Memory in Russia* (London, 2000)

Mikosha, V., *Ryadom s soldatom* (Moscow, 1983)

Mikoyan, A., *Tak Bylo: Razmyshlenia o Minuvshem* (Moscow, 1999)

Mikoyan, S., *Memoirs of Military Test-Flying and Life with the Kremlin Elite* (Shrewsbury, 1999)

Momysh-Uly, B., *Psikhologia Voiny* (Alma Ata, 1990)

Müller, H., *Die Schlacht Wolokolamsker Chaussee* (Frankfurt am Main, 1988)

Murphy, D., *What Stalin Knew: The Enigma of Barbarossa* (New Haven, 2005)

Myles, B., *Night Witches: The Amazing Story of Russia's Women Pilots in World War II* (Chicago, 1997)

Naumov, V. (ed.), *Georgi Zhukov: Dokumenty* (Moscow, 2001)

Nekrich, A., *1941 22 iiunia* (Moscow, 1995)

Nevzorov, B., *Moskovskaya Bitva – Fenomen vtoroi mirovoi* (Moscow, 2001)

Norilski, (Shcheglov) S., *Stalinskaya Premia* (Tula, 1998)

Nove, A., *The Soviet Economy* (London, 1961)

O'Brian, P., *Master and Commander* (London, 1998)

O'Riordan, J., *Sport in Soviet Society* (Cambridge, 1977)
Ortenberg, D., *Stalin, Shcherbakov, Mekhlis i Drugie* (Moscow, 1995)
Overmans, R., *Deutsche militaerische Verluste im letzten Weltkrieg* (Munich, 1999)
Palmer, A., *Napoleon in Russia* (London, 1967)
Pankin, B., *Chetyre Ya Konstantina Simonova* (Moscow, 1999)
Pasternak, B., *Doctor Zhivago* (London, 2002)
Paustovski, K., *Povest o zhizni* (Moscow, 1965)
Paxson, M., *Solovyovo: The Story of Memory in a Russian Village* (Bloomington, IN, 2005)
Pegov, A. (ed.), *Opolchenie na zashchite Moskvy* (Moscow, 1978)
Pennington, R., *Wings, Women, and War: Soviet Airwomen in World War II Combat* (Lawrence, KS, 2001)
Petelin, V., *Zhizn Alekseya Tolstogo, 'Krasny Graf'* (Moscow, 2001)
Piekalkiewicz, J., *Die Schlacht um Moskau* (Bergisch Gladbach, 1981)
Pipes, R., *The Russian Revolution 1899–1919* (London, 1990)
Platonov, A., *The Return* (London, 1999)
Pleshakov, C., *Stalin's Folly: The Secret History of the German Invasion of Russia, June 1941* (Boston, 2005)
Plisetskaya, M., *I, Maya Plisetskaya* (New Haven, 2001)
Plocher, H., *The German Airforce versus Russia, 1941* (USAF Historical Division, 1966)
Polukhina, L., *Marina Ladynina i Ivan Pyriev* (Moscow, 2004)
Ponomarev, A., *Aleksandr Shcherbakov: Stranitsy Biografii* (Moscow, 2004)
Porter, C., and Jones, M., *Moscow in World War II* (London, 1987)
Pyltsyn, A., *Shtrafnoi Udar, ili Kak Ofitserski Shtrafbat doshël do Berlina* (St Petersburg, 2003)
Radzinski, E., *Stalin: Zhizn i Smert* (Moscow, 2003)
Ray, J., *The Night Blitz 1940–1941* (London, 2000)
Rayfield, D., *Stalin and his Hangmen: An Authoritative Account of a Tyrant and Those Who Served Him* (London, 2004)
Reese, R., *The Soviet Military Experience* (London, 2000)
– *Stalin's Reluctant Soldiers* (Lawrence, KS, 1996)
Roberts, G., *Victory at Stalingrad* (London, 2002)
Robinson, H., *Sergei Prokofiev: A Biography* (London, 1987)
Rokossovski, K., *Soldatski Dolg* (Moscow, 2002)
Roseman, M., *The Villa, The Lake, The Meeting: Wannsee and the Final Solution* (London, 2002)
Rubinstein, J., *Tangled Loyalties: The Life & Times of Ilya Ehrenburg* (London, 1996)
Ruble, B., *Second Metropolis* (Washington, DC, 2001)
Rybakov, A., *Children of the Arbat* (London, 1988)
Safoshkin, V., *Lilia Ruslanova: Zhizn v Pesne* (Moscow, 2003)
Sagaidachny, P., *Dnevnik Peti Sagaidachnogo* (Moscow, 1963)

Sakharov, A., *Memoirs* (London, 1990)
Schloegl, K., *Moskau Lesen: Die Stadt als Buch* (Berlin, 2000)
Seaton, A., *The Battle for Moscow 1941–1942* (London, 1971)
Sebag Montefiore, S., *Stalin: The Court of the Red Tsar* (London, 2003)
Sella, A., *The Value of Life in Soviet Warfare* (London, 1992)
Semler, H., *Discovering Moscow: The Complete Companion Guide* (New York, 1987)
Senyavskaya, Ye., *1941–1945 Frontovoe Pokolenie* (Moscow, 1995)
– *Psikhologia Voiny v XX-om veke* (Moscow, 1999)
Service, R. *Stalin* (London, 2004)
Shakhurin, A., *Krylya Pobedy* (Moscow, 1990)
Shaw, G., *On the Rocks* (Ayot St Lawrence, 1933)
Shukman, H. (ed.), *Stalin's Generals* (London, 1997)
– *Stalin and the Soviet-Finnish War 1939–40* (London, 2002)
Shunkov, V., *Krasnaya Armia* (Moscow, 2003)
Simonov, K., *Glazami Cheloveka Moego Pokolenia* (Moscow, 1989)
– *Istoria Odnoi Liubvi (Story of a Love)* in *Collected Works,* Vol. 6 (Moscow, 1970)
– *Paren iz Nashego Goroda (A Boy from Our Town),* in *Piesy* (Moscow, 1950)
– *Stikhi 1954 goda* (Moscow, 1954)
– *Stikhi Voennykh Let* (Prague, 1946)
– *Sto Sutok Voiny* (Smolensk, 1999)
– *Zhivye i Mërtvye* (Moscow, 2004)
Smirnova, L., *Moya Liubov* (Msocow, 2001)
Sokolov, B., *Georgi Zhukov: Triumfy i Padenie* (Moscow, 2003)
– *Stalin: Vlast i Krov* (Moscow, 2004)
Stadniuk, I., *Voina* (*Works*, Vol. III) (Moscow, 1984)
Stalin, J., *Sochinenia* Vol 2 (XV) (Stanford, 1967)
Stevens, E. (ed.), *Guide to the City of Moscow* (Moscow, 1937)
Stites, R., *Russian Popular Culture: Entertainment and Society since 1900* (Cambridge, 1992)
Stites, R. (ed.), *Culture and Entertainment in Wartime Russia* (Bloomington, IN, 1995)
Stolfi, R., *Hitler's Panzers East: World War II Reinterpreted* (Oklahoma, 1992)
Storch, W. (ed.), *Explosion of a Memory: Heiner Müller* (Berlin, 1988)
Sudoplatov, P., *Special Tasks: The Memoirs of an Unwanted Witness* (London, 1994)
Suvorov, V., *Icebreaker: Who Started the Second World War?* (London, 1990)
– *Ten Pobedy* (Moscow, 2003)
Taubman, W., *Khrushchev: The Man and his Era* (London, 2003)
Taylor, B., *Barbarossa to Berlin (Chronology)*, Vol. 1 (Staplehurst, 2003)
Telegin, K., *Voiny Neshchitannye Vërsty* (Moscow, 1988)
Terentiev, P. (ed.) *Prokhorovy* (Moscow, 1996)
Thorpe, F., and Pronay, N., *British Official Films in the Second World War* (Oxford, 1980)
Thurston, R., *Life and Terror in Stalin's Russia 1934–1941* (New Haven, 1996)

Thurston, R., and Bonwetsch, B. (eds.), *The People's War: Responses to World War II in the Soviet Union* (Urbana, 2000)
Tolstoi, A., *Perepiska A. N. Tolstogo*, Vol. II (Moscow, 1989)
Tolstoy, L., *War and Peace* (Everyman edition, London, 1991)
Toptygin, A., *Neizvestny Beria* (Moscow and St Petersburg, 2002)
Trifonov, Yu., *Dom Na Naberezhnoi (Sochinenia*, Vol. 2) (Moscow, 1986)
Trifonova, O., *Yuri i Olga Trifonovy* (Moscow, 2004)
Trotter, W., *The Winter War: The Russo-Finnish War of 1939–40* (London, 2002)
Tumarkin, N., *The Living and the Dead* (New York, 1994)
Tvardovskaya, M. (ed.), *Vospominania ob A Tvardovskom* (Moscow, 1978)
Tvardovski, A., *Vasili Tërkin* (Moscow, 1988)
Tvardovski, I., *Rodina i chuzhbina – kniga zhizni* (Smolensk, 1996)
Tvardovsky, A. (tr. A. Rudolf), *Tyorkin and The Stovemakers* (introduction by C. Snow) (Cheadle, 1974)
Yakovlev, A., *A Century of Violence in Soviet Russia* (New Haven, 2000)
Vasiliev, G. (ed.), *Zashchitniki Neba Stolitsy* (Moscow, 2001)
Voinovich, V., *Zhizn i Neobychainye Prikliuchenia Ivana Chonkina* (Paris, 1976)
Volkogonov, D., *Triumf i Tragedia: I. V. Stalin Politicheski Portret*, 2 vols. (Moscow, 1990)
Walsh, S., *Stalingrad: The Infernal Cauldron* (London, 2000)
Weeks, A., *Stalin's Other War: Soviet Grand Strategy 1939–1941* (Lanham, MD, 2003)
Werth, A., *Moscow War Diary* (New York, 1942)
– *Russia at War 1941–1945* (London, 1964)
Wieczynski, J., *Operation Barbarossa: The German Attack on the Soviet Union, June 22, 1941* (Salt Lake City, 1993)
Yarotski, B., *Ne Odnazhdy Ispytav Sudbu* (Moscow, 1997)
Zakrevski, Yu., *Nashe Rodnoe Kino* (Moscow, 2004)
Zaloga, S., *Bagration 1944: The Destruction of Army Group Center* (Westport, 2004)
Zaloga, S., and Ness, L., *Red Army Handbook 1939–1945* (Stroud, 2003)
Zamoyski, A., *1812: Napoleon's Final March on Moscow* (London, 2004)
Zbarski, I., *Obyekt No. 1* (Moscow, 2000)
Zhilin, V. (ed.) *Bitva pod Moskvoi: Khronika, Fakty, Lyudi* (Moscow, 2001)
Zhukov, G., *Vospominania i Razmyshlenia*, 2 vols. (Moscow, 2002)
Zhuravlëv, P., *Dvesti Vstrechi so Stalinym*, 2 vols. (Moscow, 2004)

Films

TITLE	DIRECTOR	DATE
Vesëlye Rebyata	Aleksandrov	1934
Chapaev	Vasiliev brothers	1934
Maksim Trilogy	Kozintsev & Trauberg	1935–8
Tsirk	Aleksandrov	1936

Volga, Volga	Aleksandrov	1938
Esli Zavtra Voina	Dzigan	1938
Svetly Put	Aleksandrov	1940
Svinarka I Pastukh	Pyriev	1941
Chkalov	Kalatozov	1941
Paren iz Nashego Goroda	Stolper	1942
Razgrom Fashistsko-Nemetskhikh Voisk pod Moskvoi	Varlamov, Kopalin	1942
Zhdi Menya	Stolper	1943
Zoya	Arnshtam	1944
V Shest Chasov Posle Voiny	Pyriev	1944
Nebesny Tikhokhod	Timoshenko	1945
The Young Guard	Gerasimov	1948
Padenie Berlina	Chiaureli	1949
Cavalier of the Gold Star	Raizman	1950
Letyat Zhuravli	Kalatozov	1957
Ballada o Soldate	Chukhrai	1959
Zhivye i Mertvye	Stolper	1963
V Boi Idut Odni 'Stariki'	Bykov	
Bitva za Moskvu	Ozerov	1982
Zavtra Byla Voina	Kara	1987
Shrafniki (documentary)	Danilov	1989
Voina na Zapadnom Napravlenii	Levchuk	1990
Prazdnik	Sukhachëv	2001
Shtrafbat	Dostal	2004
Deti Arbata	Eshpai	2004
Moskovskaya Saga	Barshchevski	2004

Interview List

The first entry under 'Occupation' is what the person was doing in the war; 'n/a' means the person was not yet born at that time. Where it exists, the second entry is what the person was doing when interviewed, or their position on retirement.

Name	**Occupation**
Antonova, Irina	Student; art administrator
Anufriev, Evgeny	OMSBON special force; professor
Aria, Semyon	Tank driver, soldier in punishment battalion; lawyer
Avdeeva, Ludmila	Bolshoi theatre (contralto)
Averbakh, Yuli Lvovich	Student; chess grandmaster
Barendson	Air defence officer; lawyer
Benditski, Alexander	Musician

Bezymenski, Lev	Political officer; writer
Bolotov, Valentin	n/a; Museum of the Moscow Metro
Dëmina, Vera	8th (Krasnaya Presnya) Volunteer Division
Djambaeva, Tamara	Nurse
Donskaya, Tatiana	n/a; journalist
Dryannov, Kirill	n/a; Museum of the Defence of Moscow
Fedotov, Viktor	Soldier; writer
Frolov, Vladimir	OMSBON special force; professor
Gefter, V.	n/a; Human rights worker
Glebov, Nikolai	Underground construction worker
Golyamina, Irina	Schoolgirl; scientist
Gudz, Pavel	Tank commander; general
Gurkin, Vladimir and Larisa	Artillery officer; general
Iofin, Stanislav	Volunteer; regular officer
Jaruzelski, Wojciech	Officer; former Polish President
Kantovski, Vladimir	Schoolboy, soldier in punishment battalion; scientist
Kiselëv, Nikolai	Schoolboy; Institute of Crystallography
Kuzar, Vladimir	n/a; journalist *Krasnaya Zvezda*
Labas, Yuri	Schoolboy; scientist
Leonova, Klavdia	Textile worker
Litvin, Sara	Schoolgirl
Markov, Sergei	Dzerzhinski Division, Zhukov bodyguard 1943
Merzhanov, Viktor	Conservatoire student; professional musician
Mikosha, Vladislav	Cameraman
Mikoyan, Stepan	Fighter pilot; test pilot (son of Politburo member)
Milkova, Tatiana	Nurse
Mishchenko, Lev	Student; physicist
Mitlyanski, Daniel	Schoolboy; sculptor
Moroz, Vitali	n/a; journalist *Krasnaya Zvezda*
Savina (Naumova), Antonina	Hospital worker
Nemirovskaya, Yelena	Schoolchild; director of an NGO
Nepomnyashchaya, Anna	Teenager
Nevzorov, Boris	n/a; Institute of Military History
Ogryzko, Vladimir	Officer in Dzerzhinski Division; general
Petrov, Ivan	Bolshoi theatre (bass)
Ponedelin, Alla	Mikoyan classmate; general's daughter
Ponomarev, Vasili	Volunteer, 21 (Kiev) Volunteer division; general
Pronin, Sergei	Schoolboy (son of wartime head of Moscow

	City Administration)
Rezanov, Konstantin	Air defence officer; general
Robel, Lidia	Textile worker
Rokossovskaya, Nadezhda	n/a; daughter of general
Rokossovsky, Konstantin V.	n/a; grandson of general
Romanova, Ludmila	Textile worker
Sadkovich, Nikolai	n/a; curator, School No. 110 Museum
Saksonov, Oleg	n/a; Institute of Military History
Sandrikov, Aleksandr	Volunteer, 18 (Leningrad) Volunteer Division; general
Sergeev, Nikolai	Volunteer, Moscow Volunteer Division; general
Sergeeva, Praskovia	Nurse, Moscow Volunteer Division
Shcherbakov, Alexander	Fighter pilot; test pilot (son of Politburo member)
Shcherbakov, Konstantin	Schoolboy; editor of *Komsomol skaya Pravda* (son of Politburo member)
Simonov, Aleksei	n/a; son of writer
Smirnova, Lidia	Actress
Sokolov, Boris	n/a; historian
Soloviev, Stepan	NKVD; Moscow air defence
Sulkhanishvili, Ghia	n/a; diplomat
Teleguev, Yevgeni	OMSBON; general of KGB
Trifonova, Olga	Writer
Vanke, Elena	Bolshoi (dancer)
Volkova, Yelena	Nurse
Volynski, Yuri	n/a; consultant cardiologist
Vostrosablina, Liubov	Librarian
Yakovlev, Aleksandr	Marine; politician
Yastrebov, Yaroslav	n/a; journalist *Krasnaya Zvezda*
Zasypkin	n/a; Ministry of Interior official
Zbarsky, Ilya	Lenin mausoleum staff
Zeldin, Vladimir	Actor
Zhukova, Ella	Small girl; daughter of general
Zhukova, Ira	Small girl; daughter of general
Zvyagina, Susanna	Bolshoi theatre (dancer)

ACKNOWLEDGEMENTS

One of the greatest pleasures in writing this book was to meet so many new people in Moscow: people who were there in 1941, their friends and relatives, historians, journalists and others interested in the period. Many entertained me in their homes. Stepan Mikoyan and Daniel Mitlyanski invited their schoolfriends to meet me over supper. Vera Demina fed me, a stranger, on a day when my tight schedule had left me no other time to eat. Vladimir Kantovski took me to visit the museum in his old school, School No. 110. All these people were immensely generous with their time and their memories. Several gave me copies of books – regimental histories, memoirs – which I would never have found for myself. Their names appear throughout the text and in the footnotes. This book is the expression of my gratitude to each of them.

The bonds of friendship are particularly strong in Russia, and throughout the project I relied heavily on the support of old friends. In Moscow Lev Parshin tracked down veterans with tireless enthusiasm and set up most of my interviews with them: he was central to the project. Lena Nemirovskaya and Yuri Senokosov provided warm and generous hospitality during many visits to Moscow. Marina Tonkikh, of the Moscow School of Political Studies, slaved well beyond the call of duty in organising my programmes and transport. The project would have been impossible without them.

General Rokossovski's daughter Nadezhda Rokossovskaya and grandson Konstantin Rokossovski gave me invaluable background material on the general. So too did General Jaruzelski and Colonel Pruszkowski. Colonel Sadykiewicz was tireless in digging out bibliographical references, and wrote a special appraisal of Rokossovski's military skills for me.

Simon Sebag Montefiore suggested a number of lines of enquiry at the beginning of the project. Antony Beevor, Catherine Merridale and Margaret Paxson allowed me to see advance copies of their books *A Writer at War*, *Ivan's War* and *Solovyovo*. Lev Mishchenko gave me a copy of his unpublished memoirs, on which I drew heavily.

Academician Chubarian smoothed my way to the Moscow City Central Archive. Mikhail Gorinov and his colleagues there dug out files from 1941, gave me copies of their scholarly articles and invited me to attend the historical conference on Moscow in 1941 which they held in the offices of the Moscow mayor in December 2004.

Geoff and Kathy Murrell, Dmitri Trenin, Anatoli Chernyaev, Lev Parshin, Mikhail Myagkov and Michal Sadykiewicz read various versions of my manuscript, pointed out numerous errors and made general suggestions for its improvement. Ludmila Matthews read it twice. Peter Carson's tactful and understated comments led me to make substantial changes for the better. Lesley Levene reduced my chaotic footnotes to order.

The Wilson Center for International Scholarship in Washington, DC, provided an ideal place to finish the writing, not least because of the arrangement which enables you to get books delivered from the Library of Congress to your desk. I am endlessly grateful to Sam Wells for getting me into the Center, and for the librarians and other members of the staff who were so helpful while I was there.

Lidia Lunina of the Moscow Central Archive of Audio Visual Documents, Galina Balakireva of the Museum of Contemporary History, Maria Zhotikova-Shaikhat and especially Ralph Gibson of RIA Novosti were particularly helpful in tracking down photographs.

Jill went through the final draft with a toothcomb. I adopted almost all of her suggestions. But that was only the least of the many things for which I owe her my gratitude.

LIST OF ILLUSTRATIONS

The photographs in this book were kindly made available by the RIA Novosti Agency, the National Gallery in Washington, the Museum of Contemporary History in Moscow (MCH), the Moscow Central Archive of Audiovisual Documents (MCA), the State Archive of Cinema and Photographic Documents in Krasnogorsk, Time-Life, the Imperial War Museum, and a number of individuals. The names of the photographers are listed below where they are known. It has not been possible, despite extensive enquiries, to establish the source and/or copyright holder of a number of photographs, especially those that come from the Internet.

INDEX

A

H

O

U

V

W